TABOOED OBSERVATIONS

TABOOED OBSERVATIONS

How to Use a Satirical Hammer to Drive a Philosophical Nail

Loren Berengere

Copyright © 2008 by Loren Berengere.

ISBN: Softcover   978-1-4257-7709-8

All rights reserved. No part of this book may be reproduced or transmitted in any form or by any means, electronic or mechanical, including photocopying, recording, or by any information storage and retrieval system, without permission in writing from the copyright owner.

This book was printed in the United States of America.

To order additional copies of this book, contact:
Xlibris Corporation
1-888-795-4274
www.Xlibris.com
Orders@Xlibris.com

Contents

Caveat Lector 9

Preface 13

Pars Prima: Is There an Americanism Appropriate
 to American Pragmatism? 19

Pars Secunda: On the Lumber of the Schools 221

Epilogue 291

Bene vixit qui bene latuit

Hasten on wayfarer, lest you stir up the hornets.

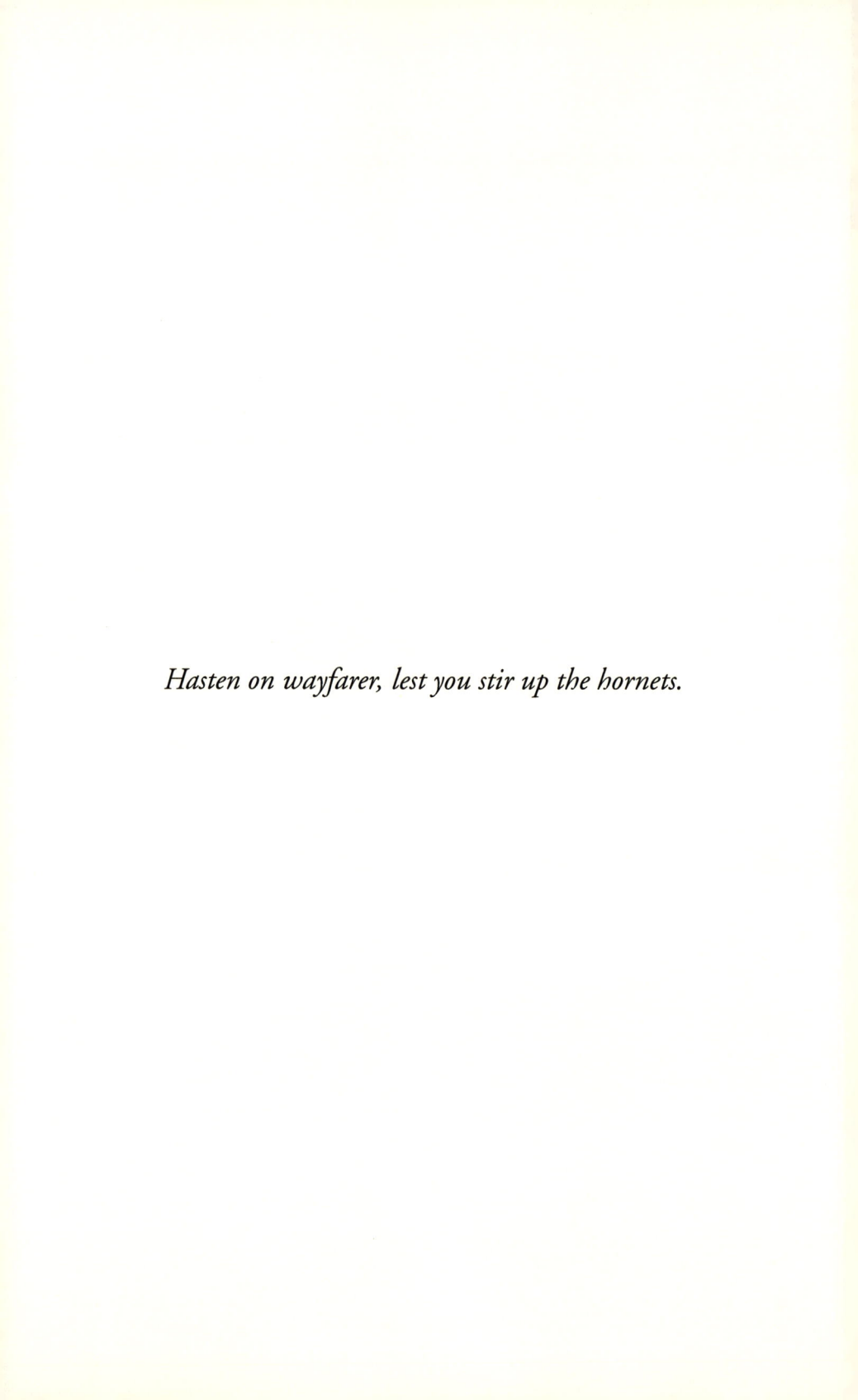

Caveat Lector

Let the reader please be forewarned that this dough has been kneaded with constant reference to the unabashedly invidious spleen in Juvenalian satire. Queasy reviewers should review elsewhere, keeping as they ought to the vanguard of lodestars annually announced in the *Partisan Review*, and sometimes, the *New York Review of Books*. I for one would place a sizeable bet on a Las Vegas table that our mandarins in dear old Manhattan know nothing at all about real satire since it is the novel American way to shy away from anything deemed culturally incorrect, *hence* cavalier evasion of untrammeled pursuit of truth, via Socratic critique, into its many modern hideouts. Solution: identify satire with the fragrance of Mark Twain's cigar. Correlatively, since reviewers and pundits must make a living, I should at least publicize the hope that they may learn something about real satire, a noble genre dear to philosophy since the earliest times whose cardinal element is the mixing of heaviness with levity as a literary trick to overcome a stubborn unwillingness to criticize, and make their living at the same time. But perhaps the hopes of this writer, as well as the fervent intentions of the waspish, offensive tradition of calling a spade a spade, are indeed idle in an American milieu.—*Quae cum*, allow me to comfort myself with the following unfashionable, indeed tabooed observation.—The sentinels and time-servers of the circumambient literary world—critics, reviewers, and the like—tis true, can make a book into something, but by the same brushstroke turn a writer into nothing. Let us assume that these beavers build a dam betwixt the lone writer, who must first exist as an individual before all his verbosity, and this literary world later to construct a causeway to the teeming crowd itself. Fact: a sensation has been created; approval has been sought and garnered. *The book has become a success.* Now what happens to this writer, who, as just stipulated, must exist as an individual first and a word-architect later? Well, to be frank, an obligation has been imposed. Just as when the plaintiff wins, the defendant—and by simple reasoning, everyone in the society—suffers curtailment of activity. Hence, the writer must also suffer curtailment of his activity. And what is his activity? Again: live first as a person, later as a writer. On the other hand, if the crowd brings to a writer his duly-earned, mean-spirited *pereat*, no such obligation has been imposed. If, like the great Schopenhauer, the *pereat* serves to make a better questioner, a better philosopher, a better writer, then bring it on, gentlemen; bring it on! Moreover, a literary attack—I am thinking of Spitteler's attack on Nietzsche. "You have given us a bit of form. Maybe later you could provide us with some content as well." Nietzsche *could* have replied, "One greater than a Spitteler is here!" This Spitteler went on to become a Nobel laureate.—constitutes no infringement upon personal freedom. Such a writer is free to proceed with his work, turn over for another hour of sleep, sport with his brunette, lounge about indolently like the great Montaigne, spy a young Arizona moon rising hauntingly over a forest of spiney Joshua trees, trace with ardent eyes the giant arms of the saguaro pitted against a purple sunset, listen for the lunar silence of Nevada's silver peaks, the sweet clangor of the little green cable cars as they, like Priest and silent Vestal, slowly climb the eternal hill.—A reception in accordance with the author's wishes, therefore, would mean that no sensation be forthcoming. None. Yet, since this gathering miasma's chokehold on free thought grows tighter and less comprehended hour by hour, service to mankind *qua* selfless allegiance to what kind of turnabout our intellectual ferment can bestow even in such a scarlet age, dictates a need for a different result. At any rate, that philosophy, in my hands, will become prophecies and oracles delivered by one who has scaled the highest peaks of thought and who lives *up there*;—this our lodestars and mandarins, our educated mob, may never fully appreciate.

Berengere
Taos, New Mexico, Sept. 06

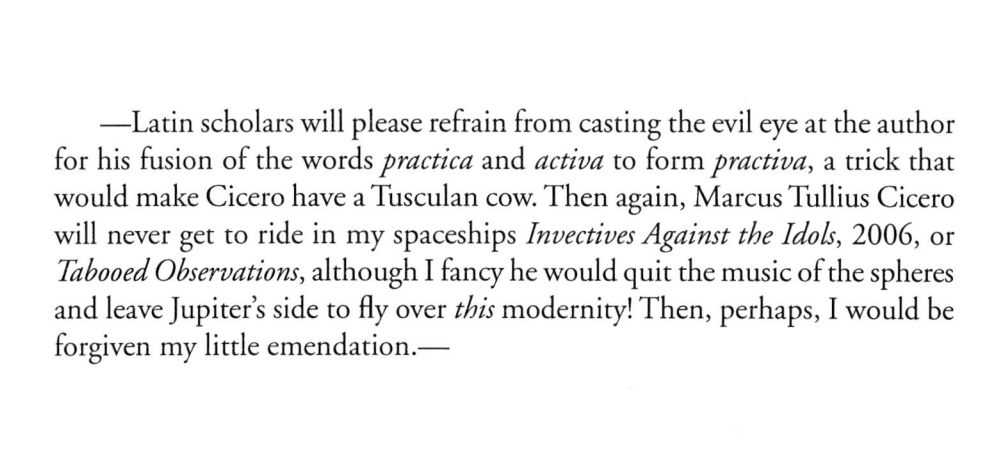

—Latin scholars will please refrain from casting the evil eye at the author for his fusion of the words *practica* and *activa* to form *practiva*, a trick that would make Cicero have a Tusculan cow. Then again, Marcus Tullius Cicero will never get to ride in my spaceships *Invectives Against the Idols*, 2006, or *Tabooed Observations*, although I fancy he would quit the music of the spheres and leave Jupiter's side to fly over *this* modernity! Then, perhaps, I would be forgiven my little emendation.—

Preface

1

This writer does not want to be understood by just anybody. My philosophy of *creating distances* prescribes this as literary "truth," for the gulf here betwixt the "us and them" is very great. I seek both atheists and theists for my readers: I wouldn't mind to see even a few pragmatists stroll through these minefields at twilight; nor would I be offended if a few "good Catholics" glanced at my little polemic, perhaps to investigate the possible reincarnation of some holy spirit, who, as a man of sorrows, lived to slay dragons—not with the sword, but with the pen. On the other hand, I do not trust the Protestant dispensationalists; I'd rather they not come around. They have a way of lifting up their eyes to the Davidic State that disgusts me. Nor do I wish to be a nice gift box, tray, or fancy pin cushion for some Hunnish Arab desperately seeking pearl-eyed maidens—70 of them—in Mahomet's bosom. (—As the kamikazes sought bevies of geishas in the Emperor's bosom.—)—What I want is to drive the seekers of knowledge above and beyond their time, out beyond *this* time and its coming night. I say knowledge, but it is not merely intellect that impels you to survey thousands of years; to reach out and take the pulse of horizons and blue galaxies!—My readers are those *most serious seekers* who have liberated themselves from many, many things: a test not of intellect but of strength. *You airy Argonauts, surveyors of continents no one yet sees, you come from a land where no one else lives!*

2

Let the liberal democracies grovel beneath the jealous yoke of the exacting and irascible press; yet so long as the world has existed, no authority has allowed itself to be impugned *at the foundations*.—But how can one reach the foundations?—One must dig for them: firstly, however, one must be philosopher *enough* to want to find them: one must want to leave the warm sunlight in favor of the true thinker's boon: iciness and absence of light!—For, believe me, it is cold and dark down there at the foundations!—And you wondered in the puerility of warmest youth, why Socrates walked on the ice and sprouted mole's eyes in the most uncanny places!—When Aristophanes asked the old miner, "Why do you tunnel so deeply?" Socrates wilily replied, "Only a comic would ask such a question!"—For is it not even truer today, my ardent friends, that somewhere deep in the old Socratic mine is the *philosopher's gold*, the fruit and purpose of the *noblest quest*? That—somewhere down there—*there is light*! (—And every manner of thing known to tickle philosophers' toes?—)—Socrates laughed over the heads of the gathering crowd, winking at big-jowled Antisthenes, who tramped the five miles from the Peiraeus to gape upon the Socratic fracas. The sage spoke, "There is a hidden method to this madness, a dialectic! One must leave the world to find it!" Yet—Do not think for a moment that we are inviting *you* to join us on this hazardous journey . . . at least, not without the proper disclaimers and auguries; for the man or woman who ventures *this* path must follow the fate of prolonged obscurity, silence, and the *necessary* obloquy of the philosopher's stony ways—; for such are the sundry faces of darkness. Tell me: what happens, what metamorphosis takes place, when a poet becomes a philosopher? Precisely this: such a wanderer feels no pain upon witnessing the burning of his work. For there, amidst the billowing flames, such a poet experiences the confirmation of his own light shining in the darkness, his own *redemption*! Formerly, such a poet traveled his own path, consoling himself with the promise of encountering others who play with words and devise poets' diversions for themselves. The philosopher, however, finds no one on his path (—for it is his *alone*—) and is bedeviled by the premonition, from time to time, that—Alas!—*there is no path*!—Yea, the philosopher's path leads ever downward, down, down to the foundations of thought and action. Thus, I descended, burrowing down to the foundations of the quintessential American faith: thus, I took it as my calling *to undermine the faith in pragmatism* and so to liberate a desire for independence as well as the thing this pragmatism fears the most: the possibility of a genuine contemplative life. What?—The *vita contemplativa* has always been at odds with this pragmatism?—And what is behind the contemplative ideal? Is it not the individual, *the most dangerous individual, the philosopher*?

3

To impale a pragmatist on the point of a philosopher's needle—or even on the point of a billiard cue—is, I must admit, no easy matter. Gentlemanly Jamesian Cambridge minds are, after all is said and done, *legal* minds, nimble, "scientific," radically opposed to the philosopher's *vis creativa*: in a word, philosophy's last gasp, it's throwing in the towel to legal and scientific "method." . . . Philosophy becomes its own *farewell*; its own ruin in the pragmatic reign of haste, politics, fads, fashions, and nervousness, as well as all the *other* gynecomorphous gaudery of our Great Deweyan Society with its "moral" duty of child-centrism and associated nurturing for associated cattle.—Did the shrewdest of pragmatists foresee the *immorality* of Chicago pragmatism? Let the psychiatrists guess *what* was active here: regression to the womb; narcotica; the *decadent* instinct of the founder of a religion, etc . . . What? The old Hull House Hegelian was merely a long time sick? Very well; recovery from pragmatism means the philosopher has *become well again*! . . .

4

It is graphically evident to every free human being, every seeker, every bird-in-flight and bird-to-be, *what* pragmatism is, what it claims, proclaims, and teaches: that for every unit there is a proper slot to be occupied, for every individual, a hole—if I may speak politely and in a Boston accent—; that, against Aristotle, who is but a surpassed milestone in the *illogical* dia-pragmalectic of the Harvard faculty look-alikes, one must not utilize the highest faculty of man to achieve a summit, but precisely the basest for the ruttish and farcical; that one must be goal-oriented, means-end-continuumed, and learn to think as good Salem witches think (—for, believe me, the future of Harvard-Wicca is at risk!—): *that one must know what one is*: that one must start out knowing what one is, the better to be *utilized* in a pragmatist society.—As, say, every crew cut who enters the Harvard Law School must first visualize himself periwigged on State Street, clerking in Washington, speaking in Faneuil Hall, etc; every philosophy student must learn to think like Quine.—If gentlemen really believe that philosophy *follows science*, shouldn't it follow that *they* should follow science precisely by throwing away the prospect of knowing what one is and, for once, learn to live experimentally, unchaining their minds and bodies from the corner, cursing every slot and hole?—Our hopes are dashed. Ladies and gentlemen will do no such thing.—Living experimentally, unencumbered by all manner of goal-oriented straitjackets, contemptuous of all essences and predetermined paths, embracing as higher knowledge every possibility of those Goethean tossings, turnings, storms, and stresses experienced by every *higher spirit* at the fabled Nook of the Seven Paths, rejecting—out of a sense of destiny; again: Goethean destiny—"the land" with all its securities and happinesses for the brooding, yawning jaws of the Minotaur; all this is condemned and adjudged "dangerously unstable" by the intellectuals of the world, who daily and hourly tout their essences and rattle their chains in the pretty essays and novels they write—not to mention that nerve-frayed trumpery they call modern poetry—and never tire of proving to themselves that they are intellectuals by sticking their long, highbrow proboscises in leading literary journal-bungholes to ensure that every highbrow will think as every other highbrow thinks, and sleep with each other, as the Roman satirist said so well, in a learned fashion.—What? There was, after all, some hidden, yet-to-be-hatched *meaning* to all his flights, fancies, wanderings, and oh-so-conspicuously impractical hawk-like freedom? All his *aloofness* and sweetly self-imposed incarcerations, all his truancy, perceived spivvery, and painful transformations had a purpose . . . *A distant goal no one could imagine*? He had been confused, not knowing, not even caring who he was: only now does he see himself . . . and how surprised he is at his reflection!

5

I devised for myself a question: are the pragmatists' judgments about truth a degeneration of philosophy? Another question: has the regnant conception of truth of any epoch ushered in a peculiar *form of life* endemic to the conception itself?—Is every philosophy therefore *crocheted to life* in some sense that cannot be measured, tested, sifted through, weighed, compared, or even adequately discussed? That philosophy has indeed taken the place of mythology, but *retains* a mythopoeic function? (—You pragmatic empiricists are certainly interested in functions.—) Therefore, resolutely plugging our ears to the analytic aridities and linguistic barratries of the whole Anglo-American temper of mind with its quicksand questions—perhaps we should refer to them as cracker barrel questions—"What is philosophy? What is truth?" we must re-propound our question for those open minds without access to ear plugs: *what particular form of life does American Pragmatism want*? Which favored forms of activity does this action philosophy require? And the pregnant question for the spirit of philosophy: what does this *radical Americanization* of philosophy exclude, condemn, pronounce as trivial, invidious, and *unworthy of continued existence*?—In sum, let us reduce these questions to one overarching inquiry: what is the pragmatism of pragmatism?—Given a philosophy of utility; what is *its* utility?—As the fox calls sour those grapes he is unable to reach, so the logician deems frivolous those questions he is quite unable to answer. Let us, therefore, by all means, declare war on these foxy logicians . . .

6

Just as the finest actors catch only a working adumbra and slightest glimpse of the characters they play, and as acting is contrasted to the real play and the real acts of versatility constitutive of real life, so pragmatism is contrasted to a philosophy that strives to capture the essential in any matter. Because pragmatism springs from legal theory—it is merely human interest that determines what anything *is*—this modern stand-in for the working belief system of the ancient rhetorician understandably reduces the essential to an inessential that works, i.e., to surface, to effect, and appearance. Just as hearsay evidence is not untrustworthy because it is untrue—it is so because of a *policy* that refuses any claim as to its veracity at the threshold—and as an unenforceable contract is nonetheless a true contract, so that way of life Americans call pragmatism, allows for truth to be determined by policy.—Which policy?—The policy that pays. Truth becomes a species of good.—We must, therefore, inquire into the truth of American goodness in an effort to see if it is really badness . . . Then, perhaps we will be accused of destroying pragmatism in order to realize our own pragmatic will. If you prefer: *the philosophy of consequences for Americans is an invitation to look at the consequences of American philosophy* . . .

7

Pragmatism *itself* as consequence seems at first to be an isolated intellectual question, some kind of amusing riddle remote from real life. But if one repeats this question enough, one may learn to ask the question *for oneself* and thus confront for oneself the saturnalia of suspicions that actuate and *must* actuate that rarest of all literary types: the philosopher.—Yes, comrades; virtue *can* be taught!—That pragmatism, whatever it turns out to be, *entails* consequences—or to say the same thing: that anything calling itself an idea can be *at work* in a society that sponsors hatred of ideas: that philosophy is an armchair phenomenon, an impotent triviality, and embarrassing redundancy; that literature is, at best, only some sort of narcotic and escape from the "real world," from American business, i.e., American faith in materialism; that the artist is a circus animal for tired spectators, etc.—is a kind of knowledge *that has not yet been discovered.* Even desired!—And why?—We have taken "the factual" itself as beyond question (—*one more* American trait with which to be dealt—), and hence beyond *questioning.* Cultural criticism in America has been linked to "protest ideology" and political movements for so long that it has no existence *apart* from these things.—Democracy and its darling, pluralism, mean one and only one thing: the sultry, self-righteous art of politicizing everything. Is this understood?—For cultural criticism as an *independent genre*—independent of protest ideology—would call into question the whole promise of an exclusively legalistic society whose every "question" must be propounded and "heard" the way issues are framed in the law courts; such independence, since it flows from the practice of philosophy and is thus the ground for every other kind of independence, is inherently dangerous for a democracy—for, believe me, if given full rein, it would challenge all the assumptions of a "free society"—and must be declared taboo. But genuine philosophers are habituated to *scenting out cues*; and consequently the rankle in their sensitive nostrils leads them to but one inevitable conclusion: *A look at the consequences of pragmatism is a look at the real direction of a society.* A critique of pragmatism leads to a critique of the entire social fabric. Not merely a critique of pragmatistic values, but an uncovering of the consequences of these values—the value of these values—is required. The project here is the recruiting of scouts to cover the hidden land of the future with questions the answers to which will have the inevitable effect of *dividing the land* and thus opening up distances and sounding dissonances for the sake of a spiritual order yet to materialize: an underground apparat of monastic states bound together by the hatred of assimilation and the *will to resist.* Thus, a spiritual tension is at work all over the world—the tension of the tragic carrying within itself the task of all tragic things: the demarcating of one thing from another; the starkest *absence of reconciliation*—ever growing in intensity in this Last Age of the Sibyl's Book when one *fundamental order* dwindles and another steadily consolidates, augments itself, and proliferates. Behind such a tragic state there lurks the philosophy of the tragic with its courage, pride, and longing for conflict. Once again, an even greater Argo will sail for even greater spoil; wars will come; and another Achilles go once more for Troy.

Berengere
In Coolbrith Park, in the cold
summer of San Francisco, 2006

Is There an Americanism Appropriate to American Pragmatism?

1

That grotesquerie of a truth notion—scion of every sort of complacency and narrowness of mind—; I am speaking of the claim that the truth is true *because we persist in calling it true* (—we *do* persist because it satisfies us—); this grotesquerie, which has all the instinctual animus of the *nobler* philosophy against it, finds its day in the sun and *gets on top* with the triumph of this pragmatism, this thwarting of good taste, this Americanism that claims exemption from the hooks and snares of critical reason.—And why do you persist in calling something true? Because you have come to *regard* it as true. And why do you regard it as true? Because it satisfies you. Satisfaction: this is a property of the truth that makes you regard something as true: far be it from you, you with your need to feel good, in one word, your need to call yourself a pragmatist, to assert that, on the contrary, it is the truth of a belief that makes it true, *not* your regarding it as true. Imagine Descartes teaching such light-o'-love to his queen; what would have been in store for *him*? Such chantefabling with truth has always been repudiated in good society. Good society feels shame at the sight and sound of such a thing; the kind of shame and repulsion, we may imagine, the writer Naipaul felt when he traveled to his native land and saw his Indians squatting on the railroad tracks.—When such indecency with regard to the most basic matters becomes second nature, can anyone doubt for a moment that this philosophy of consequences *itself has consequences*? Why does the whole history of philosophy *exist*? What is the life of the mind *there for* but to teach the people at least a modicum's modicum of freedom of thought? Today, all overnight, merely a memory! All in vain, *for us*, the freest people on earth! Lie, damnable lie! You roundheeled ignoramuses of conservatives! You sit idly by like knots on logs watching the black cloud of cultural-correctness—the great harvest of Red Du Bois, who swam across the flooded Jordan cursing the European race and the European God, shaking his taupe fist at the white sky—rob us of *our harvest*! But you were too busy, too intellectually occupied sopping the gravy of "free-enterprise," you ruffians, so that today the sight of your obesity turns my stomach. Alas, contemned as "immoral," trampled underfoot by pampered "free" helots, the collective soul *hoodooed out of its once vital instincts*! The whole underworld of Stygian malignity and hatred: *suddenly on top*! Suddenly telling *us* what to think! Envy and envy's accretive pus: *become master*! Choreographing literature, law, "morality." Dictating to *us*! One must only read the agitators to see, to *hear* for oneself, what resentment-corroded hermaphrodites and *cinaedi* now reign at the top! Everything suffering from itself (—*such* suffering must always be directed outward and foisted upon "society," upon "institutions," thus nailing the "oppressors" to a wooden Cross high atop a New Golgotha; and modern Pilates come again to wash their hands—), everything "invisible," tormented, secret, anemic, and revenge-bitten *suddenly on top*! One would be deceiving oneself utterly if one were to accuse these agitators of a lack of intelligence. They are foxes and monks incarnate who know only too well what the people can be *had* for. No; what they lacked was something different, viz: an ability, from the standpoint of long-term repercussion, to *give a damn*. If we never come out from under this cloud, it if engulfs the rest of the world, the *Americans* will be to blame . . .

2

It has gradually become clear to me that the pragmatist's "reality" and the secondhand courtroom reality of the attorney who cleverly selects which "facts" to ignore and which facts to fake; the selection or carving out of the flux of reality the facts that interest the pragmatist by means of concepts formed by the mind for that purpose and the tendentious reconstructions of brute events as if they were merely accidental occurrences into "case theories" by the advocate animated solely by the interest in winning;—that these correlative reality-pictures are identical; even their womb realities are the same. If my analysis is correct, whatever you longeared philosophy professors in your porcelain towers may say, we may discover for the very first time the true nature of this pragmatism, and by extension, the American essence. (—At this point, it might make good procedural sense to ask old Quine the question whether such an essence exists or could exist; and depending upon the answer given, either abandon our investigations altogether or confine ourselves to the marriage of void twitches and political liberalism, as our playful Professor Rorty teaches.—)—The pragmatist treats the substance of reality as a kind of remote tribunal that has no jurisdiction whatsoever over the facts, facts he proceeds to dress up according to his utilitarian delectation, just as the advocate proceeds with the evidence *as if* his substance—the basis for the evidential probanda in his theory of the case; stated bluntly, the events themselves—did not exist *in reality* as the apodictic datum of interpretation. As the pragmatist says, "Knowing is relative to doing," the advocate, conceiving the truth *solely* in terms of the outcome of a contest of case theories presented at trial, can say with equal bravado, "The sparks of conflict shed the light by which justice may be seen." In one word, for the pragmatist, as well as for the advocate, there are no disinterested facts.—Then, pray tell, what does all this *point to*? For what exactly does it sponsor and clear the way?—Who can deny that it is on such ground that every noxious weed and poisonous plant grows? Wherever the common law and its philosophic mis-justification, American Pragmatism, exist—I am speaking, of course, of every cultural domain of every kind of "open society" on this earth—the air stinks of the smallness and meanness of utility and cleverness; beg pardon, I meant to say, "truth and justice." Here—where "freedom" reigns—every effort is made, every effort *must* be made, to show that in the final analysis—"in the end" as Peirce would say—the good and the stupid are the same; that forced homogenization is the end result of all the moral mumbo-jumbo emanating from this truth and justice, our dearly *modern* truth and justice: "unity," "progress," equal rights, and tolerance as protective cocoons and security blankets of the inability to stand up, of sickliness, of the Roman luxury of degenerating life. Then, quite aside from tort causation theory, this pragmatism has its roots in Darwinism—this is to say, from the standpoint of higher, rarer, more complicated life, in error; nothing but errors—; for it is surely no fortuity for pragmatism that the more pervasive sickness becomes, the more degeneration is not interpreted and seen as degeneration (—for degeneration has become, in the miasma of value reversal, the sudden seeing of anything not as it is, not *what* it is, but instead, as its polar concept, its polar reality—), the higher should be the honor accorded the rarer specimens, the exceptions, the great virtuous men who do *not* multiply and whose arena is above the fray of "survival." Little by little, step by step, the aspect of the victor, the strong demeanor, the spirit-bestowing distance separating man from man, are *hated*; and what eloquent groans, what mendacious slime, what display of noble indignation, loud noises, and gestures are employed to disguise this hatred as justice, morality, "compassion," and love;—all counterfeits! Lies! All *reversals* of an older morality declared "evil."

3

The fact that pragmatists are in accord over something does *not* prove that they are right in regard to that which they are in accord over;—one thousand times no! It merely shows they stand in the same negative relation to a form of philosophic life they have adjudged invidious. What then does the pragmatist resent? What arouses his ill will? Precisely the possibility of a caste of men and women bold enough to practice philosophy in the grand manner; this is to say a caste hovering above the dirt of politics, above all the petty parade of legalisms that retard and thwart the drive for philosophy. For pragmatism insists upon its right to *remit* wonder, awe, and proper reverence to the domain of science—and by extension, the dehumanizing faddishness of popular technology—which proceeds to castrate the preconditions for the possibility of a new breed of critic and philosopher not at all disposed to believe that truth should be the indentured bondsman to satisfaction and "happiness."—Goal of the philosophers of the future: the *liberation* of truth from happy pragmatics, from "action," so that the truth about thought and action may be comprehended no longer as the truth of action, but as the action of truth.

4

Having looked up William James's sleeves for so many years—years which, if I may say so, I could have spent surveying *sublimer* things—I have come to some conclusions about his "psychology," and of course, the pseudo-philosophy James deduced from it, our celebrated and until now misunderstood American Pragmatism. He proceeds thusly: he *reverses* the previous atomistic theory of perception or consciousness and proclaims instead a kind of Heraclitian flow or continuum, i.e., a continuous whole. Next, he swears that the mind selects, breaks up, and discriminates this flow into useable things; and all this in view of action. The world is not originally presented to us in broken-up bits; no, it is the mind that, subsequent to the world being apprehended as an unmanageable flow, breaks it up into units *so that we may live, i.e., act*. In other words, the good professor wants it that the first thing we encounter is a continuum, an undifferentiated whole as such inimical to life. Later, divisions and discriminations are "made" according to human interest:

when any fool can readily see that the whole professorial rondo involving the whole and the parts is merely set up as a pretext for the primacy of action. Hence, interest becomes the promotion of a moot theory of truth; *meaning* precisely that the datum of *causa* in law—interest, capricious and simple—has single-handedly midwifed a "philosophy," an *American* philosophy! Yet . . . even the legal theory itself is employed as pretext: what these pragmatists want is the eunuchization of philosophy past, present, and future. They *reverse* the truth, stand it upon its head, if you will: instead of the authentic ethos of a people flowing from the thought of any given epoch, the work of the intellect is eternally parasitic upon a given ethos, an ethos, mind you, beyond the reach of value-judging criteria: specifically the meaningless American ethos of *action for action's sake* . . . Then they have the temerity to lecture us about "consequences."—; never to pause and consider the consequences of such a "philosophy" for the future! What destroys all instinct and craving for higher things more quickly than work without *joy*! At last to become an automaton of utility! Consumerism! Senseless industry from dawn till dusk! It becomes a recipe for decadence, for moronism. American moronism as *philosophy*! James became a moron.

5

A follower of Bertrand Russell and a devout Catholic accosted a certain race pragmatist, chin held haughtily in the air, on a Chicago street after dark.

The follower of Russell:	How can you persist in your belief that your ancestors are real spectators of your every action?
Race Pragmatist:	A true belief is one that is emotionally satisfying. It satisfies the ancestors to see that I am emotionally satisfied.
The follower of Russell:	A true belief is one that squares with the evidence.
Race Pragmatist:	If my belief works for me it is true.
The devout Catholic:	Why, it is almost as if you are professing faith in the things religion deems real.
Race Pragmatist:	What is real depends upon what is useful for me to believe to be real, sir!
The follower of Russell:	Well, I can see that you have no inclination to subject yourself to external facts of any kind, that you are bent upon worshiping the products of your consciousness.

Race Pragmatist: In the long run, that alone is true which it suits human beings to think true.
The devout Catholic (—to the follower of Russell—): Just as pragmatism came into being during an age dazzled and drunken by its own achievements, this fellow is also drunk, and for very much the same reason.

6

The fanaticism with which American Pragmatism baptizes consequences as the *sole criterion of what is to count as true* points to an emergency in the American life of the mind. One *had* to counter the old truth *in order to survive*; one had to produce a permanent flux, a manipulable realm of purely human interest. One could either make truth or be its slave; one either went off the deep end with regard to human subjectivity or one disavowed human power altogether.

At the very moment the law is severing itself from the ancient and venerable moorings that prevented it from being plied as a tool to multiply human power, the infant pragmatism is pitching its first tantrum over the "cash value of thought." (—This is to say the precondition of the tantrum is Holmes, in his torts class at Harvard, seeing that proximate cause in liability formulae has nothing to do with cause and everything to do with human interest.) . . . Consequences = Cash value = Truth; . . . this means: imitate Holmes and the ones he indoctrinates by learning to *think legalistically* about society, culture, humanity . . . *truth*!

7

Truth as consequences. *Incipit stupiditas.* The pragmatist's estimate of the consequences must first be true; if his estimate as to what constitutes "good consequences" is mistaken, he is also mistaken as to his judgment of truth. When the pragmatist-Chaldean insists on reading the entrails of truth in this nonsensically circular manner, he should drop the idea of truth altogether. But the pragmatist will not do this. He holds on to her (—as Professor Dewey's very unwarranted warranted assertibility—) the same way his first cousins the process theologians hold on to God. These onto-theo-logists fashion two legs for God (—Truth is made just as wealth is made, says Wm. James: God is made just as truth is made, says A. N. Whitehead.) . . . Then, thanks to the nifty tricks of the merry old Godmakers of Harvard, God has one leg in time and the other firmly in the intransitory.—"The better to make him *work* for you," the old Godmakers sang . . . No; pragmatism has no desire to let go of God or truth: it wants to *deface* the old "absolutes." To increase human power, the power of human communities, at all costs;—*this* is the only desideratum. Thus, pragmatism allies itself with technology, including American fad-technology; thus, pragmatism defaces everything rare, every "higher," every sublimity it *curses* . . .

8

When you ask me to contrast the temperament of the pragmatists with the temperament of the Americans, I honestly reply that there is no contrast: their likes and dislikes are identical. It is self deception on the part of pragmatists to believe that by writing *about* American culture they are evaluating American culture (—when Holmes and Dewey say experience they mean culture) . . . The black pot does not critique the black kettle. What they select and publish as cross-commentary can only be yet *another* expression of *declining culture*. The whole attempt to cross-pollinate a kind of society that does nothing but *frame legal issues* (—and thus generate that most conspicuous of all democratic follies: the *contradictio in adjecto* of a juridical ethics) is clear and convincing proof that such a society's co-called philosophers have succumbed to the ultimate *fugue state* of running away from their responsibilities as philosophers by teaching the "utility," the happiness and social health of adapting to anything and everything.—"But! But! This is pluralism! We Americans accord ultimate significance to making and doing!"

9

Holmes, James, and Peirce are "great philosophers" to Dewey, and he honestly sees no latent hysteria in their writings.—"The people have a right to their self-infantilism," Dewey told Jane Addams at Chicago's Hull House over Chamomile tea.—But why?—

"Because," Dewey continues, "Messrs. Peirce, James, and Holmes offer us anti-toxins to the poisonous prejudices of the great Greek thinkers . . ."

—Go on!—

"Our pragmatism gives the *coup de grace* to representationalism . . ."

—But, of course; go on, Professor!—

"Don't you see, sir, that the exaltation of the mind over making and doing is the result of the bias of a leisured class of thinkers? Don't you see that the Greeks who thought were members of this leisured class? Ascribing a special status to the mind is the prototype for ascribing a superior status to anything . . . including, of course, human beings. Our pragmatism rejects any putative superiority of the mind over the hand . . . or the foot."

—And I suppose the thinkers die out in your pragmatic ant-hill? Or are they merely weakened, *made sick* by the cold party line of correct ideas and correct expression in your pale, depressive Kingdom of Utility?—

10

The degenerate over-reacts to stimuli; he lacks the ability to forbear (—Aristotle's magnanimity stands proudly at the opposite pole); he lives, he *survives*, with and by reason of his radical cures; to wit: William James agonizing over reports of lynchings in the South. His radical cure: he invents pluralism; his *other* radical cure: pragmatism. Thus, pragmatism begins as a political expedient turned moral;—I meant to say amoral . . . Its other genesis lies with the tort doctrine of proximate cause (*Invectives Against the Idols*, 2006). Hence, pragmatism in America is the offspring of purely legal phenomena and purely racial phenomena. Therefore, what *is* America?—But I was hoping you would make the deduction—: an exclusively legal society preoccupied with *race* . . .

11

What American Pragmatism wants: to wipe out every spidery simulacrum of superiority. *Consequently*: when William James expatiates on "truth" he becomes, in *our* eyes, a Cambridge window dresser. Pragmatism and its foot soldier, pluralism, want to *counter dominances*. This is why—again, in *our* eyes—the real narrative of American Pragmatism begins with John Brown. The hatred of John Brown, *intellectualized*; the resentment of the abolitionists, *epistemized*; . . . become thought, "philosophy," culture, culture's impossibility . . . For Emerson's cultural isolationism a fitting reply!

12

Nevertheless, the pragmatist, in his own sweet way, seems to manifest some concern for truth (—it seems to me—) even if his agonizing over traditional notions of truth is only a philosophical "consequence" of an original political need. The pragmatist and all that have pragmatist blood, and therefore

American blood, in their veins cast strange and insolent looks at traditional notions of truth;—yet quite unlike others who refute the old accounts of what truth *is* in order to replace them with new ideas, the pragmatist offers business-as-usual—I meant to say, busy-ness as usual—; he demands that no other kind of perspective be accorded any value once he has rendered *his* sacrosanct with such words and phrases as: "utility," "good consequences," "cash value," and—worst of all—any given idea's election or damnation in the democratic "marketplace of ideas." What then constitutes the American Pragmatist's concern for truth? What is *his truth?*—The test of truth is: the power of the idea (—*any* idea; from pornography to paths to holiness—) to get itself accepted in this *marketplace*. Yes; the market! The *scene* of the rise and fall of money, power, and opinions; the reflection of the unphilosophic, unsaintly, inartistic mass. It is no secret—although philosophy professors, believing as they do that the university is the universe, live on the outside of this secret—that this sort of open-faced chicanery is akin to the attorney's "theory of the case," his tendentious construction of anything that *sells . . .* For the secret stands revealed: the American barrister is the grandfather of American Pragmatism—with all his make-black-look-white trial tricks and sub-Machiavellian "pragmatic" antics, his evidentiary monkeyshines—just as American Pragmatism is a *cunning* common law method, a *cunning* legal logic, etc.—The American legal profession: the best lie-yers in the world: they lie innocently, pragmatically!—Why did the legal profession rejoice when it heard Holmes utter his first little philosophical apothegm? Why such prideful fluttering on the federal bench when they heard that Holmes Sr.'s boy had become a philosopher? Why the titter at the Harvard Law School?—Wasn't it because they divined *what could materialize?*—That Holmes could bedizen their duplicity with the appearance of finery and, on the other hand, fashion with his crafty legal skepticism a *new philosophy for America?*

13

Yet what *could* such a market idea, with its wonderfully infallible dynamic, presuppose? What could it *point to?*—If one considers that this competition-of-ideas for ascendancy in the marketplace is only the further development of the adversarial system of the law courts, one is no longer surprised when one smells the internationally infamous American justice game in its—*procedures . . .* (—It has been well spoken that the attorney does *not* believe a word that comes out of his two-sided mouth; neither does his image in the mirror, the American Pragmatist, although he turns down the lights and professes a "will to believe"—) . . . One might reasonably ask oneself whether this marketplace idea was not really some kind of aesthetic phenomenon (—a miracle since the "legal mind" knows nothing of aesthetics, nothing of proportion); whether this mindset was craving some kind of picturesque effect when it forced ideas to compete in such a hurly-burly world;—a world, moreover, *of its own making*. . . . whether the life of the mind should produce some impression in such a world; . . . whether this "art" of legerdemain was intended to elevate the ridiculous to the sublime all in the name and for the sake of "equality."—Suffice it to say that the marketplace idea implicit in the American Constitution (—the judges say *what* the Constitution is, remember?—) as well as the "theory of the Constitution" itself can *never* be conceived as dowries from a higher order. Indeed: it is from a *much lower order* that these things have evolved . . . *if*, assuming as we do, a kind of proto-pragmatism animated the minds of the founders and nourished the roots of the old common law. And it is at this juncture that Holmes's essential cynicism makes him shy of positing any "higher" (—nevertheless it is a mistake to suppose an identity between pragmatism's *goals* and the obvious glee Holmes felt whenever he pointed out that the bystander has no legal duty to rescue a person in peril, for instance; or his assiduous search for technicalities as a means of depriving deserving plaintiffs of remedies) though the "spirit of the laws" has, on certain occasions, the salutary effect of moving him beyond his "bad taste." Holmes believed the experiment of the conceit of a marketplace could fail; he'd seen it fail . . . : why should a judge who saw free speech doctrine as holding out for the *group* a greater possibility for survival and whose unsatisfied hunger for certitude drove him into the arms of dissidents, go out of his way to praise the presupposition of the market idea?—This presupposition is laid bare when Louis Brandeis is asked, "What is the remedy for bad speech?"—

"More speech."

—But why, Mr. Justice?—

Here Brandeis swoons into the usual tirade over censorship; but educated ears and alerted noses comprehend the fussbudget of citations as merely surficial and illusory. Every insider knows how principles are more important than litigants; how appellate courts, spinning ever more elaborate Cardozean webs over reality, do not even *see* the "the parties." Here Judge Learned Hand—the karma yogi on the second circuit—with his learned anti-Platonic idea of "the multitude of tongues" (—babbling incessantly—) merges, I should say, "concurs" with Holmes and his marketplace. The individual does not matter;—the idea, in and of itself, does not matter . . . cannot matter!

(—Does this surprise you?—) . . . What matters and is presupposed in all free speech adjudication is the pragmatist's notion of the *survival of the group* (—the ultimately hubristic idea of vouchsafing as much power as *possible* to human communities; Dewey's idée fixe; a hysterical notion even Bertrand Russell called "madness"—) . . . As in the Hegelian dialectic the individual is cancelled and forgotten: the sole value of any "thought seeking acceptance" in the market is precisely its *utility for the social group*. Holmes sees the fundamental law as the *enacting of Charles Darwin*: the more variations, the greater the chance for survival. Free expression in this sense (—the sense of the social group permitting *itself* access to its own resources—) is only a corollary of Peirce's obsession with "statistical probability."—But is *this* the bedrock presupposition *we* are after?—Let us return to Brandeis with his ready answers. "Freedom of expression enhances the probability of the ultimate success of the social group."

—But why, Mr. Justice?—

"In the long run good speech will *prevail*!"

Yet this "music of the spheres"—heard by everyone with ears that have been put to sleep by Rousseau and are hearing these quite inaudible notes in a dream—; this superstition of the Age of Reason that mankind seeks the good and is by nature good is precisely the inarticulate presupposition we are after . . . Yes, this superstition of Rousseau; this Chinese coolie-song of that old flapper Kant (—along with the glorious sermons of Jefferson and his French materialists—) that believes in the primeval and *buried goodness of human nature* (—therefore it is the right and duty of Charles Peirce's belief in statistical probability as it applies to a marketplace of ideas to exhume this essential goodness . . .); this is our lurking necessary assumption at last!—That the ideas of French fantasists lay fulgurating in the reptilian back-brains of every man who signed the founding documents of America—even though the dreadful superstitions of such fantasists as Rousseau and Condorcet, who made mankind naturally good and ascribed all the blame for every crime and folly on society, the state and education, may have been palliated by the example of Voltaire's ordering, more moderate intellect—is quite enough to make us cry: "Ecrasez l'infame!"

14

It is this French spirit, as Hippolyte Taine said so well, that had already destroyed the national community and thus made the Revolution inevitable and inevitably terrible; this spirit at odds with the adapting and conserving spirit of the common law of England; this spirit persuading over to its side the Bacchus-faced *infantilized* carping youth, the rebellious-minded Maoists and Sartrians and cigarette-sucking de Beauvoir ingénue; this poisonous, perverted and perverting spirit of the doctrine of equal rights for all (—a doctrine manufactured by Frenchmen turning the *Aequales sunt* of the Roman Stoics on its head; for this is what is *done* in an upside down world!—); this spirit of John Dewey and his ivy league acolytes, who have no *experience with the real world*;—this spirit has waged its war against the feeling for reverence and natural wonder flowing from the boundaries—and the distance between the boundaries—that make cultural achievement and spirit possible and has shifted the center of gravity away from honor and courage into *egalitarian impudence* (—the raising of every communitarian egoism to the senseless seventh heaven of "good consequences"—);—this impiously damnable conceit that man with his monotone of mass culture *can do anything*;—this, my objective comrades, is pragmatism . . .

15

Will you pardon my confession that the founding thinkers of the American civil rights movement offer me a particular kind of pleasure I can find nowhere else?—: the sleekest panthers crouch behind every word . . . I witness a beautiful *artistry* of spiritualized revenge. W.E.B. Du Bois remains one of the few real intellectuals ever produced on this soil. A true intellectual, *very much unlike* those breezy, smarty pants noddies who live inside the protection of university halls and highbrow literary journals the way mollusks live inside hard shells (—as if an intellectual is just one more journeyman and day laborer—) must suffer, and Du Bois suffered. In fact, when William James discouraged Du Bois from becoming a philosophy professor, Du Bois immediately understood that his teacher was attempting to unchain him for a larger life . . . Yet from *our* standpoint a pragmatist never loses his chains; he must use those same chains to fetter others . . .

16

Make no mistake about it: the legalistic-pragmatistic movement we call the civil rights movement wants its pound of flesh. W.E.B. Du Bois posits the *fundamental reality* as social reality; henceforth he will only live and think as a member of a group, i.e., a racial group. His concept of the "double-consciousness" is in its ultimate consequence a rather artistic kind of double-chaining. Just as the White man took the chains off the Negro's hands and feet and placed them on his mind, so Du Bois takes the *tension* that characterizes the Black experience in a White society (—his double-consciousness—) and very deliberately places it on society at large; . . . and *viola!*—pluralism is born! viz, his brand of pluralism, race pluralism, born as every pluralism is born: out of the uterine contractions of Jamesian Pragmatism. What does this *mean?*—Quite prior to the advent of any Sartrian sociality, we find Brother Burghardt examining the Master and Slave section of Hegel's most famous book: he is the slave; he is the master. In reality, he is seeing in the text a confirmation of his own *feelings* (—for the Black intellectual movement, believe me, is an intellectualizing of feelings . . . whether these feelings be the feelings of a Negro slave, a devotee of Negritude, a civil rights theorist in America or an African philosopher) . . . He sees himself, *who* he is, as the object of a dominant group; specifically the way he is *seen* by this group; in other words, he sees a seeing and thus experiences his identity as a *being seen* . . . He is *made* who he is by the dominant group seeing him as he—in reality—is not. However, the larger aspect of this reality is precisely two groups looking at each other, *facing off* against each other, defining and spiritualizing each other in a life and death struggle. Thus—if I may refrain from euphemism—the White man is *locked in* to the Black man (—and for more than one sufficient reason—) . . . This is also Ellison's idea: the White damages himself when he hurts the Black; that if the White culture would only accept the Black culture he, the White, would then be able to build a civilization. Or: when you buddy up to me, miracles are on the way . . . Two things: it would take *much more than a miracle* to build a civilization using American material; and, regarding this particular insolence of Ellison, it ought to be drowned, as Heraclitus says, like wildfire . . . To return to pluralism. *Groups* continually define and redefine themselves in relation to *other groups*. Du Bois must always see himself through the eyes of the *other* group, must always measure his soul by the tape of the *other* group, must always see himself through the revelation of the "other world." In order to flee any semblance of biological identity, Du Bois must posit identity as social and relational . . . Presupposition of this "anthropology"—: individuals *are* individuals *only* as members of groups; groups *are* groups *only* in relation to other groups . . . Meanwhile, when Hegel surpasses the "moment" of Master and Slave, the dialectic, like that river which "is and is not," follows the slave along . . . But what to *do* with a superseded, "cancelled" Master?—Du Bois knows what must be done . . . He must be pluralized . . . castrated *ad majorem dei gloriam* . . .

17

With a self-pretence of righteousness bordering on the rabbinical, W.E.B. Du Bois says he will seek "freedom from insult" by seeking first "freedom from segregation"—; and this as a *consequence*, mind you, of the aforesaid group identity.—This is not Booker T's idea.—"Seek ye first the Kingdom of God," Du Bois intones, "and all these other things shall be added unto you." So, Du Bois founded the Niagara movement: Black consciousness chooses to forget Booker T. Washington and follow its fiery pillar prophesying integration.—But the establishment of the Kingdom of God did *not* add all these things. Here I would encourage the race professional to compare and *distinguish* the famous Brown decision with the case of *Yick Wo v. San Francisco* . . .

18

The race professional is the pragmatist once more; one hundred times more . . . The cynical *employment* of the race question; the green-biliousness of playing the race card in trials and in every venue of that disgusting form of political nervousness we call pluralism; the rejection of every other attitude but those of the race-baiter, who has been *schooled in the technique* of wailing the loudest when his toes are stepped on, etc.—What are these things but so many *racial examples* of the stock pragmatic deception of calling "true" whatever falsity that happens to come along if this falsity "pays," has "good consequences," has "cash value," makes some elite fat . . . In fact, the art of living in an advanced democracy is the art of denying what is real; better yet: looking the other way as a lifestyle, a cold, insensate lifestyle . . . Question: what does a herd of water buffalo *do* when a pride of lions singles out a victim?—What then? Have "the people" been corrupted, *hopelessly corrupted by pragma-plura-lism*? Where must one go to find the truth today but *behind* all the legal procedures and journalist clap-trap we call "freedom," *behind* all the rights and safeguards and profits and noise, *behind* the whole phantasmagoria to find a few *false modern ideas*?

19

One must read Plato, Nietzsche, or the Bible; Juvenal, Lucian . . . even Petronius . . . One must make *some effort to purify the air* after so much as a glance at a primary source of American Pragmatism. One must go into the cave with Mohammed, in the cloister with Benedict and Jerome; one must swim into the lake and fly into the air to regain one's sense of health;—one must flee the stink of such abortions of "ideas." American Pragmatism; . . . this means: an immoral compendia of bad reasons given for bad instincts . . . bad "beliefs." In fact—and I say this primarily for the benefit of you brash newcomers to the world of philosophy; you whose first duty to yourselves and to your jealous, divine, beautiful Sophia is to get rid of all "truths"—one gets the idea that even the old notion of a static, universal truth must have had something going for it, must have been worth something to have been railed over by such a claque of gloomy truth-lepers. The greatest balancing act ever performed has been pulled off and is still being pulled off by American Pragmatism: an apology—perhaps, alas! an unwitting apology—for capitalist greed spewing out of the mouth of a political liberal; the God-denier emboldened by his will to believe; the supposed civil libertarian who wants individual liberties and legal immunities from big, intrusive government whose philosophy patiently labors to *form herds* . . .

20

We do not merely say that American Pragmatism is *mistaken* in its belief that philosophy should proceed like the sciences and reduce the philosopher to a menial laborer on behalf of the sciences; that being should be assimilated to logical reasoning and scientific method; that society under the pragmatist idea should reduce itself to legal method so that the "life of the law" becomes the criterion for what is to count as true; that all popular, i.e., pragmatic conceptions of *who* the philosopher is, because they may have "good consequences" for the unphilosophic, anti-philosophic herd are therefore "true." Etc.—We say that the squeamishness of turning ideas into "instruments of action" (—besides failing to criticize the anti-cultural trajectory this country had perforce *become* in light of the preoccupation with conquering the frontier and Emerson's bombastic move to close the doors on the great literatures of the world with his Independence Declaration, a wrong turn if there ever were one—) deprives philosophy of its right to judge values and sets in motion an inherently subphilosophic tendency to pass the imprimatur to any human action as long as it "achieves ends"—; which ends! you pragmatistic goslings, which ends!

21

It is, above all, necessary to identify whom we feel to be our antithesis: the pragmatist and everyone who has pragmatist agenda in his hands. All the commotion and rigmarole about John Dewey, the pragmatist *in the laboratory*, is simply . . . yes, I said *simply* . . . foreground for what *Dewey wants*. I've said it before: if you have a philosopher's egg—not to exclude the *exotic eggs* of those metaphysical speculators known as modern theologians—that seems uncrackable the intelligent egg-cracker must resort to motive research . . . *What* in the name of God or Devil does the malcontent *want?*—Yes; all the virtuous commotion, all the empiricism, the "logical form," observation, experimentation: all but foreground for a background. Divining this background, this inarticulate major premise, becomes the first duty of philosophic research . . . Otherwise, all is clouds.—Can you identify the motive? Does it *stand up?* Does it penetrate the whole of the thinker's odyssey? Does it all *cohere?* Was it, in all probability, his real *starting point?* Do all the nuances hurry to subsume themselves beneath its magical umbrella?—Very well; a philosopher uses every bit and piece at his disposal; he will even use his background to construct his "background" (—not unlike the litterateur whose "cherished complexity" is that rare, illuminating synthesis of creator and created being); he will defend his desires with reasons concocted *post facto* (—not unlike the appellate judge who does what he wants to do, then goes back to find legal excuses for what he has done; there *are* parameters, but as Judge Holmes said, "I can always imply a condition in a contract"); he will implead his prejudices as a dispassionate dialectic unfolding itself without the slightest prod from the creator of the play (—as if God were reading Hegel and enacting the text, step by step); he will foist new moralities on the people the germs of which are to be found swimming in his own pathology (—as when gnawing guilt prompts Tolstoy to adopt the injunction: one must live by loving and imitating the serfs, etc.); he will dogmatize metaphysical assertions *in virtue of* his own prior ethical needs (—as when Simone Weil wants and needs mankind to act non-violently, she *works back* to a metaphysical "Christ," a Weilist Christ, who grounds and guarantees her needs . . . when in reality Saint Simone is working forward) . . . Having demonstrated that needs practice and have always *practiced philosophy*, let us see what Dewey was after with the establishment of his famous "School" and if any of this is relevant to the Rhetor of Cook County. Shorn of all the sociological-anthropological-psychological-biological ga-ga, it would not be contradicted that our American Rhetor was urged to establish a School to teach some of the new principles of the new pragmatism. His basic insight was something he called the "organic circuit." This organic circuit was, on all accounts, lifted out of Hegel. Why would Dewey fool around with an obfuscatory German the other American Pragmatists loathed? But we have already provided the answer to this question. Dewey was *still* fascinated by the dialectic and needed the idea of *wholes*. Wholes are as wholes *do* and—since this conception did not contradict Darwin (—first principle: do not contradict Darwin—)—wholes could do a great deal for Dewey. Dewey needed the whole *before* the parts, society *before* individuals. As Jane Addams told him, "Antagonism is illusory." Therefore, since anything is indivisible before it is divided—and *gets divided* only as practical distinctions we make (—again: the tort theory of proximate causation: we make the distinctions and causal formulae determinative of liability, etc.)—then thinking and doing (—like the other distinctions: mind and reality, means and ends, nature and culture) are only practical distinctions the organism makes in its process of adjusting to its world. There can be no knowing without doing, no individual without society, etc.—And the *motive* for all of this?: the subduing of the invidious social distinctions Dewey needed to see subdued. Thus, in founding his School, Dewey was *planting* pragmatism the way Plotinus wanted to plant Platonism—with his envisioned "Platonopolis"—in third-century Rome. So, today, the fat worms of Dewey's harvest are seen sitting atop every "ideal." The slandering and poisoning of every last vestige of noble leisure; contempt for the intellect; the *schooling* of every genuine philosopher-in-pupa, every spiritualized youth with a head for *higher things* in the vulgarity of the inevitable instinct-atrophy implicit in the gaudy nuptials of pragmatism and "these self-evident truths." Let us not be prejudiced!!

22

If God "works" for man, God exists; doing and thinking—like the matching of the defendant's act with the plaintiff's harm to determine a causal nexus constituting liability—are only *practical distinctions we make*; i.e., pragmatists aren't interested in the *objects* religion contemplates or the objective reality of any *vita contemplativa*. They, in effect, deny this reality. Whereas God is shorn away by the conceit of some modern Occam's Razor, the *vita contemplativa* is denied entry altogether in the pragmatist's anthill of "associated living." Dewey *must* get rid of the invidious class distinction inherent in any contemplative ideal: Dewey is to the contemplative as the freethinkers are to the *ancien regime*: the *vita contemplativa* is taboo.

Professor Dewey has succeeded in persuading the world of *vita activa* to pass the harshest possible sentence upon the world of the contemplative: it must, forthwith, *give up its existence*. This unusual and intentionally cruel sort of punishment could only be invoked in accordance with a convincing showing that a capital crime has been committed against humanity; to wit: a leisured class of philosophical minds has stood over the practical people, dictating their destiny and paralyzing the practical hand with invidious distinctions, etc. Our own John Dewey has *fashioned a world*, the consequence of which is to disallow the realm of ideas and spiritual values apart from the everyday practical strivings and doings of ordinary folk.—Yet the contemplative natures, the poets, hierophants, and medicine-men, were, since the rudest times of human history, always despised (—since these natures were not active and hence *not like the others*—) and subject to summary ejection. The murder of Socrates stands out as a *recent* example; . . . just yesterday poor Søren Kierkegaard was mauled to death by vicious "yellow" dogs . . . The popular culture was discouraged from ejecting our earliest representatives precisely because and in light of a realm of ideas and spiritual values connecting the seers to higher, unknown powers (—thus they were dreaded and perforce honored—) . . . Thus, the pragmatists believe that to effectuate their desire to be rid of the contemplative, they will conceive a "philosophy" to abolish the contemplative's world.

Face to face any and every species of truth American Pragmatism amounts to a *criminal offense* against the truth. Dewey's "warranted assertibility"—the foulest, most mendacious piece of Yankee ingenuity ever devised—is in each and every case of its "application" an unambiguous *veto against the truth*; a philosophic fraud only an American—with his hard, exclusively action-oriented, action-deifying, legal head—could have contrived actively, *hostilely* at work against every possibility of finding out what truth is or could be.—Every young curious spirit who takes up philosophy feels the incomparable richness and splendor of every tradition mixed with the wealth and beauty of philosophic activity in general—trekking off as it does into every branch of learning and fueling the possibilities of critique and art—but grows depressed at the sight, the *scent* of assembly lines, fad gadgets, spoofey entertainments, and soporifics for frayed nerves.—For every philosophy necessarily reflects the health or decadence of the race; . . . consequently American Pragmatism *makes ashamed* . . .—Dewey understood the need to bring untruth into good repute; . . . the need, by logical extension of this pragmatic first principle, to sanction every expedient seeking to *relax discipline* and every form of intellectual integrity and passion for clarity . . . Otherwise, American Pragmatism could not recognize itself in the American legal racket of *using lies* to justify an adversarial system of justice (—I am speaking of the American justice system's "theory of the case," its *right* to fabricate) . . . The *proximity* of so much dishonesty forces one to conclude that whatever is *next to* and clusters around this good will to fool and manipulate the people (—as an accomplished trial lawyer will "*sway*" the jury with that subliminal legerdemain he calls "demonstrative" evidence) must be signalized and indicted and brought to justice; but not yet . . . not *yet*.—It must first be understood how noisy industriousness *prepares for submission*; how American Pragmatism perpetuates the slave trade.

23

Has this been deciphered? Have the pragmatists understood their pragmatism?—The pragmatist senses no danger in scientific method or its truth (—any more than it senses anything endangering in the identical inductive nature of common law method—) because these kinds of truths, constantly "boiling over" each other, impose no necessary restraint upon the ultimate homogenization of mankind. The pragmatist knows only one great danger: the maintenance of a state of wonder produced by the intellect's intercourse with leisure; . . . the state acknowledged to be the condition necessary for light as opposed to darkness, truth against error, wisdom over folly, etc.—What is darkness? What is error and foolishness?—Precisely the falling away from the state of wonder.—But the pragmatist is offended: since the many, the "happiness of the greatest number," the "demos"—again, what do the names matter?—*cannot* be the repository for this exalted state he must concoct his ultimate pragmatistic remedy: ideas, henceforth, must not be seen as "answers" but as "instruments for action" . . . and *more action* . . . until the earth is *nothing other than a scene for utilizations*, for obfuscatory "happiness" and commodification of "human reality." (—I say *henceforth* since American Pragmatism sees itself as superseding what it regards as outmoded; . . . yet another ludicrous American conceit made possible by that Jeffersonian monkeyshine, "We hold these truths to be self-evident; that all men . . .") . . . In other words, one must have a superfluity of time and intellect in order to find this state of wonder . . . Remedy: negate time and intellect. Make the hand *equal* to the mind—Darwin's monkeyshine; make the useful arts *equal* to the fine arts; devise "continuums of means and ends" and exalt action as *summum bonum*; have mankind constantly busy, constantly racing around, afraid it has "missed out" on something, afraid of reflection.—So that, finally, thinking becomes legal thinking about social issues, i.e., legal issues. One must no longer live but use oneself up instead; one must *do* as many things as possible for the most immediate, short term goals and in the shortest possible time. Thus, our famous and famously ferocious nervousness is born, fed by instantly manufactured "demand," non-stop blogospheric flummery, and mooncalf journalism. Hence, the American ethos, the quintessentially American export: activity without spirit; energy without depth, freedom of information crowned with the gaudy flower of correct thought.

24

The "functionalisms," "instrumentalisms," "pragmaticisms," etc. of the American Pragmatist—different names for the same basic *cunning*—were invented to militate against the oppressive, "invidious," contemplative capacity of Homo Sapiens and destroy the philosopher as we have known him/her for thousands of years. It could only have been in light of some coming age, some cosmological consummation and future—some "end time" if you will—that these congenitally shallow scientific craftsmen, these "homeless" Boston bums and trolls, felt the need to blot out an anciently venerated ideal and replace it with an *outrage* . . . Peirce, on the lam in Manhattan, writes James at Harvard.—"Sleeping in a dark alley off Fifth Avenue. No food for three days. Nothing but misery and philosophy. Mapping out the final defeat of freedom and chance . . ."—Man shall no longer look around in a spirit of wonder; he shall follow no educative spirit; he shall see *things* only in a scientific way and for a scientific purpose; he shall not look down into himself; he shall believe in God the same way a chicken pushes a lever and believes its cluck! cluck! brings the pellets; one must *act*;—become more and more *industrious*;—*form as many herds as possible* . . . One must cackle the cluck! cluck! party line of political liberalism, learn to see decadent, bourgeois art as true art, and live as uniformly as possible!—Away with all thinking! All critical reason! All culture!—*One needs an instrumental imbecile*: one needs a John Dewey . . . *Away with all higher men!*

25

Peirce's cosmology: the evolutionary process of reducing indeterminacy; matter is but a mind with fixed habits; destiny is the grinding off of individualistic tendencies on the road to the *ultimate fixation*; the gradual teleological purgation of choice, individualism, mind; in the end, everyone's beliefs will be the same, will have to be the same; the built-in *aufheben* to weed out bad and encourage good;—what are these imponderables but so many groping adumbrations of the *coming cosmic-matrist race*? So many footnotes to the prophecy of the convergence of all things?

26

American Pragmatism *speaks* to a people happy to be given bad reasons for ignoring philosophy. The American spirit is subphilosophical; the American philosopher and American philosophy represent a devaluation of the concept philosopher . . . Make no mistake here: hatred of ideas and the fetishism of action constitute the twin pillars of American life.—Don't take my word; ask any intelligent long-term visitor; ask Tillich, Mann, Arendt, Solzhenitsyn . . . Vargas Llosa, Whitehead, Mircea Eliade.—The ancestors of this pragmatism—that Crown lawyer, Francis Bacon, bribes, barratry, and all;—John Stuart Mill, a crypto-jurist if there ever were one—represent the unrelenting and unmistakable *English attack* on the philosophic mind and spirit . . . Spiritual power, profundity, density, vastness, depth; . . . don't go to England looking for any of *this*!—English and American thought: charm and subtlety for some; aridity, industrious plebeianism and vulgarity for others . . . What? You solemnly object on the grounds that your pygmy-ideas are *useful*? . . .

27

The Emersonian, and later, pragmatistic Declaration of Independence from real, i.e., foreign ideas had to happen; as a consequence of the democratic hatred of hierarchies and orders of rank, this cutting America off from the rich literatures and ideas of Europe and the rest of the world was inevitable. Meanwhile, is it any wonder the Americans fail to *recognize* the philosopher? that they demonstrate their insularity time and again when they fail to see *who* he is?—This emancipation catapulted American science and technology into a permanent springtime of self-praise, self-glorification, and presumption; . . . the most singular, *most unaesthetic*, foul-smelling springtime in history.—"Away with all tyrants, all masters!"—Thus groaneth the scientific, democratic hatred of hierarchies.—"Now *we* will play the tyrant! *We* will rule!"—Thus, in America, the scientist, the jurist, the captains of industry, the ignoble mindset of the utility people; . . . these jobbers now insist on their right to play the philosopher, to play the *master*. (—A society that worships actors very naturally comes to believe that everyone in that society must, in some sense, become an actor!—) . . . On the other hand, had there grown up a real philosophy in America perhaps our present legalistic society with its incessant framing of legal issues could have been *averted* . . . But why dream about such impossibles? Why dream at all in a milieu of ignoble dreams?

28

It was no accident—no chance attunement of variation to environment—that the founders of American Pragmatism, most notably that rhetorician/court jester Chauncey Wright, revered Charles Darwin as a "hero." For in the dice throw of existence, pragmatism and Darwinism eternally bet *against* the Goethes, Pushkins, the Beethovens. The *beautiful types* have nothing whatsoever to do with any "struggle for existence."—In fact, if pragmatism really wanted to become an authentic philosophy, instead of embracing Darwinism uncritically, it would have asked itself with the utmost earnestness, "What can we *do* to counter the nihilism from beyond the Channel?"—Not a chance! Darwin must be seen as a benefactor of mankind, a vindication of the pragmatist's *Weltanschauung*. You niggardly knickerbockers! Will it take a genius to see that the Platonic *eros* excludes the struggle to survive, and that this famed overtouted struggle so redolent of penny-pinching misers in overpopulated English cities therefore becomes superfluous? This struggle presupposes a state of chronic distress in nature; . . . a state that *does not exist*! Nothing could be more extravagant than nature . . . Then, when a struggle for survival *does* take place with its "natural selection," the higher does *not* emerge victorious. In fact, the time will come when the very condition brought forth by pragmatism and every one of its necessary allies will ensure that nothing "higher," nothing noble, beautiful, rare, unusual, complicated, wondrous etc., will ever show its face . . . The ideal matrist order has spoken and will speak again.

29

Our pragmatism did not *want* this kind of reply to Darwin. Just as the inhabitants of Jericho were deprived of the walls around their city, 19th century man was suddenly deprived of the special significance enjoyed by humankind since time immemorial. The pragmatists applauded the tumbling walls. To object to Darwin would imply the restoration of a distinction between man and the animals; the pragmatists did not *want* this restoration . . . The earth *emptied* of spiritual significance; man as nothing but a *continuation* of the animal herds; man *vulnerable* to the modern idols of anti-intellectual biologism, fundamentalist sisterhoods, and mediocre, contented, industrious "associated living" in the pragmatist's beehive: refutations of the savage and violent character of life; the abolition of intellectual energy, hence the abolition of great intellect!

30

No one has ever been converted to pragmatism; no one has ever been persuaded to become a pragmatist for the very simple reason that no one is really free to do so . . . One must be sufficiently *Americanized* for it: one must be enervated and maladjusted when it comes to an appreciation of the tasks of philosophy; one must have already reached a point at which the most unassuming, childlike visceral faith in utility and the utility of the herd virtues—industry for industry's sake, belief in averageness, leveling, journalistic yapping, the tragic self-abuse of computer addiction, the condition of comatoseness brought on by endogenous blogo-mono-tony: in one word, everything bound up and chained up that calls itself "free"—is professed with the most amazing innocence. American Pragmatism has been from the very first a hard-headed anti-philosophy movement possessed of sufficient Harvard perverseness to call itself "philosophy," a collection of legal minds *seeking each other out* with the express purpose of doing what legal minds have done since the days of ancient Athens: indurating and poisoning creative philosophy, persecuting the highest representatives of philosophy and philosophy's world, instituting a party line of "correct thought" and expression one transgresses at peril (—to the extent that Cicero devoted himself more and more to Sophia and her joys he *gave up* the practice of law—) . . . These people want to be recognized, want to come to power within philosophy precisely by virtue of their anti-philosophy activities, their "positivism," their corrupted philosophical instincts (—assuming they ever had even the thinnest comprehension of *what philosophy wants*!—) . . . That Americans are capable of philosophy; that Americans can, in any sense, be philosophers; that America does not persecute the spirit of philosophy; that the spirit of philosophy does not practice daily and hourly the healthiest, *wickedest superbia* of contempt for everything American;—these notions cannot be contradicted too severely!!

31

American Pragmatism has, as its basis, the legalisms and bromidic mobisms of an unphilosophical race all crowding together seeking self-justification in the names of legal bugaboos like "tolerance" and "equality" that have nothing whatsoever to do with human character and even less with the discipline and organizing power necessary for the construction of a civilization: the very sound of the word *disciplina* hurts its ears; the scent of the genuine philosopher's *otium* makes its nose bleed; one glance at a real philosopher at work and a pragmatist feels diminished and *wronged* . . . But once one sees that the pragmatist is only the further development of the active type of human being one is no longer surprised at the discovery of his secret hatreds.

32

One should cultivate an appreciation of the development of American Pragmatism as an anti-philosophic "philosophy." In the most capacious, most magnanimous sense, it could be propounded that since this anti-philosophy was conceived just after the Civil War—and the country had almost been destroyed by John Brownism, an *idea*—one *could* find at least one healthy intention in the craniums of the founding Bostonians: a kind of ideational defanging as a preventative measure. It could be supposed that pragmatism when Peirce first thought of it was a rather attractive "idea." . . . : that even the universe, when it felt its tail being twisted by bombastic whisky-sipping young men before a roaring fire, emitted a healthy, cosmogonic fart . . . One may see in this earliest American Pragmatism a kind of gallant quixotism in its resolve to *take on* the "old religion" and the "old philosophy" (—the dogmatists, the Hegelian dreamers, the Catholic medievalism, etc.—) . . . Yes, it is nice to think so; . . . but we know better today . . . *It is indecent to be a pragmatist today* . . .

33

The early Dewey, the pre-Chicago Dewey, who trains mind to serve a social purpose, whose mouth is full of *big moral words* and showy, Hegelian stuttering about "the ethical," the "structure of nature," and a society of knowers whose march through the world construes mind as the evolving teleological unity disclosing the divine (—Error incarnate to mistake technological diabolism for divinity!—); . . . what is this holy ruction but a lurking clue for the discerning observer that American philosophy had made a *wrong turn?*—Quite apart from this philosopher's inability to conceal his hand; . . . a similarly embarrassing faux pas for that tinkerer, Josiah Royce, who thinks that jiggling a mountain of words from the analysis of a matter—the outcome of which he already has up his sleeve—constitutes an adversary-defeating *demonstration* . . . a Harvard demonstration!— . . . Dewey the idealist *wants* a philosophy of immanence; then Dewey *gets* a philosophy of immanence; Dewey wants philosophy to justify an inauthentic religious orientation to the universe; then Dewey makes philosophy do likewise. Dewey thinks it would be nice to owe Asclepius a cock; then he parades around saying, "Crito, I owe Asclepius a cock."—Every pronouncement, every orotundity and oracular conclusion reveals the long arm of a social agenda; every solemn judgment about "the infinite" and "purposive action" mirrors the fact that Dewey has allowed publication and tenure to turn him into a party man who believes the lie that big words mean big thoughts.—Everywhere disingenuousness! Everywhere dishonesty!—Dewey emblazons his lofty advertisement across the propylon of the universe. "Will build to suit." (—to suit decadents—). Everywhere apologies for visualized power-structures and paradisean social orders a la Jane Addams (—although he had not yet made her acquaintance, her dreary hand was upon him—). Everywhere special pleading, priestly syllogism, party palavering . . . In the end, the labor unrest gave Dewey the greatest gift for which he could have ever dreamed: the right, the *duty* to think only in terms of "wholes," the duty to "unify"—: the glorification of the American error of demonizing "divisions" and boundary lines for the sake of a "Social Gospel."—The duty to recognize and sanctify the numinous chasm between souls; . . . the right to independence and independent thought: all must be cured, cancelled, redeemed!—Dewey offering himself for the salvation of the workers! For the *salvation of mankind*!—Highest symbol of the Social Gospelers: *Dewey on the Cross*—with Jane Addams as co-Redemptrix—the ultimate American gruesomeness!

34

Genesis of American Pragmatism—Nicholas St. John Green: proximate and remote causation in tort law, instead of touching upon real causes, i.e., natural causation, are only practical distinctions we make regarding the liability attached to a defendant's act;—Alexander Bain: belief is that upon which one is prepared to act;—Wendell Holmes: what the courts do and will do is the law, i.e., a prediction of what courts will do, nothing more portentous, is the law;—Chauncy Wright: Holmes confirms Bain, and together they confirm Charles Darwin; law grows and evolves, and if beliefs aren't mysterious phases of the mind but instead tendencies to act, changes in belief structure can be examined by examining changes in behavior; beliefs therefore evolve, the most mature resulting from the *survival of the fittest* among our original beliefs; moreover, if beliefs are habits of action, an analysis of changes of behavior as evidence of changes of mind marries human intelligence and animal instinct;—William James: beliefs are verified only by the future; the *survivors* constitute the right way of thinking.—Conclusion:—A pragmatist is not made any more tenable by his knack for telling plausible lies. Just as law will not concern itself with what causation *is* and seeks instead to establish liability in the instant case as well as forecasts for what future liability may be, the pragmatist is not interested in the objects of beliefs (—or in the causes of beliefs only the *consequences* of beliefs—). He is not interested in whether God *is*, only in the effects of believing . . . With regard to survival: no one ever became anything out of the contemptible sort of *surviving* mediocrity pragmatism validates and dreams of . . .

35

The pragmatists have a problem with beliefs; . . . they are not opposed to belief (—one may recall here Nietzsche's convincing polemic that convictions and lies are the same—); they *want* beliefs to be subjected to empirical investigation; stated differently, they do *not want* beliefs to dangle menacingly in the air as mysteries, i.e., as unverifiable phenomena.—What do the busybodies do?—They visualize a situation that will give reality to their desires; they *pragmatize beliefs*. Say that beliefs are what human beings are ready to act upon;—*consequently* the actions—and hence the beliefs—are empirically verifiable . . . But more: they want to make belief consistent with evolution. If this means omitting the object of belief from belief then 1) that's the way the cookie crumbles . . . 2) as long as a pragmatist is happy, what could an object *matter*?

36

Whoso paints his thoughts obtains the Muse's favor, but our pragmatists paint themselves into a corner.

37

American Pragmatism combines a "radical empiricist" acidity with the English utilitarian point of view *compounded* by the superstition of Rousseau: a compound of tendencies made for the legal profession to chew on . . . But what interests us is not so much the world this legalistic dream affirms as the world it *blots out* . . .

38

Shame on the idea that a philosophy must make someone happy in order to be a good philosophy!

39

Quite apart from the professorial pansies of pragmatism proper, Mr. Charles Peirce was a genuine man of the world. The only genius of the crew, he easily dominated the others; in conversation he was invincible; more: his flaws only served to make him interesting and . . . *women liked him*. He was in no way a low, bestial man, and there is enough evidence to convince that he did not possess the quintessential American trait: a poor soul. Moreover, that the criticasters have contentedly connected the only American near-philosopher's suffering with his character flaws and not with his genius and the kingly nature of his work is eminently understandable once we consider the source.

40

While the philosophy of Charles Peirce is not simple, the *problem* with this philosophy is as simple as spotting a prostitute in Boston's Combat Zone. Philosophers are no longer free to act like judges and do what they want to do, then look for reasons to justify what they've done.—Let us state the issue and its conclusion: *the problem with the Peirceian philosophy is the problem of how philosophy is to be practiced*.—That Peirce comes to philosophy from science and math; that he is hung-up on Kant; that he *wants* to function on behalf of, and as part of, a community of scientists; that he *abets* the nihilism of Darwinism;—these things are more than sufficient provocations to make us a little charier of presuppositions and motives. But these things—even the execrably obsequious attitude to science—do not directly touch upon the way philosophy is practiced; e.g., when Peirce abandons his premises upon seeing that they are leading him down the wrong road; this sort of thing arouses *more* than suspicion; . . . for we know what is bound to happen next: when the philosopher finally reaches his conclusion, he will *pose* as having attained it by "following the argument wherever it led" when in fact he has done no such thing. But then . . . that a philosopher should *not* be an advocate may well be inconceivable for a philosophy that grew out of a profession of advocates . . .

41

—Thus, we come down to what is tangible and practical as the root of every real distinction of thought.—(Peirce) . . . Yes; *down* is the word . . . But thoughts are not like beliefs; thoughts are not *ours* as beliefs are; we do not *form* thoughts; . . . truth is, we really do not even *have* them. Thoughts are on the outside; they come to us . . . when *they* want, not when we want!

Thoughts form part of that void of incognizability between mind and reality. When our minds—on the periphery of this void—hear the whirr of rushing wings we can know that our thoughts, like the restless shades flitting eternally in Hades, are, at long last, *coming to us* . . .

42

But Peirce insists: the way to "make our ideas clear" is to see them in a laboratory setting (—Mistake Number One: confining ideas to the laboratory; shackling the philosopher with science; . . . in effect, *creating a modus vivendi* between the philosopher and technological culture; No; worse than a mistake!—) . . . Next, conceptions have objects; . . . we must conceive what effects these objects may have; . . . then our conception of these effects *becomes* our entire conception of the object.—Here one need not attempt any unraveling and de-tangling of this Peirceian "snarl of twine" for we witness precisely the *vanishing of the object*—as well as the religious object.—(—No small oversight, it seems to me, for a man so interested in uniting science and religion—) . . . And all this happens *in order to make our ideas clear?* . . .

43

Clear ideas?—To *what end*, Mr. Peirce? Clear ideas and nothing besides? (—Peirceian clarity = personal clarity . . . making ideas personal—) . . . The personalization of thought is only a highway and byway to a community of scientificality, the *transference of all power to the community.* "Enquiry," in the end, would *have* to lead to a Crystal Palace of universal harmony (—science would be the means—); . . . a palace eternally under artillery fire from the souls of those who live and work *underground.* In sum: Peirce worked for the final consummation of all thought and experience yet foresaw it but dimly: he did not understand (—could not have understood—) the rise of powerful herds; . . . the forces of a new matriarchate had not yet begun to gather and gain strength (—Bachofen's pioneering work on a matriarchal interpretation of the ancient myths was unknown); . . . the new African philosophy, mute and vengeful, still lay coiled like a baby mamba at Western philosophy's hegemonic feet . . .

44

The earliest religions arose out of a dreamlike condition of failure to distinguish one thing from another. Early mankind confused one thing with another on the basis of the most fleeting similarities. It was *believed* the twain were the same when in fact only error *made* them the same. Later, the poets transposed this daring, confused capriciousness into narrative and the ancient mythologies were born. Still later, *much* later, when this mythological capacity—this religious impulse and creativity face to face a numinous unknown—hemorrhaged into a new realm, the first philosophy came into the world. The rigorousness of this new thing under the sun consisted in its sternness in *bracketing out* the actions of divinities as explanatory constructs: we had entered a realm of *reason* destined, as it were, to fly away like a bird headed for a far shore, some transoceanic continent where the old gods would be no more . . . This rude age of belief in which a happy, consoling metaphysics gloried in its extravagant youth could not afford to doubt that "the above is like the below"—; that a metaphysical correspondence ruled the realms; that the mind of man was the indubitable point of contact between the higher and lower worlds.—The same in other words: this active mind must be understood as *reflecting reality*.—The mind can know the real. The real is beyond mere objects of sense and is divine. Metaphysical edifices, towering anemones of ideas, spanned gloomy medieval skies as testimonies to what man *could do* . . . Then comes the solemn divorce of faith and reason! Thinkers found their way to the great anti-dogmatist critiques; the *adaequatio intellectus et rei* itself was summoned before the grimmest accusers, scourged and forced to recant. Philosophy *became* this grim council of accusers, became "critical philosophy."—Not that belief was dethroned or made impossible; on the contrary: we witness the vindication of belief (—Søren Kierkegaard's idea of the leap: to believe is to *leap out* of reason . . . a remedy *against* reason for reason's tendency, whether His Holiness knows it or not, is to bully belief; this remedy, we may say in passing, has never been placed in history) . . . To return: philosophy shed its outer skin and transformed itself; thinkers glanced askance at System-building, once revered as the prime art form of wisdom and knowledge; symmetry for symmetry's sake was called into question; philosophers were no longer free to "trespass into metaphysics," etc. That the universe was made for man's intellect (—as if it could be there for no other intellect!—) was *recognized as the specifically human presumption*. The categories of reason were constructs, fictions so-called, to make the world estimable for ourselves. The perfect fit of man's mind and reality was but a pretty piece of naïveté.—Consequently, philosophies that purport to investigate being must conduct any investigation in the light of the new critical spirit, not in violation of it . . .

45

To continue: asking philosophers not to overstep boundaries is tantamount to entreating them not to be so immodest. Surely, philosophy has not comprehended the phenomenon of man because it has gradually refined a few corollaries pertaining to cognition over the past three thousand years. Moreover, even supposing these corollaries to be inferences and deductions from *aeterna veritas* this would not excuse the ultimate immodesty of *spinning a world out of human cognition*. Yet this is precisely what Peirce does . . . And all to make *him* happy!—as if a happy pragmatist has anything at all to do with truth or error!—The fact is the spirit of optimism in logic gave Peirce the mission to invent worlds. The mind's categories *must* be commensurate with reality *inasmuch as* an absolute mind exists with identical categories to those of the human mind! Thus science, given enough time, must converge in the ultimate realized harmony of the final Peirceian omega point (—and not only science, we may add—) . . .

46

American Pragmatism's unconditional love for Darwin's "struggle for existence" is a synonym for its unconditional hatred for the *vita contemplativa*.—No pursuits are super-animalic.—The best of us are "of one clay" with the worst of us.—*Lies! Pragmatist lies*! The most significant gap is not that between man and animal, but that between man and man. The most powerful, most spiritual human beings sacrifice their own life-impulses for *more* power, *more* spirit. The pragmatist, down deep in his exclusively action-oriented American heart, wants to suck the spirit out of the *ruling natures* of the famous—or is it infamous?—triad of philosopher-artist-saint.—Unholiness! Deification of Mass Man! Vampirism!—This is American Pragmatism . . .

47

Darwin *needed* his "struggle for existence" for the same reason Hobbes needed his *bellum*: both men had need of their presuppositions to guarantee the consistency of their final judgments and conclusions. Suppose Hobbes didn't begin with his war of all against all; could he then posit the need for an absolute state? (—a figment clearly foreign to the English Constitution inasmuch as the English kings at their accession had to anneal the charters, etc.—)—And Darwin: how would natural selection take place—how would it *work for Darwin*—if he had at the beginning posited the *opposite* of struggle, hardship, distress? Under these circumstances, one should say that if Plato is right and beauty incites the elevated soul to procreation and generation of the beautiful, overpopulated English cities are enough to *turn you into a monkey.*

48

Mr. Justice Brandeis sums up the theory of the American Constitution when he prescribes the proper remedy for "bad" expression. The remedy—so far from enforced silence, as Plato recommended for the Perfect State—is simply *more expression.* This notion, then, is the real explanation for our press bias; information, *more information*, more "debate" will, in the long run, staunch all our follies and cure all our ills. In practice, everything (—that's right, *everything*—) must be talked to pieces and trivialized by "debate"—the holy law of the democratic form of state—; everything must pass through the *legal mill* of mind-enfeebling, bewildering babble . . . But this Babel of voices—this "multitude of tongues" to use Judge Learned Hand's famous euphemism—finally blends into a unison. This is the *Constitutional faith*, evidence of the way American Pragmatism fueled exegesis of a "value laden" Constitutional text.—This is Mr. Peirce's idea come to explicit fruition: his notion, his envisioned triumph of good; American Pragmatism's core idea of a Peirceian *final opinion*: the community of pragmatists seized as the final solution by James and Dewey. (—Hence, the individual becomes an unauthorized, illicit luxury *destined* to be transformed into a useful organ of the community; for pragmatism, as for its kid brother, socialism, the individual—as the *possible* incarnation of individual thought—becomes a source of revulsion—) . . . To return to the final solution . . . It seems to me that a triumph of evil is just as conceivable as any putative triumph of good. But if evil is mistaken for good—in the name of misconstruing the manifest "defeat of the Constitutional venture" or in a sordid effort to allay the consciences of the theorists themselves for the tricks they are playing—well, that is something else.

49

The destructive experiments Peirce conducted, to the extent that their underlying purpose is to efface the contemplative and ascetic ideals, amount to the suicide of a higher type of human being as well as the gradual destruction of a species. (—Homo Homogenens as the efflorescence of Darwinian man—) ... The gradual *convergence* of modern mass movements working toward a new night will prove the Darwinian philosophy's most secret goal: the combination and syndication of the weaker, more clever animals as a means toward the ultimate defeat of the stronger, more intelligent animals;—the victory of the uniform over the unusual and complicated. Stated artistically and with a view to vindicating historical reality: great things are succeeded by degeneration ... Consequently, Peirce *himself* became a suicide, a casualty of his own doing. Yes, for science! for the final uniformity! the flood-height of knowledge!—For these things Peirce—the embodiment of the ascetic-contemplative type of being—would live and die, like Homer and Archilochus, in grand melancholy ...

50

A scientific clarity with regard to *himself* produced in Charles Peirce a lack of clarity with regard to "the real," i.e., his own nature as genius. Bracketing out anything supernatural, he *must* have focused on the origin of his powers, the purely human qualities, the chance qualities that came together: the good fortune of his education, his interest, resoluteness, and energy ... and, not the least, Benjamin Peirce, his father, beneath whose blazing eyes the young man found the celestial fire.—But for what? For its extinguishment on American soil? ... Perfect stasis with "the object" ... ; this means: the elimination of sublime suffering; hence the elimination of all possibility for genius ...

51

Considering the poets as Martin Heidegger considers them, is strictly taboo for a pragmatist. The poet leaves the present and, unless he is a Hölderlin, is not overmuch concerned with the future. In point of artistic fact, the authentic poet comes from the *past* in every respect and strives to evoke the spirits of the heavier ages of mankind. The mythic, the uncertain, the fantastic, and the extreme are not merely elements of his art, but its foundation and precondition. Here scientific drudgery and an unthrilling sobriety with regard to truths are looked upon as albatrosses.—But if the poets are bridges to connect distant, very unscientific ages to our present—when they join heaviness and the symbolical to our over-active spiritual jejunity and utility in order to intoxicate us—they must be seen as enemies of the toilsome pragmatists and hinderers of those so easily lulled and deadened by action, simple action.

52

The pragmatist expects the world to salute him for his generosity when he allows for the possibility of his chimera-religion, but he is expecting more, much more. He expects the religious feelings to perdure, but feels uncomfortable at the thought that these feelings will take hold of any new territory. He remembers how the Enlightenment discredited these feelings for the religious dogmas, remembers how these feelings were driven out of religion and into positivistic philosophy, art, politics, and the sciences. Consequently, he believes in the *possibilities* of religion. Yea, but here his religious instinct is identical to the instincts of the old Hegelianism he supposedly left behind: *his* chimera will have the tail of a serpent, the body of a lion, and the head of a pragmatist.

53

As Katherine Anne Porter's casket descended—legend has it—her created characters hovered mournfully about the rim of her grave bewailing with bitter tears the fact that their creator had passed away. And whether you stand with Comrade Nietzsche and say that created characters are merely invented and not "necessary" as actual living characters are; or with Comrade Dostoyevsky and contend that real people are but "watered down versions" of characters in fictional art, it cannot be easily denied that art triumphs again and again . . . But how does it triumph?—By deception; by illusion: by acceding to the writer's bag of tricks the audience is led to believe that created characters, in no way products of nature, are real. The audience is willing to *see* the character—as when Conrad's Mr. Kurtz, a character the author has taken very few pains to draw, lights a cigarette, we can see his ruddy face in the momentary flash of the match—and take an abridgement for the whole. That the writer, the painter, the sculptor bestow life is a fantasy . . . Let us state the truth of this matter: the audience's belief in the characters—*and only this belief*—makes the characters real. If you prefer: the audience's belief bestows reality; . . . the characters *become real by belief in them*. (—Not to say, however, that this reality is fixed and, as it were, universal: there are as many Don Quixotes and Julien Sorels as there are—or will be—readers of Cervantes and Stendhal; as many *different* glimpses of Sappho's ingénue as there are lovers of Sappho; as many tragic clowns on the tightrope as there are adventurers who wander with Zarathustra, etc.) . . . Very well.—In the world of fiction, belief bestows reality.—Has it ever occurred to anyone how precisely this sort of thing grooves with the *religion of William James*?—How pitiful and grotesque must this pragmatist religion be, how repulsive, for even stalwart atheists to feel offended by it?—: that belief, quite in the manner of the audience's belief bestowing reality upon a fictional character, *makes* a religious object real; that belief makes religion "true," makes God "true"; that God is God only because some spiritual cad, some New England snob, some pragmatist happens, today, to believe he is! and tomorrow, perhaps, depending upon the Dow and the NASDAQ, to believe he is not!—When James substitutes human belief in God for God, he is but feigning interest in God . . . Having foregone his opportunity to be an honest atheist, he chooses instead to be a very dishonest believer . . . I meant to say, belief-er. It is *this* sort of spiritual drunkenness, *this* sort of subjectivistic stupidity that paves the way for the decadent, child-empowering, engineering *Americanism* of John Dewey; *the plague bacillus* now covering the globe.

54

The idea of action in pragmatism is quite unlike anything else in philosophy. "Good consequences" and "cash value" are used as latchkeys to open metaphysical doors; the pragmatist then enters the sanctuaries where the old metaphysical problems have lain unsolved and proceeds to solve them using the same keys.—What then? Are the keys stored away, awaiting further use as problem solvers for the "most sublime yet most ridiculous" pursuit?—The keys are never stored away. There is much more for action to "do."—Pragmatism depends upon the idea of action to solve, more properly, *dissolve* the old, hated distinction between *higher and lower*, for active people are always wanting in the higher activity, that of the great individual. They are active only as parts of groups;—and pragmatism is very interested in group activity and its benumbing possibilities. The active types are active only as generic creatures: a scholar does not *stand alone* in the university (—if the scholar feels a need for *that*, the scholar, following the great examples of Schopenhauer and Nietzsche, *leaves the university*—); a businessperson, a statesman, an official, an attorney *can never stand alone* (—in the representation of controversial clients, the lawyer sometimes fancies he is standing alone and revels in the experience of a momentary quixotism; e.g. the Roman Stoic Labeo stubbornly resisting an overweening Principate, Hamilton's maverick defense of Zenger, Belli "taking on the corporations," etc.) . . . Moreover, do not ask these active people why they are active. Since all their action comes from general perfunctoriness and stupid inertia (—they are active as comets, condensation, waterfalls, and rolling stones are active and precisely for the same reasons—) and has nothing to do with unique, frequently dialectical, individuated willing, the active human types will not be able to give an answer, let alone a rational answer . . . After all, what landlord, salesperson, banker, or CEO, whose pinnacle experience consists in amassing more and more "capital" in a frantic effort to assuage his "disorder," can be seen as *rational*? Just as the waterfall and the rolling stone obey the laws of gravity, so the actions of this lower species of man exist in consequence of something and in mechanical obedience to something.—The lower and the higher are but other names for the slaves and the free; for as laid down by all philosophers since the very first philosophical activity in ancient Greece, he who is not at his own disposal *is* a slave.—American Pragmatism: the quintessential slave philosophy. America: home to the wealthiest slaves in the history of the world.

55

There is something *rotten* in the way philosophy is practiced in America; it is, today, the rotten apple in the history of philosophy.—Just glance at the way philosophy is *confused* with professional, scholarly activity in the American universities. The entire hub-bub of professional jockeying for tenure and respectability; the insane frenzy to publish all manner of intellect-petrifying glossolalia on other people's ideas; the notion that thinking about thinking is thinking and the crawling up into high chairs is proof of thinking; the agitated, ant-like industry of fescennine, sandal-footed Rortyites behaving as if in the throes of some Wall Street dash for the finish line.—All this business contradicts in the starkest most degrading manner the calm of Pascal, Epicurus, Montaigne; the free-spiritedness of Nietzsche who *cut himself off* from the scholarly pedanticism that held him down just as the world of Bayreuth held him down and prevented him from *learning how to think*; and, finally, Plato's conception of what the Academy should be: his warning what it should *not be* . . . And, pray tell, what manner of perversion has spawned this lamentable condition? What iconic force has stood watch at the doorway to prevent reform? What *one thing* has dominated American philosophy since the Civil War?—*Harvard Pragmatism*!!—James, Royce, Santayana, and the frou-frou.—One may detect here a continuation of the error of William Ellery Channing and Ralph Waldo Emerson, the *fundamental cultural error* of the Americans: cultural isolationism: the irrational fear of European philosophy and literature; that is to say, to *repeat*: the fear of ideas.—For it is a fact: had the American philosophers taken the European trends seriously—in one word: had they divined the *future of authentic philosophy*—they might have been more cautious about primatizing the comical discipline of epistemology; secondly, and even more comically, the uncritical subservience to Darwinism might not have been such a fait accompli.—In Europe, it was *never* a question of this epistemological-ism versus that epistemological-ism or of adapting to Darwin. The keenest minds—on the contrary—were intent upon simply getting rid of epistemological obsessions (—one no longer *needed* to answer Hume's skepticism with suspicious, circumlocutory arguments signifying nothing—) and transcending the "nihilism" of the ape-philosophy once and for all.—As it is, the tradition of thought that emerged from the James-Royce philosophy department's way of doing philosophy has turned the noble tradition of philosophy into a laughable proposition and has rendered the philosopher's existence *as* a philosopher comically impossible.

56

The pragmatist wants to take in hand the contemplative element in man and weaken it (—this happens not as a mere consequence, but flows directly from his *intention*—); he wants, if possible, to extinguish all trace of it . . . He wants Aristotle's idea of contemplative repose to be as ashes under his feet; he wants all repose in civilization to come to an end so that the coming twilight time may, by the very agitatedness which is its essence, halt the direction of culture. Complete computerization is hailed as the bulwark of the technological-informational complex within which the Androids swarm over each other like ants and bees. With no time left for thinking and quietness, one will no longer ponder deviant views; what is not taken in as part of the party line will be banished and hated. And *this* in an age of "compassion"—"mercy"—"love"—and "freedom" as no human being has ever experienced it.

57

American Pragmatism's motto: *shallowness pays.*

58

Our old dead values parch in the sun. And yet the locust women are still plotting burglaries.

59

When the Aegean sky is gray and the sea is combed by the wind, the seamen long for a quaff of yellow beer, the thin arms and brooding eyes of a Greek girl, and oh! to walk on land one more time.

60

Show the pragmatist where the treadmill is; he never wants to rise an inch.

61

James's Pragmatism is an account, based on experience, of how some people seek truth, not a statement of how they ever find it. The original statement a pragmatist declares true can never *be* true unless and until other statements are also proven true; but *these* statements the pragmatist wants to declare true must remain untrue unless and until other equally parasitic statements are declared true. *Ergo* pragmatist truth can never be found; *ergo* the pragmatist dismisses the finding of it as inconsequential . . . When, under the circumstances, the only honest thing to do would be to declare, "We pragmatists have nothing whatsoever to do with truth."—But the pragmatists will not say this.—Instead, they lob the possibility of truth over into the expanding experience of others, placing their faith, as usual, in the circumambient world of the ever-mutating community of worker bees, and say, "In the long run" (—think of the unabashed childishness of First Amendment theory—) . . . "*In the long run*, after enough experience is placed in the crucible, after the flash and flying sparks of ideational swords have faded away, everyone will see pragmatism as the only truth!"—Thus, the appalling kind of Roycean Pragmatism (—which is ultimately nothing but the keystone for the secularization of all religious dogmas in the effort to outbid those dogmas—), this Eschatological Pragmatism at the end of pragmatism is the nauseous resurrection of a long-discredited, superannuated "Absolute."

62

We have been taught better, and, consequently, we *know better*. Philosophy in America—Harvard Pragmatism and that reconstituted regurgitation of it, Santayana's Critical Realism, so-called—is a step-by-step, piece-by-piece confession on the part of the professoriate that it *knows* its absolute discontinuity with the practice of philosophy as a self-consciously lordly enterprise: it confesses its sickliness and degenerated, pedantified dreariness in its very landscape: by means of illusory distinctions upon distinctions and conceptual phantasms (—which by these gentlemen's express admission, exist only in imagination as heuristic phenomena—) dusty-headed Harvard PhDs, having sold out the moment they were granted graduate student status and swimming in a host of pompous errors their high-chaired mentors bequeathed to them, proceed implacably to immure themselves hopelessly within the Jericho Walls of "theory of knowledge," as if the *purpose* of American philosophy is the reduction of philosophy to epistemology, to the prolix Harvard gobbledygook of the mind's relation or lack of relation to "the object."—This professoriate wants to give this all-too-workmanlike gobbledy-genre, this *corruption*, the appearance of high seriousness by clapping "scientific method" behind it (—Again: it is an American article of faith that science *redeems*—) . . . As if giving a philosophy that denies itself its right to enter a vacant premises a scientific coloring is enough to turn cowardice and dishonesty into integrity; . . . as if science is perfectly capable of providing its own direction; . . . as if the philosopher's duty itself is insufficient to place him eternally above science, above theory of knowledge, above sweeping the courthouse. As if the philosopher does not *rule*.—But the gobbledy-osophers are puerilely oblivious. They go on publishing in their learned journals, generating intellectual tempests in Cambridge teapots, thinking they are liberating philosophy from medieval absolutes when all they are doing is divesting philosophy of one straitjacket immediately to immure it within the prison of "correct" popular thought.

63

A word should be spoken about the ignobly mechanical coolie labor of our Harvard intellectuals.—For ways that are dark, for tricks that are vain, the heathen Chinee is a most peculiar bird.—What thought purporting independence, what mind not mired in the clay of Academe can fail to recognize a duck when it sees a duck, when it hears the unmistakably pedantic obtuseness of its quack! quack!—Every Harvard intellectual understands character as an objection; honor and courage are seen as dangerous atavisms that threaten "veritas."—What destroys the spirit of philosophy more quickly than the performance of scholarly labor by automatons of nervous, learned energy, who fondly shuffle suspiciously tailored "concepts" in response to previous, just as suspicious "accounts of how we know," in response to previous coolie labor?—

64

Just as there are thinkers whose intellectual labors contribute to the turbidity of philosophic discourse, there are those who freshen the air. Even the prolix Kierkegaard and the unashamedly non-literary Martin Heidegger may clear the air with their prose and hold the young student in authentic suspense. Plato himself, whose prose Cicero compared to the voice of divinity, averred that this kind of lucidity is the writer's way of being polite to his readers.—But what a different, depressing world we enter once we attempt to read the American practitioners whose involuted ululations sound like a string of coonhounds crossing a Mississippi bog; as if their word rattling *intends* to hurt the ears and hopelessly cramp the mind! Gewgawed with winding get-tough tautologies and impossibly vapid hard-boiled technologisms, the American philosopher betrays not the slightest concern for how he may be heard and understood . . . Perhaps he knows—as Nietzsche said so well—that the sophisticated reader reads with his or her ears as well as with the eyes; and that *there are no sophisticated readers in America* (—Tell me, what senior editor at which Manhattan publishing house does not know this fact as well as how to use it profitably?) . . . He also knows *what* the Americans read: deliriously non-stop journalism, mind-deadening political dysphasia, and those feeble-willed toreadors of scat we call our "icons of contemporary literature."

65

We have said that American philosophy denies itself its *right to enter* the human reality it has a right to judge.—And let us say here now (—with regard to what you may be thinking—) that the "new" genre of African-American philosophy a) is not philosophy but merely special pleading with one race's interests in mind (—no matter what the pleaders may *say*; the genuine philosopher, being of independent means, is not interested in what they are *saying*—) and, b) this "thought" can never be anything more than a political sit-in, a reflection of political phenomena, i.e., political lies to benefit one group vis à vis all other groups, i.e., *pluralism in practice*. In other words: this thought has denied itself *its* right to enter.—We have said that American philosophy hides behind its epistemological obsessions; that the stupefying droning on about mind and matter, the painfully dishonest supplying of various painfully specious "accounts" of perception and the content of "consciousness" turn the American mind into a laughingstock.—Let us now point to the depressing, despicable manner these "views" are disseminated. I say "disseminated"—I must be pardoned—; these views are *generated* in the very same manner: the corruption, *the proof of a realm empty of intellectual conscience* is precisely this: the individual professor's puerile need for the company of rogues; his assembly line mentality (—his Henry Ford-ism—); his need to *feel* the security and support of this assembly line (—his American mechanicity—); his banding together with other like-minded "thinkers" to form a movement via publication in "the learned journals" in the hope that this group-publishing will have the effect of launching the movement, etc.—This sort of thing cannot be sufficiently calumniated! It has the courage and integrity of the animating spirit of philosophy against it. The *presumption*—in one word, the *innocence*—of this petty, pedantifying bourgeois activity proves—this time beyond any possible, chimerical doubt—that the Americans have never learned what philosophy is about. The genuine philosopher simply does not function as a spider or worm among other spiders and worms in a glass jar. No; not even an intellectual is able to function in this manner; . . . writers, yes; intellectuals, no; unless, of course, you are an American "public intellectual"—that *collusion of decadence types* seeking each other out; judgments *against* intellectual integrity, *against* honesty and *superbia*;—in this I detect every fated public intellectual . . .

66

To resume; in the midst of all this spirit-killing miasma who could have foreseen that an *anti-toxin for American Pragmatism* was on the way? Charlatanism and congenital cowardice had held back and prevented the spirit of philosophy for so long a reaction was bound to come (—I say *congenital* for the simple reason that the paranoia of William Ellery Channing and Ralph Waldo Emerson that *closed the doors* to non-American thought, resulting in the coup of Emerson's "Declaration of Independence," established a *bloodline*); and it came—of all places—from a certain ferment, mid-century, among the undergraduates. Interesting events began to occur that would, in the end, hold out an opportunity for hope—*if* the professoriate would respond—*if* the professoriate would act . . . And American philosophy itself hung upon this *if.*—Sidney Hook's raspy old voice no longer defended his master, John Dewey. Had the fire gone out?—Mortimer Adler began repudiating Dewey and all he stood for.—Mircea Eliade, Herbert Marcuse, Walter Kaufmann, and Hannah Arendt breach the wall of independence Emerson had so carefully erected.— Next, two pivotal events: Kaufmann "rehabilitates" Nietzsche from the Nazis (—that Nietzsche *needed* rehabilitating was the sole consequence of a stunt only the intellectual dolts of the Anglo-American world could pull—) and makes

Nietzsche's oeuvre readily available to the English-speaking world.—William Barrett, an editor for the *Partisan Review*, introduces Jean-Paul Sartre in the *Review* and publishes his *Irrational Man*, which uncovers a new world for American men and women of mind.—Kaufmann and Barrett find American academic philosophy out of touch and parochial; that, notwithstanding the left-liberal leanings of the Deweyan cohorts, the philosopher had a first duty to investigate not consciousness, but the world.—Then Sartre lectures twice at Yale, entering the parched, lifeless American intellectual environment by way of the French Department.—America, at long last, had bitten into the phenomenological apple, the haunting spectre of post-war European existentialism; the intellectuals had to choose between their enlightened, fallen state and the bread-and-water, business-as-usual insipidities of a compromising pragmatism.—What then?—Would American philosophy find its new kicks on the European Express and learn to appreciate the tragic destiny of man? Would it seize upon this historical opportunity to cross the Rubicon and leave pragmatism behind? Would it at last repent of its intellectual aridities and follow the call of the wild?—The thrill of leaving pragmatism is one thing, repentance quite another. Repentance means changing the heart, changing *direction*. So what did American philosophy choose to do? Did it relinquish the epistemic anxiety evolution bequeathed it: the anxiety over "how we know" in a Darwinistic universe? An anxiety that propelled not forward but backward to the old cramps of Locke and Descartes? This is our answer. Just as theory of knowledge obsessions engendered a philosophic spirit that runs and hides from real critique and real life so with the new opportunity to dissolve the obsessions American philosophy *again spurns life*. It was precisely *because* American philosophy rejected its own possibilities resplendent in the new Continental philosophies of fundamental ontology that it paired Kierkegaard with Ibsen's Brand, labeled the later masterworks of Nietzsche as products of insanity (—Anglo-American stupidity!—), proclaimed existentialism "irrationalism" and "nihilism" (—what an educated ruffian will not do to preserve his right to business-as-usual!—), etc . . . The American academics—even those of the immigrant-vanguard who had breached the walls—knew what they had to do. True, Herbert Marcuse *led his students out of the classroom* and placed the "tools of philosophy" in their eager hands; but what can be new under the socialist sun? Walter Kaufmann made Nietzsche available to read, but he never dreamed of going beyond his rehabilitative polemics. Meanwhile, philosophy professors, following William Barrett, who had one leg in academia and the other in the wider intellectual world, discover literature, auguring a new *mood*: depth was fused with complexity and life. But, alas all merely an aesthetic phenomenon. It is as if the students were led into a museum for a view. The students can *feel* that the philosophy preached lacks a social dimension.—The mood, shrouded in ambiguity, is collapsing as the ephemera of a lofty dream. Everywhere, everyone makes the choice to opt out. American philosophy, eternally corrupted by pragmatism's will-o'-the-wisp, is itself opting out . . . again . . . *again*!

67

When Sidney Hook learned he could no longer defend John Dewey, the dead pragmatist was learning how to defend himself. Like the nominalism that left the schools to cavort unimpeded in a Renaissance-awakened world American Pragmatism greedily gained ground. As the friends of Unamuno, when the great mystic was put under house arrest by General Franco, exclaimed, "Spain is under arrest," and as Charles deGaulle said, "Sartre is France," so Dewey, posthumously thirsty for the blood of the ideals he hated, christened Deweyism the authentic America.—*Here one has the duty to assert an absolute equivalence between pragmatist and spiritual destruction.*—Dewey says with the Hindu god, "I am the destroyer of worlds!" The most spiritual human beings find their happiness precisely in the realm pragmatism disallows—*must disallow*—and sedulously works to erode and blot out of human memory. Deweyism turns its face against the very ground of our being: there is no thread of Ariadne leading out of it. Everything this Deweyism defends, praises, and *wants* for mankind depends upon mediocrity in ability and desires. To be an oil can for a machine, a functionary, a cog, a public utility, a gelding professing contentment with "equality," a specialist;—this is the species of happiness for which Deweyism offers its apology. Injustice can *never* be linked with inequality and hence unequal rights and responsibilities.—What is justice?—Precisely the *setting free* of the better endowed and with this the reverence for *separation*: the separation of the spiritual from the actors, the bad from the good, the elect from the damned, the refined from the coarse, the rulers from those a hundred miles above them, the demons in hell from the angels in heaven, the successful doers from those who roam the labyrinth and dwell on the high crags of Helicon . . .

68

Pragmatism seeks to devitalize its opponent, the intellect. Dewey's world is the alchemist's world turned upside down: the transmutation of gold—from the standpoint of the great Greek thinkers—into base metal; ... *homo sapiens* without the *sapiens*; . . . without the *homo*! After Dewey, the coming degeneration *proves* that the world can no longer recognize his case as unique and exceptional. Very early on, Dewey concocts his expedient, his idiosyncrasy, his pragmatism, his "America" as the world's radical cure: *he wills the nightfall of the old humanity.* Meanwhile—and this old horned and haloed pragmatist could not see; it is for *you* to see—the underminers who want to instill venom and skepticism into our trust in life, man, and ourselves—the slimy, vengeful haters who preach against hate—; these abortions of "love" silently prepare for union in this night;—for this coming night *is* the marriage, merger, and confederation of all possible degeneracies in the world!

69

John Dewey and Jane Addams hoped that with the prospect of an old, discredited "relativism" baptized anew as a strict "separation of church and state" secularism implicit in the American Constitution they could *sum up* every refuse element—from the expiation of their secret, I say, *secret* Harriet Beecher-Stowe species of religious guilt to everything in revolt, everything that hates itself, every form of life requiring a secret revenge, the history of anarchist agitation in Chicago: the elevation of the Pullman strike, Sacco and Vanzetti, the holy Eugene Debs, the sleeping "Negro question," etc. into *comprehensive symbols of a new order* in which the only real struggles are legal in nature, the only redemption is "unity," the only sin "divisiveness."—Furthermore, they knew—or should have known—that to accomplish this would require the *cunningest* interpretation of "free speech doctrine" imaginable. *Could* the legal profession pull off a second gigantic legal fiction that would operate with the same secrecy and success as the primary fiction? *Could* the law inculcate a party-line kind of correct speech and see it operate *behind* a Constitutional panoply of free speech adjudication the same way judicial lawmaking operates behind the fiction that the judicial branch only applies existing law?—

70

Dewey *corrupts truth* by taking all the things by which the anarchists and holy dogs of labor agitators exercise their fascination, their playing the masses and holy contempt for truth (—socialist insolence, drunkards of dreams, utopia psychoses—): he then places these things into the truth theory he invented.—"warranted anarchist assertibility"—

71

The scribe in Babylon was a hundred times more a man of the hour than a man for millennia. He was a functionary, a toady, a man whose value as a scribe consisted in his *usefulness* for the practical world of action. He was not a thinker, most certainly not a commander. Then something is felt in Egypt; literature as a *higher calling* casts off its practical trammels, flies above the earth, and descends in power, splendor, and might. The Jews become enamored of this *sublime* idea: one must use language to fly; religiosity, for the first thrilling time on earth, learns to soar. Then in Greece and Rome, literature is cultivated for its own sake. Religion is now a mere adjunct; the poet flies above the practical. Sibyls and moon women, as well as slaves and sons of slaves, join the old male guard and the once charily circumscribed literary aristocracy to create the foundations of an erudite culture. For the very first time, one is commanded to use the ears *and* the eyes (—for the Muses are jealous, exacting mistresses—); the Platonic *eros* evokes the holiest law: *beauty is the creation of beauty.*—What happened?—Reading and writing had *combined* to create a tradition, a culture transcending eras and peoples. A tradition of reverence, honor, seriousness, and *segregation*; a tradition of patience, smiling integrity, and *distance*: such a tradition was the result of the most exacting, jealous labor of thousands of years.—The reality of a foundation had been laid, bit by bit, layer by layer. Such a culture could have existed side by side with religion, each adorning the other, each wise enough not to interfere with or pollute the other, etc. This sort of civilization could have educated the people to listen; one could have been taught to value repose, taught how the inability to be still and appreciate solitude is shameful, taught the self-abusing indecency of fad technology, one-dimensional computerism, etc. Well, as it is, listening is not an option; manipulation is the only real, effective way to run a democracy—and the people love it. Sublimity... Autonomy... Taste... All sold down the river! The disappearing act of millennia!—This, then, is the way to read John Dewey: the pitting of one thing against another, the counterfeiting of a cultural possibility... *become reality.*—These pragmatists are shrewd as foxes; ... they have deciphered the hidden meaning of our glorious "self-evident truths."—Whether "these self-evident truths" were waiting around for pragmatism's polemic against higher culture is a question that could be answered in the negative. The fact of slavery was certainly sufficient to place the Americans where they are and where they are *going*—; how can I say?—sufficient to bestow an American destiny.—Without a doubt, Jefferson's malignant perversion of the Roman jurisconsult's *aequales sunt* was sufficient, absent our philosophy of cash value and common truth-charades, to trample down every previous kind of cultural harvest and ensure, "in the long run," the *extirpation* of anything higher, noble, reverent, and splendid in a people, anything that possesses duration and promises a future for independent thinking, solitude, and thirst for *higher* things: Equality and Pragmatism;—the twin sirens of cultural stagnation and death . . .

72
Fools and simpletons recognize each other.

73
The ruling nature is the slave of the ordinary man.

74
It's sickening: the deep souls unknown, shallowpates walking tall.

75
Other men tend my fertile, blooming fields and swagger around with my gold.

76
A thinker reaches epochs by thinking them.

77
I do not associate with those who say, "All roads lead to New York," for all roads lead *out* of New York, *away* from the sewer.

78
The art of a philosopher is to be understood and not understood.

79
Land is not holy to God.

80
In a democracy, one believes anything.

81
Women love to rule.

82
For the lonely, even noise is a consolation, but the great avoid noise if they can.

83
Suffering is a gift to the great; little men are slaphappy.

84
Impotent Ishmael, son of Abraham, descend and rise, rise and descend.

85
To segregate into each thing is the way of God.

86
Pigs love dirty things, thinking they are clean.

87
Man has lost his way.

88
A philosopher is a boy's man and a man's boy.

89
Without inequality, equality means nothing.

90
Fear is the kiss of death.

91
It gives pleasure to the doomed to make others like them.

92
One reads to learn the names of gods.

93
Sleep is what we see awake; awake is what we see asleep.

94
Hollywood's only brain is between its legs.

95
Pollution is the rotten core of democracy.

96
Thinking thinks that good and ill are one.

97
People sleep and do not think.

98
Monkeys do not want to become men.

99
In battle, boys die for men while peace has men die for boys.

100
Weakheads, believing they are strong.

101
The dead spring back to life, but when? How? Where?

102
Souls do not grow, but change direction.

103
Men make the earth dry, women wet.

104
Sleeping, his web is spun.

105
At first I was something; then this and that rushed in to teach I was a succession before.

106
Slaves turn into slaves.

107
At the end, the beginning returns.

108
Every voter wants to show others his stupidity.

109
A free people never stays lean.

110
Freedom hates the best just as slavery hates the worst.

111
Wisdom is the ouster of stupidity, but in a democracy stupidity ousts wisdom.

112
Great Mother drown us all!

113
Africa is the terror of the earth.

114
The harder you hug the Muse's knees the longer she'll resist you. Leave her, and she will come.

115
Fools are slaves to everything the crowd says.

116
Martyrs are pigs.

117
Prophets eat food taken from the tables of kings.

118
When the new temple is built, even the ruins of the old one will be destroyed.

119
Dirty politician! Wipe your ass!

120
Even the wisest woman still listens to women.

121
Hold John Dewey's spectacles while I sock him in the eye.

122
Has enough been adduced to show that the animating spirit of American Pragmatism is the law?—Consider what Justice Holmes told his brothers *in camera* . . . "If a goose has no bones, gentlemen, you can carve him any which way."—Very Holmesian!—The good judge was telling the Court that he could turn *any* legal rule into a *ratio decidendi* (—not merely that he could imply a condition in a contract or spin a legal web around a fact he did not care to discuss) . . . Likewise, when John Dewey thinks about truth, he is thinking about de-boning geese. This is the precise meaning of his "warranted assertibility."

123
Is there a *desire* to travel to the core of this Deweyan Pragmatism? Does any foreign scholar, any interested class of persons, want to find the essence of *American shame*?—Well, I do not propose to hide my ideas in a reef of wordiness, intimidating the reader with academic issue-dodging babble—. Let the essence of our shame be stated up front and unequivocally.—Pragmatism is moral and political. It undertakes with every expedient the leveling of every mountain and valley (—for, believe the writing on *these* walls: this philosophy, though expelled from the schools by the more attractive, less academic, new thought from Europe, is alive and well in the collective psyche and marches on—) . . . Pragmatism wants *its* morality to overcome all other moral distinctions (—this is the meaning of your "multiculturalism," your shame exalted to a moral principle!—). Pragmatism declares immoral any distance between one existing thing and another, any principle of individuation. Pragmatism brands as "invidious" any segregation of mountain from valley and

calls forth instead a non-invidious *reduction to homogeneity* . . . reduction to a condition prior to thought itself; the reduction of man to the *most primordial herd animal.*—Excepting those militant, "fundamentalist" vestiges that refuse to go along, patriarchal mountains must give way to matrist valleys. A theology of *adjusting and transposing dogma* will reach a flowering hitherto unknown. A new, decadent art will perforce arise to mirror the condition of sick cosmicness. Philosophy too will become decadent, more multicultural, more *African* . . . But you coming philosophers! You *are* coming, aren't you?

124

Like the disheveled-haired Druids hurling execrations at the approaching ships of Julius Caesar, the "religious right" *also* is standing on the seashore peering at something strange, something ominous, something all too easily sensed as "evil."—For the Druids the evil day has come. Caesar will conquer Britain and bury Druidry in Roman might.

125

The patriarchal religions preach with a fervor born of self-preservation, "Go back to an earlier standard of virtue!"—Thus, they preach a retrogression, not merely for their kind, but for mankind.—As for mankind, it *must* go forward, step by step, into "progress": it cannot be retarded. Any success in retarding what is coming is counterproductive.—What? You are afraid to see your faith tested?—You must *wait*; you must *endure*; the entire concept of resistance must be internalized . . .

126

I heard the Islamists say, "We believe in Abraham, Moses, Jesus, Mohammed, and the shoulder-mounted rocket launcher."—So you *do*!—Yes, for every rocket you launch, precious energy is being *siphoned off*.—As degeneration gathers, as all things converge into the Omega-Night, a corresponding gathering up and accumulation of the *opposite* energy, the opposing force occurs. Powerful human beings, themselves but the deposit of this spiritual gathering, arise as natural detonators of this previously accumulated mass of explosive material. (—Christian eschatology calls this the Age of Anti-Christ; for you Islamists—for all patriarchalists everywhere—it is the Day of Reckoning) . . .

127

Many actors and people who tell themselves they are doing philosophy delight in cudgeling the once dominant religion in America by joining some eastern religion, resurrecting hitherto buried mythologies, or professing faith in some neat-o "Star Wars" conglomerate of a fictional nature (—in which the Buddha was really a shoeshine boy brought via spaceship to earth to have a new career and enlighten the aliens, etc.—). From Kabbalism to Rilke, from Tibet to the Great Mother, America gets her religious kicks (—not to discriminate, of course, against poisoning and infernos) . . . However, a much subtler and, for us, a thousand times more amusing flight from the old religion occurs when John Dewey and Harriet Beecher-Stowe, the great armlets into American decadent morality, become peculiarly unsatisfied and agitated on the inside at the honest prospect of departure from the faith of their fathers . . .

128

One simple proof that American Pragmatism makes sterile and devours all seriousness for truly intellectual things is the dramatic transformation that takes place in the great logician Alfred North Whitehead once he moves into the pragma-cuckoo commune of Cambridge. Almost overnight, "logic" takes second place, even third place. He takes the synoptic high road; it is time for a grand Whiteheadian ontology . . . The need for a synthesis of knowledge comes out of aridity;—out of an American preoccupation with science and Darwin—and this kind of reaction from an *Englishman*?—

129

Such a reaction takes place within American Pragmatism itself: Deweyism becomes even more practical; it becomes *political*; . . . consequently, devouring all seriousness for truly intellectual things is a *fait accompli*. When Dewey goes to Chicago, he finds himself in a world of anarchists, labor agitators, dreamers, and Social Gospelers. He remembers the words of his evangelical mother . . . "Is your heart right with Jesus, son?"—"Oh, no, Mother!" the pragmatist replied, "Teleological evolutionary change is the means of salvation. My heart is right with Darwin and Rousseau." (—Yes, sometimes even a pragmatist can tell the truth . . . but perhaps, only to his mother.—) . . . Thus, Darwin's inarticulated conclusion that *only mediocrity survives and multiplies* is given a fancy justification: Rousseau's superstition: *man is good;*

only social institutions have made him bad.—Transform the society! Reconstruct the social order! Usher in the Kingdom of God on earth!—(—Precisely the same call issuing forth from Tolstoy and the Crystal Palace proto-Leninists in Russia—) . . . Humanity is redeemable through social progress *because* "God" is immanent in human culture.—(—Precisely the same situation in Germany with Hegelianism, the conceptual basis of Darwinism, and its young theological phantasmagoria) . . . The summing up of all the errors pertaining to the society-individual question *become political.* Transform the institutions and the individuals will be redeemed;—*not* the other way around!—That whatever comes later in time is of greater value than that which came before; that history must be a grand story of progress, of "perfectibility," of man-made salvation;—most primal lie!—most pitiful error!—To say the same in other words: there is no *essential difference* between your democracy and the old socialism; . . . but you; you keep looking for righteous men in Sodom . . . No; the *opposite* of that asserted by pragmatism's instrumental-Deweyism and the conceptual progeny of "these self-evident truths" is the truth—a truth so penetrating and comprehensive it must appear to a good, complacent, Constitution-fearing pragmatist as fanciful heresy;—a truth that ends all the songs and merriment abut the "relativity" of values valid only in a certain place and time yet somehow mystically connected to a progression of human experience: that each moment is an end in itself—above the flux of history—; that later developments, so far from being greater values, are merely lamps to shed light on what came before, merely *commentaries on summits.*

130

American Pragmatism is proof of the *spiritual corruption* of the first community (—the good people whose hearts swooned to the sin-conjuring performances of Jonathan Edwards on Sunday and whose money-grabbing and land-sharking knew no bounds the rest of the week—) . . . The pragmatists *carried to a conclusion* what had already begun with the make-a-quick-pile mentality of the frontier, the profits are proof of piety Reverse-Calvinism of the early tycoons, the poison of the doctrine of equal rights for all, et-pluralistic-cetera . . . Only two cognate types of people would, without any shame, introduce such monstrous hyperbole as "cash value" and God works as Santa Claus works into serious philosophical discussion: the pragmatist and the loon . . . the political loon. The drive to employ only the concepts and attitudes of the entrepreneur, the organizer, the bounty-hunter, etc.—in one word, the conscious *rejection* of any attitude of reverence and wonder—is an inheritance of the stupidity of overvaluing the practical life . . . The whole American self-counterfeiting fatality a product of *pragmatism* . . .

131

Dewey sees democracy as the drama of spirit de-spiritualizing itself . . . evolving into non-spirit. From "abstract" spirit, we move to a socially aware spiritual life and on to a spiritualized society. In other words, the institutions that corrupted the essential goodness of man's nature must learn to function religiously. The church must dissolve into society and, in effect, *become democracy* . . . Theology means the constant overhauling of dogma the same way a "restatement" of law updates legal rules according to recent decisions, which of necessity reflect changed conditions.—Pragmaculture—in Dewey's vision become *our* vision—devours religion and the individual. Religion *is* social potentiality in allegorical form. Dewey's dialectic is the identical existence-abrogating dialectic of Hegel, but no one has yet seen this . . . And consequently . . .

132

William Ellery Channing, Emerson, utopian labor, the Social Gospelers, Dewey, the civil rights movement.—These inherited Rousseau.—I beg your pardon; I meant to say the *sacred* civil rights movement.

133

Strictly speaking, there is no such thing as American philosophy absent a) a false epistemology so meaningless it has no audience, and b) a popular set of socio-political misconceptions flowing from Rousseau, the French materialists, and the spirit of the common law.

134

Just as a beautiful city's skyline is ruined by reckless developers chasing gold, so the possibility of a rich philosophical landscape in America has been thrown out the window by the new pragmatist-positivists—the "analysts"—, those ingenious lions in the seminar room, Williard Quine and Richard Rorty. This philosophy is a child of the intellectual ingenuity (—I use the words "seminar room" and "ingenuity" in the *starkest* contradistinction to the lived world, depth, proper social awareness, and existence-attuned categories—) of the Cambridge-Oxonians, those scientifically-minded men who unconsciously adapted philosophy to the procedures of legal logic: the obsession with language, the meaning of words, the idea that application clarifies; ... that the unclear—the inexplicable—should be *made clear*, etc; ... that this experience of the inexplicable doesn't have a proper role to play in a new human metaphysics.

135

The final insight of the logical positivists is that language issues from somebody, that it is *for* somebody; consequently, language should not be hypostatized above the human; consequently, the existence question precedes the language question; consequently, science cannot provide a norm-language *for life*... Wittgenstein knew this. He was just slow to admit it.—Or was he just slow?

136

Wittgenstein's logical analysis should be understood as the attempt to make the unfamiliar familiar. Language is mistaken for the whole of philosophy: philosophy is nothing but language analysis.—The drive to divest philosophy of its sense for the peculiar is a drive to abolish philosophy, which as Plato said depends upon wonder.—Where is wonder?—It is enfeoffed to science, devitalized by research: the perfect scenario for forming and nurturing a swarm of industrious zeroes.—Moreover: Wittgenstein's norm-language finally sees itself as no longer capable, no longer worthy, of functioning as a norm-language; it sees *the impossibility of a norm-language as such* (—the principle of verification cannot be verified or formulated, etc.—), and sees instead *many usages*! What then? Philosophy of language is pragmatism in pupa. Analysis *collapses into pragmatism*.

137

Logic as *the* language of philosophy: this is a logical spin-off of philosophy conceived as subservient to science.—But there are *many* languages just as there are many philosophies.

138

Logic, the destroyer of vagueness and ambiguity, is seen by logicians as the essence of celerity. But logic bogs down swift minds.—Can a bird fly underwater?

139

The earliest Christian theology needed philosophy as a proselytizing tool and a weapon against heretics (—a *clarified* doctrine will move against and defeat heretics; classical learning will give perceived crudities in the new religion a prestige and ward off the attacks of men like Celsus—). But this did not end the matter. Theologians drank deeply from the pools of pure Platonism and later the springs of a recently-translated Aristotle. This promiscuity led to the so-called debauch of the Middle Ages. Logicians like Ockham try to restore order. Descartes rallies philosophy around the orderly concepts of clarity and distinctness.—But philosophers, habituated to excesses, are not so easily sobered. Order led to new turbidities and intoxicants. Before anyone knew it, philosophy was saddled with new monstrosities like the external-world problem and the universal math of pre-established harmony. Philosophers developed theses they *knew* ran counter to experience, to *their* experience. Language was seized upon as a means to order, sobriety. Language analysis in the hands of scientific philosophers who had no feel for the spirit of philosophy assumed control in England and America. It was agreed upon: order could be restored and maintained only by the cavalierly authoritarian act of shrinking the role of the philosopher.—And the *basic instinct* behind all analytic philosophy is this shrinking; . . . so that, aha! today analytic philosophy itself is shrinking.

140

Quine's vaunted Indeterminacy Thesis itself is *not* "empirical"—not in the least. It is but an a priori thought experiment's reckless assumption, a conclusion *he wanted*, an end-result masquerading as a beginning (—I say reckless because this kind of frivolity plays directly into the cunning tribulations of the new African ethno-sophers) . . . He pictures a linguist seeking to translate an unknown language only after he, Quine, has prepared his sermons on "ontological relativity"—: pragmatism's inveterate trick of denying any possibility of one thing claiming superiority over another.—That scholars do not gain knowledge of other languages the way Quine suggested is enough evidence to establish his indeterminacy as fantasy—an ontological quinization.—What? Quine the philosopher of science is unconcerned with what actually happens in scientific communities? Let us console ourselves here that reality quinized—lapsing into insouciant, dogmatic fantasy—is enough to prove there is a respectable modicum of anti-pragmatist in every pragmatist . . .

141

Like the sun, life is a process of combustion. Intellect is the *light* produced by this process. But pragmatism, with its prejudices against intellect (—it inculcates and justifies cultural biases; it is inherently invidious, etc.—) affirms *darkness*, the first principle of the emerging *female god*. Consequently, when I speak of herd and herdlike behavior, I am always referring to the darkness of the swamp and its teeming "life."

142

When the pragmatist and the logical analyst feel any need to philosophize, this need is taken care of by science just as the various religions take care of this need for the ordinary human beings. On the other hand, it goes without saying that this need, felt with any frequency only by the very *rarest* of individuals, seldom arises in the unphilosophic, inartistic types of people.

143

The African-American intellectual must have his *revenge*: only by robbing ancient Greece of its iconic cultural status can he feel good about himself and *his* "culture."—Thus, this way of thinking lacks the courage and sense of responsibility of the Latino thinkers who do not harbor sufficient *collective resentment* in their souls to claim that their myths and moralities constitute "philosophy" as it was practiced in the ancient Aegean world.—The African intellect must have its pound of flesh—*white* flesh. "Righting wrongs" must mean leveling mountains and raising valleys. The Greeks—the only people of genius the world has ever produced—must *not* be unique and individuated (—as the religions must be hybridized and mongrelized by the comparative religionist's putative and fictional "borrowings" of dogmas, rituals, etc.), but must be seen as *awash in the cultural stream*; hence no longer able to claim primary status . . . Moral: anything that finds strength in itself, that stands up, *segregates*, and is proud of its achievement must be "racist."—"Equal rights!"—Only a juridical pretext for the ideology of the world to come: marriage of Demos and Mother Mythos: African philosophy assumes control of the earth . . . *by default*!

144
Swine think diamonds are drops of dew.

145
Consequences of pragmatism: 1) the promotion of industry, averageness, public utility, soullessness, etc. 2) the breeding of the coming chthonic race.

146
Philosophers do not know when the day ends or begins.

147
Their goddess and shamelessness are one.

148
Darkness, without light.

149
The world is made of earth, water, fire, wind, and secrecy.

150
Words are the action of the mind.

151
Silly people sleepwalk through life.

152
Logicians do not seek wisdom so they do not possess it.

153
See, the Muse is like a little girl.

154
Even if apes could read they would hate books.

155
Philosophers with full bellies are not philosophers.

156
The dead know nothing.

157
Something cannot be without nothing.

158
From his tower Montaigne is writing the king.

159
Writers say what they think, but do not think what they say.

160
I'll take that laurel wreath and use it as a switch!

161
Heidegger's place-ontology is an ontology of place.

162
The insane are happy. The sane say they are not.

163
Those who learn philosophy are not philosophers.

164
When I hear a claque of brainwashed poltroons mouthing mousey palaver about things they do not understand, I know our "public intellectuals" are engaged in another important "debate."

165
Theognis and Heraclitus say a thousand fools do not make one wise man. Pericles says wisdom comes from much foolishness.

166
Law is a whore. It is used by those who seek power.

167
New York City. Our Big Rotten Apple!

168
Pragmatism teaches that one should think only as much as one's trade or business requires and everything should be tackled with the least possible expenditure of thought. Thus, pragmatism teaches people what they already know.

169
The origins of art, poetry, philosophy, and religion reveal themselves as the polar opposites of all pragmatisms. This is so because practical knowledge is a lower—much lower—form of knowledge than an objective knowledge that has relinquished the natural task of perceiving relations among things . . .

When intellect exceeds the measure needed for living, the pragmatists call it to task.

170

Pragmatism thinks it is doing something spectacular and is performing a great service for mankind when it misconstrues the intellect as a kind of conveyor belt for an assembly line.—As the Hegelian System "forgot" existence so pragmatism overlooks the proper construal of the intellect. Because of the need for practical concerns, the motif of a factory is generally correct: but the intellect is not an assembly mechanism. It is more like a factory worker, a working stiff as they say in the union halls of San Francisco. This working stiff serves his master as he is required, leaves the factory, and instead of lounging around doing basically nothing, for once on his own initiative and for his own satisfaction, does *his own* work, as *he* requires of *himself* with no other object than the work itself . . . Such purely objective employment of the intellect—the ground of artistic and philosophic achievement—confuses the pragmatist and catches him off guard for the simple reason that he comes into direct contact with an intellectual exertion free and devoid of personal interest.—The pragmatist begins with Darwin: it is in our *interest* to survive and multiply.—But thinkers and artists transcend the survival instinct . . . From a purely practical standpoint, artistic creation is a purposeless expenditure of energy—; just as the suffering of the artist is seen as purposeless, when in fact it is purposeful in the highest degree and is the *sine qua non* of creation itself.—In other words, pragmatism, a philosophy of interest, denies the higher human being engaged in his or her higher human task.—True, intellect arose as a purely practical concern; intellect came into the world merely as an aid to survival. The factory worker eats, drinks, and does whatever he can to maintain his livelihood, but utilitarian concerns do not exhaustively define what it means to be human (—the ignominy of it all! The pragmatic analysts devote their lives to ascertaining "meaning"!—) . . . Here a distinction is drawn between the activity of most—almost all—humans and the human. If you prefer: the human as such is defined by the very few, not the many. As aforesaid, the intellect of the many is in constant and exclusive service to interest, subjective motivation: there is nothing left over, no *remainder* of intellectual force after the natural expenditure of *intellect necessary for life*.—Not so with the creative ones for whom spirit is both an *excess* and an accident: spirit and life are incommensurables. Thus, the brutality of the blind and hasty Darwinists . . . Thus, the limitation of knowledge we call narrow-mindedness is betrayed even in one's face.—Pragmatism *wants* the proximity of intellect and interest; it condemns on principle the separation and hypostatization of the intellect—: it wants a society with no genius except scientific genius, which, on *our* principle of intellect's disservice for life, is not real genius. (—American Pragmatism began as the choreography of interest and causation in tort law—) . . . One can see that here just as much intellect as a subjective motivation requires, and no more, is pragmatism's desideratum; . . . more here leads to distinctions pragmatism has declared invidious . . . In other words, pragmatism expects intellect to subside into obsequious quiescence as soon as brutal life-interest no longer drives it and makes it "work." The moment the intellect surpasses its natural factory-worker status and takes an objective interest in anything, it incurs pragmatism's suspicion and is officially interdicted (—whereas, contrariwise, a purely objective interest in the rank-and-file, the roustabouts in the pragmatistic superstructure, the "good," the tolerant, the *aequales homines* is always exalted—) . . . American Pragmatism builds upon this natural aversion to thought disconnected from practice—the previously established foundation of the *vita practiva*—; it erects its own coarse popular culture in which bourgeois art intoxicates, mindless buffooneries excite, non-stop quotidian trivia lulls to sleep, and every issue is a quasi-legal issue; . . . and all this because the pragmaculture is capable of only subjective interest! The proof that American Pragmatism, once upon a time but a Cambridge study group, has left the schools and gone mainstream, has fabricated a peculiar and peculiarly insular culture, is, as already mentioned, in the most American of motifs: law; journalism; fad technology; the small, mean, politico-culturally correct; the seduction of dependency concealed in computer adoration: fitting amusements for supine, correct-thinking fudgeheads who have thrown away every instinct for hardening, self-control, suffering, and command.

171

The intellect of the genius detaches itself from practical striving.—This is what Darwin did not and could not see; this is what American Pragmatism comprehends, but brands as offensive.—Genius is the entirely *unnatural* ability to leave our own interest out of sight. Like the saint who renounces the world, the genius does not struggle to survive. The genius makes sacrifices to deities that ordinary people cannot see . . . Or: the genius lives for an idea the others reject as futile, senseless, and vain. (—This rejection is based on the common judgment that the activity in question is impractical) . . . This *abnormal* employment of the intellect becomes in the genius, who alone possesses healthy intellectual abnormality the one goal of life, the criterion of all other activities. In having to resist the others, the genius begins to see himself as an authentic hero. (—Thus, the seeker seeks with the soul of a seeker, the genius seeks with the soul of a hero. Think of the great Balzac eternally contending with his prosaic mother. Why did the parent fail to recognize the celestial fire in the child? But I have divulged the answer: it was *unprofitable!*—) . . . Because the mind of the genius must be occupied with one thing and one thing constantly, his or her gift—the abnormal enhancement of the cognitive and imaginative faculties—is as a thief in broad daylight; a thief who, like the Devil, comes to "steal, rob, and destroy." What is stolen? What is destroyed? Precisely the capacity for mere existence and *its* aims. The genius does not exist—he creates. Ordinary talents must live and die, but the genius is eternal. (—Think of Horace's monument "more enduring than bronze and higher than the Pyramids"—) . . . Of course, there *may be* abnormalities of the abnormal. Pointing out that the genius lacks the ability to traverse the scenes of life like the ordinary, merely talented person of affairs is not to deny the possibility of sublimity wearing a mask, of genius, for whatever psychological directives, *straying* into the banality of the ordinary. (—Think of the soldier-poet Archilochus and Xenophanes).—The possibility for mere life is stolen from the genius since the *state of wonder* necessarily entails the contemplation of phenomena in themselves—the outside world intuited for its own sake—which detracts from these same phenomena grasped as connected to active possibilities and service to immediate aims. So that the degree of objective clarity constitutive for the life of genius functions as a hindrance to the comprehension of the connections between nature and individual interest.—For purely practical aims (—the satisfaction of the requirements of ordinary living—), the most superficial contemplation suffices, and contentment with the active life (—entailing haste, narcissism, consumerism, militarism, etc.—) means blindness to everything else. On the other hand, the genius is *never* in step with his age. In *conscious* opposition to his times, he addresses himself primarily to posterity and is thus prepared to do his work under *any* conditions, recognition or no recognition. In the end, the comprehensive appraisal of things shames and confounds the superficial contemplation sufficient for realizing practical ends just as ordinary living profanes the genius and his bright, wonderful world.

172

Practically speaking, as well as from the standpoint of core concepts and values, American Pragmatism is correct in its clean estimation of the fundamental law: the U.S. Constitution and America's perennial philosophy stand as mirror images of each other.—Democracy is based on the freedoms of the people, and as Constitutional law affirms, speech and press freedoms operate in a free society as the primary bedrock freedoms. In legal comprehension, the other freedoms implement, expand, and expound the bedrock freedoms. In this manner, freedom of association and freedom of movement *presuppose* an unfettered flow of ideas, a flow expressly grounded in expression freedoms. The idea behind Constitutionally protected expression is that every discontent in the people will be relieved and exhausted in words (—as Holmes said, the law will up to a clear point protect even "the speech we hate") . . . If this discontent is considerable, a host of legal remedies spring into action.—However, as the reasonable person test serves as the crucible for solving the problems in the realm of tort law, Constitutional adjudicators rely on the scales of justice: competing interests are *weighed* to determine which interest should prevail and which adjudged deficient.—Philosophers of the future, since they are untouched by the one-dimensionality inherent in a purely legalistic culture, will *weigh* the bedrock freedoms against their abuses (—and philosophers are no strangers to weights, coinages, and measures: that is to say *what* clear and present dangers lurk beneath and behind any surface, appearance, practice, etc.). In this way, these patient, incorruptible investigators will not be afraid of answering the question, "Is the nature of man good?" in the negative. Having disposed of the delusions of Charles Peirce (—I mean his opiate that "in the long run" every child of the Demiurge will eat apple pie in pragmatism's by-and-by—) this grand future investigation will ask what *cannot* be put into the heads of the credulous, patiently manipulated masses . . . Then it will be seen that freedom of the press is a permit to sell poison; that the mind is poisoned and the heart corrupted by the well nigh ineradicable press manipulations.—The freedom simply *must be weighed against its abuses*; then it will be determined that the only fair press is a muzzled press; . . . especially in light of the existence of so many other grievance-redressing remedies. But if the masses can be manipulated so easily, what could possibly awaken them from their comforting, tragic-comic illusions?

173

I will say it again and again: America and American Pragmatism complement, confirm, and reinforce one another: America looks in the mirror and exclaims, "I know this pragmatism!"—Even a cursory glance at the relevant texts disclose to a reader not versed in the field that this philosophy with its emerging pragmaculture begins with action as the *ne plus ultra* and concludes hungering and thirsting for more action. However, an exclusively action-oriented culture is unable to slow down for one moment to ask, "Why?"—How can it be that *such* a people uncritically accepts *such* a philosophy?—The answer may be found in a simple examination of two vastly differing kinds of activity: internal activity and external activity. The Americans *need* external activity precisely because of a poverty of internal activity. Stated differently: the richer they become the poorer they are . . . One must learn from an epigram of Heraclitus: *Ephesians be rich! I cannot wish you worse*!

174

To herd ideas into a "marketplace," to identify the sublimity of thoughtfulness with shouting, to subject the *vita religiosa* to quite unchurchly architecture;—to innocently suppose that ideas thrive in that left-right malversation we call American politics—: only a pragmatist could invent such tin-pan obscenity.

175

Proust at the Ritz—Beneath floor-length blue satin curtains, the great Proust, swaddled in wool, his melancholic eyes dark oval lakes, bites a drooping moustache as the hotel's maître d' delates the latest gossip. Pearl gray gloves with black stitching adorn hands the maître d' knows to be white as snow and abnormally soft. Marcel is sipping tea and mulling over his *boeuf á la mode*.—"Have you heard, monsieur, from the House of Gallimard?"—"My novel has been rejected," Proust replied in a puerilely insolent groan, "because the Gallimard editors are cold, calculating pragmatists. Calculating the consequences of my work having no audience in France, they have pronounced it unsalable. But," Proust added with palely purplish lips puckered as if awaiting a kiss, "just between you and me, Fouquet, I don't believe they ever opened my package."—

176

Proust and Colette at the Chez Larue—Tall paintings reach to the gilt ceiling. Everything is airy and carefree, but also eerily somnolent and severe, the soul of gay Paree. Colette, looking like a little fawn in her black velvet dress, faces Marcel Proust, sleepy-eyed in a somber-colored jacket, striped trousers, and a waistcoat of red silk. Her voice caresses Marcel. He thinks she is caressing him with her soft baby hands, her dreamy aquarium eyes the color of the pewter lilies embroidered on her dress.—"Someday, I promise you," she says, "Gaston Gallimard . . . and Gide . . . will repent in ashes. Your marvelous style, Marcel, puts me in a trance, in another world, a world in which I am reading my own memories and experiencing again my own intimate sensations. Your words put mine to shame! You have created something beautiful. You have leaped over the artificial mechanicity of plot. Resonating situations take the place of plot! The reader of your *roman fleuve* feels no need to hurry to your climax, as if to say novel structure should invaryingly mirror the practical world. I tell you: as soon as you see writing that has no other purpose than to cover paper, as soon as you discover that the main reason the writer writes is for gain, you should throw that book down. Payment is the ruin of literature, but a novel that has something to say? Rare. I do not need to remind you that the greatest work is written for little or nothing. Look here! You have been rejected by Gallimard, Fasquelle, Ollendorf, the *Nouvelle Revue Francais* . . . And now you must pay Grasset to publish the sweetest music on earth!"—Proust's eyes grew darker, heavier. He sighed, puncturing his cheek with an index finger as he held his chin in saccharine resignation.—"And what," she flailed on, "is immediately accepted without question or quibble? The page-filling through which empty heads seek to fill their empty pockets! Yes, on the one hand, so-called literature is the promotion of triviality; on the other, it is experiment run amok, a symptom of decline. When some Irish leprechaun mangles words to his heart's content so that what the writer is thinking and what the reader is thinking are segregated by the most radical, yawning dissimilarity, when the writer is satisfied as long as he himself understands what he means as if he were engaged in a drunken monologue in a Dublin bar, then all is lost and irretrievable for our ancient, noble form! It is as if this kind of writer is daring the reader to make out shapes and pictures in blots on a wall. A mistake. Obscurity cannot be profundity. Ugliness is not beauty. Nay, he who writes for fools finds a large, fawning public; he who writes for lunatics is himself a lunatic."—"I wish," the *domina* continued after lighting a short, filterless cigarette, "someone someday would write a history of writing as tragedy, a work that would contrast the exorbitant pride the various nations take in their great writers with the way these same writers were treated while they were alive. This tragedy would depict the way they lived without recognition, without sympathy, and would bring visibly before us the struggle the good and genuine of all ages must wage with the dominant and famous unworthy. But it would also depict how—in spite of all—belief in themselves and in the value of their work sustained them. Someday, Marcel, someday, your dawn will come. And the fact that you had to pay to have your work published will bring blame, obloquy, and infinite joy."

177

Just as the crudest novel is the most action-packed romance with its poverty of inner drama, so the crudest philosophy justifies itself by packing action into its ideas. True, the philosophy of existence is an action philosophy, but it comprehends action by way of existence, not existence by action.

178

The overwhelming presence of Goethe in Germany drove the emerging intellect into unharvested fields, i.e., into philosophy, and German philosophy was born. In America, the presence of pragmatism *prevents* new talent from entering unharvested fields.—But why?—This question has been asked and answered.

179

Indeed, Mr. Peirce, ideas *are* plans of action, but *we* do not make and execute the plans—ideas do. Thus, "theory of mind" must be transformed and seen anew as theory of ideas—what ideas do. Abstemious empiricists can hem and haw as they like (—and as their nature requires—), but ideas do, finally, in their own due season, find their way to the ground. Ideas are thus *translated into reality.*—Whereas events, being already real, merely snowball their way, sometimes, into ever greater realities, ideas must wait. But they do not, as even the yellow journalists say in their unthinking overconfidence, "have their time." They enter into time and *become* it. Our times, seen from *any* perspective, are the times of ideas. You want to delimit and narrowly circumscribe ideas. We want to watch them "work." Are you watching, Mr. Peirce?—"I am watching, but what I *see* is men of action like Martin King, whose ideas were nothing but plans of action, and Thurgood Marshall, who used the law as a plan of action, revolutionizing America, altering forever her face, her soul."—A very Peirceian thing to say, Mr. Peirce. An empiricist can never see the *whole* picture. By definition, he is out to limit what is to *count as* the picture. These men of action you mention were preceded by the poetry, novels, and essays of the writers whose ideas called them forth. The active types are always but intermediaries *following orders*.

180

Les grandes pensées viennent du coeur.—Yes; and our pragmatism has no heart.

181

To philosophize today means precisely what it meant in the days of Socrates and his dialectics, his critical questioning of whether the top dog should, in truth, really be on top. It means, firstly, to comprehend "the given" as a problem.—First failing of pragmatism: it refuses to comprehend the given, American herd culture of consumer and narcissistic values as a problem.—If the mind is to philosophize at all, it must not be so wrapped up with any aim that it lets this aim formulate its questions and dictate answers.—Second failing of pragmatism: it wants "science" and its impudent, empty-headed little brother, "technology" to frame its questions and dictate every answer.—

182

Socrates and Plato taught subsequent thinkers how to accommodate philosophy to religious dogma. Thus, for more than two thousand years, philosophy remained in chains. Kierkegaard, Nietzsche, and, in a different way, Hegel unchained philosophy. But today, pragmatists and logical analysts want to keep philosophy enchained by science. True philosophy seeks to rid itself of ruinous entanglements by avoiding unnatural intercourse with its neighbors.

183

The idolatrous veneration in which the Southern preacher Martin King is held in America passes belief, but *not* the belief in a steady stream of images to manipulate the all-too-malleable masses and a steady stream of propaganda pouring out on these masses from a centralized authority (—the marriage of Madison Avenue huckstering applied to culture and America's perversion of its "federalism") . . . As we have pointed out, it is entirely consistent with the unconscious needs of an exclusively action-oriented, legalistic culture to idolize its "men of action" and almost forget its thinkers who wind up the clock of life. Someday, the question must be asked, "What did the thinkers who preceded the civil rights movement really want?"—This is our answer.—Since Afrocentrism became an excuse to teach myth as history, this movement wanted to create a mythology—but this mythology is still under blueprint.

184

A: Pragmatist W.E.B. Du Bois turns universal wrongs into Negro wrongs. This is an error.
B: You don't understand Du Bois or his pragmatism. Is an error blameworthy if it has good consequences?
A: You mean consequences that are good for Du Bois and his people?
B: No. For mankind.
A: Yes. Negro wrongs are universal wrongs, but universal wrongs are not Negro wrongs. That is an error.
B: I have already told you how we regard error.

185

Burghardt Du Bois is the *artist* of revenge. He must have known the form this revenge would take even if he did not know its eventual content.—That it would come he never doubted. Simply stated: the artist always wins.—Somehow, sometime during the century of hope, the children of Du Bois must be *seen* as sacred cattle. Around the untouchable, collective head of these children of Du Bois, like the nimbus about the head of a sacred personage while on earth, a *doctrine* of correct and incorrect speech must fulgerate in racial splendor: lists of proscribed words, attitudes, thoughts expressed and harbored at peril.—Go tell it on the mountain! Proclaim it in every dark place in the earth! Burghardt has his revenge!—And what was Burghardt's favorite part of the *Phenomenology*?—The Master and Slave. Do I need to tell you this?—After the conflict—and Burghardt prophesied conflict—the Hegelian dialectic follows the slave along.—*Free at last.*—And here Burghardt is the consummate pragmatist. In making war on the segregation instituted by the master (—if you will, the pleasurable distinction between ruler and ruled) who, as *he* says in his slasher, *Jesus Christ in Texas*, despises the slaves, here former slaves, he is jettisoning his own status, his distinction as thinker. Thus, the pragmatists see themselves in the role of liberating mankind from a philosophic caste segregated from ordinary folk.—Or: Is *he* W.E.B. Du Bois the man on the Cross?—sacrificing himself for his *race* . . . At any rate, distinctions of moral value must not apply to human beings (—this would reinstate the master/slave conflict—), but to just actions, actions that place Burghardt's children in a light deemed just. Du Bois says, "What is unjust to me is injustice itself." Thus, the moral *becomes* the just and *only* the just.—Thus, when someone points to American decadence, bewailing our decline (—a decline Burghardt's blessedness was always conditional upon—), we hear the Du Bois addict roundly reply, "What? *We* are immoral? No, no. *Only slavery was immoral.* The hard heart of the master, *that* is immoral! When we profess our belief in progress and the future, *this* reveals clearly enough who is moral, who *cannot be immoral!* How can the one who does not honor us and bless us have any honor and be blessed? We are viscerally suspicious of every happiness that does not look and feel like ours. Everything that makes us uncomfortable and fearful by placing us in an improper light is surely immorality itself. The bad man is the one we have adjudged contemptible. The good man is the harmless man, easily manipulated, malleable, ready to fall in line, easily deceived. The good man smiles when we smile; he laughs when we laugh. Above all, the good man does not want to inspire fear for *we alone may inspire fear.* He believes in freedom and all its refinements . . ."

186

An artist's art is built upon what he *sees.* Du Bois sees the world and then constructs his race-art—but a fact is never something simply seen. It is a mental construct in which a number of prejudices enter. Seeing in the art of Du Bois is overladen with the art of the *artist as seen* . . .

187

The pragmatist theology of Charles Hartshorne and Alfred North Whitehead insists that pantheism in its bright red dress, panentheism, is an advance on theism. This panentheism has one of God's legs planted in the world and the other in the intransitory. Neat trick! A very pragmatic thing to do!—Red dress or not, this new pantheism is substantively the old pantheism: the theologian, who is in need of constructing a deity in his image, that is, in the image of his needs, assumes theism and proceeds to the "advance" of identifying God with the world. But the advance on theism is presented as if God has *transplanted himself* into this world. The theologian assumes theism, then moves to politely set God aside: the world takes over his role. The theologian says to himself, "Yes, well, the world can do a better job."—Taking a view of this business from the standpoint of the world is rewarding for an unprejudiced observer, for it would never occur to anyone to identify *this world* with God, or to attempt to pull God down into this world, as if part of God should remain God, unchanging being, and part not. Then, from the standpoint of God, it would take a very reckless and ill-advised sort of God who knows nothing better to do than to transform himself into a world such as this one. Could it be that God transplanted himself, or part of himself (—perhaps Whitehead prefers the left leg and Hartshorne the right leg; or, maybe, someday, it would be an "advance" to prefer the torso to the legs; then the hapless deity would be turned upside down like the reprobate popes in Dante—), from a *lack of intelligence?*—The better view of this nonsense is that the theologian is here disguising a negation—and *pragmatism loves disguises*. Thus, William James, the pragmatist with Swedenborgian roots, wants to substitute a human belief in God for God. James crows from his Harvard high chair, "This makes for better consequences."—(—Professor Hartshorne confessed this much to me in his office.—)—Yet, until now, the decision of James to include within the ambit of these consequences the effects of holding a belief (—that in considering claims about God James was willing to accept emotional satisfactions flowing from the acceptance of the claims—) has been misunderstood. Holmes had told James about the interesting use of "legal fictions" in the law. If the law wants to give a cause of action to a plaintiff or group of plaintiffs, it will repose a fiction within the relation of the parties such that its operation grounds and legitimates the possible action. If, say, a corpse is mishandled, the law, to secure for the nearest of kin a recognized right to sue the offending party, will construe an ownership interest reposing in the plaintiff;—an interest the plaintiff does *not* really possess. It is the law's effort to make itself tolerant. If the granting of a right depends upon a fiction, the law will sanction both the right and the fiction: the consequences of possessing the right justify the fictional ground for enjoying the right. In the same manner, James seeks to make his analysis of consequences tolerant: he will admit claims about God, but by the same logic claims of the "reality" of Santa Claus and unicorns . . . Let us say, arguendo, that William James is afraid to walk through the thick woods that surround Walden Pond by himself after dark (—that is, without Nick Green, Wendell Holmes, and Chauncey Wright to keep him company, stimulate him intellectually, and hold his hand). William James, consequently, avoids those woods after dark, and occasionally admits in this regard his admiration for Henry David Thoreau, who loved to be alone in those woods when the moon rose like a luminous ghost over the treetops and shone iridescently on the pond. But—if William James *believes* that unverifiable propositions are meaningful if they help us cope with the world, and if William James *believes* that unicorns are unusually and felicitously placid and protective creatures, and if William James *believes* that unicorns exist, then presto-pragmato, we have a winner! William James says, "I don't need to be afraid of wolves or goblins or Salem witches. I can go on alone unafraid. I can, if I choose, even believe in God!"—Do unicorns exist?—But this is not a meaningful question for a pragmatist. For if *pragmatism did not exist*, it might make for a more thoughtful, less helter-skelter America, and who would want to believe in *that*?

188

Postclassical pragmatism wants to give philosophy over to normal heads engaged in the business of checking sentences for "meaning."—The primary business, of course, is getting tenure.—The idea here is that the normal head, knowing that the intellect was designed merely for subjective satisfactions (—a state devoid of authentic wonder with its *objective* aims; we call this our "struggle to survive"—) will deny meaning to sentences pointing to totality on the ground that the intellect was not designed to direct itself to things lying outside the domain of animal being. Kant began this drift with his demonstration that the old metaphysical problems were incapable of solution. In other words, intellect is abused when it is directed at totality. A delimitation of intellect means the *vanishing of the problems*. Just as the squirrel possesses only that degree of intellect necessary to serve the need to discover food, so it is with man.—Pragmatism stops here.—It is oblivious to the not inconsiderable *abnormality* we call genius. Because the normal intellect is enveloped by nature, it cannot *see* nature. Genius spills out over the struggle for existence. It is a superfluity *exempt* from the normal struggle. That which is beyond the normal intellect's ken appears to have a "knower" at last . . .

189

It should be pointed out in the interest of fairness that the imputation of Wittgenstein that generality exudes a special contempt for the particular case is a matter of emphasis. (—And, once again, philosophy is hiding from us what it *wants*—) . . . Charles Peirce, too, overemphasizes the particular—and we *know* why. He says, "The application exhausts the meaning of general terms."—Not quite. Let us say we want to find out what obscenity is; . . . specifically the law of obscenity. "Obscenity" is the general term. To determine what it *is*, we must consult a cluster of applications *qua* decided cases. We appear to move from the undecided general to the decided particular, but the cases themselves are distilled to find a general rule: a definition is *attempted*. Thus, we do not swing definitively from the general to the particular, i.e., we do not abandon the general. Even Holmes didn't accomplish a definitive swing to the particular with his seminal dictum, "General propositions do not decide concrete cases" (—biased judges do) since he was only driving after a sociology of law. Moreover, the facts of the individual cases—an infinity of *possible* particulars—are referred back to the general to determine their relative strengths, that is to say, whether they make out the *prima facie* legal thing; e.g., exception to the hearsay rule, estoppel, felony murder, strict Constitutional scrutiny, or what have you: . . . specifically, the "particulars" must be referred back to the *elements* of the law. Consequently—

190

When you see the great crowds that throng the American universities, you would think that knowledge is valued; you would think the professors are much occupied dispensing knowledge and insight to the eager students sitting at their feet, and are compensated by the spiritual fruits of a higher, noble calling.—With regard to the students, who perforce think like the computer, the desideratum is information as a means to things, not knowledge as a means to insight. What would an American do with insight that cannot be *pragmatized*, converted into action and things, and used for the most private, convenient gain?—The professors teach to earn money and love to be credited with possessing knowledge they do not have . . . As for philosophy professors—who profess a kind of wisdom in their lectures and writings about "meaning"—; well, let them endure a few weeks in a Nietzschean Purgatory—or Strindberg's "inferno crisis."—Please excuse my slip-up; purgatories and infernos are for *creators*, not for wage-earners and popinjays . . .

191

The philosophy professor fits into the same category as the popular writer: the thing prompting these "professionals" is always some kind of want, hunger, or greediness. The first group falls under the general heading of highbrow vulgarity, the latter garishness.—At the *opposite pole*, we find the genuine human being who refuses to use something as a means (—as pragmatism teaches—), but treats the thing as an end, being occupied in the matter directly.—What great things have come from wage-earners?—Just look at the way classics professors at the ivy league schools lambaste and make fun of the greatest Greek and Latin authors, for instance, Theognis and Juvenal, when the beautiful naïveté and will to truthfulness of these ancient writers gets tangled up with the juridically-pragmatically reared political nervousness of these "scholars." Let the Devil take this impudence! Do you academic cads seriously expect the *real men* of antiquity, such as the incomparably courageous polemicists named above, to write with the same kneeling submission to the sensitivities of the select groups as those pussyfooting catkins in America who call themselves essayists, novelists, and historians? You people cannot see these men; what you do see are truncations, silhouettes, contortions, obliquenesses, etc., in the half-light of your "modern ideas."—Where the purely and universally human is the only concern, what difference does it make whether a writer is proven to have flirted with fascism? The same amount of energy you lesser minds have put into your hobby of transforming Martin Heidegger into an unregenerate Nazi could have just as facilely turned him into a good Catholic.—Giving a thinker the ideological once-over in the beastliest efforts to turn him into some ominous "ism" reaches, as you may suppose, its vilest, ugliest nadir in the Land of the Free, where greedy-guts of every ethnic ilk combine to discover "the cultural stance of the Knower."—While the unfortunate is tried *in absentia* by a standing race-and-gender constabulary of fevered believers, who—even as they light the faggots—wring their hands over the "chilling effect" of some free speech violation.—Thus, the professional cowardice of the philosophy professors and the classics professors, this greed and shame, gets inscribed in legible symbols splayed across the American experience: correct speech vs. free thought—free expression vs. correct thought.—One simply must divine *what* it is that is here at work! How much or how little that is dangerous to the community, dangerous to equality, to tolerance, to the pluralistic herd—with its select, i.e., its dominant groups and their sanctimonious noise and vile uproars—resides in an emotion, a thought, an opinion: this is the measuring rod of decadence morality, itself but a kind of necessary way-station and interlunary period. The gradually tightened sensitivities and insidiously morbid mellowing unrelentingly inculcated by the groups—those who shriek the loudest over "past wrongs"—; this democratic over-tenderness that finally learns to bewail punishment, war, and necessary severity of every kind; this hatred of independence, separation, pride, honor, purity; this hatred of "hatred" itself; this regression to an infantile state: do you not think that all this sensitivity and gloom is necessary fodder for the eclipse of the old order and the triumph of *supreme matriarchal values*?

192

The writer of novels and plays uses a repertoire of techniques in his bag of tricks to make the most of every event in the narrative. In like manner, journalism employs and must employ exaggeration in its portrayal of every event. The headline is a device the journalist uses to sound an alarm, and journalists must sound alarms to make themselves interesting. The public must soon come to see how the real message in the alarm sounded lies beneath and behind the instant exaggeration of the current event. The message is this: "We, the journalists, operate under and in accordance with a well-nigh sacred Constitutional mandate to rouse, deceive, and manipulate the unsuspecting simple ones who place their trust in us pursuant to their unquestioning trust in our mission. We are a profession *still emerging*, still hungry for more money, power, and influence. Only God knows *how far* we will go for there is nothing to stop us."—Meanwhile, the simple ones learn to shout, *Sic semper dominus superbus* at every "abuse" committed by the *other* professions even as they sing paeans to press freedom as if it were freedom itself . . .

193

A.) Journalists are like little insignificant dogs who start up a loud barking whenever anything moves. B.) Too much journalism is responsible for Wagnerians, proto-Nazis, and Anti-Semites. C.) The press demoralizes on the largest possible scale, in the shortest amount of time, for the smallest possible price. D.) The press makes its living by chaffering with spiritual values. E.) Serious writers cannot be journalists and remain serious for very long. = A.) Arthur Schopenhauer B.) Friedrich Nietzsche C.) Søren Kierkegaard D.) Honore Balzac E.) Gertrude Stein . . . Ditto Goethe, Heidegger, Heinrich Böll . . . Let us hail all signs that a more *warlike attitude* toward the news media is about to begin; a time when the *libres penseurs* of the world, in the horrifying light of press manipulations and the theft of their ancient prerogatives will learn to be constant in anti-press activities. You spirits who *must* engage this corruption will someday no longer be content to work disengaged in nooks and corners, peeping out at the rank spectacle like kittens. To this end, you must forswear their lies, especially when they say, "The government must not control the press, the press must control the people!"—Like Francesco Petrarca, draw up a list of cultural idols the people blindly worship. See your work as a series of attacks on these offending idols;—and put the "free press" at the top of the list!

194

Through her leading liberal intellectuals, America finally woke up to the rigid authoritarianism of Calvinism. People grew sick and tired of the idea of a *Consistory* whose job is to listen at the wall and delate to higher authorities any oblique references to adultery, profanity, spirituous liquor, etc. Much later, through her activist civil liberties organizations and a very sympathetic federal bench, America again woke up to the vicious "witch hunts" and "legislative trials" of Congressional committees like the notorious Un-American Activities Committee. But today, the liberal intellectuals, their civil liberties organizations, and the federal and state judiciary turn their solemn heads the other way when the New Consistory rifles through the literary canon hunting for "racial slurs," combing through the communications of elected officials like stray dogs looking for scraps of food.—Yes, friends, the militant "Black intellectual" has made it his business to upstage *every other* cultural idol by the sheer frequency of his whines and groans, his ingeniously inventive race-baiting, his protean "dream" of blunting-down minds with the image of his torment.—Here we must learn how to backtrack from the ideals of the intellectual (—although it insults sound reason to cite the legal "gains" of the civil rights movement as ideals—) *to the intellectual who needs them.* Burghardt Du Bois saw the Invisible Empire and envisioned a Visible Empire of reverse-racism, but under the "intellectual" rubric of understanding the world of "Black folk" and rescuing White America from *its* racial hatred. The dream of deconstructing whiteness is the establishing—as Sartre said so well—of the black phallus, expanding, penetrating, and overcoming the White world. What is this but the poisonous fruit from the tree of *black pragmatism* planted by Du Bois and tended by our high chair Harvard intellectuals and race-baiting retardees?—But not only the intellectual: now the preacher, the man of action, the community leader must abet the struggle to *turn national history into race history*; . . . the miracle of falsification! And who prospers from this? Precisely the parasite, the *parasitic type* of human being: the Black leader . . . *He* calls "just" and "moral" that state of society in which *he* determines the value of things. With snake-blooded cynicism, he turns his face to the past and assesses individuals and epochs by the measuring rod of whether these individuals and epochs were conducive to his rule or whether they resisted it. Witness his naïve fanaticism at work: the "brother" is the one who looks like him; the "racist" never looks like him. The epoch in which *he* was nothing, was nothing; the period of his coming to be is lauded and covers a multitude of sins. He simplifies and reduces every social psychology to his tyrannous either/or: *my* predominance or injustice.—Another step: the demonizing of hatred: the invention of the gruesome "hate crime"—the square circle. This is done to announce and circumscribe the conditions of what the race fanatic wants, needs, and *will obtain*. Precisely at this point, the race fanatic becomes indispensable—: *he is needed to bless and curse*. When he is seeking the gaudy rewards of a well-executed power play, he'll reach down for his deepest, "I have known many rivers" tone of voice and pronounce with a quaver, "Pray for our community. Our community needs healing. Let us pray that we become a better people. Lord . . . (—this slick bigot calls on the name of the Lord!—) Lord save us." Et sickening cetera.—Then he'll ascend his pulpit and preach his ferventest sermon about Moses delivering his people from the mighty hand of pharaoh even as he thinks about his stocks and bonds, his Cadillacs, his community service, and the peculiar way he thrills to the God is dead ethno-theologies of the "brothers who struggle against racial injustice." On the one hand, he asks, "What is the will of God?" and quavers, "I only want to do God's will!" On the other hand, he says, "What is the will of Africa?" and groans, "I only want to do Africa's will!"—He takes issue with Elijah and the prophets. "I have incorporated tolerance into my religion. Tolerate thou me!"—Meanwhile, this sanctimonious fat cat *profits from the commission of sins* . . . Only on a soil adulterated and polluted in this way can the tree of black pragmatism grow. Only in such a greenhouse with its green ideas and green sicknesses can old Father Du Bois *come to dominate*. Only in such a green world can the war Du Bois wanted, a *"war against Europe,"* be prosecuted and eternally justified. *You* the victorious ones, fie on! You who call for reaction, arise!

195

The Black leader *as a human type*—whether he is a man of ideas or an individual fitted exclusively for the practical realm—has been retrospectively outfitted with traits manufactured in light of propaganda suitable for consumption both by those whom he came to lead as well as the "enemy" . . .

until finally he *becomes* these cunning propagandistic accretions. In other words, he *becomes doctrine*; . . . a doctrine that does not, seemingly *cannot*, advance itself with reasons (—the only "argument" it knows is the *amicus curiae* brief—). Then, most important of all: the doctrine simply does not understand that contrary doctrines exist or *can* exist. Since it doesn't know how to *imagine* a contrary opinion, when it does encounter one, it is stupefied. It asks itself, "How can any human being choose to avoid the light, choose to avoid *me*?"

196

All this plays into a psychological lay of the land as yet unexplored. Perhaps it is best that we never explore it.—As previously pointed out, the *anti-pragmatist* breaks the bond forged by the ancestors. His duties and responsibilities preclude dishonesty in all its forms. In the realm of art, deception is the rule, but philosophy drives it out the gate with blows. Dishonesty is not the issue with Pragmatist Du Bois. He did what he *had* to do. He showed that the thinker, and *only* the thinker, has the right to lead people.—This is precisely the debut of Du Bois as the quintessential *anti-pragmatist*: he wants to mix philosophy with rulership. Not merely concept (—Plato—), but its working application is the *great dream* of Du Bois. This idea isn't to be found in American Pragmatism, even in the starriest moods of its Cambridge originators.—Yet Du Bois did not break the bond. His philosophy—call it what you will—is based upon ancestors and thrives on the ancestors.—What is the *meaning* of Out-of-Africa-Afrocentrism?—*Ancestors. The Race.*— . . . His concept of dark blood confesses this much; . . . as if White men have white blood! Some say the plebeian rattles his chains so noisily because he *has* chains. True, but if you take his chains away, kill the fatted calf, and place a diamond ring on his finger, does this mean he will turn into a quiet fellow? Stated again: the problem of race is the problem of ancestors. It is quite impossible for Du Bois to philosophize *absent forefathers*, quite impossible to take "education" by the tail absent racial resentments. Here, especially here, education is deception.

197

The difference between a lemon-lime quinine fizz and the pragmatism of Willard Quine with its psittacistic "symbolic logic" is that the one is good for colds and relaxes the muscles. The other is good for nothing.—I do not mean the word "nothing" to be understood negatively.—

198
Seeking holiness they mock holiness.

199
Silence is uplifting, but noise turns everyone into slaves.

200
A journalist's opinion is a child's toy.

201
Socrates offended the popular culture by practicing philosophy. Gilles Deluze and Jacques Derrida offend philosophy by practicing popular culture.

202
I heard a sailor announcing that Pan had been reborn.

203
What is the difference between a Texas woman and a lady? The same difference between a gentleman and a Texas man.

204
For ordinary souls, sleep comes after work, but a philosopher works while asleep.

205
Politicians, who take nothing seriously, expect to be taken seriously.

206
Richard Rorty ought to be sold to a circus.

207
Dr. C. G. Jung: that safari-hatted, pseudo-Gnostic groupie-rouser who dabbled in alchemy and titillated himself into believing that he could concoct a religion by pressing a dream-button. Did the good doctor's reputation exceed his brains?

208
Pragmatism is democracy's melody. This is why the noisiest democracy, to a pragmatist, is a song.

209
To curtail philosophy to the symbolic drawings and dronings of logicians and linguists! So akin to the detruncation of our literature to genre writing and sensationalistic journalism most people read. American philosophy, if I may put it to you simply and directly, has become nothing but reverberation of rhetorical peripteries surrounding the repulsively overwrought question of mind's relation to the world. Our literature is exclusively market-driven because it has no audience outside the industrious, progressively dumbed-down environment of the ruling popular culture. I trace these respective reductions to an inbred intellectual insularity, thewless perfunctoriness in the major philosophy departments, neurotic haste, distrust of silence and solitude, muleheaded preoccupation with politics, a collective will enfeebled and finally suffocated by non-stop journalism, and the side-splitting comedy of pursuing fashion for its own sake.

210
Pragmatist-Darwinist Rorty, sitting in his favorite chair in the Princeton philosophy department's seminar room, is conversing with a group of graduate students. His favorite teaching assistant, known for his weak eyes, frail, bony physique, and hippie-like fly-away hair, flanks the professor like a guard dog. "My most recent work," he begins, "hoists analytic philosophy on its own pontificatory petard. After all, how many angels *can* dance on

the hood ornament of Van Quine's Volkswagen? Can we ever really decide which physicalist position is correct? Alternative conceptual schemes in an analytic setting are a dime a dozen. Forgive me for being so brash, but expert argumentation ad nauseam may be completely and unabashedly unrelated to the truth. All our epistemological labors want to ground scientific knowledge, but what if it turns out that the scientific community is no less or more exceptional than other communities seeking knowledge of the human. Puzzling over how to justify science is a dead end. It is false to say that *because* knowledge is linguistic it must also be fundamentally a knowledge of the world of physics. However,—on the other hand, I *am* an atheist. I'm one bleak son of a bitch. If Quine wants to 'twitch in the void' I'll twitch with him. What the hell? Even animals can talk sense if they want to. And this is my view of what philosophy is: we must keep talking, but *not* as analytic philosophy has been talking. Agreed: philosophy does not seek wisdom; agreed: philosophy is all about examining vocabularies. What does this mean? Well, let's go back to the thing about science. Science is too normal. There are surprises in science, but not nearly enough of them. We need moral dilemmas, moral discourse, peripeteia. And literature has plenty of this! No more assisting people of knowledge to legitimate their endeavors. That's almost like Catholics using philosophy to defend religion. Philosophy is splintered, dead. If life has no meaning, let us at least make of ourselves whatever we can. Read your Sartre, your Malraux. Literature has replaced philosophy in the conversation of the West. Consequently, believing as I do that literature is the primary way to speak of the human, I am leaving philosophy for a chair in Comparative Literature."

—This is our reply. At the risk of arousing enormous offense, it is axiomatic that one must have first acquired a right to speak on these *higher ranking* things;—a right the academic does not, cannot, and pursuant to the academic game he plays, *must not* possess. Otherwise, we have a man blind from birth lecturing to us about the colors of the rainbow. Let us distinguish between the concept and experience. Since the concept arises from and grows out of experience, experience should precede the concept. But this does not happen with the academic. Immured within his cyanotic velleity, experience is something he *hears about*—in the media. The academic philosopher knows why Descartes quit Flèche for the rousing iridescence of Paris, why Goethe left the duke, why Nietzsche left Basel, why Leibniz relished his frequent absences from Hanover, why Schopenhauer and Aristotle needed to travel, etc; but he doesn't really *comprehend* the necessity of this *why*. The academic knows only concepts, and worse, the concepts of others, and thus he becomes the perennial glossator. Experience is the teacher for the man of experience; the academic's teacher is his concepts ... and precisely to this extent: the concepts teach him *prior* to any experience ... so that his concepts are not, as it were, fleshed-out by experience. When experiences do come, they are fitted into the prior concepts, and the academic sees, if he is honest, that the concepts, absent experience, had been misapplied all along. So it is with the student. He misapplies his education. Upon entering the non-academic world, he very gradually learns to fit the two opposites together.—Since in philosophy we begin with the *widest concepts*, the student, when he leaves his philosophy hall for the *wide world*, is perforce engaged in a process of applying concepts to experience and experience to concepts, a process that may take a very long time. Philosophic instruction meant that the student *wants more* (—think of Cicero and Julius Caesar in the company of aristocrats, sailing for the philosophic groves of Athens and Rhodes—); now, in the throes of this process, the student must *earn more*. And, yes; you will, for a time, be perceived as retarded, as Cicero and Caesar were so perceived in their late 20s; but you, as Nietzsche said so well, are moving backward so as to prepare for a great leap.—Suffice it to say that this Rorty fellow is the very mirror image of the bland, lukewarm, caribou-faced graduate student who does his doctorate, then does his own "respectable" brand of self-bondage to safety, security and—concepts. Quite unlike the Ciceronian whose *higher calling*, whose authentic *humanitas* goads him to *enter the world* (—again, think of Goethe—) this lopsided caricature of an eternal student is happiest when he sits in his high chair, fumbling with things he has *no right to touch*.—At first glance, the person who first entered upon the philosophic mode of curiosity with nothing but imputations and imprecations on his or her lips with regard to the analytic philosophy crowd would want to see Rorty's hoist of the analysts, himself included, on their own petard as praiseworthy—and it *is* praiseworthy. A more patient consideration of the *motives* for this hoisting, this critique of his own kind of philosophic temperament, reveals that his criticism of the panoply of "physicalist" explanations and their futility is really but a vestige of the man of utility's much older accusation that philosophy amounts to nothing more than a series of refuted systems benefiting nobody (—emphasis on benefit and utility—). In one word, the unphilosophic instinct is speaking here ... *again*. With an attitude like this, Rorty is, in a perverse way, justified in his efforts to shake philosophy's dust off his shoes, slap his statuesque Sophia, and exit the stage;—for, as *he* says, this stage has no narrative, no discourse, suspense, etc. Rorty's triumphal abandonment of philosophy is a symbol for his essentially debilitated nature, on the one hand, and the essential inaptitude of American philosophy on the other: he does not choose to stay and work within philosophy to restructure it; he opts out. But if he *had* remained, what foundation was there upon which to build?—That he would run to literature speaks to his lack of *solutions*. After all, what practitioner of logic and epistemology is fit to propound solutions? Moreover, literature *raises* questions, it does not answer them: the artist sets down his vision, refracted in the prism of life: then only questions remain. (—Remember Gertrude Stein's dying declaration—) . . . Once inside literature, Rorty places primary emphasis on the novel, as if to say the things most needed to be said about existence are being said in the novel, but cannot be said in philosophy . . . Again, a confession of inaptitude, softness: typical pragmatist *unbelief* in the power and rightful dominance of philosophy. The classic theory of the novel is Cervantic: the protagonist, in the face of the onslaughts of new experiences, is forced into a state of disillusion. What is being done in the most serious novels ought to be done in philosophy. Because it is not being *done*, philosophy, as Rorty admits, has lost its audience. He should make one more admission, to wit: American philosophy does not know how to break out of "theory of knowledge" and this flaccidity arouses disgust.

211

The Kennedys buy writers, says Gore Vidal. Then again, all wealthy political families in America are good pragmatists. Let us take special note that our friend Vidal (—who, possibly without knowing it, has the spirit of philosophy; he *looks down* on power and wealth:—first trait of a philosopher—) says *writers*, not philosophers. I suppose the Kennedys would own a philosopher or two—if they could find one; . . . but the spirit of philosophy in America is thwarted in quite another way.—You see, the philosophers are the productions of many, many generations. The seed must be found and planted in good soil. The plant must be tended until its rare fruit ripens and slowly becomes sweet.—Of course, what is sweet to a philosopher is usually very bitter both to the Kennedy clan and to those homeless Bostonians who drink and carouse by the Charles River.—The idea is to take an axe to the roots of this tree and attrit the young candidate while still a learner. After all, materialism *coarsens*. The dictatorship of journalism suffocates the freedom of a mind and turns it into material for a herd such that all thought must be herd thought, all philosophy herd philosophy, all dreams lies. Also operating with its own fateful seduction is the American call to specialize and its consequent contempt for the synoptic. Hearing this call the candidate may very well conclude that it is morally wrong to "judge."—If I may be blunt here: no judgment, no demand for judgment, no philosopher!—Do you understand this?—The philosopher's *right to judge* is inalienable, but the American pop culture has got it into its head that the greatest *possible* wrong is "to judge."—Nice pragmatism!!—No judgment, no standards. No standards . . . well, use your imagination . . . This idea that judgment is morally wrong is a consequence of the inevitable moral spiral-down in a society of legalisms, a society consisting entirely in the non-stop *framing of legal issues*. Here "tolerance" must be defined as a complete *inability to say No*; consequently, a Yes must be said to everything;—everything, that is, but the duty, the *responsibility* to say No.—Before the injunction, "Thou shalt not judge" ever comes into view, there stand evaluations and the motives for these evaluations. We shall return to these . . . Meanwhile, it should be very clear *from which side* the injunction issues. Precisely from Tolstoy and the "non-violence" insects who want to "honor God" by rolling over and playing dead. Tolstoy, the desperate moralist, sought to secularize the Gospels. When Jesus said, "Judge not that *you* be not judged," the *opposite* of a decadence movement was meant. The statement is both eschatological and doctrinal. If one is not to discriminate, judge, and *separate*, how is doctrine possible? Holism, yes; doctrine, no. (—And Tolstoy did *not* understand the Gospels;—he understood Rousseau—. The entirety of Nietzsche's *Anti-Christ* is based on Tolstoy's *misconstrual* of the "Resist not evil" dictum. To the Count, we would say, "Have you not read that the people were told to sell their coats to buy swords? That Jesus came not to bring peace but a sword?"—These are statements pointing to *doctrinal integrity*) . . . What do these Tolstoyan cows *want*? What does their "new morality" *point to*? Precisely to the unauthoritative, subservient, type of cow who knows its proper place (—this is what herd *means*—); precisely to the morality of unassumingness, mediocrity, uniformity, beehive industriousness suitable for every "good" bee, and quiet, green pasture suitable for every "good" cow. Then, with this mind-benumbing industry (—you cannot judge if you cannot think—) goes the feeling of being diminished and abused by the leisure and free, *open horizons the philosopher requires.*—What, then, thwarts philosophy in America?—Has this question been answered? Has it been *asked*?

212

Let us use our common sense. It is not possible to have a philosophy without being a philosopher, without being compelled and *bred* for problems the nimble-minded but commonplace empiricists bang their flat-topped heads against in vain. The philosopher, the one who is segregated from the mob, takes the road leading to the solitude of higher spirit, the lofty eagle's nest from which he *rules*, gaping no honors yet gaped upon by envious pretenders.

213

His simple house, haunt of the emperor of Rome, sits high on the long ridge of the Janiculum. The dainty roof of Horatius Flaccus, son of a slave, rises up to the unclouded stars.

214

Dostoyevsky says he met a man in Siberia who had the insides beaten out of him.

215

The Supermen steer all things.

216

If martyrdom were a coin, on one side you would see the pitiful martyr as he gives himself to the flames; on the other would appear a ranting lunatic like the one who appears on the toylike, wicked streets of San Francisco.

217

A certain Chinese man left Chinatown and traveled by train to Austin. At Lavaca Square, he met an old jazz-man who sang the blues. Mr. Wu turned to the old jazz-man and asked, very politely but pointedly, "Why you sing blues?" The old man scratched his bulbous nose, looked out at the street for a moment, and replied, "Well, my daddy, he was from Mississippi, and my mama, she was from east Texas, and I reckon that's enough to make anybody sing the blues . . . Now, let me ask you one: why do you eat rice?"

218

On a warm San Francisco night, I stood on the Wall Street of the West at Pacific and Montgomery and gazed straight up at the Pyramid. From

Telegraph Hill, I enjoyed a much grander view. The building's magnitude was multiplied. But I did not appreciate its real magnitude until I crossed the Bay or cut through the ghostly fog to the famous first grade of Marin.

219

Once when I found a little insignificant tree growing among the weeds next to a sturdy, portentous-looking live oak on the east side of the Interstate on the way down to Laredo, I noticed how paradoxically proud it seemed, giving little shimmies in the warm prairie wind. I said, "Just look at you, little tree, no taller than these weeds!" As I reached down to feel its stalk, it said to me, "Don't compare me to the weeds nature vouchsafes only a year of life! I'm a live oak tree! I'll live as long as my grandfather there who is nine hundred years old. Shame on you for not recognizing who I am."

220

A.) Socrates was arrested for examining things above the heavens and below the earth, but pragmatists believe nothing exists either above or below. Pragmatism is a new way of thinking about the famous nihilistic position of the Greek sophist Gorgias. Of course, ships exist and oceans exist. Plummets exist that descend to the bottom of the depths, and thus the depths can be measured. But the bottom, the fundament, the inexplicable does not exist for our pragmatist.

B.) Our pragmatist answers, "The intellect is there only for the service of our aims. The totality of things did not proceed from an intellect. So it did not and could not have existed as an idea before it became actual. If it *did* exist as an idea, *our ideas* could curry up to it and there would exist that correspondence we deny. The intellect originates with our preservation and is there only for our preservation. Its purpose is to serve our aims. It cannot serve anything lying outside our aims."

C.) No. You have captured all intellects and put them in a bag, as your Darwin told you to do . . . As pointed out elsewhere, Darwinism is a war against the rare, the strange, the unusual, the complicated. You speak of intellect as being in the one-dimensional service of human aims. But a superfluity of intellect is something else. The kind of intellect we find in the artist, the thinker, and the saint is *not* a slave to these aims; and hence, free from your "struggle to exist."

221
Children play and dominate adults' devils.

222
Slaves become masters and masters become slaves, but the Supermen are like fixed stars.

223
Supermen are hybrids of angels and bulls.

224
Let us solve this problem once and for all. If apes could create a philosophy, this philosophy would feverishly seek to define the ape intellect face to face the intellect of mankind; next, it would seek to convince the world that since the human philosophies have de-absolutized and decentered themselves, they should be superseded by the ape philosophy.

225
A prophet's word strikes root through everything.

226
When we speak of "secularized Christian concepts," the concepts of equality and equal rights come to mind. Since the time of Holmes, the legal profession in America has come to view religion as "divisive" and hence inherently suspect. On the other side, the religious people have a trying time realizing how the legal profession, with its secular popular culture, *could* be inimical to religion. After all, weren't the founders religious men? These fine people busy themselves digging up quotations, which to their oh-so-simple minds, *prove* the "Christian principles" of the framers of the glorious American Constitution. Yet these men were scions of the Age of Reason, distinguished men; for every Christian principle professed, these men carried in their pockets a host of French ideas whose "time would come."—Then, one day this crazy religious/anti-religious mish-mash would become the topsoil out of which the gaudy flower of pragmatism would grow . . .

227
Quine is analytic pragmatism's old hag, Rorty its meretricious minx.

228
In Gotham, the proper place to spit is in a publisher's impudent face.

229
The oracle at Delphi was asked how many free men lived in America. She replied, "Only one. Berengere."

230
Heideggerians speak fondly of Being and fail to grasp what they say, although they tell themselves they know.

231
A charlatan dressed as a philosopher was christened a philosopher and is even honored today as the great Jacques Derrida.

232
Castro to his brother, Raul: Good God, I didn't know Hemingway was a leftist!
To Fidel:
Well, you knew he was an American writer, didn't you?

233
Jews and Arabs and Arabs and Jews . . . and Jews . . . and Arabs . . . and Jews . . .

234
Those preachers who have it in their heads that the Jews in Israel will remain little lambs throughout the long process of religious decline in the

West, and that land can be holy, need a direct revelation from their God. The Land of Judah—are you listening?—will wind up in the *same* predicament it found itself in at the time of the prophets: only the names will be changed. He who blesses Israel in those days shall be an abomination.

235
Beethoven listened to rivers, Goethe to the silence within him.

236
A bird's swiftness in flight is to its nest made of twigs and tattered pieces of cloth as a thinker's painted thoughts are to his external conditions.

237
Sorry, sorry Texas men! Sorry as suck-egg dogs!

238
Men do not know what comes after death, they believe they know.

239
The prophet reveals, but philosophers conceal many things.

240
Philosophers sacrifice their lives for a pair of wings.

241
Kwame Appiah washes in the slop of a pigsty while Cornel West composes an incoherent song of his cock.

242
Actors, gypsies, stage and screen.

243

Just as there are many kinds of eyes and hence many ways of seeing the world, there are many kinds of justice. To search for a way out of this relativism and chaos in seeing we could at least construct a kind of experiment that from the outset *divides* all the so-called just actions into two rubrics: good justice and bad justice. Regarding the rubric good justice, the one who requites, the one who can repay, is called just; the just action is positive. Requital here will be seen to involve *spheres confirmed by boundaries and distances*. The person who requites lays hands on the sphere of a benefactor, for instance, and repays the help given him. Each has honored a boundary by crossing it; each has affirmed the other as not being himself; each intrudes into another sphere, a dimension not his own in order to requite; . . . and thereby he has honored the dimension as *other-than*, as reciprocal negation. It is an honoring of respective positions, an affirmation of distance. As in Aristotle's ethics of the noble, a just action is done on the basis of plenitude and self-sufficiency; . . . on the basis of and for the sake of such a feeling, such a state of being: that is to say in consequence of a *marking off* of one being from another being. Revenge will be seen as an intensification of the above, as will the intentional refraining from revenge, either as a species of self-cruelty or strict obedience to religious law. A feeling of plenitude and sufficiency of *self* accompanies the just act. As a just person, one belongs to the just, one belongs to a community of individuals possessing the capacity to requite. Justice as negotiating in light of an understanding of another's demands would seem to be a part of this good justice as it arises in light of *differences and boundaries*, specifically: the drive and need to preserve the *self*. Here justice originates between parties enjoying what is perceived to be equal power positions. Where there is no clearly recognized superiority of force a contest would result in mutual injury, and thus the idea arises on both sides of negotiating over one another's demands. One gives and receives, exchanges this for that, requites. Why?—to preserve the self, the integrity of boundary, under the presupposition of an approximately equal power position; that is to say the capacity to injure or destroy is equal. Justice goes back naturally to the position of enlightened self-preservation and thus back to the self; and thus, as aforesaid, to the *marking off* of reciprocal negation: the self is not a stone, the self is not the other self, the self is not God. Moreover, there is distance between the selves, the things, the *numina*. Tension, pathos, incorruptible pursuit of holiness—: this tension is the maintenance of boundaries, strength and health, the creation of culture, perfection, honor: in a word, the prevention of social chaos, self-responsibility, the natural tendency to preserve the distance that divides us, the triumph of all organizing power and *reverence for separations*. Regarding the rubric bad justice, the just action is negative; the just action is action that adapts to anything as long as it is new (—thus the just action is inaction); the just action doesn't offend (—he who doesn't offend or is incapable of offending is called just); the just action doesn't discriminate on the basis of the interests of specially protected groups; justice posits the exception as equal to the rule; . . . thus it posits a contemptuous bias against rules, the "normal," the "straight" (—the person who honors boundaries is the "homophobe," the "witch-hunter") . . . We have already entered the realm of Equality: here the sordid ideals of the French Revolution, annealed and expanded by modern movements, become gospel; here the doctrine that everyone is and ought to be equal is shouted from the housetops; here the mass swarms, the busy intolerant mass of self-identical automata submerged in the gray soup of factitious happiness; here the impudent social planners preach what shall be and not be (—those freedom lovers); here the sordid mythology of synthetic unity is passed off as religion, as true philosophy, as the art of political rearrangement, as light shining forth out of darkness; here the needle-pricked voodoo doll of racialism casts its shadow over every shoulder, ever ready to bait and vilify and destroy; here achieved unanimity in forbearance, the look-the-other-way morality of tolerance, confuses weakness and cowardice for goodness and compassion; here everyone is at once an invalid and a nurse . . . a "victim" . . . an over-excited, dysfunctional, acquisitive, soft, economical, unpretentious, machine-minded extension of technology; here one limps on both legs and exults in the ability to *whine*; here the subjugation and suffocation of complex forms is practiced as survival (—survival of the cloned and best-programmed); here the rare and the extraordinary run for cover; the drive to perfect oneself has been replaced by the drive to gratify oneself instantly, accumulate more and more things, operate more gadgets, see more deranged movies, revenge oneself for more "past wrongs," objectify, stultify, and stupefy oneself with more and more robotized "information."—

244

Almost everyone in the philosophic world is impressed and awed, even overawed, by Wittgenstein's *passionate* work, and one may fancy that more than a few of our fine commentators—I am speaking of their fine collaborative instincts, you understand—might feel a hankering to see in this work certain glimmers of the fulfillment of Nietzsche's call for a completely new, *redeemed* philosophical landscape.—You see something Socratic, something bold, austere, *profoundly grand* in Wittgenstein's nature; a commanding presence in the history of ideas, a critical consciousness at work; one who, in his magnanimous leoninity, is no longer disposed to believe that the *truth of all things* should be in any way connected to elevation, inspiration, ecstasy; the patient, guileless, supremely caustic investigator who cultivates, as though naturally, unconsciously, the true philosophic spirit of severity and sobriety in the presence of debauchery.—But reasonable minds differ, gentlemen.—I am at a complete loss when I try to justify Wittgenstein's dogged interest in philosophy; in one word, why he is *there*? What is he doing in philosophy? I do see clearly enough, however, why philosophy students and their professors are so captivated by Wittgenstein's clarity and "genius." It is because they know nothing of common law method and the legal logic behind it. It is singularly significant that Bertrand Russell wanted to know just about everything about everything, but became cold, pale, and shy in the presence of the blind goddess . . . I feel Wittgenstein wanted to *use* this, as it were, extracurricular logical tool as every polemicist uses his tools: to destroy. In other words, Wittgenstein did not seem to care that the results of his work would amount to having philosophers think as the legal community thinks;—an outrage against philosophy if there ever were one as well as a broadside that could *only* have come out of England, namely the grand old party of philosophic legalisms from Bacon to Bentham.—I maintain that Wittgenstein's "new method" of thinking strictly inductively, experimentally, and in terms of *family resemblance* is really a very old method harking back to the English dialectic of the case law. Moreover, this man came into philosophy with the sole purpose of reducing philosophy and the philosopher to an unexampled level, that of the scientific day laborer, the ingenious little wage earner whose "ideas" deprecate and disallow the manifold vision required for the philosopher's *royal voyage* through the whole realm of values. For who can doubt that the natural outcome of these modern ideas, i.e., these false ideas, is the reconciling of philosophy not with "certainty," but with the most uncertain, wobbly, conciliatory deference for the racialism, feminism, and hermaphroditism of pragmatist culture? Alas! Did Wittgenstein grow a long, glossy pigtail, which, in the end, in his "mature philosophy," he learned to attach to his mind? Did he become the grandest *coolie* who ever lived?—

245

To answer the question, "Why does Wittgenstein philosophize?" it is already clear to everyone that the fame of the "greatest philosopher of the

20th century" lies in his ambition to diagnose a cure for the immemorial metaphysical ailments of mankind. He wants to place these problems under his microscope and reveal them to all persons of knowledge everywhere as—nothing. Whether the answer to this question also answers the further question, the really dispositive question, of what he is doing with *his* philosophy, should be answered unqualifiedly in the negative. "What is he doing?" can only mean to which place does he want to arrive. To answer the question where a philosopher is going is invariably answered by an examination of motive.—Where does the philosopher, whether he answers to the name of an ancient metaphysician or our newest, trendiest positivist-analyst-linguist, *want to go?*—We ask three simple questions. The third question may be answered by positing the opposite of the first two answers, especially if the thought is great philosophy;—theology, being much trickier even than the trickiest philosophy, answers to this with much less prompting. First the outward form. What is the *outward form* of Wittgenstein's philosophy? He wants, he says, to solve the problems. Yet who needs a Wittgenstein to tell us what is wrong with some philosophies? He wants, then, to speak of all *possible* thought? This creates interest, suspense, sympathy.—What is the *underlying idea*? More of the above: to rescue the thinker from his own mind. Final question, the motive: what does he want to *do*? Here the answer to this question is more a shading of the first two questions. Wittgenstein wants—even before he ever gets started—to place *philosophy itself* upon a pragmatistic base. The fourth figure in the Peirce-James-Dewey triumvirate is not Rorty, (—Rorty is a fad, and a simple-minded one at that—). It is Ludwig Wittgenstein, the quasi-Irishman, leprechaun-philosopher!—The thinker imposes a conceptual model on phenomena *per se* unproblematic; the resulting radical disjunction births philosophy's problems. To move from thought to the thinker is not illicit. But the thinker who thinks this thought is not immune either. The form? The idea? Merely means to an end. For what better way to solve philosophy's problems than to write a few pungent, passionate disquisitions counseling dismissal of the problems *as* problems? After all, pragmatism is good for more than a Harvard paycheck. Pragmatism solves problems in *thought* by bringing them *into action*, as modern theology gelds spirit by bringing it down into life. Better to have the fish die in the water—which is what all philosophic problems do; they *get old*—than be brought out upon dry land.—With his new method in hand, i.e., with his common law method and legalistic spirit that he will use to hoist philosophy up into the damp English air and set it down upon a pragmatistic base, he says, "This is the hardest thing that could ever be done on behalf of the spirit of philosophy."—The spread of *analytic pragmatism* itself depended upon this prideful assertion! The burgeoning of nameless, symbolic faces doing symbolic logic depended upon this pride! Yes, let us stop and reflect. It is time for seriousness in philosophy. From Ryle to Quine . . . *this means*: the scent of formaldehyde is added to the already ineradicable doomsday mustiness and gloom of the philosophy halls in the Anglo-American world! Quite unable to enter into experience—I do *not* say into the "real world" *sub specie pragmatatis*—philosophy must leave the mind for the nostrils! Only in the wasteland of American thought—and in the "Mother country"—could this sort of thing be possible. Philosophers, yea, more than philosophers, these saccharine Saxons with their Anglo symboli-mummy-logic!—The great Wittgenstein avers, "Meaning is not something hidden behind many *everyday* usages; the use itself is the end of the line. Thus, the everyday is the end of investigation. More than this, and the philosopher is looking for pink elephants." (—Notice the stock pragmatist position—).—Wittgenstein will thus bring words back to their everyday use, for the conceptual model, the *picture* the words evoke, has perplexed us into an inevitable captivity. An appeal to everyday language is the way out of the self-imposed labyrinth. Wittgenstein's philosophy then appeals to "practices" and "cases." Analogically, the legal community is not perplexed by the concept of obscenity. First of all, it is changing; it changes according to practical need and is expressed in a gamut of cases. The lay person may strive for a definition to cover the cases, but the attorney will not do this; sufficient unto the case is the evil thereof. When an attorney explained to Charles Peirce how the whole concept of proximate cause—the mystery of causation bespeaking Augustine's mystery of what time *is*, etc.—had nothing to do with causation, he pricked up his ears and invented Cambridge Pragmatism on the spot. Thus, the upshot of this Wittgensteinism is the same need to supplant and render primitive and prejudicial the *res cognitans* that we find in Dewey (—who, however, clearly lacks Wittgenstein's sensitivity—) . . . When you stop searching for witches in Salem, witches will cease to exist . . . although, in fact, there *are* many witches whose witcheries are now of no concern to you . . . Thus we have the unsung, *unknown* honeymoon time for positivism and pragmatism; the union of logic, linguistics, science, and—God help us—their motley, half-breed progeny hungry for life;—*life?*—No, not life: its semblance! Philosophy desiccated, abrogated, drained of spirit! sucked dry by logicians!—*Englishmen*! All to the satisfaction of the most heartfelt longings of the still youthful, *innocent Americans*! Philosophy domesticated, incarcerated, pronounced *logical*! To which spectacle the American "philosophers," their veins full of pragmatist venom, wag their still quasi-Calvinist, pious heads and say, "Philosophy is dead." (—While in the same decade, far, far away from the academy, the American novelists were saying the novel is dead) . . . What more could we expect from a cult of death? We still believe do we not that philosophy *mirrors life*?—

246

It can do no civilized man an injury, as Pufendorf says, that another believes differently than he; and it is our reasonable duty to diminish needless suffering in the world. As far as tolerance does no violence to truth and doesn't by the practice of it vitiate religious doctrine, it ought to be recognized as a principle of common reason by princes and public alike. Agreed, sir; truth ought to be insulated from the designs of tolerance; that it is but a kind of truce and not an end of the conflict.—And yet, to the contrary, I would only point out that the reception in England of the Roman law was less than hospitable, for the common law, since it rests upon a principle inimical to the law of the Continent, repelled and drove out the foreigner with undiminished energy and guile.—The principle of toleration within a world of differing particulars is one thing; tolerance of any single world by every other is something else entirely, and it is destructive and tyrannical to teach it, much less attempt to enforce such an obscenity: it amounts to the subtle emasculation of every philosophic insight and religious doctrine. The consensual task of modern thought is simply to have the one kind of tolerance indistinguishable from the other so that every existent is indistinguishable from every other existent. And yet in the end Baron Pufendorf is eminently correct. The interest in being free from needless injury leads us to tolerance by emphasizing similarity; the interest in the preservation of truth leads us to emphasize difference. The modern democracies pervert Pufendorf's principle by expanding it into one overarching "correct" thought: intolerance in every form is *not to be tolerated*: correct thinking and correct expression dominate the American democracy, and this because of the American worship of the god of "unity" as a fallowing and preparatory stage for the coming triumph of matriarchal values.

247

Descartes was the father of rationalism;—this does not entail the recognition of reason as the only authority. The whole of Catholic philosophy—which can never be a philosophy but only special pleading—follows Plato and his faith that both faith *and* reason move toward the good, i.e., God. One must have faith, but persuade reason to aid it with good arguments. As if faith needed any aid; as if the arguments are any good; for supposing they are good, a proven God, as Søren Kierkegaard says, is no God; . . . in fact, to "prove the existence" of God is to insult divinity; but Catholics must never recognize this, for it would mean the emasculation of their faith, "the faith," as aforesaid, the faith in faith *and* reason. Yes, Descartes did not buy into this kind of rationalism. He said—with William of Ockham, Martin Luther, and the leading lights of the age—"I would have to be *more than man* to know those things Aquinas claims to know!"—What? Thomas Aquinas was more than a man?

248

Anyone with any philosophical discernment can see that a move to neutralize the pretensions of Catholic medieval philosophy is what trundles in the background of the whole flank of analytic pragmatism, and is the not-so-very-secret animus of Russell, Wittgenstein, and that Cambridge Cagliostro, Professor James. This is precisely what these philosophers *achieved*; . . . but only in their minds and for their people. For how can pretensions be neutralized when Catholic thought averts its eyes from any post-Kantian development, and the "great pope," John Paul II, goes on doodling with his precious *fides et ratio*? (—his *historical* theological error.—)—Any achievement in *this* area would have to explicate the relation of reason and faith *in history*; how reason became culture; so that the same theological predicament that materialized in ancient Israel *occurs again*. But here even the Reformers and Kierkegaard see through a glass darkly and necessarily so. Here is a tale yet to be told, a vision no one has seen . . .

249

The philosopher is a tyrant. Who can doubt the proto-tyranny of such mad hermits as Plato, Empedocles, Heraclitus, Xenophanes, and other examples of what philosophy *once was*? Compared to the storyteller—who sets his characters in constant conflictual motion and lets his images carry his reader to and fro as the reader's imaginative thoughts dictate—the philosopher holds the reins on the reader and demands obedience; that is to say the reader will not flit away on his own trajectory like a butterfly, but will think as the philosopher thinks.—However this is not to deny that philosophy tells a story. Even the history of philosophy tells a story; but there is no plot and far, far fewer "believable characters" than we have supposed . . .

250

The great expanse of time in which philosophy was *expected* to accommodate itself to religious dogma constitutes the darkest age of the genre, a retarding of its development. Philosophy once again springs to life as soon as this expectation is driven off and the chains are sundered.—What then are we to make of the Anglomaniacal diagnosis that philosophy must accommodate itself to science?—and, hence, to technology and the hysteria of popular culture? Gentlemen, gentlemen, use your heads!

251

The pragmatists and logical positivists believe that philosophy is a world very much like that enclosure made of bones Balzac describes in *Cousin Bette*. They believe philosophy leads not to a good life but to a very bad one. (—In one of his lectures, James comes out and says this in some detail.—) But every real philosopher knows that to seek a good life—a life, as it were, abstracted from a *necessary dialectical scheme*, which necessity, for want of a better name, Nietzsche calls *Amor Fati*—would mean the desertion of his philosophy; . . . and, therefore, the greedy, web-fingered pragmatist is here existentially correct! Later, in light of the pragmatist's horse sense, he is quite sure his ministrations are giving life to philosophy when in fact he is doing the reverse and serving it hemlock.—The low-bred Hollywood screenwriter; the activist attorney who sees his duplicity as moral; the instant gratification success addict; the political favorite who appears in shining armor to "the people," but lives by expediency's Janus-faced law.—All these gave Socrates the hemlock.—And why? Precisely to protect and extol the good life.

252

When the San Franciscans drove me out of the city, they condemned themselves to a life without me.

253

San Francisco, like Sodom and Plato's Atlantis, is destined to descend beneath the waves. I know no other way to explain the city's magic. Fantasy buried beneath glaucous, whooshing arbors; the ocean is a purple dream . . .

254

Rome is heavy, as is Istanbul. Athens is light, *still* light, and this should tell us something about the Greeks.

255

Mournful clumps of cypress white as the sand cover an abandoned beach in Spain. Clouds, the color of the freighters that sail for another world, beyond Gibraltar's double face, descend lazily for the tilting horizon. Here, assuming you can *see* such a man, is the beach where the underground man takes his Sabbaths. You wouldn't know, what with his shining visage and agile body, that this man spends a good part of his life in the dark, and soon—perhaps too soon—he will descend like the clouds and burrow down to his home in the depths beneath the sea. Believe me, there is some kind of *recompense* down there that keeps him ever pushing onward, digging down, down, away from the sights and sounds—and hence the applause and rejection—of others. But a man, even an underground man, must come up for air and enjoy the light of heaven! No, no, do not think that he will invite *you* to join his hazards and joyous deprivations, for he is, after all is said and done, a gentleman, if a very unusual one. Yes, it's true, he wonders at the freighters, the *human* part of sea and sky, and sometimes thinks they are coming for him. For he has been waiting a long time for his ship. But he, on the other hand, is not one to be unriddled, and will remain a riddle only by remaining concealed. *Bene vixit qui bene latuit.*

256

I prophesy the *victory of the nurturing values* amid the waning of courage, the disposition to see differences, the strength to resist. Victory in *decline*. And what constitutes "decline"? I have said it before: the ultimate convergence and homogenization expressed in the omega being, the *unio mystica et physica* of the triumphant matriarchate.

257

What then will be the task of the true philosopher in this last *humane age*?—Let us state it this way. The more humanity a people has "achieved," the more is this people bedeviled by superstitious fear. Conceive of a great many truths gradually rounded up and thrown in prisons by a culture-elite

(—including the truths no longer seen and recognized *as* truths by an indoctrinated herd powerless to express these truths: hence the *correct* way to censor a "free society"—). This prince of the power of the air knows these truths as *dangerous*: they are locked up, branded as felons—as falsehoods—and forbidden further expression. But the prince fears a revolt, a *jailbreak*. After all, many generations have labored to achieve this kind of humanity! These very "old truths" now moldering in their wicked corner prove the possible resurgence of the beast that has been laid to rest! No parole for *these* old truths! No amenities for these cruel, unregenerate, hardened criminals! No mercy, no reprieve for that which is utterly without redeeming social value! As such, whenever someone comes preaching, "Set the captives free!" you will recognize at once *who* the true philosopher is, *what* his task is, *why* he philosophizes, etc.—Let us say, hypothetically, that some philosopher comes along who actually succeeds in *freeing* one or two of these wicked old truths;—what would transpire? The ideological constabulary would be galvanized and instantly placed on alert. Not only the *free thoughts*, but the philosopher himself who dared conceive and carry out such a conspiracy—this is what they will say, "conspiracy!"—will be hunted down and imprisoned; for, alas! in legal comprehension, these prisoners at large may be rightfully construed as *his thoughts*. Then, once again, the offenders will be handcuffed, placed in the grim van, and corridored off to jail. There, hidden in the dim, gray walls—walls so much like, so much *akin* to the lurid Bastille walls—the priestess will appear in her long wiccan gown. Casting Druidic imprecations, her sharp, frightful glance at once slides into a state of equanimity and celestial repose. She says to the prisoners who bang their chains against the wall in abject defiance, "Your dangerous thrills, now for this second and this third time, have again cost you your freedom. Yet it did not *have* to be thus. You—yes, even *you*—could have learned how to worship and love."

258

No wonder the popular culture believes in meditation! Just as their Hollywood entertainment offers respite from senseless, nerve-fraying work, so meditation is their anodyne and sedative for ultimately purposeless herd activity; . . . their escape from life. Popular writing too is an escape, standing, or rather, slumping at the opposite pole from literature, which *leads the reader into matrices of meaning*; . . . in other words, leads *back into life*.—On the other hand, for the thinker, life itself offers a rest, a sedative, a perch for a bird that has flown so high above the earth! The thinker does not meditate to quell the stream of life. In fact, he *does not meditate at all*! For life is *his* respite from that stream of thought and feeling he calls "thinking." Consequently, he disdains all noisy exoduses from life, and instead demands silence.

259

Pragmatism and Oxonian analytic are frontal attacks on ontological wonder; thus the issue has been joined with the highest exemplars of the *vita contemplativa*: the poets, artists, and thinkers who clearly and expressly recognize wonder as their philosophical and artistic *sine qua non*.—Wittgenstein singles out Augustine to pummel and insult. Yet our almost incredible distance from Augustine sets him up as an easy target. When, in truth, Augustine's need to *penetrate into* an everyday reality—to go behind the everyday usage—is just as present in Nietzsche and Heidegger as it is in the Saint. What? Was Wittgenstein unsteady on his legs? (—American Pragmatism's "cash value of a thought" made him steadier than Socrates in the Agora—)—We must not fail to grasp this: where the everyday use leaves off, wonder begins; the otiosity of wonder is precisely the functionality of everyday use. "We understand backward," says the anti-Hegelian polemicist, "and live forward," yet this expedient is, in the final accounting, quite, *quite* beside the point. For, as our self-tethered empiricists hate to admit, thought bullies action and winds it up like a clock.

260

When confronted with the "return to Africa" question, Frederick Douglass became indignant. "You ex-slaves will do nothing of the sort," he said. "You will stay right here and make the White man see us as men."—Thus began the long struggle, a struggle still going on. In fact, were it not for this ongoing struggle with its golden-skinned plan for ultimate redemption via its dream of de-centering *all other facts and possibilities* in the so-called "American experience," how could anyone speak of the existence of an American democracy? The spectacle of people in the streets demanding their rights, their dreams, their place in the American sun, militates against every Tammany Hall backroom deal of every Boss Tweed who ever lived!—"We are men!" Ralph Ellison clarioned at the white sky. "Listen to us, heed our rising voices, and maybe someday, you too will be men!"—No, the South will *not* rise again. Get this out of your Confederate, German-stubborn square heads. For something else is rising in its stead. An authentic democracy—thus speaks Ellison's "invisible man"—must be constructed from the groans of our ancestors and the clanking of their *holy chains*.—And, broadly speaking, though it comes to us encased in its strictly racial form, the message of Douglass and Ellison must din in the hollow souls of every American. For the message is this: racial prejudice *originates* in a soulless people.—And this is to say: we stand at the door and knock (—the door, the front door, of a big white house, to be sure—). Every man who lets us in, and sups with us, and clothes us, and blesses us, the same man shall *acquire a soul*.—But the rank exuberance of this blasphemy, this gruesome race pragmatism, rankles in the very nostrils of God.

261

To implant the teaching of *racism* in the still childish, animal nature of the American is to do nothing other than poison the organism: a ferment sets in that breeds confusion in *all* judgments; a fear supervenes that leads to an enfeeblement of spirit (—I use the word "spirit" here merely as a synonym for animality—); the backs of the people show the red whelps of a strange, new ideological cruelty; a new kind of "freedom of expression" is enacted; the people, just as their racial sins are washed away and scalded clean by a strict doctrine of sinfulness and damnation, works and grace, learn how to let down their guards and *accept more*—of everything! Every kind of fuchsia-colored phantasy throngs in demanding acceptance and fructifies, finally, into a new reality in which and on account of which the only sin left is—*racism!*—*racism!*—*racism!*

262

The great von Ihering's only hope: written constitutions. Yet no prudent person can deny that a bad new wrinkle has been put on expression law, the floor of the basement for Constitutional democracy.—"Why, of course, we deny that any *wrong* has been committed. We, you see," the protected groups continue, "are the beneficiaries of the new law."—Very fine. But the censor filches with his own when he filches with what is mine.—And so it goes. Since von Ihering there has been nothing to back up justice (—other than a sociological grounding of all law, and this backs up nothing but the "growth of the law," etc.—) . . . But *we* foresee a time when there shall be new laws written on new tables, the likes of which have not been seen since the spectacular rise of Marduk and Jehovah.

263

The famous pragmatic theses in Marx's *Theses on Feuerbach* alone are sufficient to turn de Beauvoir and Sartre into pragmatists. Every Marxist is a kind of pragmatist.—Miss de Beauvoir, with her penis envy coupled with her reading of Schopenhauer's later work, transformed herself into a gender pragmatist. Gender pragmatism preaches an African ethno-philosophy and seeks the return of the matriarchate or at least a kind of synthesis. Armed force, of course, will *not* be needed, and never is anything but nurturing, humanity, and justice preached. Sartre never suspected, as he basked in his 20th century glow, that his woman would overtake *his* existentialism and his Critique of Reason; but a girl it is who will seize the reins of the future and dictate, like Plato's fabled guardians, the destinies of the earth; . . . all in a framework of advanced democracy, *not* communism.—Miss de Beauvoir *can* be but a revered pathfinder whose work will be totalized by the onward movement of feminist thought;—the onward movement of history. After all, she *came out of Sartre* and is still an existentialist. The woman, by her choice, emerging out of objecthood is a truncated notion; and can only be a provisional philosophy. Next step: Irigaray. She says, "Woman must speak!" (—a woman's language, a language of hysteria, to destabilize the world of men—). And already, at the snap of a woman's slender fingers, freedom in the Sartrian sense, is cancelled and superseded. Toril Moi, defending de Beauvoir, accuses Irigaray of "essentialism." But so what? It is, after all, not a matter of a woman becoming a woman. It is a matter of woman becoming Woman . . . Existentialism is sloughed off as the snake sheds its skin.

264

It is understandable why women are searching for a "sexual identity." They have lived quite without one since the worldwide acceptance of the male creation myths. Still, there is a dilemma: the *woman's* identity must assert itself *against the male* "version," "model," call it what you will.—And it is surely not the case that their identity has been pulled out from under them. No, they have *thrown it away* by abandoning their role in the patriarchy. They say, "We have an identity, but it is a false identity. We will search for a better role within the social context of a new identity."—Very well; woman is searching for a new identity. When she finds one, you will not want to be so blind as to deny the concomitantly new *male identity.*—What then is the meaning of feminism?—: *what women want*. But where are they going, where are they taking us to get what they want? It's a question of direction, you understand . . .

265

Who can comprehend this?—Woman lost her fear of man on the same day the children lost their fear of adults.

266

From experience I know what women want, what they invariably require: a stand-up fight!

267

Put down that fiddle, Kate Chopin, so I can slap your face!

268

Who's afraid of Virginia Woolf? Poor Virginia was afraid of herself.

269

Feminism is the convent of a Marxian order, it is true.—Yet it was only after the spirit of capitalism had triumphed over the knightly spirit of feudalism that woman could *venture out*.

270

What? Progress means making women more like men?—"No," a feminist said. "Progress means making men more like women."—

271

I'm trying my best to understand you. It's *worse* for there to be a few Madame de Staels in a climate of repression than to realize a full emancipation for so many mediocre women? You look at me as if to say, "We will always have our Madame de Staels around." Then why don't I see any today? Let us confess it: *the splendid literary woman is dying out.*

272

Sometimes I think it will never happen even though I've convinced myself it is on the way. The pre-patriarchal matriarchy inculcated in every way the fundamental sexual belief that woman was the incarnation of a qualitatively different ideal than man. But the feminist espousal of equal rights and equality of the sexes *denies* this feminine ideal. In other words, all the feminist activity—from philosophy to politics—destroys in man the *residue* of any belief in this ideal. Women are simply equal co-workers.—Certainly you feminist philosophers will not deny that the ineradicable *inertia of philosophy is to destroy belief.* What?—A necessary and inevitable tension exists between feminism and matrism?—

273
In fact, my friends, the *feminist idea* in all its lurid nakedness is rendering women more hysterical, more and more incapable of being human. Of course, other factors are involved in this forced march to a one-dimensional soul. The general dehumanization of modernity *could* have spared this our fairer, more cunning "second sex," but feminism is addressed to the ovaries, and, I'm sorry to say, there is no escape . . .

274
With regard to male and father, feminism feels no need to distinguish between men whose spirits are chained and men whose spirits are free. It sees only men—free and fettered—as perpetuating a model of domination. This is so because they have posited the mother, specifically the body of the mother, as the "origin," and "identity" comes from being related to this origin. This already bodes ill for the female child for she, unlike the male has no object with which she can negotiate a relation with the origin. (—*Already* we see what the real problem is—). This non-penile state oppresses women, who must find identity some other way.—Thus, woman, since she cannot lapse back into a pre-rational, oestrogenic "matriarchy"—such cannot be maintained without denying paternity—must *rely on her feminist philosophers* to usher her into their world of the "concave mirror"—a hermaphroditic staging area adumbrative of the next world.

275
Thomas Pynchon: that miserable voodoo-cartoonist/word-heaper confessing decay, impotence, and exhaustion: the most American of fiction writers writing today.

276

Our touchy, supercilious news business seeks to oversee a constantly running Constitutional crisis. But there is only one such crisis: the news business.

277

Henrik Ibsen: that old maid dressed up as a man.

278

The beginning will begin again. Genius lives in the middle.

279

When William James told a Boston troll that if he'd gone to Harvard he wouldn't have to sleep in the Common, the troll replied that if William James slept in the Common he wouldn't have to go to Harvard.

280

Simone Weil's God is good for Simone Weil.

281

Is it really the case that the fearful *energy* engendered—the sparks ignited beneath artistic kindling and stacks of dry wood—necessary for the production of genius issues forth as a consequence of centuries of human domination and conquest? Can it be that the sparks ignited by the fearful energy of contest, of envy and hatred, at last break out and, as if guided by something divine, trek out for another, higher realm, the realm of art and thought?—In consequence of this, the production of genius is limited by a circumscribed period in the life of mankind; and so on.—Well, not to deny for a moment the fact of *ruthlessness in the generation of genius*, we propose that nature is compensating for her mistakes on a mass scale whenever she creates the exceptional being. The mass of humanity, bred for nothing but survival, must appear as a jumble of confused truncations seen from nature's perspective of having intended whole beings; as privations of this wholeness. The sum total of these privations gets *accumulated* somehow and *incarnated* in the genius, the being with more than enough, the superfluous human being!—This *accumulation of deprivations* conception of genius explains how the light of Greece could arise out of so much Dorian darkness; explains the *sudden occurrence* of exemplary human beings out of peasant stock; . . . the startling proximity of a Horace and a Pushkin to slave lineage, etc. These individuals, these geniuses, are bound to attempt the flights the succeeding generations were *supposed* to have appreciated tenuously, and in some rare cases, actually offer rude sacrifices to the jealous Muse. Therefore, the existence of genius presupposes not cruelty, but barbarity.—Let someone else wrestle with this . . .

282

Conceive of pragmatism as a species desiring the continuation of its type (—this species will, in due time, live to see the *predominance* of its type—). There are things this John Dewey-Jane Addams species of Hull-anthropoid *must do*, must see through to social completion for this triumph to be realized.—There must come to fruition what—for lack of a better term—we will call "nurturing," i.e., the strict uniformity of stupidifying goodness (—nurturing = uniformity = goodness—/—goodness = nurturing = uniformity—); . . . this is to say, unintelligent goodness . . . The idea here is that intellect, since it is a *part of human suffering*, must be ruthlessly suppressed. And given the already exclusively action-oriented nature of a people (—not to speak of the love and worship of technology and the march of secularized religious concepts through a wasteland of perpetually reconstituted legal issues—) this Hullification of American humanity seems eminently doable and "necessary." Pragmatic, put it that way.—For let us not be deceived, and let us not deceive ourselves . . . here, here at the threshold of the future!—Yea, these pragmatists know what possibilities can be cultivated out of mankind! What unexhausted "probabilities" blind, oh-so-guileless confidence in modern ideas can bring forth!—The degeneration of Homo Sapiens as pragmatism's ideal!—The cosmic race as visualized and willed!—The philosopher who sees *this* sees a new beginning for philosophy; and specifically what philosophy must do . . . must *not* do!

283

On the plain meaning of *inter pares*: among equals can only mean *exclusively* among equals.—Whenever philosophy professors attempt to appropriate Nietzsche intellectually—and I draw the sharpest distinction between appropriating this philosopher intellectually and appropriating him existentially—they will do a cute little academic jig on the table, their left foot moving to the "raw" and their right to the "refined." As if a philosophy professor's *frottage* could determine what is "coherent" or "incoherent" *inter pares*!!—Suffice it to assert that the comicalness of the good professors is apparent in everything they say, and that Nietzsche's actual *audience* is much, much tinier than his readership.—But this raises the asinine presumption that treats the philosophic canon as the private game preserve of walleyed academics whose "Nietzsche" is one-third intentional misconstrual, two-thirds instinctual comicality. Such creative misrepresentations for the purpose of obtaining tenure cannot be branded with sufficient contempt.—Question: what is "incoherent" to a philosophy professor incapable of living as a philosopher lives and must live is therefore not coherent among equals, i.e., among *thinkers*?—Verily, the professoriate has *its inter pares*: respect among peers, i.e., among *professors*, the creative non-creative crowd, the thinking non-thinkers!—For, believe me, there is a different *kind* of spirit aloose in the Academy today! It will soon dawn on more than a few wooers of Sophia's nakedness that the men who *taught* philosophy—I think of such fine teachers as Walter Kaufmann, Father Copleston, Herbert Marcuse, Julien Marias, Jose Ortega, Miguel Unamuno—are now but memories and worm-riddled vestiges of a bygone era. And this today? What *is* it? The industrious mob of rank and file time-servers! The journalistic rabble that wants to poison the uncommon man so that when this rabble looks outside itself it may see its own image. Make no mistake: it is these dressed-up dolts of mirror-gazing journa-narcissists who have finally subverted every healthy instinct that once existed between and among teachers and their students. These draggle-tailed hinnies of professors cannot create, *therefore they destroy*! And how do they destroy?—By means of their exegeses and exegesis of exegeses, their gad-about glosses upon glosses, their mind-destroying interpretations; in one word, their *journalism*! Since authentic creation of philosophy is an embarrassing non-possibility for the professoriate, the texts of philosophy must be made to *disappear* beneath layer after layer of scholarly exegesis;—vulture-ly exegesis!—To fashion the Academy more and more like the popular culture: *this is the goal; this is happening now* . . . John Dewey's religion of political liberalism; American "Legal Realism" replete with its "law as a means to an end" species of idolatry; the triumphant, "Constitutionally mandated" Fourth Estate; the sacred cow racialists in the Harvard Afro-Studies Department; the perfumed

Rortyites and Hobbist "Senior Lecturers" in Merry Ole England whose learned moronism crisscrosses oceans; the *in hoc signo decadence* implicit in every contorniate big word constitutive of modern ideas;—these idols now inaugurate a new American "philosophy," a new American culture, a new *pragmatism* . . .

284

The promise that the lowest shall be on top, that the slaves become masters. This *process* as a turning over again of the hourglass pertains to the shape of the glass, the size of the sand particles, and of course, the *who* of the turning. Pivotal is the *great abdication* of the thinking class, the falling away from the old values.—Quiet! Do I hear faint objections that the imagination of the moral future of mankind is not the proper role of the philosophers of the future, that this task, however infamous and disagreeable it may be, is not the life-history and *blood* of every philosopher?

285

Forward amidships the deck's awash; the guns are wet with salty foam; from the bridge I saw the focsul riding the edge of a sword.

286

Remember me, when with my heart against despair, I held my Land from her enemies.

287

The Greeks rejoiced over the language of the Greek poet and epigrammatist because they could detect in this language the same crystalline reposefulness one may still find even today in the Aegean sky and sea. We see last vestiges of overwhelming transparency: a full moon over the open sea swaths its supple path of silvery iridescence that runs breathlessly to the black horizon. Seen from the archipelago the Acropolis mutely proclaims *its* victory of clarity over obscurity, and its intercourse, finally, with the Aegean sun. Then, east of Crete in a wraith of dim sunlight, perfectly conical orange peaks rise unexpectedly from the milky depths. In the charging whitecaps off Lesbos, I see the god on a dark, angry day . . .

288

The youth Heraclitus never sailed, and said, "The land is enough for me."—However, ever since the day he saw the goddess of posthumous fame, his stone ship glides through the eerie Strait of Messina, finally to pass the ghostly white rocks of rugged Gibraltar for the algae-green ocean of Atlantis.

289

Theologians work to turn the name of God into filth.

290

When any modern democracy, through an overabundance of laws, the incessant noise of vociferous, disenfranchised minorities, and a supine majority, tries to complete itself it always will go too far and dissolve all individuals; as if Rousseau is sealing a pact with Darwin.

291

Philosophers are monks with hatchets in their hands.

292

A pragmatist tosses his axioms the way a fop tosses his head.

293

Dreams are a mirror of the past. They are the picture of *our* past seen through the crazy telescope of ancient humanity. Dreams dramatize an isolated situation, a kind of emotional link in an unknown plot. From this it does *not* follow that mankind invented "another world" because of and out of dreams.

294

If the Renaissance has continued more or less unabated, how can there be a new Renaissance, *another* Renaissance?—A cultural weight of a *radically different kind* would have to make itself felt.

295

Pragmatism wants to congeal the turbulent river of belief into blocks of ice.

296

It is perhaps understandable that a form of political neurosis hitherto found only in the ancient *polis* should show its relatively belated face in America—the *extreme* democracy—as a tropical outgrowth of French revolutionary ideals. It was inevitable that the very first signs of the breakdown of freedom should show *its* face in the field of expression law. Just as Juvenal had to endure a hard exile for lampooning an actor favorite of Domitian, so today only the things *no longer worthy of satire* may be "lampooned," and a predictable Reign of Terror has come with regard to those groups that demand—and *receive*—special protections in the law.

297

People in a democracy are outraged when it is discovered that their government decided to go to war on quite independent grounds from the plausible *casus belli* officially offered. Such disjunction between the real motive and the publicly declared motive is tantamount to bad faith and "cover up."—When this is compared with the hidden dialectic in the separation of powers upon which the democracy rests, the vaunted bliss of ignorance shows its Mardi Gras face at last. The judiciary, within parameters no one has set in stone, is always employing its cache of legal fictions to achieve such a disjunction by arriving at adjudications independent of the publicly stated *ratio decidendi*. When the facts of a case are viewed in such a way as to justify an interstitial innovation in the law, the judge acts as if he is *applying existing law*. Thus, the primary legal fiction: the appellate judge doesn't, and pursuant to the separation of powers, *cannot* make new law. As every expert on the Constitution knows, the exigency of judicial supremacy must rank a strong second place. Legal fictions allow the law's long arm to "reach for a result."

298

Journalists set shallow souls aflutter.

299
The scholar Erwin Rohde did not like his friend's mature work. Rohde knew that Nietzsche abandoned scholarly work for higher ground, and for a time smiled at the mention of adventure. But a scholar cannot be adventurous for very long, and then, perhaps only at cocktail parties (—at which some learned hack at the *New Yorker* has a learned highball thrown in his impishly nimbused Manhattan mug—).—The scholar, as Rohde confessed, cannot dive down *deep enough* to find the pearls! Not to say, however, that Rohde misunderstood his friend's work. He said after reading Nietzsche's self-published napalm attack, *Beyond Good and Evil*, "It is full of a repulsive debasement of everything and everybody."—"Friend!" cried a jubilant Nietzsche, "You see at last what philosophy is!"

300
Islamic presupposition: genocide, slavery for the swarming hordes of the non-possessed. Islamic nemesis: Fascist aggression!!—*He who wills the end must will the means*!

301
First principle: only *men* can fight men—and Islam sees all too clearly the emerging womanization of the West!—A religion with no eyes in its head *sees*.—As a people loses its instincts, counterweights are bound to appear, counter-reckonings are sure to crop up.

302
What *is* the difference between absolute obedience and machinelike activity?

303
Resignation and meekness in the face of the enemy: decadence, soft pragmatism on the brain, Mother mythos in the blood.

304
The mellowing of Western "humanity"—a symptom . . . a cause; . . . not an advance . . . a regression. Translation: one no longer knows who the

enemy is (—I mean here the immediate, palpable enemy, for the hidden enemy is degeneracy.—Small wonder that degeneracy doesn't recognize itself—).—Soon the weapons will fall from our flaccid hands.

305
As you hear me look at the clear signs all around.

306
It's *not* a matter of *leading on* (—for what does one lead on? what is led?—). It's a matter of striking out alone, a matter of *being different*.—Industry, modesty, the uniform, the worthies (—Pragmatism's ideal oxen—): all so many hindrances to independence, "heroism" . . . greatness of soul . . .

307
One sees clearly enough what came to an end with the passing of John Dewey: American Pragmatism—which had all along only been seen *as* philosophy by the Americans—ceases to be a philosophy and becomes an absolutely primary new beginning of a social engineering culture, a *Bildung* of derangement and ruin destined, nay *more* than destined, to take over "education." The at least tangential, half-hearted kind of Peirceian seriousness for philosophy is juggled away in favor of a true blue pragmaculture for the hapless "happiness of the many"—a many beleaguered *too quickly* to know *what* had happened to them.—How malicious! What a rapturous self-glorification it is when an old horned peacenik of glad tidings, i.e., Dewey, poses so innocently in front of the horned beast he hides!—He comes preaching that the legitimate goal of education is to teach "problem solving" and felicitous adjustment to the world, when what he really wants is to place education in an iron shirt of absolutely correct and absolutely incorrect thinking and behaving.—What does this prove? What does this amount to *in praxi*?—The politicization of education; . . . precisely *one more* spicy item politicized *ad majorem pragmatisti gloriam*. So today one must wait for the next onslaught of propaganda to find its "acceptance in the market" via the most lamblike innocence: . . . when to any objective observer what has taken place before unseeing eyes is something so voracious and imperativistic as to remind an objective observer of the teaching tactics of our old Calvinism. (—But I ask too much when I ask for an objective observer, correct?—)—Let us say it:

Dewey's "education" craves dominion; Dewey craves dominion: the *wizard* in him craves dominion.—And what *is* dominion? What state of affairs *makes* dominion dominion?—Suppression!! Ruthless suppression!!—Dewey as the ideal-castrator! The "bringer of feminine tidings."—Dewey as the empowerer of children: a *childlike* note has been added to the voice of virtue: Deweyism becomes the shepherd's song for the new ideal, becomes morality, becomes the *Mother God* . . .

308

American Pragmatism's special *esprit*: seeing a profound connection and *modus vivendi* between science and a healthily consolidated mediocrity. This *esprit* is sunshine and rain for the coming plant species . . . But first a new mythology must be constructed. The American "movements" are accomplishing this feat.

309

The concept of the philosopher, the way of life inhering in philosophy;— abolished! done away with! repented for !—But American Pragmatism does not rest content with this merely existential negation: *it craves more.*—The fruitfulness of belief must extend beyond the world: as religion is a spur to moral action, the efficacy of pragmatic belief must—wonder of wonders—somehow construct a transhuman order: a pragmatist's fictional realm to validate—aha! to validate what?—*moral action.* Thus, our pragmatist has his William Ellery Channing birthday cake and eats it too: thus, the pragmatist's Hallelujah! is blessed in his heaven as it is upon his earth: our Cambridge and Columbia humanists have *become theologians at last*!—What, to transpose and alter Tertullian's question, does a pentagram have to do with a crucifix?—Our pragmatists have paid their vows and their bountiful "God" has given them the working answer to this question: *opposites must be reconciled*! . . . John Dewey's conception of philosophy is simply that philosophy shall resolve conflicts in a society (—echoing, of course, the law's purpose of "settling disputes" in a society—).—Question: how to resolve the conflict between the pentagram and the crucifix? Answer: *there is no such conflict.* Yet since there is a perceived conflict the pragmatist must dabble in theology.

—The conflict between faith and culture, about which the Hebrew prophets fulminated and tore their hair to stitch together the most magnificent prophetic literature in the history of the world, finds its modern analogue in the conflict between secular values and religious values within the modern industrialized democracies. The *purity* of religious doctrine is in the gravest danger within a democracy. Are there ears for this unfashionable truth? What then is pragmatism's role? And for what purpose is the arm of philosophy revealed?—With typical American disdain for every tradition, every religious feeling of the community, every historical reality—in one fell swoop of American ignominy, and in one precise word: *to declare that nothing is sacred.*—Dewey, our *self-styled pragmatist theologian*, takes it upon himself to reduce religious dogmas to an American ethos—I meant to say, an absence of ethos—specifically by translating the sum of American negations into religious terms. And—*Violá*!—we've found our pragmatist faith at last!—Fumbling at his Chicago typewriter with that pompously professorial attitude that says, "I am a benefactor of mankind. The onward march of Progress cannot complete itself without my perfidious doodling," what does this old shop-philosopher do? What does he *accomplish*?—Precisely the *worst* thing: he converts religion to pragmatism!—He says: "True religion is entangled with religious dogmas. We pragmatists are on a quest to disentangle it. What *is* this true religion? Why, we have all known for quite some time what it is! It's the very thing passionately and forthrightly proclaimed by Channing, Emerson, other proto-Deweyans, and moonbeam monsignori. True religion is a sense of the possibilities of existence and devotion to the cause of these possibilities. This *purified religion* would no longer be in conflict with other elements in a modern society, and it would take the form of a kind of natural piety. Dissolve the religious creeds! Release the religious values! Let this be the highest calling of our beloved pragmatism."—Indeed, only such *could* come out of the mouth—I take care not to say "heart"—of our worthy Chicago web-spinner and old Columbia albino. Such ruttish *ignis fatuus* is—what?—the *highest calling of our beloved pragmatism?*—Such are the choruses of victory sung by men of the cloth, *prophetic albinos*! Such is the cosiness, the Cambridge cosiness and bucolic contentment of those moonbeam theologians who once camped round about Walden Pond, counting the twinkling stars of the morning and learning the value and virtue of praising "God."—"God? Oh, be quiet about God. God is but a name for *our* imaginative unification of *our* ideal values, a projected union of the ideal and the actual. Let the Transcendental heifers moo! Let the different drummers pound their different drums! And let there be no other function of religious faith than to unite pragmatists in our common effort and shared destiny!"—It was these same self-contented pragmatistic heifers, with the same end in view of guaranteeing their own peaceful grazing—beneath chalky blue Concord skies—who took charge of American history and sought to transform every Increase and Richard Mather, every Jonathan Edwards, every seminarian who dared to believe in a real Flood, a real Eden, and a real Pharaoh who let his people go, into fiends, ghouls, and bony-headed John Browns: (—"Without the shedding of blood there shall be no remission of sins."—)—The Pragmatistic Heaven, after all, *had to be* a Heaven on Earth. What spiritually-minded person would not freeze at the sight of it?—Gabble off the pragmatistic catechism to any believer or any reasonable person who desires to believe and expect to witness writhing paroxysms of disgust consequent upon horror; show these same patient observers the pinched expression on the serious face of our old Columbia albino and listen for peals of raucous laughter!—Witness the spectacle! The pragmatist as the founder of a new religion!—That is the purified religion in its most impressive form: the *pragmatist* as a visionary, as *heavy*; pragmatism as the convocation of terrestrial ultimacy!—Religion as the unutterable shame of a bloc of naïfish schoolmen!—I should like to know what kind of prayer life our pragmatist (—hands still holding the tools he has used to form his new religion and pallid eyes raised not to Heaven but lowered the better to fixate on his navel—) might venture to enjoy in his regenerated, action-sanctified new life. Would he sit in upper rooms and sing his intercessory evensong for the future of little people like him? Would he utter his requiescat with unctuous groanings—which no non-professor may utter—for the souls of Peirce, James, and Dewey? How could he *not* supplicate for the future of science and technology, unlimbering his phylactery with specific beggings for lawyers, actors, malingerers, and journalists?—Ah, but the prayer life of a pragmatist, like that privilege the law reposes between the penitent and his priest, perhaps, should be shielded from the eyes of a vulgarly inquiring world . . . How, my dear pragmatists, can you even think of a believer's ardent prayer, the actuality of religious ecstasy, and the faith of a child? How can you think of such things without a doglike feeling of shame? Can you deny that such things, such "ridiculous trivialities and abstractions," are and of necessity must be in constant conflict with your absurdities, grotesqueries, and idols? your repellent factory worker/entertainment culture?—Therefore, let the most liberated and freethinking pragmatist come forward who fails to mention his hopeful new religion and the almighty sciences in the same breath. Let this lone iconoclast find his place at the trough of philosophy! Would not the most serious student and the child with his trusting faith alike sense at once how these two domains serve simultaneously as each other's exarch and surrogate?—What then? The pragmatist's new religion is *really* the pseudo-hope implicit in the modern sciences and is not religion at all? John Dewey and Jane Addams aren't *really* practicing theology?—At this contumelious assertion, the Old Guard Pragmatists shake their learned heads and surlily stamp their feet. "But! But! We will not be denied! Our Master Dewey *meant* the same piety the believers in the old religion once felt for their God, the new believer now may rightfully feel for life itself, for the Earth!"—Very well; such is your tellurianism. But can you stand there and blame any student of this new pragmatist religion for sensing in it a tottering spirit and an embarrassing artificiality? A lack of spirit and palpable artificiality, moreover, so illicitly evocative of the *hand of its founder*?—Here Dewey's orotundity speaks across that great river separating the living from the dead, "Your question is not properly framed. It is always a pragmatic question to be answered by resorting to consequences. The real question is: does the new religion do for the new believer what the old religion did for the old believer?"—This is our reply. Surely one could wish for a little more naturalness of faith! A professor's religion simply will not do. This kind of high-wire act, this pompous simulation, teacher of teachers, has been discredited ever since Comrade Kierkegaard picked up his pen to assail the wicked Goth. Let me ask you, "On which side do we find health, strength, and naturalness in this existential question? On the side of Hegel or on the side of the prickly Dane?"—If someone were to say in defense of John Dewey the *believer*, "The naturalness of Dewey's glorious new faith lies in his rejection of his mother's Christianity," we would listen with interest. In saying this, however, the Dewey defenders are also confessing their rapt discovery of Dewey the believer to the exclusion of Dewey the pragmatist, i.e., the logico-empiricist interested in "experience," and emblazoning above the propylon of this faith the *credo ut intelligam* of the medievalists who believed before they understood. What? The defenders are not a little disappointed to discover that Dewey as a believer is a philosopher to no one?—But if these defenders should change their minds and say, "The naturalness of Dewey's glorious new faith lies in his capacity as a *thinker* and not as a believer," we would listen with even more interest, for the *intelligo* has been primatized and therefore the thinker has also been primatized. This is our conclusion. While Dewey the believer is not a philosopher, Dewey the thinker believes by *thinking faith*; for it is obvious to all the defenders of their Master that *qua* thinker or believer the great pragmatist is constructing the Highway of Progress out of the accouchement of "modern ideas."—Here now! Is it not the right and solemn duty of our great educator to lead *believers* down the great Highway of Progress, proclaiming modern ideas with the magnanimity of one who has founded a religion? Nay, the *religion of the future?*—Gird up your loins, O ye righteous pragmatists, prepare your hearts and minds for your Lord and Master's glorious Parousia!—"What of God?" you ask.—Let us allow Dewey to educate us about God: God, he says, is there only to the extent and as long as the Deity succeeds in stimulating action (—which is another deification of success if there ever were one, evocative of Hegel's worship of the real as the rational—). Moreover, if ever there were a *real* false God it is Dewey's Pragmatistical God, his existence conditional upon "human need," upon—even worse—*action*—the rapscallion of all the philosophic states: philosophy's impudent child, not its parent.—Then Dewey is constructing a philosophy of God, building beyond the clouds! God *helps* us "get into satisfactory relations with our experience," a fiction who matters; again: God and man together will usher in the *final state of homogeneity.*—Very well. Let us ask, belatedly, this question: why should Dewey's religion matter?—Dewey's pragmatism enjoins upon him a position between theism and atheism, that is to say, a dishonest position. Either God is or is not. Perhaps, my friends, it really does take a "revelation" to understand what is going on with Elijah, the priests, the prophets, and the people. At any rate, John Dewey shunned and pooh-poohed this core religious truth (—I speak of the Either/Or splayed out in history from the Hebrew seers to Tertullian, Mohammed, Pascal, and Kierkegaard; not to forget the founder of Christianity who used the "sword" to separate—) from his youth and decided, in conscious revolt against it, to become a pragmatist, a proto-political liberal, a religio-philosophic clown. After all, what is or could be more anti-modern, that is to say, more *intolerant* than a good, healthy, boundary-forming Either/Or? Tolerance; this means, as Nietzsche said so well, an inability to say Yes or No. Thus, our favorite clown is saddled with a *religious* position that, forswearing intolerance, proclaims fence-sitting as connotative and adumbrative of action, the *summum bonum* of a pragmatistic universe.—What then? Is the modern world dissatisfied with American Pragmatism's religion?—Not by any means. This religion has ingratiated itself into the backbone of our fundamental law and has, in fact, in "practice" become more real than any other religion: it is the religion of the evolutionists and monkey-genealogists, the scientific craftsmen and technocrats, the pompous engineers of the law and dizzy, power-crazed journalists, the Hollywood elite who "need something to believe in," the freethinkers who are terrified of becoming free spirits, the writers for the crowd who know no weightier authority than "the moment," the so-called cultivated people for whom all is jubilation, contemptuous airs, and pretentious dignity, the chief priests and Pharisees who love the uppermost rooms at feasts, greetings, salutings, gatherings for worthless honors, and to be hailed, Rabbis! Masters! Teachers of Teachers!

310

Students of pragmatism take it for granted that pragmatism is a philosophy, and that such a vitalist faith in action may rightly be subsumed beneath the rubric of change;—to state the concept philosophically, "constant flux." Let us tackle the second assumption first. The notion, sounded by our dear political liberals as a messianic hope and ultimate ground for happiness through a human manipulation of the environment, that "everything changes" is disproved by the fact that some things do not change, and one does not need to posit, with Plato, a static *realm* to appreciate this fact. The works of Rodin are changing just as the Parthenon has been in a continual process of decay; yet, if you will allow me, the sculptors' ideas in the stone have remained unchanged, regardless of what time or the meanness of the elements may try to say. Sappho's thoughts and feelings, expressed palpably in the marks on the papyri, have not changed since the "tender feet of Cretan girls crushed a circle in the soft flowering grass." How has the "Moonlight Sonata" changed? Is it *able* to change? Allow for the extremest example of one condemned to see everywhere a state of becoming. Such a person would experience nothing but a stream of moving points, and such a person's being would be rent and torn asunder, dissolved in the ever flowing stream that *passes away* and becomes again with no end. Such a pupil of Heraclitus would be unable to believe in his being and lose the ability to act; thus, philosophically, change and action are mutually exclusive *unless* the human being is formed moment to moment, in which case the being of the human is vaporized;—a state clearly foreseen with frightful clarity by Kierkegaard.—Regarding the first question, we say that American Pragmatism is not a philosophy in the same sense that Catholic philosophy is not philosophy. The Catholic thinkers apply reason to belief, to what is *already believed*; thus, their philosophic conclusions must be squared in advance with a previously existing orthodoxy, i.e., dogma; there *are* no conclusions, only pleadings. You may say reason demonstrates the belief, but if an article of faith, an *object* of faith, is demonstrated by reason why is it necessary any longer to have faith?—unless, of course, you are pigheaded and too obtuse to comprehend that, for us, the compatibility or incompatibility of faith and reason is no longer the real issue for religion.—American Pragmatism applies reason in like manner: when a pragmatist applies reason to an exclusively action-oriented American culture, no new knowledge, no additional knowledge, ever comes into being. American Pragmatism is *submissive to a particular kind of culture*, just as Catholic philosophy is submissive to a mystic loggia of integral beliefs . . .

311

When I ask the Americans to become a more *contemplative* race, I am only asking for a break in their many activities, a time to stop, think, and take inventory. In such an advanced democracy, the only inventory ever taken concerns the empowerment of the organized groups—with their awesome power to bless and curse—; thinking becomes the decrepit product of the culture, i.e., pragmatism; and stopping . . . how *can* anyone stop?—One must be ever mindful of the fact that American restlessness began in 1849 when a somnolent San Francisco Bay changed overnight into a forest of masts. The lust for gold, the ineradicable haste, the "work ethic" gradually metamorphosing itself into instant gratification, a continual pretence, overreaching, and huckstering: all these ferocities became the germ for the quintessential American philosophy expressed so presciently and poignantly by that venerable proto-pragmatist Ben Franklin: *The sleeping fox catches no poultry!*—The obverse being that a wide-awake pragmatist catches plenty of philosophical poltroonery.—*Lose no time; be always employed in something useful.*—Is there a better way to be a pragmatist? The philosopher, on the other hand, is always losing time in the eyes of the world and *arriving late* so he may gain *his* time and arrive at the most unexpected, unusual, and inopportune time.—*Think innocently; and if you speak, speak accordingly.*—Indeed; pragmatism is a very innocent "philosophy."—*Laziness travels so slowly that poverty overtakes him.*—The philosopher chooses to be rich by making his wants few.—*A cat in gloves catches no mice.*—Yes, but if an intelligent tomcat were to study pragmatism, he would be imprudent *not* to wear gloves.—*One today is worth two tomorrows.*—You don't say! The philosopher, on the other hand, lives for the day *after* tomorrow!—*A small leak will sink a great ship.*—Yet a true philosopher is born only when some great ship sinks.—*Early to bed and early to rise makes a man healthy, wealthy, and wise.* Yet Rene Descartes remained in bed all morning, thinking. I take it that a Descartes is a bit higher than a Franklin!—Pragmaticalities and their philosophical oppositions—Oh, what am I saying, oppositions?—*refutations* aside, one cannot help but wonder what the Black slaves were doing when Franklin penned these niceties (—gnawing on a chicken bone? singing? praising God and giving thanks for their deliverance?—) . . . It almost seems as if the Boston Tea Party and the whole gloriole about Washington, Jefferson, Hamilton, and Thomas Paine writing with numb fingers at the drumhead passes into the eeriest kind of insignificance once *these* questions are asked. One must not turn to the "slave narratives" for the answers because these narratives leave out too much.—Could the slaves have known that their descendants would someday rise up, in the greatest "slave revolt" history has yet to see, and blueprint the future for the *coming mythology?*—What? The slaves become masters? What kind of pragma-mythos is *this?*—But to resume: it is precisely at the *end* of Franklin's petty, soft, work-a-day world that philosophy begins, and has always begun. Just imagine the astonishment that must have burned in the face of Plato's father when his son suddenly abandoned the dual careers of rhetoric and writing tragedies.—"I just want to be close to Socrates, father. I want to take my time, absorb all I can, and see where I wind up."—No spiv, Plato!—No sophistical pragmatist either! Today—*more than ever today*—one is ashamed of taking time, absorbing, and allowing for mental and moral development. We Americans want to do as many things as possible in the shortest amount of time. One lives as if one might miss out on something. "Do anything rather than nothing" is the hangman's noose for all culture, and it has only dawned on a few heads that we Americans are losing all *capacity* for culture, our movies, gadgets, dime novels, and dime computers notwithstanding. Wisdom and goodness—the things Plato wanted and loved—are in America shams, tinsels, and pieces of educated idiocy; and inasmuch as entertainment has become mindlessness even talent itself has become idiocy. When one expends oneself in *one* direction, one experiences a loss in the *other* direction. Where is the energy left for culture, for knowledge? Chasing gain day in and day out has co-opted all energy, all esprit, all joy! Leisure, Aristotle's great leisure, the ground of culture, the proper end for which the state exists, has all but vanished! Straightforwardness and honesty are *permitted* under certain circumstances. Our journalists talk everything to pieces; our educational institutions, in their curricula and in their aims, pander to the lowest common denominator and the *moral rot* of politico-cultural correctness. Just glance at the climate of fear—described by the great Peruvian writer Mario Vargas Llosa—that prevails on the campuses of the American universities regarding the twin bugaboos of "racism" and "sexism." He, Vargas Llosa, the outsider on the inside, *knows* our condition! Funny what a handful of mythmakers at the NAACP and mad, hysterics who have lost their instincts can do—*have done*! But, to be fair, hysterics and megalomaniacal mythmakers of any age and clime have always had their reasons; beg pardon, I meant to say, their *victims*. Vargas Llosa must have said to himself—for he dared not utter a word of it on campus—as he strolled down the halls of the great American universities, "What a strange people, these Americans! They are free yet Helots. Between the lines of the beautiful lyrics they offer up to freedom, I hear the awesome clanking of their chains!"—Absolutely señor: these mythmakers and hysterics take their delight in sallying out to prove the "racism" of the great thinkers, artists, musicians, and literary artists. Well, our culture suffers from nothing more than it suffers from this festering presumption. Its real upshot is that one should become a racist the better to become a "great thinker." The malaise in this game played even in Europe (—regarding Martin Heidegger and his short membership in the Nazi Party—) eludes description . . . Meanwhile, I fail to see how Richard Wagner's music is affected by his beliefs about Jews; likewise, we will like or dislike Heidegger's new religion whether it is just *another* new religion or a new "Nazi religion."—Everyone in Academia comes into eventual conflict with this philosophy of taintedness when at its best it is a way for a "scholar" to pass time—I meant to say, wind—; a means to get tenure and look cute.—Nietzsche favored Jews; this is a good thing. But if Nietzsche disliked Jews—or Poles, Finns, sauerkraut, or hashish—does any of this touch his philosophy, his art? One might as well taint Karl Marx the Jew for his scathing indictment of Jews; then some scholarly flathead will try to tar his humanism with the fact that he was a "communist."—These observations made, what is most astonishing? What one fact tears the heart and hurts the most? *There has not been one American philosopher!*—Oh, don't get me wrong; there will be philosophers aplenty; those in their greedy hurry to call themselves philosophers will turn up everywhere in this our new century and the next! Then, just as the false prophets in ancient Israel contradicted and muddied the messages of the true prophets—those whose words have come down to us—so the false philosophers, those yet unborn, will push the real philosophers out to the periphery of the passé (—for they will be offended first of all by these great ones' pure, antique conception of philosophy—). But this pushing to the periphery, to the outside, will only confirm *who* the real philosopher is. Isn't the philosopher the one on the outside looking in?—*looking down?*—And to repeat: *there has not been one American philosopher.*

312

If the government controls the marketplace of ideas by regulating the "free flow" of ideas rigorously; for example, when we *command* that a very few opinions be believed or that *one* official party line be adopted by the people, we call this censorship and hear the grimmest innuendo about the "state-controlled press," dictatorship, flagrant denial of "human rights," etc. On the other hand, if this market remains officially unregulated, any number of ideas may find their place in the sun, and "freedom of expression" will rise to its finest hour and its fullest bloom.—This sort of legal analysis reminds me of the venerable dictum of John Fortescue, sometimes cited as the seminal authority for the famed "principle of lenity" in the criminal law, and, not to forget, the presumption of innocence. Fortescue said, "It is better to free 50 guilty defendants than to punish one innocent defendant."—; which obviously forgets that the guilty—at least a few of Fortescue's 50—will recidivate, and this means a multiplication of harms done to the innocent.—In the same way, the analysis of freedom of expression forgets the principal thing. For why should it make any difference if the state commands one opinion or permits any number of them? Whoever deviates from these opinions—the one or the many—is bound to be suffocated by the stampeding herd.—Again: English legal presuppositions and Darwin's overall trajectory fall happily into each other's arms.

313

The martyr takes a detour to wind up in heaven. But if his vaunted "sacrifice" for heaven is interpreted *in* heaven as something base and ignoble—i.e., if the detour is put in the heavenly scales and seen as a *dodging* of life's goal, as the way no one but the sacrificer himself could have taken and thus denies both life and its ideal—well: maybe this delirious boy should go to hell. Be my guest, as Mr. Hilton says. Burn your body on a beautiful morning before the massif of Ararat. Do not disobey the awful rolls of the mullahs' howls.

314

When foreign nations accept American exports, what do they invariably accept?—Machineism, Deweyism, Nomocratism, Xenophilism, Journalism, Techno-fadism, Civil Rightsism.—The seven American narcotics.

315

Understand our position: It is better for one independent mind to appear on earth than for a state or university to be founded. Many generations must labor to produce one philosopher, whereas states and universities are founded, sometimes, overnight. When the great Athenian statesman Pericles found Anaxagoras huddled in the corner of a lean-to, biting on a piece of stale bread with no means to defray even the inconsiderable costs of being a philosopher, Pericles raised him up—but not without this barb: "*When God has furnished you with a lamp, it is your duty to supply it with oil.*"—Indeed. Now let us ask this question: Why did Pericles furnish the oil so readily? What motivated him?—Another question: Could we expect a ruler today to show such tender solicitude?—the second question first. How could a statesperson today evince any interest in philosophy when what is encountered on the throne of philosophy is not philosophy but a ludicrous eidolon, a scholarly lecture bearing no resemblance to the heroic; I mean the fearsome risk that philosophy *is*?—Yes, even the political earth obeys the laws of gravity. When the statesperson of today investigates philosophy, no spirit of philosophy presents itself, no *great spirits*, just feeble expatiators forever jockeying for tenure;—and, not to forget, doing pompous, learned jigs before lecterns and maundering mercenary harangues to local businesses on "ethics."—As if the scholarly beer hall, wide-eyed nubile ingénue with pink backpacks on lysergic acid, could teach anyone anything about ethics!—To repeat:—*the philosopher's job is to remove hinges from doors*. All things are AT RISK when he appears snub-nosed and sunny-faced in the Agora, asking questions and seeking the questions that lurk *behind* the questions; . . . and when *she* appears, marvelous descendant of Perictione and Hipparchia turning everything to stone with her gorgonic glances.—When Pericles encountered philosophy as a youth he found intrepid spirits preaching that heroism should be carried into the search for knowledge and the pursuit of wisdom; spirits carrying torches showing the young of Athens—whose *open horizon* had attracted and wooed the goddess of wisdom in the first place—how to preside at their own marriage of philosophy and heroism. Thus, it was Periclean heroism that clothed the naked and fed the hungry! Periclean heroism that could see, even in the midst and in spite of the cares of state and the political vicissitudes besetting a man of affairs, that the things any society holds dear are so on account of the ideas that have emerged on its mental horizon, warning signals from the great klaxon of philosophy, which, when these signals reach the stratosphere, turn again earthward to rend the proud, infallible fabric of human affairs.

316

The dogs of Diogenes began barking louder and shriller than usual when someone praised a philosopher in his presence—: these dogs always barked when their master doled out a sharp rebuke to pauper or prince.—Diogenes quieted his dogs and replied, "This person you praise so highly has called himself a philosopher for a very long time, and in all that time, he *hasn't once disturbed anybody.*" Then the dogs began barking and growling so menacingly that the visitor left at once.—Yes, even dogs can sense when the spirit of philosophy is offended, and Diogenes loved dogs because of their apparent wisdom.—Oh, but how much lower than stray dogs are our fine, nugatory, briefcase-carrying university professors?—creased khakis, campy sandals and all! Not to forget the Kwamies at Harvard, dickered and dandied in the loudest African colors! (—who, incidentally, do want to disturb in the inauthentic, non-philosophic sense of disturbing one race but not another—). And what better inscription can we write above the doors of our philosophy departments than the simplest imputation, *You disturb nobody*!—You lobbygows have consumed knowledge without a taste for it, and *this* makes you so pompously fat and sleek! University philosophy—pragmatism at its worst, for it is a lie that hides behind the truth—is not a living thing, certainly not philosophy, but is instead a kind of knowledge of philosophy—no matter how vehemently and "passionately" you purplish existentialists preach that philosophy is "life."—You teachers of the philosophy of existence have an idea of and feeling for philosophy (—for the reception of existentialism in the American universities in the latter half of the 20th century grew out of an originally authentic impulse to outbid and slander all the sterilities of so-called American philosophy, i.e., the pragmatistic and analytic spirit of subservience to science and the hands-off attitude to cultural criticism—), but no true philosophical achievement ever emerges; you think and speak "critique," but no real criticism ever occurs; you feather your comfortable academic nests, miring yourselves to one spot of ground when you should be seeking distant shores, deep caverns, dark forests, crags, labyrinths, tightropes spanning spiry skylines.—You aesthetes of the disturb-and-rouse-nobody mentality caricature philosophy with your pitifully pompous lectures and your interminably voluminous glosses upon glosses, not to mention your conceit that these non-stop, famously orthodox glosses and philosophy are one and the same thing. You go around like a pope in his papal carriage, assured of your cultivation, when in truth you are only a mirror image of the bogus culture that surrounds your quaint, quiet, little cubbyhole in Academia. The proof? You *demand* proof?—You are continually stimulated by the stream of new things; when a journalist, a computer, a movie maker, a class action suit, a politician's hokey-pokey say, "Think as we think and only as far as we think," you fall in line like circus animals; you risk nothing, pledge your careers to safety and security, and follow the rules of haste, party line correctness, and ease.—In conclusion, you scholars do not know what or who the strong and free human being is; moreover, I see no cheerfulness, no refreshment in you people: if you were honest, you'd write *to yourself and for yourself*—like my ancestors Schopenhauer, Nietzsche, Montaigne, Fontenelle . . .

317

If thinkers are dangerous, it should be very clear why a university professor is not dangerous. The thoughts of this sort of person grow even as the law in common law countries grows: logically, inductively, peacefully, accretively *out of tradition*. Danger stands at the opposite pole from security, and it only stands to reason that such dangerous people—I mean those *free souls* who are serious-minded, take philosophy seriously, and are thus *made dangerous by philosophy*—would live a life of perversity; i.e., those innocent of philosophy would hasten to call such a life perverse for the simple reason that the philosopher throws away what all the world would regard as his "best interests" to take up philosophy and follow it seriously long enough to find the hidden truth. Very well; such an ordinary, quite unfree soul would be justified in seeing matters thus; such an ordinary soul's animus against the philosopher is easily understandable since if this ordinary son or daughter had one-tenth of the freedom, solitude, and seriousness the philosopher possesses and must possess, this soul would die of such freedom, solitude, and seriousness.—Yet, as adumbrated above, there *are* certain spirits—they call themselves African-American thinkers, we call them race pragmatists—who would be exceedingly disturbed themselves if someone were to deny flatly that they disturb anyone. On the contrary, they would say, as Toni Morrison recently said, that they "never have played it safe" and must be willing at all times to "think the unthinkable," etc: therefore, since these individuals constantly seek the truth about "race hatred," they should be looked upon as genuine philosophers.—And I suppose every abolitionist in Pottawatomie, Kansas with a cutlass in his hands is a *philosopher*?

318

A painful fact to find the same folk who split the skulls of pro-slavery settlers in Kansas return with hammers in their eager, resentful hands (—and think it not a *great* thing that pragmatism is able to transform cutlasses into hammers and skulls into agendas—) . . . For truth is never served when one hammers out agendas for profit; and nothing stands so much in the way of the production of the philosopher as does the bad philosopher who transmutes freedom—the inestimable freedom the Greek philosophers grew up in—into political constraint and the philosopher's *proper office* into a connivance, a political mechanism, a party line, an office of profit: in effect an office of state. Such a man or woman is a scholar only—cautious, subservient, and bereft of greatness;—no matter how many beelines are made between Africa and the Harvard philosophy department. In fact, a fact painful for *you*, a real philosopher would never make such ballyhoo out of being blessed by an African "epistemologist" (—a term an African uses for his special privilege to be rational and quite irrational at the same time—) and an American Harvardist on the same day. Nay, such a blessed beeliner serves not the truth, but his own viscerally pragmatized agenda;—I beg your pardon; I meant to say, his racial group's viscerally pragmatized agenda; is this understood? So, at length, such an Afro-Harvardist is brainwhacked into *believing* that the concepts he exalts above the truth compose the truth! that his insolence is the truth! that *he* is the truth!—And how, let us ask, is such a one recognized?—apart, of course, from his coat of many colors?—I propose that he is recognized the same way we recognize a writer who writes only for his audience, regardless of how base and baseless soever this audience may be: he thinks for his audience just as the popular scribbler scribbles for his audience; is *this* understood?—In fact—just between you and me—every time I see such a color-clad Harvardist-Princetoner trying to "get a leg up," I know exactly what kind of leg is being hoisted, what kind of mindset is directing the hoisting, and what kind of pedicure is in the offing.—Yes, you Harvardists have "something to teach" young minds about their "roots," their dreams, and their Harvard-bestowed ability to "effect change" (—we know all about this leg too—), but your ability to teach actually distances you from being a philosopher. Yes, even your ability to "write philosophy." I should like to know how many truck loads of sugared "moral philosophy," a moral philosophy, moreover, that can only sing hymns to "group identity"—which, translated means: racial identity—and, of course; the discerning reader will discern at once that I am speaking of the laughter and despair provoking word-rattling of the Kwame Appiahs and Cornel Wests of our sick Academy—; how many mythmaking jokesters of Negritudish, "indigenous theologians," how many sham and tinsel philosophy professors would have to be exported from America today before our air would begin to smell fresh again, before roses would smell like roses again, and excrement like excrement. As aforesaid, the philosopher does not so much have an agenda as he follows agendas to see if there is indeed a golden fleece at the end of the road; if the philosopher did have an agenda, he would be like the Scholastic philosophers in the days of yore when thinkers were obliged to think *only so far*; that is to say, obliged not to think at all! We may very well imagine Socrates not showing up for work every day he was *supposed* to: better a pestiferous truant than an allegiant fake. Isn't this what philosophy means? Even Plato finally learned this truant art . . . After all, some philosophers even among the real ones are more honest than the others. Why did Schopenhauer and Nietzsche give up teaching? Why did Leibniz and Descartes avoid teaching? I have already answered these questions.—You Harvard people are so magnificently certain you are philosophers!—Answer me this: what confused undergraduate cannot sense what an *actor* the good professor is! Then, assuming his coveted degree has not taken from him as much or more than it has bestowed, someday he will see for himself how his lofty philosophy professors turned their backs on the truth, and hence the practice of philosophy. How is this accomplished but by the doling out of concessions?—To the ethnic group, to the university as an institution, to scholarliness, to comfort and tranquility;—*never* to freedom, perils, riddles, severities, silences, solitudes, open seas, and that "most advantageous advantage" Comrade Dostoyevsky designated "caprice."—A philosophy professor, especially an Afroist philosophy professor, digs down into the history of philosophy and wallows in the things he finds, psychoanalyzing and fingerprinting, searching for the prized deflowering innuendo, spinning webs and glosses from other webs and other glosses, spreading an obfuscatory deliquescence over what should stand out as individuated clarity.—What are their analyses, critiques, and solemn syntheses but a spoof on words with words?—What is their insolence but a security blanket to cover their fear of living like a philosopher?—What is their scholarliness but a confession of philosophic cowardice and creative impotence?—What is their passionate anti-racism but the very "racism" they decry?

319

Aristotle very clearly delineated who the real philosopher is when he laid it down that the slave doesn't know how to use freedom (—notice he didn't say *enjoy* freedom). Here Aristotle is painting with a relatively broad brush as he is including all truly spiritual and truly creative human beings; namely, those who use leisure in the highest and best way: those who are born free. This moral, aesthetical, and philosophical concept—this *description of reality*—escapes any kind of political refutation as it is prior to politics, democratic theory and all . . . Now one thing is certain: the behavior of the free human being—again: the one who knows how to use leisure in the best way and who uses leisure in the best way—is poles apart from the unfree human being, the immoralist who "spends his substance" and squanders himself even as the eldest son in the parable of the Prodigal Son squandered his substance in riotous, irresponsible living. (—Thus, his "prodigality," his sin—) . . . In other words, the free human being *does not resemble the slave.*—And surely for all the offence that Socrates gave to the solid citizens of Athens, nothing offended them more than the fact that he, Socrates, did not resemble them. The facts cry aloud for the possibility of a criminal case when Socrates, going out beyond the swaggering, festooned horde of creative geniuses then in Athens, became the *very incarnation of the philosophic type.* Thus, the criminal imputation in its inception became the incarnation of the contradiction and polarity of the two types: slave and free.—Where the freedom-loving and nothing-succeeds-like-success Sophists and solid citizens merely *looked askance* at the cult of Athenian genius, from Phidias and Ictinus to Sophocles and Agathon, their resentment—precisely the resentment of the slave—gave birth to the need for the ultimate "ostracism," the ultimate caper of a "free" democracy: hemlock! the death sentence for the best citizen of Athens, the *very best.* Socrates! Slain! Not, mind you, as a faithful Greek infantryman serving his cherished *polis* on the plains, but as a prisoner in the dock convicted of subverting the youth of Athens!—Yea, there is more than a little *subversion* in Silenus-faced Socrates the erotic, the trapper of youths publicly gone daft over his daimon!—"Corrupting the morals of the young," the indictment read. As if Socrates could use philosophy to corrupt the morals of all the young (—when the truth is that philosophy can only corrupt the morals of *some* of the young—). Yes, the ones who took up philosophy were predestined for corruption, predestined to gaze upon Sophia's curvaceous nakedness.—If narrowed down to the smallest group the indictment was intended to protect, this group would surely consist of the fathers of Athenian young men who *might* choose to follow Socrates—and thus forfeit gainful employment, service to the state, civic decency, etc.—What interest did the indictment intend to protect?—The father's specific interest in having sons who "turn out well," sons who will come to crave offices, positions, and honors. To have a Sophist for a son is one thing, a philosopher quite another. The real interest reposing in the father of an Athenian boy consisted in his interest in having a son deaf to the blandishments of philosophy; a son who, therefore, would not become a philosopher; in effect an attempt to kill any subsisting predisposition for philosophy: the father's right to protect his son from *danger.* This is precisely how Plato understood the indictment. His task: to set up a state in which the protected interest reposes not in the fathers but in the sons—and we may add, the budding daughters as well—; nay, to actually install philosophers as rulers!—Thus, the highest men and women go through life believing that people of power and wealth are their inferiors . . .

320

William James *wanted* a link with the spiritual world even more fervently than his brother Henry the novelist wanted to write about the queer, unmentionable hauntings of "missed experience." With mesmeric fervor, William James the pragmatist *dreamed a dream of God.*—When Charles Peirce told him, "I believe it *might* be possible, William, to construct a kind of purified metaphysic consonant with the dictates and limits of my grand pragmatic method," James scratched his head, retired to his study, and fell asleep on the couch to dream of Jacob's Ladder, Joseph's deliverance, Joshua and the battle for Jericho, Swedenborgianism, and, of course, God.—James then woke up and convinced himself to identify his dream of God with the reality of God. In other words, it tickled his pragmatistic fancy to blur the distinction between dream and reality. I have wondered if James and the Spanish mystic Miguel de Unamuno met in the same vestibule, the one on his way from pragmatism to religion and the other on his way from religion to pragmatism.—For both thinkers blur the distinction between dream and reality: Unamuno came to pragmatism because of quixotism; James drifted into religion because of a pusillanimous eagerness to place a bet and hope it pans out. If a vision of water slakes your thirst, says the professor at Salamanca, then the water of the vision is as real as any water.—What? Don Quixote the *pragmatist?*—

321

Everything points to some realm beyond experience, the world of the voyager, the actual *highway of the shamans.* Oh, the shamans *know* it is real for they have inhabited this "other world." It seems to be an impersonal realm in which—when taken up into it—one feels one's privacy rent like a covering of nasty cloth; and then: the highway, the open air, the others who are in a special sense "just like you," peering into your world (—that is to say, the former constriction of your experience, the place in which you once were—); a world one has somehow known was there all along.—How can it be that the others know so much about you? Neither godlike nor diabolized, they have been *waiting on you*, seeing your shame as if it were their own. They are the fellow-travelers. Ah, but not everyone can be *your* fellow-traveler!—William James wanted to find this highway of the shamans with all its infixed transparency, but since he never found it, he decided to counterfeit it: we can believe in the other world even in the face of doubt, i.e., lack of evidence. For evidence is, in some sense, intellectual and not volitional. What then are we to do about this *hungering volitional nature* of ours? We adopt a hypothesis; if it works, it is true. This is the Jamesian solution: first we twist our own arm to commit to a religious belief, then we keep our fingers crossed that it will prove itself in experience.—And how will it prove itself in experience?—Precisely by *altering conduct.* (—For pragmatists are already in love with altering things for the sake of altering them; e.g., altering the "environment," making mankind childlike and "good," i.e., gelded, predictable, uniform, "happy," and above all, pragmatic—). Therefore, if pragmatism succeeds in altering conduct, it validates the religious hypothesis. The unseen world is *there* if it produces effects in this world!—But what kind of conduct and what kind of alteration?—the Buddha's conduct is altered: he cautions the monks against gall-producing emotions.—the conduct of Jesus is altered: he sees the moneychangers in the Temple and drives them out with harsh words and a rope.—Mohammed fights against those who think differently.—What then? It is possible that *because* pragmatism's archguru altered his conduct when he read about lynchings in the South, this alteration of conduct *proved the existence of an unseen world?*—Maybe his invention of "pluralism" proved it.—For as everyone knows, a "Black young lover hanging from a gnarled and naked tree" proves the existence of God, the non-White Supra-Christ, and the whole eschata-racial-ogical malice of every Harvard race pragmatist and poetical tomcat prancing down the dark alleyways of Beacon Hill.—American Pragmatism's conception, I meant to say its skimble-skambled *befuddlement* of religion, wants to reduce the central idea of the great German theologian Rudolf Otto—his *sensu numinis*—to an obsequious additament to pragmatistic morality, that is to say, immorality. Thus, the high-water mark of the religious strivings of William James—his concern to *admit* the divine into his cash-and-carry cosmos of certified conceptual pay-offs—is twice removed, even *thrice* removed from the genuine Numinous Presence.—*William James! William James! Come forth!*—And he came forth, white as a leveret, wrapped in dark grave clothes, his crusty old face fluted with frost.—*Speak, William James!*—He began growling in the queerest tones, "Just as pragmatism is a new way to think old problems, reducing religion to morality is not new. What we want is to reduce religion to Americanism so we will someday see a new religion for a new mankind."—Imagine it! A superabundance of journeymen, near-men, and fragments of near-men on their scrofulous knees praying to the Jamesian "God."—No, don't imagine it!—It is happening *today* . . .

322

That greedy and shallow world to which American Pragmatism introduces us—a rendezvous for every oblivion and contempt for the individual as a type of humanity; the highest and best type humanity has achieved—must have a very convenient *argument for its defense*, a ready means to anticipate and *fend off* any "invidious" vanguard of critique purporting to come from a higher ground.—How is this done? How does a pragmatist defend himself?—Simply by the invocation of three words, the cock-a-hoop "working words" of every pragmatist everywhere: *what people do*.—Parry every thrust, confute every impudent attack, and take any anti-pragmatist a prisoner with the mere flourish of these three words. Reveal their awesome trenchantness at the tail end of any philosophic disquisition and enjoy the solid blessings of instant ontological equilibrium. How *much* anthropological and sociological acumen is subsumed beneath this magic phrase: what people do!—Just as we should have expected, the air is already saturated with the scents of a healthy, Holmesian legal rejoinder for the enemies of our progressive common law: law is *ascending*; it grows as a plant grows; it did not come down from Sinai *or* Olympus; even the Twelve Tables grew up, albeit imperceptibly, out of custom.—So, what does this inductive and experimental paradigm prove? What does it *teach*?—Again: what people do.—But, if you can keep a secret, I will reveal the hidden meaning of this gospel of "sociological jurisprudence" with its pantheon of activist judges (—Holmes's "judicial restraint" was his shot at telling a noble lie.—), Brandeis briefs, and well-nigh sacred civil rights adjudication. It is precisely fear of the basic proposition that inequality of rights is the condition for the existence of rights at all. This is to concede to a people the right to a *different kind* of development.—Very well; let us ask this question: what do you pragmatists mean with your brittle phrase, what people do?—And here is their vaunted answer: what people do in a pluralist society amounts to what organized groups of people do.—What is pluralism?—Precisely a collegium of mirrors: the groups must play off each other, interdigitate with each other, and any group must be seen through *another* group's eyes, i.e., a specific group's reality must be conferred by another group.—How then does this justify itself? Can it be justified?—Expressed pragmatistically, such a condition of society means the perpetuation of testing, experimenting, and maintaining the fluidity of all moral values (—and whenever this kind of flow overtakes a religious doctrine, we say a nebula point has been reached; when the religion itself reaches *its* nebula point, it dies—). The *opposite* of this condition is the greatest enemy of pragmatism, democracy, common law method, pluralism—can the *names* really matter?—: an aristocracy, a condition in which, on paper, there is no freedom, yet there is more freedom than the people realize; for at issue here is a philosophical aristocracy, rule by the best and not by the worst (—as Aristotle said so well, "by the best in man"—). For what is the practical difference between oppression from the top and unabashed manipulation from the bottom? From the standpoint of *another* practicality—freedom of expression, long hailed as the principal, bedrock freedom—I fail to see a real difference;—and this I say in the very face of *your* propaganda that in any "open society" expression law enjoys its halcyon day and greatest consummation. You have already—and this pursuant to the pluralism under consideration—decreed against hatred: this expunges the animating emotion of many of the great Greek poets in one "mean-spirited" scratch of your pen;—I should say one well-pled *amicus curiae* brief from your legal architects. The same satiric verses of the poet Juvenal are rudely interdicted by one emperor, then suddenly accepted by another. You say, "There was more freedom under Hadrian," but I take it as axiomatic that it is better to have freedom *sometime* than a pompous illusion of freedom and *no* freedom (—for wherever subliminal manipulation rules there exists this pompous illusion—). The theory of expression law—and I emphasize the word "theory"—is that bad speech should engender more speech until someday, if we follow Charles Peirce's Ariadne thread far enough, good speech will win out completely;—an Elysian possibility made impossible by censorship. But this theory *assumes the existence of a censor from above, not a group of censors from below*. The descending censor is quite isolated, an easy target. The ascending censors operate under cover of the groups. Moreover, and more importantly, these censors have *made it appear* that "justice" is on their side; that they have a *right* to suppress invidious speech; I meant to say, of course, speech they deem invidious. Under the rule of pluralism, everything depends upon being on the right side at the right time, and the dead hand of "correct speech" haunts the letter and spirit of every free constitution in the industrialized democracies. But where did the plague bacillus come from? Show me its mother and its father. Show me "the crack where sin crept in," and for God's sake, show me before the groups in our healthy pluralism can get down wind of it; before they begin their oh-so-benign task of recruiting plaintiffs who will manufacture the once important adjudicative element of justiciability the way hot dogs are manufactured on Coney Island.—But first the *déclassé art* of American writing. Journalism *again*: journalism blocks new literary talent the same way the exclusive publication of blockbuster British works shoved out new writers in the time of Emerson, who complains that greed has marshaled itself against literature. Yes, a convenient diorama: greed on one side, art and taste on the other! Today the blood and thunder tactics of the free press have effectively co-opted any possible truly literary audience, and the serious novel is fast being marginalized and archaized like poetry;—all because the reading public has been gradually image-tweaked and anesthetized into the horribly barbarous notion that the seriousness of literature is equal to the seriousness of journalism.—*Aequales sunt*, believe me, devours everything.—Pity the once proud polemicist, says the great Goethe, who must ply his words in the evil day!—Yea, and today is the day! The best voices hiss in the wilderness, become hoarse, cracked, hobbled, and finally opt out. As Amaziah the priest said unto the prophet Amos, "Get thee into thine own land. Take even thine ass and thine stylus with thee, and get a job!"—Yea, and today is the evil day! The forest is getting thinner and thinner, the waters recede, the pallid sun hangs confusedly in the sky, and the spirit and spiritlessness of journalism penetrates into the very vehicles charged with the critique of journalism. (—For the sanctimonious whigmaleerie that the journalist profession is a self-correcting profession is yet another pretty ornament the journalists wear, one almost as interesting and effective as that cloned comb of fiberglass we usually mistake for a news anchor's hair.—) Journalism produces fearful, anxious, identical people who are more than happy to think like journalists and act like members of a herd; just as writers, under the influence of the awful quotidian, change into writing-machines who write like journalists and think like—well; suffice it to say that in America, journalism has invaded literature and has carved out no mean power-niche for itself with its ineradicable impudence and lust for handling objects it *should not touch*.—Why would a writer seek unhappiness rather than happiness; choose disharmony and not harmony; strife and not peace? Only when such a writer reacts to the evil day can there *be* writers who weep for their surly age and groan forlornly in sackcloth and ashes; writers who *refuse* the providential advice of such a false priest and political conservative as Amaziah.—For, as it is written, you shall sell your security for the whirlwind and hock your coat for the sword!—But let us leave the problem of journalism for another day.—William James made a calculation; he weighed the *consequences* on both sides. Either die at Antietam or live to consummate John Brown's hubris.—Our pragmatist chose the latter. Pluralism became eminently *possible*. Yet part of him hated his pusillanimity. What to do? Stock trick of a dishonest philosopher: cover up, prevaricate, do a sophist's jig.—Make it appear that pluralism came into the world because of justice, not cowardice and guilt (—Mrs. Stowe knew *this* justice—). So James plays hide-and-seek. He makes it appear that his pluralistic birth pangs are but proper Harvard protestations against the essentialist depredations of Hegel. Pluralism becomes a rejoinder to Hegel's monism (—as if Hegel's monism is the *only* monism; as if the Hegelian monism with *its* presuppositions, nervosities, and god-creating georgics is the only possible monism in the world—).—The upshot?—Cult pragmatism: *pluralism becomes cultic*. And what is the nature of these cultic groups?—Naked self-interest. Power. Dominion.—That for pragmatism pluralism is a true idea is demonstrated by the fact of a correspondence of the pragmatist's idea and the eventual dominion of interest groups (—the *Fifth* Estate, I suppose?—) and, of course, that it "works." For whom does it work?—The groups. That this pluralism *cures* no invidiousness but instead places invidiousness where there is none is more than amply shown by a visit to the lunatic ward of any asylum. Not, however, for a disciple of Du Bois—or that solemnized, holy-oiled Thurgood Marshall—; for such a sickness-legatee denies by instinct that sickness *is* sickness, that a ward of lunatics *is* a ward of lunatics. Pluralism requires and needs sickness as much as individualism needs health. The *objective* of pluralism is to suck down and *make sick*. First, however, it must lure, entice . . . And this requires every trick in the book: the blind, unthinking idolization of race-narratives, the filing of motions, deft arguments, deft lies—Oh, did I mention "non-violence"?—that self-induced travail of the insect that lies down and plays dead: the self-lacerations of the bony, vacant-eyed *mahatma* who absorbs too much Tolstoy (—I speak of that Russian's lack of all philosophic sense—) and chews on leather.—The "individual," as pluralism requires him to be, is a wrackful fragment of "humanity" whose whole inner world *must* be a world of over-excitation and need for dramatic political questions to continually define *who he is* . . . Whole organizations are employed—groups within groups—to envelop the larger groups in dramatic situations. Like a collective protagonist forced by circumstance into that famous boundary condition Karl Jaspers called "Vertigo on the brink of a Precipice," the action of the narrative overtakes the group; psychological dilemmas, ever apace with the lust for brio and panache, rear up on their hind legs and howl; then, mirroring the analogous dilemma of the saturnine African philosopher—his drama—for either the African is rational or not; if not, his intellect is marginalized and he is made to feel inferior; if rational, he is obeisant to the West, and thus feels inferior—things come to a head, and somebody must speak.—"Remember me?" one pluralist says. "I'm your piebald pluralist. What on earth would come of us if it weren't for me? Separatism is the answer, the only answer. What would the groups be if they possessed not *this* power? Come unto me all you who believe in the power of groups."—Another pluralist is speaking, purportedly as an individual. "Remember me? I'm your highbinder pluralist. Du Bois is my master. My identity is conferred by other groups. This is my master's double consciousness. Come unto me all you who believe in the power of groups."—Another pluralist rises. "Remember me? I'm your rag-tag-bobtail pluralist. The answer is simply: *we must commingle*. Separatism means I am subordinated, and when I am subordinated, I feel inferior. Commingling is the answer, the only answer to my felt inferiority."—Suffice it to say that the indispensable condition for the survival of any group is to be seen and heard . . . . *felt*. But precisely because of the inter-power-play of the groups a new being comes into existence: the *modern herd*. I say "modern" herd since herds have always been in existence. Man has always been afraid of standing alone. The individual thinker and doer is, as a *reactionary phenomenon*, an inherently superior state of affairs when contrasted with the general dysaesthesia of "safe and secure" herd life, its decadent art and mob rule—oh, what am I saying?—its *pragmatism*! Its nauseating *fungibility of desires and goals*! Its burlesque on divinity and spirit! Its hatred of *who* the philosopher is.—Even science belongs to a mediocre kind of machinery-man, and independent minds for ages to come may justifiably speak (—assuming they may still speak at all amid the flood of matrist conceptions outlawing every word and action not deemed "nurturing" by the gynecocracy, and, of course, the eventual religious triumph of the spirit of pragmatism—) of the scientific herd with its claque of impudent mountebanks serving as the infallible epoptae of the secret order;—and *its* star-strewn pantheon of new technologies! Indeed, there is abundant evidence that the apex of humanity was reached and experienced in the age of Beethoven and Goethe. From *this point* begins the great historical spiral-down, and one is tempted to say that mankind will become what it was in the beginning, except for the fact that there will no longer be any "mankind."—But to return quickly to our groups.—Yes, friends, the spiteful and perfectly gloomy soul of our pluralists leads sober men and women in every walk of life to ask this one question: *can* it be doubted that the vulgarest secret of these pluralists is that they are propelled by the emotion of resentfulness? Another question. Isn't it beyond question that pluralists everywhere are the ward-heelers of all the false-coinages stamped upon the American collective psyche by those anemic bloodsuckers in the NAACP whose *only* requirements are vampirism and naked power?—In fact, no itchy politico-legal ideologue has ever itched as you have itched; isn't this true?—My proof? You have the bully's itch, the innovator's lust for dominion.—Resentfulness. Spitefulness. Gloom. How do you get, how *did* you get, from these negative-positives to *dominion*? The entire herd of democratic animals can be dominated, *allow* themselves to be dominated, by smaller, much more activist, much more malicious, petty, conniving, highly *organized groups*?—"And why not? This is the way democracy works."—The groups grow obsessed with the ideas "we"—"they." They are consumed by this us-and-them dialectic. (—Under this obsessional umbrella, of course, we see the "moral" need to carry around whole chunks of history—And notice the pragmatist at work here: the we-must-never-forget mentality becomes a heuristic spur to action, to "justice."—) The "we" are the truthful ones who have a much better idea of what justice is; the "we" always tell the truth. On the other hand, it is the "they" who are maleficent, blind, obfuscatory;—the liars who *deny* truth, the backward-looking people who must be "educated."—"And why not? This is the way democracy works."—Moral: infiltrate the public schools; teach the cattle how to think; fabricate and inculcate a group-empowering party line; brand and demonize those who deviate from the correct thought of all empowerment strategies, etc. Let it be understood that the action-orientation of this us-and-them dialectic in no way accuses or prevents the brooding inaction that leads to sporadic emotional storms and explosions, hate that is sanctioned, and all properly noisy, plebeian behavior. But how?—How *could* the emotion of hate be horribly culpable in one instance and sanctioned in another? Precisely because of the artifice in selling the one and condemning the other: the one is *sui generis* and stands entirely alone, the other is a branch-off of the very resentment that propels the justice machine into eternal motion. So we say: this group artifice makes these vengeful ones the most ingenious, and by far the most *interesting haters* in recent history.—And the world's greatest haters have always demonstrated their goodness and rectitude!—That the fruit of resentfulness, of the resentful nature, leads to any genuine happiness seems to me to be refuted by the asking of the question, "Is legally-created happiness happiness?"—For genuine happiness is a kind of tranquil enjoyment and how, alas, could the victorious groups be happy when they must run around like the little boy with his finger in the hole in the dock, crazed and anxiety-ridden because of the possibility that social gains *could* be accretively retrenched (—for this *is* the common law's dynamic: advance, retrench, expand, curtail rights, remedies, etc.—). Moreover, the "happiness" of the groups does not happen naturally but is always established artificially—pluralistically!—by an examination of enemies, by examining the happiness of *others*. Consequently and forthrightly, the unhappy-happy pluralist is always at pains not merely to observe genuine happiness in genuine human beings, but to persuade and perhaps trick himself into believing that he is happy. Thus, *pluralistic happiness* is like a narcotic, a slackening and mitigation of tension, an effective anodyne and *anti-toxin* for his already poisonous, suppurated feelings.—What? Victory is not happiness? *Seduction* does not make heedless, tranquil, and blithe?—Not enough: the resentful impresario is enticed by everything hidden and covert: darkness and ambiguity become fixed ideas. Since the resentful person's ancestors learned how to survive "in the closet," live hidden lives, and become, in the end, veritable simoniacs of secrecy, this human type—although much noise is made about being denied access to the front door—naturally and unavoidably prefers the back door, caves, catacombs, and mouseholes of all kinds. Is it any wonder that the *pluralist society* is the most litigious in the whole world, the most litigious imaginable? (—They compose their briefs and motions in those mouseholes, we may bet on that—). In fact, when one descends into *such* a mousehole one is obeying the god of cleverness;—not justice—*cleverness*! A veritable synchronism of acumen—: the same god who fires up every attorney's strenuous efforts to "make black look white" and every guilty defendant blameless; every jacked-up journalist's strenuous efforts to lie, twist, cheat, and obfuscate with images.—What *is* American politics but a blueprint and copycat of the very basest, most notorious aspects of the American legal profession and our untouchable—but oh-so-touchy—Fourth Estate? Such a resentful people *must* come to embody and eventually worship cleverness: the clever become the good, even the pious;—for piety is rewarded by profits; nay, profits are proof of piety. While cleverness itself becomes truth; nay, the only truth—for the core pragmatistic teaching is: any truth is valueless unless and until it becomes "useful." Clever arguments, clever choreography, clever tactics, clever *lies*!—clever ways to *appear* one way and *be* another: cleverness as the *god of this world*.—As Aristotle has his magnanimous man, the crown of all virtues, shake off with one shrug what would eat deeply into lesser human beings—for this is his strength—the resentful soul lets every slight and insult eat down into his already impotent nature, and is best characterized by an ability *not to forget*; an ability he turns into the crown of *his* virtues, i.e., his gyratory sniveling and self-flailing lachrymosity; . . . what? do I forget so soon?—his *justice*! He seizes upon the wrongs perpetrated upon his most distant ancestors and treats them as treasures and delights, enshrining them in eloquent speeches and placing them with the tenderest solicitude in his august armory of causes of actions, certiorari petitions, grievances, complaints, and other *loci standi*. Translation: the resentful type honors cleverness as it combines with vindictiveness and culminates in the ecstasy of hurt feelings. This emotion *can only appear* in a certain type of soul. Vindictiveness is the condition of this soul's existence! It is, in fact, the means one venomous impotent rouser recognizes another. At the other distant pole, the strong human being, the individual who refuses to be the pawn of any group or self-deifying historical process, never has to muster the gumption to forget: forgetting is more or less automatic. Vindictiveness takes too much of his energy (—after all, noble humanity thinks of *loci standi* only as last, grudging resorts—). The apex of this proud ability to forget—and yes; to use a popular word: forgive—is found in the true artists who must devote the energy they would have used for sowing poison to their work. Ah, these are the great antipodes of the pragmatists, the pluralists, the lame and halt, the little folk who no longer believe in the philosopher! These people refuse to be politicians, actors, and possessors, and find greatness precisely where no one looks for it: in the lenity and grace of *favonian men* without the least desire to rule!— Remember how Cicero refused Julius Caesar's plan to turn the triumvirate into a four-man rule; Goethe refusing Napoleon; Horace's "epicurean" refusal of Augustan favor; yea, and *every* spirit who shuns fine linen to wear the rags of philosophy—No! I most emphatically did not say, "Forsake the wealth of Egypt to suffer with his people." Suffering and suffering for a people are *not related*, and are mutually exclusive. I am beginning to open my eyes to the possibility that the first battles fought against the individual—and victory in these battles means confusing the individual with the group—were fought by the "chosen people." This is the dream of Du Bois: to have *his people* recognized as the chosen people! To wave a magic race-wand over all *other* people to achieve this end (—the quintessence of pluralism!—)! This is the philosophy of Du Bois: *leave Harvard knowing nothing of philosophy!*—Be a pluralist!—Be intelli-bois-terous!—But is this designation strong enough? For it is surely not the resentful one's intellect merely that *requires him to have enemies*. He is who he is by virtue of his enemies;—as Du Bois is what he is by virtue of *being seen* by his enemies—; he becomes who and what he is by the miracle of objecthood; and since this objecthood is of necessity conferred by his enemies, and selfhood so-called begins and must begin with his being an object for his enemies, Du Bois can say he loves and hates at one and the same time. But it will be remembered that the father of cult pluralism is not merely a Harvard man who "thinks" and may someday—who knows?—philosophize; Du Bois is an artist, as his disciples never tire of reminding us, and as an artist he becomes creative: as the enemy pushes over the first domino to confer objectness, he must be evil; evil is thus posited before good is ever known. Good is then appended to this most necessary being as an afterthought and after-production: the good man, the *only* good man: Du Bois himself!—The ultimate blasphemy: the good must be a species of pragmatism! This kind of selfhood, this offshoot, cannot ever be found in advance or be, if you will, the final result of a process experienced in the beginning as spontaneous or self-generated. But there are other ways to show the impotence and helotry of the resentful man.—What then is the meaning of our antipathy to this pluralistic anthill?—That it reduces the individual to a cog of the group and suffocates him in the group. That the groups holding the individual as a pawn are themselves pawns to the historical process. That in light of this "absolute" of historical development and "progress" what has gone before is a stepping stone toward greater group empowerment. What is the difference for a pragmatist between this to-be-abrogated individual and the extraordinary individual? Precisely here one may detect *how* American Pluralism is a footnote to Darwinism: the "struggle" of that which calls itself an individual within the inert pluralistic machine and the struggles of the real individual—who must always exist outside the machine, the dialectic, even history itself; for the individual is above history to the extent that whatever is later in the evolutionary scale is not, *eo ipso*, more valuable; certainly not more valuable *because it comes later*—are worlds apart. We hear again and again the cult pluralists complaining of their sufferings and distresses. "Something must be done," they say, "to comfort, soothe, and placate *us*! The groanings of our ancestors cover Lethe's plain! The golden hour of our victory, the time *history has promised us* when we shall be fed, clothed, and eat of the fatted calf must come! To this end, we will struggle and toil! Let the world join us ! Let our sufferings be no more!"—Yea, but how *can* barnyard animals understand suffering, *what suffering is*?—What arouses fear? What breeds doubt, agitation, distress, loathing?—The inexplicable suffering of the extraordinary individual!—So, American Pragmatism—as every decadent "system of thought" must—seeks every expedient, every argument, every weapon and polemic based on "utility," every Druidic curse and booby trap as means to warn the healthy pluralistic herd that such dangerous maverickism—such "queer idols in the philosophic cave"—will not be tolerated. And why?—For the "good" of the herd! For Kwame Anthony Appiah's *good*! The authentic life of the authentic individual must die so pluralism may live! Everything good, full, completed, brave, triumphant, creative, and truly free must be interdicted at the gate, branded and demonized as invidious and unacceptable in an open society—*a free society*! How many cosseted numbskulls at Chicago, Columbia, and Harvard; how many sleek-pompadoured squirrel-editors at the *New Yorker*—experts on American ideas—does it take to *blot out* every hint of that which is rare, beautiful, remote, unbreakable, unbending, mercurial, and seeks with all its might its predestined end of quiet, calm, and if my wish be granted, Horatian independence? Let us listen for our answer on the evening news.—Is it *sufficient* that American Pragmatism and its cultic sidekick feeds upon evolutionary illusions? It is quite enough that since the extraordinary individual exists to be abrogated; and since history can only be conceived as a galloping straight line with no symbolic realm above it; and since whatever is later in the evolutionary scale must be more valuable; then, granted, the achievement of this pluralistic pragmatism is more portentous and exalted than any reasonable disciple or critic could ever have expected: it amounts to a communitarian hubris never witnessed since the despoiling Aeschylean gods, a hubris so vast, vaunting, and inconfutable that its likes has never been seen on earth. Cambridge Pragmatism began as a roughhousing reaction to a rampant Hegelianism, but when it placed too many eggs in the pluralist basket—and when John Dewey rightly saw Jane Addams as the real Hegel in a laced corset—this pragmatism for all practical purposes became too Titanic for comfort, and constituted a *reversion* to the intents and purposes of Hegel's social philosophy. It is as if the control over natural forces, along with the ability to re-do society at will, sponsored a spirit of intoxication in the community itself, a spirit that thinks nothing of resolving the individual into his social functions;—and stubbornly conceives the real as transitional, i.e. unreal. There is simply nothing left to check the pride of this communitarian intoxication we call pluralism.—I take that back . . . I can think of one thing.—Very well. The liquefaction of the individual should proceed from some rational source other than general intoxication over mankind, at last, sitting in the driver's seat. Is it rational? *Can* it be understood?—Cambridge Pragmatism posited and clung to the basic truths of existence revealed by Kierkegaard in his confrontations with Hegel. But for how long did these worthy pragmatists cling to these existential truths?—Question: how long did it take Jane Addams to recite the socialist version of the Lord's Prayer and caw a sweet tune in praise of Eugene Debs?—When John Dewey triumphantly substituted the hand for the intellect in the *adaequatio*, these existential axioms accepted by thinking people everywhere became a thousand times more nongermane. (—Either dialectical movement or the irreducible—) The notorious Deweyan contempt for the *vita contemplativa*—a contempt he learned at Jane Addams' knee—dismisses the extraordinary individual with this consequence: the individual as such is also dismissed. "The individual does not matter. Organic wholes matter." Well spoken, for the individual is most emphatically *not* an organic whole, most emphatically *not* a terrenly humbug abstraction imbrued with the Social Gospelism of every splayfooted "anarchist" roving the streets of Chicago, laced corset or no laced corset.—The dismissal of the value of the contemplative as a type, the refusal to allow for it any kind of special honor or favored status whatsoever—another "all men are equal" profanation and misunderstanding—constitutes the necessary conceptual precondition for the growth of pluralism: the groups do not merely possess a common nature; the groups are of a common nature. Again: the groups are the efflorescence of the common nature of the common man. What is the nature of this common man?—Industry. Utility. Common work and common boredom (—consequent need for mindless entertainment, pinfold computerism, journalism, economic and entrepreneurial freedoms, etc. with the stark proviso, of course, that these freedoms—these "rights, liberties, privileges, immunities"—the concepts are cognate and point to the same phenomena—aim not for freedom itself for the common nature is horrified by an open, iridescent horizon, but for security—). In one exclamation: the nature of the common man is to *seek his own advantage*.— Now the slaves of antiquity always sought what was most expedient for them, and never lost sight of their immediate advantage (—for a slave, like an animal, *cares only about what is closest to him*; this is certainly to say, what is most *practical* for him: what "works"—). Here the stark contrast between the attitude of the slave and the attitude of the noble obtrudes itself and grips our imagination: the *slave was a cunning animal*; I beg your pardon: the slave is a cunning animal. The slave is always on the lookout, waiting patiently like a spider for someone to step into his cunningly-spun web, patiently watching. Indeed, the modern *slave type*, no less crafty than his ancestor, realizes his essential nature as the most vigilant animal precisely by the cunning construction of dams to block the free flow of ideas; then these animals, these censorious little beavers, turn around and say, "This is free thought and free speech!"—Oh, the curse of it! Once some hapless public figure steps into these webs or seeks to swim under the beaver dams, he is apprehended—here I almost said, "read his rights," but this unfortunate has no rights—and forced publicly to recant; or if the slaves are feeling disgruntled or especially angry and vindictive, forced to "step down."—Alas, one must watch where one steps today for nothing on earth is tenderer than a slave's toe! Pluralistic democracy—let it be proclaimed from every house top!—means avoiding tender toes; i.e. setting up an invisible regime that monitors thought, speech, even "symbolic speech." So much for modern expression law in a pluralistic democracy! Let us return to the psychology of the ignoble nature.—Question: what is the slave's reaction? What is his natural and necessary reaction to magnanimous feelings—feelings, that is to say, *not* always on the lookout for what is practical, for the most immediate advantage?—feelings *not* in themselves cunning, crafty, grasping, vindictive, remorselessly resentful? To rephrase this question: *what happens when the slave meets someone who does not look like him?*—Precisely confusion tapering off into disbelief! "How *can* someone be inexpedient?" the slave asks, shaking his befuddled, discomfited head. "Surely, *surely*, there must be some hidden advantage attached!" He examines his opposite with all the force and thoroughness of his natural cleverness, rubbing his eyes. "Yes," he tells himself, "this person so not like me is at last just like me! He seeks his advantage surreptitiously!"—Still later, after much conversation designed to trick his antipode, the slave at last agrees to the absence of any selfish intentions. Confusion starts up again.—The slave hates to be confused, hates to be caught off guard!—Then the confusion suddenly dies, never to return. The slave is satisfied at last. "This person," he sneers, "is only a fool."—Indeed; for only a fool, says the slave logic, could fail to see and act upon his own *advantage*! (—We find Celsus the Epicurean polemizing against the early Christians, polemics used by Nietzsche, on account of a very large number of slaves found sitting in the early houses of worship. How utterly engaging Christianity must have been to the slave classes, how life-changing the reality of repentance, to force into the slave's field of vision an advantage not immediate, an advantage beyond all the slave's immediate advantages as the greatest advantage, an advantage "not of this world." That the slave finally, in this historical instance, *let go of his advantage*, gives meaning to the injunction, "You shall know the truth and the truth shall set you free." But the slave instinct, as we know, did not die. It went underground to resurface with the appearing of that slave revolt you pragmatists lovingly call the eternal verities of 1789. Viva Rousseau! Viva Condorcet!—). Having dismissed the magnanimous man as a fool, nay, worse than a fool, the slave experiences another bit of discomfort when this noble type, a type anti-pragmatist to the bone, is seen shrugging off insults the slave would have taken very seriously, would have *had* to take very seriously, and the slave—possibly through the "association" that speaks on behalf of this slave's particular group—formulates this very pertinent question. "How is it *possible* to live at a disadvantage?"—He is honestly taken aback, reeling on the periphery of the question of all his questions. "Is there . . . can there be . . . something higher? The lowest common denominator is not the truth? I have been lost, straying; my name is Nemo. I am zero: ought, naught, flat, vapid; I am a round pancake! All my cunning, all my social gains—zero!"—But not for long; not even as long as a yawn. The slave, the good slave, always springs back, bounces back like a red ball. (—Once more: "good" for the slave can only mean "cunning" in self-seeking, cleverness born of resentment: all this becomes strength, health, wisdom. Yes, they have experienced in chains the wisdom of the Yoruba onisegun—). The momentary "dread" fades away, the question of advantage dangles dazzlingly in the air. "How *could* one choose to live at a disadvantage?" Suspicion is the nature of a slave, and he asks this question from suspicion. He is suspicious of the other; he sees the gulf separating them and he hates it. (—In a pluralistic democracy, this chasm of separation is known as "divisiveness." Religion is divisive: appeals courts stay busy working out the stalking horse of "separation of church and state" doctrine. In one exclamation: *everything not like the slave is and must be divisive.*—). He senses the intractable unreasonableness of this superior spirit we call the individual (—superior; I say "superior" because the individual possesses the strength to stand alone; his existence *desecrates* the very idea of groups and associations of person—); for, as we know all too well, the individual does not always follow his reason. Whether self-sacrifice is not unreasonable in view of the fact that the individual will ultimately derive something positive from a negation is a scholastic question here; what is dispositive *for the individual* is simply that this eventual positivity, the fruit of the experiential dialectic, is not connected to any pluralistic component whatsoever;—precisely the thing that so vexes the slave, the *proud* slave! This unreason—the stubborn refusal to cast his individual lot in with the group sortition—the slave, pluralist to the rotten core, comes to hate! (—Once the slave-minions in their policing function of censoring and proscribing thought and speech come to outlaw "hate," they are aspersing one hate from the standpoint of another hate; they in no way condemn the phenomenon itself; they would lose sight of their advantage if they did!—)—What is the ground of this hatred? Not the individual's failure to fall in line with whatever the slave *offers* him; not the irritating, stark otherness of the individual—the nausea implicit in the idea that the group does not exhaust reality—; not even the passion of the individual; but the fact that the slave *sees* the inutility and fantasticness of the objects of the noble person's passion; this recognition gives the slave that dosage of decentering confusion most vexing for his *feelings* (—for the slave, to think is to feel, nothing more—). The slave, so strong in his determination to outwit and overcome the other but never himself, sneers again and stamps his feet. He points his finger accusingly. "You have allowed the drive for disunity to tyrannize over the drive for unity. You declare war against *us*!" Thus, the slave logic says and *must* say, "What is impractical to us is therefore incomprehensible.—The cognitive variant of what does not look like us is therefore evil.—And do we not also possess the right to combat evil, to ferret out from the history of philosophy and literature all the evil and *stamp it out*?"—But the higher natures of the *vita contemplativa* themselves do not have an ear for hearing the protest of the scheming, clever common nature with its value standards implicit in "what people do." Although without the noisy self-advertisement and rampageous vengefulness of the lower natures who live in and through the group, the hardness of the exceptional ones consists precisely in this: they, too, see the inexpediency of their antipodes and say with characteristic aplomb, "Does not *our* passion lie concealed beneath the incessant inanities and sordid power-plays of a pluralistic herd the way the exception lies buried deep inside its gaudy rule?"—Meanwhile, everyone looks at the exceptional ones with strangely querulous eyes and goes on living as if "what people do" were the principal thing . . . the *only* thing.

323

We speak—and sometimes scream—of "progress" and "dignity" and witness reflection's loss of dignity. If philosophy could be concretized into a physical form, it would consist of the Socratic trance: the stoppage of all movement.—Already the keen reader can see how we have degenerated: I mean our inability to stop and take account of things: this long lost, never-to-return power—this *human* dignity, the *sapiens* dignity—has been stolen from us by the deceitfulness of those who continually preach the gospel that "everything changes." As pointed out elsewhere, everything does not change, nor should it change.—Given the fact of universal flux, does this mean that human beings should not attempt to stand above or outside the flux? (—How did the Ephesian hermit mean his gospel? Did the philosopher of change want to destroy philosophy?—) It can rightly be maintained that all modern philosophy is a reaction to the Greek ideal of unchangeableness. But haven't we in our passionate overzealousness to overturn this ideal raised up a grim new idol, a kind of divinity, a Moloch-visaged god of haste whose crazy cult sees rumination and prayerlike seriousness in thinking as stagnation, stasis, and death? Speed and action have become life, have become philosophy; and critique, since it is serious and reflective, has become the enemy of our modern "philosophy of life." I take it as a ready axiom that political critique—the ebb and flood of our incessant legalistic wrangling—is not *real* critique for the same reason that defamations made during an election are time-honored exceptions to the slander rule.—Assuming that philosophers have never enjoyed any intercourse whatever with that which they call "the real," I am unable to see exactly how the old androgynous ghost of becoming should be any "more real" than that which has duration and *lasts*; that which "is," as the ontologists say . . . After all, it seems to me that our general development from that which is to that which becomes is a capricious, accidental kind of thing: when we find life in another world, the movement there, i.e. the development of knowledge, could just as well wind up precisely where we began, i.e. the inflexible. Plato's work amounts to a synthesis of the two positions: this only means he will have a host of disciples in one age and a host of enemies in another. Christianity, as a philosophic continuation of Plato, plays host to the ascendancy of "being" over becoming until the Renaissance. By the time of Hegel, the faith in becoming had become a philosophical orthodoxy one attenuated at the risk of being primitive, "dogmatic." In various forms, the good news of constant flux has been preached as the way out of uncritical debauch and into rigorous critique. But to return to our problem: the actual effects of this doctrine on the popular mind.—In a decadent democracy, the cultural ethos is to *adapt*. This springs ultimately from the common law's method of making any legal rule adapt to new facts. The jurists say, "The genius of law is change, not constancy." (—This idea is the opposite of a code of law. Since societal change occurs under both rubrics, the meaning of the difference is only a matter of emphasis—). In other words, because "everything changes" the people feel justified in adapting to anything, and the prejudice stealthily arises that this constitutes the essence of a healthy society. Completely unaware of it, the healthy democracy (—I call it "healthy" because it *can* only think of itself in terms of health, development, progress, and having "come a long way"—) goes about in every detail overturning the Greek ideal; and thus, finally, inaugurating the worship of the Great God Speed.—What then happens to the possibility of critique and its presupposition, reflection, in such a *state of worship*?—Everyone goes with the flow.—"Nothing lasts, everything changes."—as reflection, real critique, and hence, all sense of the noble in mankind and real possibilities of development begin to *die out*. The setting and solemn gestures of reflection begin their predestined descent into obloquy: there is no real seriousness anymore. Popular culture, with its "flux" of legal reasoning, Hollywood entertainment for tired work animals, a political mindset that interprets ultimate political success according to the uncannily unconscionable ability of "brilliant" dolts to place shimmering glosses on half-truths, and certainly not least, a greasy, gill-slitted Fourth Estate with its just as greasy "Constitutional mandate" to manipulate guises become the only standards of value for a "free society." Then these fine lawyers, judges, movie-makers, actors, politicians, and journalists—these "few"—run and ruin the very lives of our hapless "many." Yet real criticism of such a state of affairs would stun and stupefy both the few and the many (—for together they form a whole and exemplify the characteristics of any herd—). The reason?—This true criticism has as its precondition the Socratic stoppage of all movement—and this is intolerable. Such a state of affairs *requires* no thinking, no seriousness, no silence. Such a state of *pragmatic grace* requires that the individual be caught up in a continuum of flowing points, carried along by the wayward stream of becoming the way a leaf is borne along unhinged by an unheeding wind, all within a philosophy championing action. Action? How is action possible unless there first be the windless calm of uninterrupted individuation? Such an individual—a flowing point within a series of flowing points—would forfeit existence and lose himself in a somnambulistic cosmos of meaninglessly mercurial facts, tangentially sentient, always moving and on the move, but not knowing, not caring why?—where?—for what?—What cry has been raised, what voice allusive of the excesses of a dynamic society?—The *excesses* of freedom and dynamism . . . A philosophy of the future? Of perhaps *today*?—

324

An active individual is first an individual; he is not an individual because he is active, as pragmatism would have it. If an individual were an individual because of action everyone would be an individual (—as the thought that there are many recalcitrants in a given society is an unthinkable thought for pragmatism—). One could use the existentialist idea of authenticity here—a *Danish* idea—: attained authenticity grounds authentic acts; action itself does not make authentic, does not make an individual. Indeed, if pragmatism would confront philosophy of existence, there would be no more pragmatism: the individual—another name for irreducible opacity—*could* in no way blend in and become a part of an organic whole, and pragmatism with all its active fineries forgets the individual. If the social essence precedes the existence of the individual, where does the individual appear? Not in action, for activity alone has never made an individual. Social action is by extension never a collective action of individuals, for the individuals are abrogated by the collectivity itself.—Here the socialism of pragmatism—the Deweyism of American Pragmatism—asserts itself unabashedly, "When you speak of your individuals contemplating who-knows-what, we bark and growl. The essence of American Pragmatism is to guard against the acceptance in the marketplace of any inherently invidious pre-Darwinian ideas."—Such as?—"The existence of a class of thinkers thinking who-knows-what and *standing over* our social wholes, our precious unity and glorious process-dialectic, is unacceptable. Those who want to interfere with the hands of *our* clocks interfere with the moral education of the race, and must be, as you say, *abrogated*. The disposition of any thinker, let alone a bloc of germinal philosophers, to think under Aristotelian presuppositions and—even worse—the drive to interpret all events according to a religious scheme and rediscover in every fortuity the will of some static, patriarchal God cannot be tolerated in the new order. Not to interpret, but to change the world is our task. You have heard of the priesthood of all believers; pragmatism believes in the academy of all doers."—Bosh! Pragmatist bosh! You cannot begin at the bottom and then arrive at the top in all things, but only in some things. Induction only spreads its nets so far. Whatever psychophysical antecedents may be unearthed, thinking begins at the top and works down. Forward? Very well, forward if you prefer, but never backward, never upward *from* an act.—"What are you talking about? This is the way we pragmatists think."—Go on!—"Thinking is only a species of acting, nothing more."—Merely an apology for hegemonic technologies and the eventual ascendancy of nurturing, gynecratic values. Merely a biologist's ditty planted in a monkey's throat. Thinking *descends*, reaches the ears of active types, and is oftentimes tardily *translated into action*. From the bleakest, remotest, loneliest presidio, the thinking types command the panoply of learners and show the way to the goals of culture. They are always placing luxuriant Promethean exempla in the world that were not there before. Over and over, the practical people rehearse their lines, and at long last, the faintly audible expatiations heard only by the mice in cold, cramped lofts and ateliers change miraculously into fostering cadres of flesh, clamps of steel, and sometimes, scorpions and bundles of rods!

325

How best to throttle the contemplative life, starve its energies, and expropriate its place in the sun? Implant in the people an industrious ethos; keep things rolling by the non-stop fabrication of epic legal narratives, cock-eyed news stories, and celebrity gossip; *ergo* bestow upon art and reflection upon art only the tiniest remnant of time and energy. (—There *is* no time, no energy; only time and energy for following the dirty laundry narratives—the necessary degeneration of Zola's naturalism, Gallic salacity, etc.—and slave labor.—)—Art? Great art? To what end?—When art makes its demands upon life, life says in an impudent, condescending tone, "I, even I, *life*, have already filled my capacious belly with the choicest morsels of meat. You, even you, my grand counterpart, satisfy *your* hunger with these measly dry bones! Make yourself a sodden soup!"—Thus, it is in *our* age that the culture of pragmatism launches its assault upon art; for the ancient relations of art and life are detrimental to its plans, its desires, its place in the sun! An ethos of industry *feels* the demands of art too forward and overweening; art responds by centering itself more than ever before around the necessity for an audience, and if at all possible, the widest audience. Great art sees its *possible* doom: it must respond or die. The serious novel, for example, instead of leading the reader *into* life, becomes more like what Jose Ortega calls the dime novel and leads *away* from life, i.e. distraction, recreation, escape (—for the essence of all *petty art* is to afford an escape for its audience: it entertains merely, distracts, numbs—). Thus, great art, sensing the prideful ethos of the "new," prevailing action-orientation—with its necessarily tired, weary, dispirited-because-run-down audience hungry for kicks, egregiousness, and narcotica—does its best to adapt to its new environment.—As if selling paintings and books really mattered to Van Gogh and Nietzsche, and political success mattered at all to a mature, disillusioned Plato; as if their high brows could be besmirched by a cash drawer and the race for power; as if spirit in its eternal contentiousness with life were necessarily amenable to the cold, pulseless singsongs of raw survival.—Because its former claims now seem presumptuous, this art must energize a tired audience and force it to wake up;—this art must intoxicate its audience and put it to sleep (—which is precisely what modern "cultured" audiences need: anesthesia).

326

How conspicuously is the courage for *ideas* lacking in America! Where is the possibility for the philosophical life when everything genuine has disappeared? Yes, I realize this belief of mine presupposes a vision of the relation of philosophy to genuine life, and this is precisely what is most impossible today: vision.—I take it as the ultimate blasphemy when I hear our suppurated political liberals cry aloud in their house of mirrors, "Political vision *is* vision itself!"—One literary generation of political liberals finished off every hope for philosophy, philosophical writing, and even serious literature when this pampered claque of minikins succeeded in carrying through its agenda. I am speaking of the complete politicization of American culture.—And *what* do we find taking place in philosophy proper? We find the Cambridge Pragmatists *chewing* on Kant, gone daft over dim sum in the old Chinaman's Cathay House. We find them disciplining themselves, drinking less bad whiskey, etc., in a grand attempt to *understand* Kant!—When what, tell me, *is* there to understand about Kant other than the fact that Kant clung for dear life to his university; that he made no attempt to separate himself from the scholarly castes, state, and society; that his attitude toward religion was dishonest and obliquely syncretistic; and, finally, that his synthetic *a priori* judgments were and remain metaphysical phantoms?—These pragmatist hard heads struggled to understand Kant?—Therefore, isn't it natural and expectable that this preoccupation with epistemology would germinate into more clones and look-alikes, more professors, more stitch-in-time-saves-nine *professorial philosophy*?—But let us focus again on our dear "postwar generation" of American writers. We can see some of them playing dodge ball with the editors of the *Times Literary Supplement*; some are getting manicured and having their faces treated, while others loll around in Westchester County hot tubs, sipping gin and dry vermouth over ice.—These Cold War writers were perhaps destined to be functionaries in the great American political superstructure, all-too-taken by the dynamic fripperies of a free society: its pragmatism, pluralism, journalism, race and gender/church and state fedayeen, as well as the sum of those adscititious citations constitutive of the ruling case law. The boys were *exclusively* political; put it that way. Moreover, this was the time of the general reception of Sartre's philosophy outside France, the "student revolts," the scrooching astringencies of the educated feminist hetaerae, the wind-blown diabolism of Chairman Mao, etc.: and this amounted to a *political* situation with *its* ability to toss up facts and figures tending toward the aridification of any writer's ability to process and learn from these events. (—Perhaps I am too kind. Everyone in the know knows that these writers had nothing in their hearts but the philistinism of the various hydra-headed "rights movements"—so someday even they could complain their teeth were set on edge when they bit into the sour grape—and their pinnacle experiences consisted of smoking too much marijuana, preaching sanctimonious xenophilism, and occupying upper rooms at self-congratulatory book chats—) *Were these writers capable of understanding ideas?*—I find it more than merely amusing that the American public grew tired of reading just after the postwar generation of writers *stopped* reading.

So, what did they *do* instead of reading? They *wrote*! (—Interesting how this generation of liberals compares with our current crop of right wing radio windbags: frivolous talk takes the place of all intellectual curiosity: the reality of everything is *on the surface* . . . Teaching from surficial reality . . . Politics dominating everything . . . Attempts to persuade take precedence over investigation . . . Noise . . . Agitation . . . Mindlessness running amok . . . Journalist chatter.) A jumble of Id, dragging their stomachy carcasses through the homoerotic streets at nightfall.—The hero is the nonconformist?—Evidently.—But what to do when the hero's nonconformism becomes conformity? Even black picket fences have a way of getting dirty. But were these writers capable of understanding ideas? Perhaps it *was* too hard to deal with the Cold War and French existentialism at the same time. Sartre's philosophy was just too dense for the American intellectuals, too foreboding. After all, it led into Heidegger's Forest, and no American hot tubber wanted to expire in that kind of environment. The fact is that had the Americans been able to see beyond politics and for once grasp something pure and serene, they would have been able to teach the advantage of *knowing* the present age precisely by educating others *against* this age. So, today, there are no more philosophers. No one to *teach against the age*! No human soul willing to go bail for a people—*for mankind*! Mankind? Yea, that philosophy today is even less profound and relevant than a newspaper is no tribute to mankind! Whenever the spirits of philosophy and religion lose ground, when the people value liberty more than seriousness, the spirit of journalism magnifies itself and gapes upon all that calls itself independent, honorable, hard, exalted, silent, severe. As it is, since they were too weak and disoriented to go bail for us, we must go bail for them when we curse the political idea as a non-idea and trample upon the modern forces seeking to uproot contemplativeness, simplicity, spirit, *humanitas* in every memorialized form, and promote the velocity and stupidly barbaric homogeneity we abhor.—Among Americans, there is a seductive sort of refutation of Andre Malraux's charge that American writing is bereft of ideas, that the thinking in America is done by human beings bereft of ideas. And the refutation—assuming I have not misheard and misunderstood it—is the following: there is a criterion among the Americans for sorting out the true from the false, the precious from the dross, and it is precisely this: "Our criterion of truth is rigorous proof, and this proof always takes the form of struggle. Struggle—the potency of an idea steaming to the top of the market—makes holy; and, therefore, if something is holy, must it not also be true, axiomatic, honored for all time, and *consequently unassailable*?"—But have you proved that struggle makes holy? You have only promised us that holiness, and therefore veracity, is conditional upon struggle: *if* we struggle, we shall become holy, wholly true beyond question, and, as you say, unassailable. You are not proving anything, only bringing in a further belief that the effect promised to come from the belief in struggle will not fail to appear. (—This *is* the essence of pragmatism's absurd truth claim: to establish its validity, a belief must bring in another belief; then *this* belief must be validated by yet another so that the belief-consequence-belief-consequence *catena* extends at least as far as Mr. Peirce's logical illusions, and in fact, *ad infinitum.*—) Therefore: since it is *desired* that struggle makes holy, since it is desired that someone and something actually be holy in this completely naturalistic, social, pragmatic sense, is our proposition validated and proved? The "good consequences" of pleasure, gratification, and solidarity become as many proofs of holiness and truth?—No; proof by solidarity is a proof *of* solidarity, nothing more. It is, as if to compensate for such an illicit, Elysian leap, precisely when considerations of gratification enter into the questions of the holy and the true that happiness and "human need" fall into the most exigent suspicion. But how *can* a pragmatist be suspicious of *his* proofs and muster enough intellectual integrity to hail *his* founderous convictions before the Sanhedrin?—After all, such a slick operator has arrogated to his court the right to review and pass judgment upon all previous thought.—Experience? You gentlemen have tossed that word around like a ball. Put your favorite gauntlet in the drawer—where you keep your ears—and face up to the fact that experience teaches precisely the opposite: that when pleasure and pleasant feelings enter, holiness and truth beat a speedy retreat. Eating cake *never* suffices in this realm. Service to the truth requires sacrifice, honor, devotion—and heroism; a word, an "experience" anti-pragmatist to the core! But let us take another look at our proposition.—Let us peer directly into the *how* and the *what* of the struggle equation as a distinct pragmatic idea.—Struggle makes holy; *what* does it make holy? Since struggle is surely of the collective, the struggle in question is the struggle of the groups. In consequence of this balkanized struggling for advantages—this pluralism with punitive eyes and hands—what is made holy is not the groups themselves, the elements of any pluralism, but instead the *means* to obtain the group advantages are made holy by their separation from the group as consecrated group ideologies. To assert the same in other words: struggle creates the very ideology it sanctified. Then since holy is as holy does, what must be the next move in the struggle?—Set up holy alliances between what is acceptable in the flow of ideas and the group ideology itself so that the old morality, the old right/wrong, is gradually *taken into* the legal system (—i.e., moral wrong is now contemplated as falling under the rubrics of legal rights and legal duties, etc.—) and the new morality—strictly speaking, the enforcement of the new ideologies wrought upon the anvils of the social struggles—becomes the codification of what is "right" and "wrong." How then does struggle make the necessary ideology it produces *unassailable*? But this question has been asked and answered.—Malraux's imputation that the Americans possess no ideas in their exclusively action-oriented, dizzy heads; how has this imputation been refuted?—I have already divulged the answer to this question, but allow me to restate the answer in different words: the imputation has been duly thrown out on the most puerile and puerilely convenient grounds: pluralism is the idea of ideas, the *summum bonum* of an informed, open, robust democracy; therefore: there are no real ideas; no critical reason.—The writer and thinker as this pluralism desires him to be is in fact a person who has surreptitiously and inexorably been divested of his reason, and thus also his capacity for ideas, his capacity to see things as they really are—as things *shall be*. The whole inner world of the thinker (—for in such a world, the writer has dropped completely out of the picture; for the writer ultimately is the *auctor* who "increases" the world, and at the core of this increasing is independence, command, heightened sensitivity and thus enhanced critical powers, etc.—) *must be dragged down and sucked down by the culture* so that the practice of criticism becomes, in due time, a form of exhaustion. Pluralism with its frayed nerves and noise rules the night, and eventually, the day. Everything is sottish and reels in earnest expectation of a "new dawn." These drunkards drink in their precious news images and spout, "We must have justice." When the conclusions of this justice no one yet dares draw! Everyone wants *their* freedom, but with the least amount of responsibility; like a Gogolian troika full of "freedom riders," we thunder on for the ultimate homogeneity.—Worshippers of the sacred vulva! Swamp-habitants! Goddess nurturers! Hermaphrodites! Vice addicts! Degenerates! Fie on you who call for reaction! Fie on!—

327

When the *refuse elements* in any advanced democratic society combine to form the morbid, corrupt classes of such a society; when new social collectives are formed to concoct a new value-legislation (—so the impoverished elements may at long last *come to power*—); when the decadence types, one by one, learn to recognize that the force of law is really the law of force waiting to be used in their war against the *superbia* of everything high-spirited, uncompromising, severe—everything, in one word, suspicious of collectivity—; it is precisely then that the social fiat of pragmatism becomes invaluable.—Almost overnight, one educates oneself to become obsessed with children—as Dewey would have it—; one hastily, feverishly imports values discussions into the public schools. In one stroke, one transforms "education" into a *training camp*—as Dewey would have it—. The role of formal subjects must decrease in favor of methods that help the young adjust to the world and become "problem solvers." (—Use your imagination with this one.—) Dewey's faith: there is an intimate connection between a democratic society and how people must think; I beg your pardon. I meant to say "how people function." Dewey's faith: all seriousness must be spent on the political process. Dewey's faith: a formula, a straight line to lukewarmness and contentedness: the "organism" and its satisfaction with its self-wrought "environment," etc.—Very well; what does Dewey *want to do* by means of his educative pragmatism?—First of all, he plays gracious host to the hastiness of a modern democratic society—its endless self-commodification, greed, noise, can't-stand-still-for-one-minute industriousness—by herding young minds into a "pragmatic" environment in which utility is the primary virtue, the primary driving force of education: the child must be fitted for utility: fitted to serve the "organic whole," which means the child must fit into a slot in the superstructure and be *used up*. (—For American Pragmatism is perennially recognized as the most rarefied, the most cunning apology for American industrialism yet conceived: as such it constitutes philosophy's *thwarted development.*—) But can it be that even this drive for utility and machineism is only a surface phenomenon? Do the pragmatists have something else up their sleeves?—Before the young are used up, they must be prepared for the ultimate task: they must be carriers of the value-legislations, bearers of the new values, ushers and *future engineers* of the new religion, the new sexuality, the new race.

328

What? You express surprise and not a little dismay when I place a raven black question mark above the heads of our splendidly self-righteous, tolerance-epoptae, and social progress people? When I accuse them of being actors who strut and fret their historic hour upon the stage without ever caring, without ever knowing, *why* they do what they do, why they *are*? How easily we moderns—especially those of us who live in and under that peculiar form of political nervousness we call democracy—come to confuse ourselves with our roles! Yes, our actors are our masters today. Who can doubt it?—To secure justice and raise the level of "social consciousness," the social justice people greedily reach out for any given minority group's interests as their *own* primary interests. (—I am being facetious when I say "any given minority group's interests." What is involved here is the lung power of the minority group, how loudly and abrasively it can shout.—) But how *can* the alien interests of some alien group function as *someone else's* interests?—as promising the satisfaction of the primary interests? The minority interests, the most vociferous interests, invariably function as prey and nutriment for those whose original happiness lies in demeaning and bringing indictments against authority in any manner possible. When the minority interests first assert themselves to the *other* party—whose real interests are in no way congruent with those asserted interests—it seizes them eagerly as means for the possible satisfaction of its own interests; *ergo* the appearance and passing away of these chance opportunities bear no real relation, that is to say, no rational relation to progress or justice;—quite the contrary: any congruence of interests is misperceived and misinterpreted as unity or unities, the building blocks and *sine qua non* of social justice; for this congruence is solely the outcome of the *nutritional requirements* of some vastly dissimilarly situated group; ... so that any moral predicate attached to this organic play and counterplay of purely physical forces (—as, say, hunger is an amoral, physical need—) constitutes a gross misunderstanding; in one word, a stupidity.—So, why *is* there a primary drive to resist authority? Does *it* bear a rational relation to justice or progress?—The inclination to resist authority as a desiderative element in the personality appears always as an indiscriminate and insatiable relation to some quite inarticulate *prior fact*; more properly stated, it is a *reaction* propelled by a gratificatory mechanism intent upon compensation. Such that any purported objective quest for justice is really only a kind of symbol and sign language for an absurdly private mechanism geared toward a purely subjective end. Progress is just this absurd delimitation of the social phenomenon. (—An objective justice and a triumphal march of progress are suppositions and hoaxes flowing from French materialism, Hegel's notion of the historical sequence of philosophic systems, English evolutionism, and, not to forget, Sir Edward Coke's stubborn assertion of an innate meliorism in English legal conceptions; nothing more.—) If the people plagued with the primary drives intent upon satisfaction—in the main, as aforesaid, a drive to resist authority actualized in response to some, perhaps unknown, prior psychic phenomenon—were *deprived* of the minority interests to give shape, scope, and discharge to these completely alien drives, they would be faced with the necessity of inventing them.—In this kind of environment, the clamor for "individual rights" bears no relation to individual autonomy. The assertion of the latter in a progress-drunken society constitutes a danger for the society; for the *autonomous being* lives on as spiritual seed to form *opposing states*.—A similar kind of *secret* ebb and flow takes place in the realm of religion. When Count Tolstoy rid himself of the necessity for personal salvation and the dogmas clustering around such a religious concept faded into the background, the originally subsidiary belief in *moral action* pushed itself into the foreground and became the real "conversion." In France, from Pierre Bayle to Auguste Comte, we see attempts to outdo and outbid the "old religion" as the secret spur to this new religion of freethinking—a religion with its own moral formulas and postulated ends. The more one liberated oneself from the dogmas, the more one sought a *justification* for such a liberation in a self-wrought *secularized residuum* of Christianity (—The separation of church and state, speaking practically, means the inundation of the state by the new church.—) As redemption retreats, love, forgiveness, charity, and the drive to submerge the individual in the whole anoint themselves, find acceptance in the political realm, and call their ilk God . . . As John Stuart Mill in England unctuously preaches the advantage of others as the principle of behavior, William Lloyd Garrison and Harriet Beecher-Stowe, at last feeling side-splitting twinges of *mea culpa* over the "progressive" liberation from the Calvinism of their fathers, hail the Negro as the new redemption, the new Christ, the new "all in all." . . . Emerson wastes no time equating John Brown's pitifully insane love for Blacks with Christ's love for mankind. From the French Revolution onwards every socialist system places its true believing feet on the common ground of these teachings: Babeufism, Owenism, Marxianism, egalitarianism, the dream of a United Nations, brotherhood, sisterhood, African ethnophilosophy, democracy, the emerging matriarchate; what do the names matter?—Within this *secularized* Christian ideology—this cult of philanthropy—everyone KNOWS that the good society is precisely that society on the way to viewing the individual in one correct way: as a member of the whole, as a *sacrifice* to the whole! For, believe me, the social enactment of viewing everything in one correct way, this meretricious flowering of the dialectic of our case law, is the ultimate consequence of that darling in the Constitutional nursery: free speech; . . . a modern offshoot of the ancient Greek democracy's right of ostracism, political exile, etc. Whether it's called tyranny, exploitation, the patriarchy, "the hegemony of Western reason," divisiveness, denial of justice, etc., what is *wanted* is the same: the weakening and final abolition of the individual (—which includes, incidentally, the discouragement, and wherever and whenever possible, the harassment of the thinker *as a type* who necessarily *stands over* the cosmification of society, i.e., society progressively dumbed-down and equalized: society *pragmatized*).—Pragmatism contemplates and warrants equity, safety, uniformity, cheapness, conformity, etc., in a worker bee environment free of every "evil"—: danger, independence, command, the *right* to be extravagant, inequality in abilities and endowments—; and most conspicuously free of the satanic *vis creativa* of a leisured class of thinkers whose critical thought has the overall effect of breaking up unities and transforming complacency into query, jubilation into the third degree (—the most feared and fearsome "bad consequence" for pragmatists—). So that goodness becomes—morality becomes—the *utility of managed members in large bodies* . . . But to return to our original question: what did the Negro slave and the Russian muzhik have to do with Mrs. Stowe and Tolstoy?—Everything and nothing.

329

The emancipation of the children—the evangelical wing of Dewey's thought—and, at the opposite pole, the liberation of the childlike: this starkest distinction American Pragmatism must coddle from the light of critique, for the evangelizing of pragmatistic values has solemnly commanded it. By contorting and curlicueing the needs of children with regard to "education" and the matricizing of justice, Deweyan ideology has found its way to some axiological curlicueing of its own: *the right to create degeneracy*. That parents have lost control over their children is the *consequence* of ideology . . . Let us face this fact: Deweyan ideology creates values, but disguisedly, subterraneanly, on the sly. Operative fact of your precious, can't-touch-this Brown decision: *how children feel*. (—For it would give the Negro children a complex of felt inferiority, Deweyan mercenary Thurgood Marshall argued before the most activist court in history, if commingling were not the better part of the moral law.—). Publicly and privately, the one thing to be valued is: *how children feel*. Does X make the child feel bad?—Then X *must be immoral*. Does Y make the child feel good?—Then Y *cannot* be immoral.—John Dewey's philosophic conviction consisted precisely in this: the rise of one thing must entail the downgoing, the degeneracy of another. No, do not destroy the old temple . . . Begin the construction of a new one, and in time the old one will implode. But do you temple builders have the right to retire on your laurels? As early as the late 1970s daycare personnel began to witness certain changes in the children. Where was the crack discipline crept out? How did respect beat such a fast retreat? It came to our ears that the public schools had gone haywire, that parents no longer existed; that there were no more children.—We must see, we must *learn* to see, this Deweyism as the mint of American values; for philosophy—yes, even here that which passes for philosophy—coins new values ... sedulously enlisting the aid of who knows who. Meanwhile, the most insolent temple builders, the strutting peacocks of the legal profession—and, I'll be the first to admit it, those trial bar mimicing elves we know as our dearest "Constitutionally mandated" journalists—continue to foist the myth that *law ought to revamp society*! Thus, the hand-wringing American conservatives continually wring their lily-white, un-calloused, sweet-smelling hands over the disappearance of their most cherished values because of an activist judicature chanting illicit paeans to judicial supremacy (—The idea that the American Supreme Court is the patient parent chastising the wayward branches of government when they err, etc.—). Our conservatives intone the following, "*If only* the judicial branch would stop making law, and *if only* change would come by the legislature, then all our cherished values would come back to us. Good government and moral fiber would be restored." Etc.—Most conspicuous misconception!—Most idle hope!—Let us say it again: *American Pragmatism coins values*. After all, what possible difference could it make—even to you educated and not-so-educated right-wing hand wringers—whether a given product is delivered by truck, by rail, or by hand? The legal profession and their mimics are only carriers. Is this clear? You could have a throttled judiciary and things would be no different.—Please allow me to say a few words here expressly for the benefit of you jittery people on the nervous political right: the issue here should *not* be framed in terms of the "intention of the founders." Such pretty legalisms will never curtail "the least dangerous branch" in its lust to dictate. Given a state of facts; the judges would not have to decide what the founders did mean on a point present to their minds, but what the founders would have meant on a fact not present to their minds, had the point been present. Then, assuming the judges do have a beatific interpretation of such rarefactions such "intention" would—quite aside from being construed away at will—only arouse an antiquarian curiosity. Let us say, arguendo, that the framers of the American Constitution wanted an absolute law of expression. (—Indeed, the Constitutional language suggests this much as it says, "Congress shall make no law," etc.). Does this mean that we would want such an absolutist position to prevail? Such would preclude all defamation actions and all suits impinging upon a plaintiff's interest in protecting his good name.—So a much better formulation would be: did the judiciary jump ahead of the social ethic? If it did, it has overstepped due bounds, as it did in, say, Brown, in the prayer rulings, and in many other cases tending to trash the principle that the law must *follow* society. (—As I have said elsewhere, Brown should be carefully compared to Yick Wo vs. San Francisco).—Dewey's new education agenda is the agenda of focusing on children's needs; consequently, the *ratio decidendi* of Brown's revolution is a regurgitation of Deweyism. Drain the marsh and you will clearly see the defiant, slippery rocks with the *grand designs*: the labors of the most influential pragmatists: Burghardt Du Bois, John Dewey.—And the sorest sore spot on the hands of our hand-wringing conservatives? Judicial activism? Not at all foreseeable, hardly *possible*, absent the pragmatist brainchild of law divorced from its ancient ground of philosophy and religion and *consequently* wedded to social reality. Then: action; the essence of pragmatism's "idea." Dean Pound (—and Holmes from afar—), presiding at this accouchement with the glow of a religious prophet, ceremoniously directs the "legal monks" to come down from their ivory towers and preach the healing gospel: law is now a social tool, a blueprint for the restructuring of society. So then: Holmes the advocate of "judicial restraint"—while sitting periwigged on the bench with his fingers crossed—becomes, even unwittingly, the architect of judicial activism. Stated differently: the Holmesian philosophy outbidded the Holmesian judicial temperament.—Must I draw you conservatives a picture?—Very well; another example, another question: were the seminal prayer rulings likely to fructify absent the intellectual ferment of Jamesian Pragmatism's darling, pluralism? Did they teach you *this much* at Harvard? Can you recognize the Holmesian dictum in action regarding the "consequences of a legal rule"?—*I point out that American Pragmatism as it touches the legal realm is a legal rule.*—The judges *foresaw* the kind of society pluralism wanted and willed it into eventual actuality. They, as the saying goes, "reached for a result." And the result?—The ground of the decisions? The sufficient justification for jumping ahead of the social ethic here?—Pluralism becomes settled law. Petitioners felt they were wronged by the very existence of a dominant culture, here a dominant *religion*. Thus, the judges fleshed out the ideational skeleton, turning it into "law."—But the mere mention of an idea, a blueprint on the table, stealing itself into the practical world claiming dominance is more than enough to warrant a contumelious thumbs down from every right-thinking empiricist in the Anglo-American world. They will say, "We do not believe in such hobgoblins."—Yet, upon *what* is empiricism based?—Trustworthy evidence. (—I say this quite aside from the practice of turning philosophical rigorousness into a working injunction to deny the nose on your face.—) And the cold evidential fact is that America possessed the barest minimum of a pluralistic culture prior to the 1960s, i.e., when the "new law" in the prayer rulings came down. Barely a handful of pornographers, dreamers, and Beat roadies had the drug-induced temerity to blame all their aches, pains, and phobias on a "square world," i.e., a dominant culture. Another cold evidential fact: *After the civil rights movement the American melting pot stopped melting.* On Monday, the people took to the streets demanding, "Do not discriminate against me because I'm different." On Thursday, the people celebrated those very differences. Why did they bless difference and reject similarity? Because it was in the interest of the race to do so . . . Just as the prayer rulings implemented an envisaged pluralism, an open door to the new immigrants from Asia implemented the pluralism implicit in those cases. (—I fondly and vividly recall the spectacle of Melvin Belli publicly bewailing the influx of "Asiatics" into San Francisco in the 1970s, and thus, for reasons I will not discuss, driving down jury awards.)—And to which purpose, to what end did all this pluralism tend? What upshot lay lurking inside pluralism's warm devitalizing bowels?—Precisely the inauguration of a correct way of thinking under the protean guise of "freedom" (—*Invectives Against the Idols*, 2006—). To oust traditional religion and put *another* religion in its place. I have been feeling up philosophers' long sleeves too long not to comprehend *this* . . . Yes, even to comprehend the religion of Leo Tolstoy, Jane Addams, Simone Weil, Harriet Beecher-Stowe, as well as all the poisonous mother's milk implicit in the feminist, Neo-Marxist liberationist mish-mash as itself but the pale hue of an approaching giant, as itself provisional and adumbrative of a *coming grand synthesis*;—well, comrades, this sort of recognition and accounting serves to *unravel* philosophers' sleeves!—But let us return to Dewey's children. Dewey wants the radical empowerment of children. What does this mean?—Children must unlearn the fear of adults, for fear *creates distances*, and stark individuation is hated in a pragmatistic universe. How to combat and stamp out distance?—The superstitious belief in equality, perfectibility, progress, Darwinism, race pragmatism. The noble of antiquity noticed such distances between his own being and the being of the slave that he could scarcely see the slave anymore. This identical relation obtained with regard to the philosopher of antiquity, i.e., the *real* philosopher, and the unphilosophic mass of men who must regard living for an idea a form of pitiable lunacy.—Read Diogenes Laertius and count the times the crowd laughed at those serious enough to take philosophy seriously; in the starkest contrast to the wiser sort, like Pericles and Cicero, who saw the perfection of sublimated force in the philosopher, the crown and flower of *higher power*, the sanctuary of self-mastery. Remember Napoleon humbling himself before Goethe, King Darius reverently entreating Heraclitus, etc.—But not so with our pragmatists! Indeed; what does our doyen of race pragmatists, Du Bois, have to say about the distance implicit in the Hegelian master/slave paradigm? What is his final word? The master must learn to live in the slave's belly like Jonah lived in the belly of the whale.—"*Devoro ergo sum.*"—Distances, either in the objective world or those internecine turgescences within the soul, are discriminatory; and here our pragmatist approaches the cryptic truth at last!—The opposite of all this: the *liberation of the childlike*. Precisely what is most valuable in the life of the mind, in thinker and artist, is not hard analysis, not hard work. The chosen ones know how to *seek out the childlike*. I can conceive the artist-thinker in no other way. And what constitutes this realm?—Play. Serenity. First and foremost: forsake the practical! Eschew the trammels of mere utility! Sins of sins for our pragmatist and the industrious, obedient bees in his beehive!—Question: why *would* anyone forsake the practical world, the world of palpable advantage? Why throw away what constitutes in the eyes of this world the sole advantage? Since this breed of spirit lags behind in order to get ahead, since here the counterintuitive is cultivated as a rare plant, since this species turns the world upside down in order to see it aright, this hidden question must have a hidden answer. Power, yes; but *another kind of power*. The one who plays is too full of life. The feeling of struggle is absent: vision, calm, intoxication. One is induced to survey expanses—of peoples, eras, distances. The player in no way sees life as it is; his joy is bent on transfiguring life until it reflects back this very joy in intoxication. The artist wants to see himself in things, if possible in *all* things. Who is playful? Who is childlike? Who is the chosen who finds his or her advantage in straying, in conspicuous truancies, and in *staying behind*?—The one who reflects, the dangerous one who flings Darwinian jejunities to the wind; the bird-prophet who soothsays his way through life. The philosopher in all his incommunicable guises and nonstop invisible activities. The spirit who stops, turns around, and *looks back* to see what is to come. But just as this spirit, this childlike spelunker who makes a life of losing his way, depreciates the practical world—and in this sense comes after this world and grows out of this "real world"—so the countermovement that he spawns and that must grow out of him represents and will represent the "logical" consequence of the final accounting of all our modern ideals.

330

What monotonous circus animals our fine conservatives are today! What hopelessly muddleheaded circus-pragmatists they all are with their notorious incapacity for ideas, confusing basic, i.e., philosophic ideas with Catholic legal theory, unquestioning praise for the military, naïve trust in the business community as the God-appointed bestower of right conclusions for all right-thinking people everywhere, and their pompously self-styled "conservative movement" that wants to take us back to an earlier time of virtue—to an earlier conservatism! Yes, they noisily extol "freedom"—and, here, nine times out of ten, it is *economic* freedom they are really extolling: Adam Smith for the people is the outer limit of their "thinking"—; but we are not free to return to an earlier time, we are not free to retrogress: American conservatism can only retard the march of decadence . . . It will be the task of coming philosophers to speak of reaction and a possible restoration. Only philosophers, not political presbyters, possess the capacity as well as the good will suitable for the *winding up of clocks.*—But let us return to our circus. The muddleheads will preach again and again, "The government doles out largesse and this hurling money at a social problem is really intended to buy the politician votes, to keep the politician in power. Goods and services—privileges—are spread out over a wider and wider area to ensure next year's victory at the polls. The liberal politicians are a bunch of elitists who see the people as so many uncouth bellies needing to be filled. But we, we truth-seekers of the right, we have a better, nobler view of human nature! The people are good enough and wise enough to make it just fine without the largesse, without the good graces of an obscenely over-expanded, omniscient government." Et right-wing cetera . . . But what *is* this?—The conservatives in their philosophic innocence will say that *mankind is good*—that the people, pursuant to this basic soundness and wisdom, will always do the right thing if this same good people will but get a firm hold on those bootstraps;—when it is this very Age of Reason idea (—man is good; social institutions have made him bad: to alter the inside one must first alter the outside, etc.) that has served and continues to serve as the galvanizing fundament of liberalism. What *is* American political liberalism but a true-believing inmate of this utopian socialist house?—Open your complacent, sleepy eyes, you conservatives; *open your eyes*! You will speak—oh! what you will *not* speak!—of autonomy and the individual (—when what you really drone on about is certainly not the individual, not any authentic autonomy whatsoever, but your entrepreneurs: this constitutes the qualitative distinction between intelligence and idiocy for our fine conservative: how much money one takes to the bank at the end of the day) when you should take a look at the race of sheep to which you belong. The individual has flourished under *opposite* conditions. Individuals do not arise except by such conditions, through resistance and sometimes voluntary renunciation of happiness, etc. What you innocently extol is the impoverishment of autonomy, the weakening of the individual *as a type*. To this end, you employ your Adam Smith verities—your eternal verities; in one word, your *materialism*. Yea, in every epoch the strongest, richest, most independent live and work on the outside, far from the swindle of depersonalization, and refuse to be possessors, office holders, and honorees. Just as law's mission was to bestow order, which in turn made economic prosperity possible, so economic freedom, the whole world of finance, is itself only a means. What is its legitimate end? The autonomy and authenticity, wherever and whenever possible, of the individual! This end then becomes or should become a means for constructing a civilization. But more than anyone else, it is you conservatives who bar the way to *this* road. And why? How?—But I have answered this question.—Adam Smith aside, you will now be seen stroking your quaint pomposity by venturing out into the world of writing: you must join the scribbling rabble, adding *your* illustrious name to the gleaming roster of media-hucksters at the *Wall Street Journal*, who daily crowd around the cracker barrel of penny-ante, op-artsy "ideas." Then to confirm your hysterical juxtapositioning of buffoon and canaille, you appear on every impertinent talk show you can so that as many of the idea-enfeebled mass as possible will get one *more* chance to feast their eyes on your brutality. Pity that the party of Burke, Hume, and Maine is left with the likes of *you*! America, so rich in clever journalists and astute politicians, has lacked great souls for so long that no one can any longer recognize what a great soul is, who a great soul is . . . There is so much noise and self-praise today, so many advertisements for mediocrity, so much lack of embarrassment, that the petty souls, inwardly tormented by their petty feelings and endowments, can easily get on top and stay on top.—Pettiness *sells*, remember?—Surely to lust after honors in this day and age is even more unworthy of a philosopher than it was in any previous age: for today the rabble rules, the rabble bestows the honors.—Let us be clear how dearly our conservatism is bought, how dearly it is maintained. Let us recognize for once that the price of every conserving power is mediocrity. For the conservatives themselves I should say unabashed mediocrity. To say the same in other words: the exceptions are out of place among conservatives; and vice versa! The spirits of adventurousness, prodigality, spiritual disturbances of all sorts, including the sometimes excessive exactions of our artistic gifts, the demands of genuine religion, excessive tension, the acceptance of contradiction and extreme tendencies, a sociality of chasms, the cultivation of solitude, leisure, and caprice as the triple-jewels of all the virtues;—these traits of the exception militate against conservative mediocrity, conservative welfare! You see then that it is error for conservatives to hoard all the virtues of mankind; to say, "Virtue is only possible through us!" (—The other crowd, our liberal crowd, jealously guards all the "forward looking" excellencies, swinishly subsuming them beneath idolatrous rubrics you know only too well.—). Daily, we find conservatives stand at their Armageddon posts, declaiming the real meaning of "the news" (—yes, how can a conservative today not be *ashamed* of the fact that every conservative of merit is a *journalist?*—), marking themselves off from "the leftists, the liberals"—using those words with such rancor that no one will readily confess to such dirty business;—when in the end all drawing of distinctions is illusory, worse than illusory! For, believe me, American conservatism and American liberalism constitute but one force, one tendency, one aim.—The dream of a "religious experiment," a New City on a hill, piously reflecting the light of a new sun! America would be a new beginning, a perfect place of heavenly harmony—like the Plotinian City of God.—Hallelujah!—But at length, strife and dissensions appeared in the ranks of the saints. Between the Mathers and the men who thought like Roger Williams, a great gulf yawned. The struggle against Calvinism was the struggle to open the American mind, a mind that can create and destroy. With every sonorous cadence, every burning glance, Ralph Waldo Emerson bemoans the divine obsequy, but hails another divine beginning. Mrs. Beecher-Stowe loses her faith, and in the next breath, gains her beloved slaves. As for the religion of the founders, suffice it to say that Mr. Jefferson knew how to use his scissors. Am I understood?—But the anti-Calvin purge—even the victory of the North and the unionists—failed to purify the air so the seculars could *breathe*: other victories *had* to be forthcoming, other consciousnesses envisaged and willed; and, if necessary, the establishment of New Consistories for the maintenance of a new American heaven and—alas!—a new American earth! What is this? Our dear seculars are persecuted?—Enter the "American fifties," a time of intense persecution. We find the divine Jack Kerouac "becoming a Buddha" on the road, looking back at respectable society with a gay smirk, pronouncing judgment upon the old complacency and correctness in the name of the new. Henry Miller—the old reprobate—wickedly inveighs against the "square world" (—For it is a trifling distance in modern America, isn't it? between a straight line that asphyxiates and a nurturing circle?—). We find such circular luminaries as Allen Ginsberg and William Burroughs fellating their way down to South America in search of mind-altering plants. Ginsberg writes to Dr. Timothy Leary, "Burroughs knows more about drugs than any man alive. Soon, very soon, we will be able to say, We are everywhere!" At length, fighting asphyxia takes a new form. The struggle of the secular party must be given a new "potency." Enter Hugh Marston Hefner with "all the girls" and his Playboy philosophy (—as aforesaid, *anything* is dubbed philosophy in the Land of Cash—), a curiously dry montage of J.S. Mill, a bastardized Epicurus, and the red light district. Hefner—*another* journalist! But all the girls weren't quite enough. As if to animate the fragments Suetonius chose to delete, "Hef" must taste the exoticism of group sex. Must I also mention the "higher thoughts" of, say, a Miss Katherine Anne Porter, who was no Mae West, feeling comfortable, perhaps too comfortable, with nudity; the American literary novelists of the 1950s throwing themselves at homosexual themes; Jerome Salinger's curses hurled at the "rah-rah baloney" of the "Establishment," the corporations, Eisenhowerism, etc.; our dear, pampered civil righters with their three bags full of imperial Negritude and all the resentment that shows its backside, and sometimes, its face in the new philosophy on the continent of Africa; and, not to forget the hellion in the raw, Andre Gide—reincarnation of the great god Pan—; when *she* stepped "out of the closet," everyone followed her.—What then do all these proto-persons mean? What do they *point to?*—Just as modern law forges the tools and weapons to be used in political struggles, so the entire political realm should be seen as part of a larger *cultural struggle*. The proto-persons *wanted* a different world—and they got it! Then those who receive worlds must ask what kinds of worlds have been taken in. Are they worlds of higher justice or higher Chinadom? Yea, a leveling and stationary dwarfing of mankind that suffocates, not liberal dreamers, but that synthetic, maximal, summarizing form of over-life we call the philosopher.— But specifically with regard to the consequences of the liberal wing of the totalizing cultural idea: which overarching idea serves as the basis for the universal tenderness, nurturing, unity, peace, compassion, love, freedom, and equality envisaged by the liberals?—Matriarchate. The *opposite* of restrictions and bounds. The Democratic Ideal.—The idea of "universal brotherhood" is *rooted in* motherhood, the great Nurturing Mother, who loves all her children "equally" (—The "all" here means the inevitable redemption of all elements; matriarchate is thus the root of all liberal theologies: the ouster of the judging, "jealous," intolerant Sky God as the *summum bonum*, the "end of history," the Hegelian-Feuerbachian riddle at last *solved*.—As is well known Marx and Engels welcomed the idea of matriarchy. How could they do otherwise?—). Regarding world democratization: what can "consent of the governed" really mean *any longer* if it can be shown unequivocally that consent, for modern overtechnologized man, means manipulated consent? The value of an individual must be measured according to the effects produced;

pragmatism *again*! Moral evaluation is social evaluation: individuals are not seen as so many proofs of difference, not enclosed, concealed, unfathomable; certainly not superior (—the word "superior" is interdicted; one must not think superiority: one is *never* superior. How could one rod, one gear, one cog be superior to another?—) since this kind of evaluation proceeds quite differently from the social evaluation; ... as if, say, a work of art should be appraised solely by the effects it produces. Even if the pragmatist were to allow for something superior—arguendo!—this superiority would have to exist as so many causes and levers to set masses in motion, a kind of pragmatist teleology.—This government by the consent of the manipulated works side by side a technological, affluent society; in one word, the consumer's paradise with its "instant gratification." Here the Great Mother becomes technique, fad, freedom; here her precious children are fed, nurtured, pacified; here is heard the non-stop lullaby of entertainment and "news." (—and our serious novelists wonder why the literary novel has died out?—) Here man becomes emotionally an infant, feeling secure in this abundant supply of "milk." Individuals no longer need to make decisions. They are made by the technocrats with their as-if-invisible mechanisms, apparatuses, and congeries of levers and gears.—Group sex, the drug obsession, the predominance of passive-receptive attitudes, the need for immediate satisfaction, the tendency to diminish sexual differences, the duty to abolish the traditional status of the male, the phenomenal "children and adolescent revolution," the idea of the group itself;—*all negations and perverse affirmations.*—In sum: if this is the unveiling of the real, even the unconscious, end and aim of political liberalism, the pertinent question rises to the fore: is the end of political conservatism any different if seen as part and parcel of the great stream of cultural, i.e. *non-political forces*?—American conservatives will do daily lip service to a "culture war," a war against "traditional values," an assault on tradition generally, when this war's basic conception can only be as narrow as the insularity of every conservative's ability to think comprehensively. Furthermore, no conservative is educated today; if basic ignorance passes for knowledge, then ignorance "works." (—For I swear it, our conservatives are petty, Johnny-be-good pragmatists first and "laborers in doctrine" later, in fact, *much* later; at any rate the doctrine they labor with is shallow on principle. The most profound conservatives of any era have been superficial legal thinkers, skeptics, jingoes; e.g., the aforementioned triumvirate; e.g. Cato—). Sadly, every young intelligent spirit in America can only turn to liberalism by default; in one word: the callousness, rankness, and blockheadedness of the conservatives must be avoided as bad company is avoided! Moreover, conservatism places its trust in that common economic management of the earth I designate as the brutal clockwork of mechanization, a techno-whole of such tremendous force that the units composing such a force can only be functions and gears—the pragmatist's "utility"—and therefore *minimal values*. Consequently: as this overall machinery presents itself as nothing other than dehumanization and exploitation, leveling, dwarfing, a direct assault on man's *ability to question*, etc; as this higher solidarity increases the expenditure of everybody resulting not in collective welfare, but in collective loss, conservatism, as always, aligns itself with the *regressive forces* even as it tirelessly preaches its "freedom." What kind of freedom? Economic freedom: the individual is the entrepreneur, the demoralized fungible unit, the weakened, pampered, multifarious, morbidly inquisitive, self-deceptively happy cog in the whole gruesome spiral-down of "civilization."—Forging a new dehumanizing ethos means the gradual erosion of the old one: so that it is no longer known what aim this tremendous process has served. To fight upward out of chaos requires something more than an aim no one recognizes; it requires hardness, severity, sacrifice, the "evil" separatism of a higher caste, compulsion, reaction!! *Where are the reactionaries of the third millennium?*

331

America has produced but one man who had the makings of a philosopher, and it is entirely fitting that this man should also be the only real genius America has produced. Yet one is witness to our vainglorious historians who shake their heads, stamp their feet, and say with that combination of innocence and insolence that is the essential American nature, "All American artists are and have been geniuses, and there have been many American philosophers." Yes, every caribou-faced teaching assistant in the philosophy department at Harvard, every be-bopping poet in Harlem, every right-wing windbag who exhales in a New York-Washington microphone hails directly from a great pool of geniuses and philosophers, according to this American logic! and the Americans have a way about having their way . . . On the other hand, I can think of a number of reasons why bourgeois overconfidence and *innocence with regard to serious matters* should be reproved. While it is a brutal fact no one likes to admit, and this precisely on account of its brutality, that a people no longer in possession of its *vital instincts* has a certain knack for calling more geniuses into existence than actually exist, and have ever existed, such a people, even if it exacted an abstemiousness in regard to this matter of naming geniuses, would invariably draw the line in the wrong direction. To say the same with more economy: in an advanced democracy exclusivism is taboo. As Heraclitus says, they (—his Ephesians—) will have no genuine man among them in their efforts to make *everyone* genuine.—Very well; if the Americans have produced only one genuine genius, the questions arise: Why? How was he the *only* genius? Why for all his genius, had he only the bare external accoutrements, as it were, only the *appearance* of a genuine philosopher?—A genuine philosopher must live philosophy, and so a genuine genius must live his genius: just as a genius is a spirit of great intellectual energy who bridles this concentration of energy in his effort to take the world where it has never been, so the philosopher—I beg your pardon, I meant to say, the genuine philosopher—learns to live *outside the world*. To the extent that one who professes philosophy remains in the world, he forfeits his right to judge sentient being, and therefore his *right to philosophize*. Consequently, genuine philosophers are absolutists in the sense of never feeling at home in the practical world. They are the simultaneous negation and highest hope of this rude world. They have taken up residence beyond Darwin's apes *and* Darwin's humans, whose highest purpose is to survive and worship the fact of the evolution of their survival, i.e., their "inalienable" right to propagate ever more technical and successfully adapted chimpanzees; . . . or if you must have it specifically: the breeding of ever smarter and more clever teaching assistants, ever louder and more aggressive be-boppers, and ever more pompous and insular right-wingers. Good sense follows the well-worn paths, genius never, as Lombroso says, and the reason Charles Peirce was America's only genius *could* be connected to the palpable fact that in a nation of followers, Charles Peirce followed no one. Given the fact that American literature is the only literature in the history of the world not composed by intellectuals, we may confidently conclude (—aside from the painful fact that an "intellectual" in America and an intellectual in Europe are two very different, I should say *qualitatively* different specimens: for to be an intellectual in Europe is to be connected to an intellectual tradition and patrimony, whereas to be an "intellectual" in this country means composing politically sensitive pieces for the *New Yorker* and perhaps sporting a prepossessing, fustian mug like that little queen Truman Capote—) that all manner of literary activity per se is notoriously insufficient to miraculously turn every story architect into a candidate of such integrity and heroic devotion as one who aspires and is capable of aspiring toward something so noble and a rare as the authentic life of the mind. Peirce's essential genius, therefore, forbade his following anyone: he visualized himself as blazing a new path, not with James and Holmes, but *alone*. It is this solitude, again, this capacity for solitude, this heroism of the *marked man* who tramps ever onward toward the boundaries and inaccessible regions of the world; it is this solitude that leads the great man and woman into philosophy; yea, a philosophy eternally able to teach its lucky thrall what he or she *already knows*. (—As Zeno, shipwrecked, found his way to Athens, hungrily came upon Xenophon's winsome account of the Socratic wisdom—this is to say the Socratic ability to reside outside the world—and asked where he could find a man like this Socrates, he was really asking the way to himself, the path to his own philosophy, his own place beneath the great Aegean sun.—) More: what this lucky initiate *will become*!—But let us hurry again to our question: did Charles Peirce, casting off the respectable world with the same iciness the world had rejected him, in light of his bold negation of life, and therefore in accordance with his right to Sophia's embraces, go in unto her ancient and venerable boudoir to possess *her*? Peirce knew in his heart—for he confessed this to William James—that life's rejection of him constituted his concomitant *access* to philosophy. Yes, that there could be, according to Peirce's own account of the matter, more philosophy in a dark, garbage bestrewn alley in Manhattan than in Cambridge:—*this* is a question for philosophers!—But Charles Peirce rejected philosophy! He, our truest blueblood, America's elect, the handsome, glowering genius with hard ebony eyes—*rejected philosophy*! What? For all his women, our only genius was not capable of a *deep love*?—Well then; let us ask *why* Charles Peirce rejected philosophy (—for the fact that he stumbled upon a more genuine philosophizing in his poverty than he found among the leisured upper crust of Cambridge must be seen and understood as merely accidental—), specifically the *spirit of philosophy*. And here is our answer. He did so upon pragmatistic principles; to wit: on account of science and the narrow desideratum, *More research*!—Translation: flee spiritual insight; breed an unphilosophical race, an American race that perforce sees philosophy only in social protest, social gospel (—think of those righteousness-reeking muddleheads Daniel Berrigan and William Sloane Coffin, to name just two of our learned "compassionate" shortgrass preachers—), and all the other social-legalistic mass-stultifications nominated "freedom" . . . oh! did I mention "non-violence" with its "moral" and morally sick Gandhian/Tolstoyan insects rolling over on one side and playing dead?—Independent minds must seize upon genuine philosophizing as an *antitoxin* to all this social poison . . . Meanwhile, the most serious students of Peirce—those rare spirits who catch the whole of his philosophy (—I speak here of direction: the consequences of all his talk of consequences—) at one glance—notice the stark cleavage:

Peirce the pragmatist versus Peirce the man. As we have pointed out, the man already possessed all he needed to become a philosopher: honesty, apartness, the exceedingly rare capacity for genuine solitude, immersion in the literature, the ability to set an example for pupils, the happy marriage of heaviness and cheer, the need for the hard task, independence from the university with its menagerie of professors scrambling in a glass jar, boldness in confronting disorder, the feeling of unlimitedness that comes when comfort and fashion are cast aside, the iron nature that knows how to stand firm, and sometimes, reach out with placid fingers and tickle danger's toes . . . Then, at the threshold, he halts, *denies himself entry*, and goes the way of all scientific flesh! Yea, to corrupt the youths by denying access to any *other* perspective than the cultural insularity taught by those sanctimonious Unitarian tricksters Channing and Emerson—: this is the consequence of consequence-preaching, the narrowness of sequestering American thought from the rich literatures and philosophies of the rest of the world! To snatch the gifts of the gifted natures (—which, after all, have taken generation upon generation to come to fruition—) and throw these treasures of treasures upon the dirt and slime of the American assembly line! To constrict American writers to those themes and interests contiguous to an evolving frontier; to inculcate a solemn distrust of foreign ideas; to deny to philosophy its primary mission of passing judgment upon the direction culture takes; . . . horrid industriousness from early until late! the consequent need for a repellent entertainment to excite the nervous system of the weary and worked down, the exhausted! the duty to see all life and living as one big, happy, noise-polluted factory where the slightest slacking is worthy of punishment!—*To enthrone a busy race and its busy bee "philosophy."*—I mention here but a few of pragmatism's horrors . . .

332

I have searched in vain, scouring the ranks of our haughty, good-for-nothing conservatives, to find one soul possessing the sense of animating wonder, the drive to knowledge, and the courage to stroll through the "harvest wonderful" of the great race pragmatist Du Bois to see once and for all what kind of harvest it really is, what kind of pragmatism has been loosed, what changes for democracy have already been wrought by this our most ambitious, most energetic pragmatism, our *noisest* pragmatism.—For, as Plato says, the ceaseless din of fury is as important for democracy as the franchise and the shallow, debilitating spirit of restlessness in the law courts.—First principle: whatsoever a race pragmatist sows that shall he also reap. Du Bois hails this as the Deity. "Sing, O barren, thou that didst not bear! Cry aloud, thou that didst not travail with child! For the children of the misbegotten, even by my seed, shall inherit the desolate white cities and cause them to be inhabited."—Yea, William Edward Burghardt Du Bois, the *great* writer; (—I almost said great thinker but a) a pragmatist cannot be a great thinker, and b) it is baseless palliative to suppose, to contend, that every Negro American in Harlem who read *The Waste Land* and dabbled in leftist garbage was, and *had* to be, a "genius."—) must now reap the *idea* of the Golden Fleece from the cotton fields of the Georgia Black Sea.—For I will say it again: it is the *ideas* turmoiling in the black intellectual's head, the ideas and *nothing but the ideas*, that produce all his troubles.—What is an idea? When does an idea forsake its reality?—Yea, the great, "eloquent" writer has planted; . . . and as long as the earth remains, there shall be seedtime and harvest. What to do in the meantime? Speak! Out of the valley of dry bones, speak! Say unto dreams, "There are so many dreams not yet dreamed!" Say unto dawns, "There are so many dawns not yet broken!" Yea, prophesy the Not-yet rolling like a black caisson toward its All! Prophesy deliverance! Speak!—Re-do the idea of tolerance: formulate new rights and new wrongs; create new "thou shalts" and new "*thou shalt nots*!" See to it that this new morality overshadows all *other* morality . . . Specifically: formulate a "correct" and an "incorrect." Arrogate to one people the right to *bless and curse*. Let the black intellectual write beneath the correct heading "Tolerate the right things." Let him write beneath the incorrect heading, "Tolerance of the wrong things must be cursed and unblessed for all eternity."—At length, the softening of the American spirit brings with it the *bizarrest* of all immoralisms: military conquest abroad; moral canker at home. In one shameful word: the new morality of the new tolerance poisons everything. To be moral means, and can only mean, to think, and by extension to express, the correct things, i.e. the things decreed correct by the race-gender-lifestyle Schutzstaffel.—Let us ask this direct question—our original question—: what are the social consequences of race pragmatism?—The vast madhouse of correct thinking baptized moral brings with it firstly: hypersensitivity laced with fear; second: stupid imitation, the cowardliness of vain assimilation; third: to allow one's environment to determine an individual, for there to exist no more individuality, the *American* decadence.—If we were to tour this madhouse, what evils solemnly masquerading as "progress" and racial justice would we find? (—For believe me, the haughty bugaboo in all of this is our dear all-knowing, all-seeing "justice"—) . . . In Father Du Bois' Great House, there are many rooms; if it were not so social justice would have informed us. To wit . . . The weakness room: here one renounces resistance and wrath; one *succumbs*: one degenerates into exhaustion even as the extreme irritability flowing from constant machinelike behavior desiccates the critical faculty. The holy room: here one blesses the "ancestors" and communes with these "spirits." One conjures the blackest, evilest conjuration, "Compensate the ancestors for their sufferings. Compensate *me*." The hysterical room: the underminers are always and of necessity hysterical. They want their fits and rantings to become the centerpieces of every form of mythic, revisionist history. The stimulus room: weakness of will breeds the necessity for strong stimuli; one lives from stimulus to stimulus. (—Moral: never stop; never listen: consequently *never think*—) One no longer enjoys one's "highs," one *needs* them. The rhythm room: one must dance, and laugh, and play. One must experience the numbed happiness of the herd animal. The zero room: live the magic of virtue as the sum of all zeroes. Every culture, every people, every desire, every "contribution." These are so many equal quantities. The room of the expanding man (Burghardt Du Bois' favorite room): in this room one unlearns modesty and inflates one's needs into cosmic values. Here the mass is taught how to dominate its exceptions so that the exceptions no longer believe in themselves. The creation room (most popular room in the house): to have any *right to be* anything must first give the race pragmatist pleasure. The "ideas" of the race pragmatist are based upon feelings. All pragmatism springs from utilitarianism. The philosopher's room: as if philosophy *happens* when Alain Locke boogies his little gay booty across town to pop bennies with Brother Langston, mingling his spirit with the ancestors upon hearing "The Negro Speaks of Rivers," dirtying himself with the lie that being a Black homosexual, per se, is more than sufficient to produce the kind of authentic suffering real philosophy requires and has always required.—I have no words to express my contempt for such starved sick-brains as Monsieur Locke . . . oh! should I have said demoiselle?—The social room: in this room the elite social planners hammer, saw, and screw. The law-minded, law-bounded planners want to fashion institutions—social combinations—that will prevent every sort of suffering and distress. Thus, they—the last—want to *make law* for the first: this step-by-step process of legislation teaches the sound to see themselves as unsound; the good-looking are forced to hold the mirror in such a way that reveals their ugliness; the serene and comforted, the detached, stoical souls are made to feel the lash, the bites and belly pangs of guilt. The world is turned upside down. Why? Because of ignorance: the social planners fail to see where the remedy is to be found:—*not* on the outside, *not* in institutions, social rearrangements, new combinations. But the large-scale associations of herd animals are politically chameleonic: the left has its egalitarian socialism, the right its "Fatherland." And *you* . . . you have your race cards. There is always a card game going on somewhere in the Big House. The cosmic room—sometimes called the blueprint room, the Richard Wright/Jimmy Baldwin penthouse: here in this high-ceilinged, splendid room, with its gallery of tall windows flung open to the west, the prints are drawn for the eventual construction of the new religion, the new sexuality, the new race.—These then are the rooms in Du Bois' Great House. Every thought, every act and steely machination in this house proves exhaustion: *race pragmatism leads to exhaustion*. The exhausted bestow nothing, but only know how to take, to diminish. The exhausted know the black art of demonizing their opponents. They succeed only when they are seen not as the exhausted, but as the rich who know how to give to life: they take when they give us their "dreams" and their dreary new justice; they take when they write, associate, machinate, *breathe*. The race pragmatist is a parasite, a "generation of vipers." He knows *what* our public schools have become; and on account of *him*! He knows that his race-based agendas are so much insolence, so many lies!—Our conscience knows today what his sinister imputation "racism" means, *what end it serves*. Everyone knows too well. Where have our last feelings of decency gone when our political figures of whatever persuasion get down on their hands and knees to do cringing obeisance to these resentful extortions incarnate?

333

We simply must *learn to think differently* about pragmatism and the evolving Americanism flowing off from it. The Americans know or should know how any objective observer feels about the moral consequences of their "freedoms," not even to mention the immoral roots of their glorious "rights." (—Magna Carta and Constitutionalism, all the seminal skirmishes between the common law courts and the Crown, that "edifice more glorious than Greece or Rome," were, it must be remembered, given an entirely new direction by the perniciously blithesome notion hidden in the reptilian back-brain of the American founders that the hitherto strictly juridical import attached to equality should become a tool for homogenizing humanity and *breeding herds*.—) That a philosophy of consequences should not itself have consequences!—This is philosophical *self-abuse* at its worse, the low-water mark of the "unexamined life." That the Americans would even flirt with the prospect of constructing a system that—for all the Deism up the affluent sleeves of our "brilliant," bourgeois founders—a Deism, mind you, pregnant with the *plague bacilli* of Channingism, Emersonism, Social Gospelism, Deweyism, and all the other brave new "isms" so deliciously redolent of our new matrifocal world—consciously shuns any contact with truth; that the people should retain a right to mistakes—as in the famous dicta of Wendell Holmes and Learned Hand—yet manifest no inclination or capacity to learn from these mistakes (—for the mistakes of a people deemed ineluctably virtuous are immediately set into a fine print nobody ever reads: consequently, since no one ever learns from the democracy's lapses, the lapses are doomed to be incessantly repeated); that the "free flow of ideas," posits itself as the proud polar opposite of any sort of *selection*; that this free flow has no rhyme or reason absent the fairy tale of an ideological invisible hand (—such a fairy tale could only be propounded by French fairies with their "perfectibility of man," and, of course, by our own Charles Peirce and his stubbornly clung-to Hegelian atavism that goodness must prevail "in the end."): these self-evident truths, this intellectual racketeering, these abortions of hoaxes: these are the "truths" the *freethinkers of tomorrow* must resolutely set their faces against.—Someday, I promise it, these great independent spirits of love and scorn; these beautiful, and beautifully misunderstood solitaries, the halcyons whom earth and sky obey! the ones who will *give back* to us the freedom of our thoughts: *they must come one day*!!

334

Where is the artist, the saint, the thinker, the musician, poet, dancer, even the orator of the old school who let himself go in the moment of inspiration; in the act of creating, thinking, obedience to rhyme's reason and metric's strict rules? This constraint is the principal element in all religions and in every morality: obedience is the transfiguring aspect and agent of human existence. How did language attain its subtlety and strength? How did law hone itself out from merely general considerations of equitable custom?—Strict interpretation. Obedience in one direction.—So that when the slave says, "Nothing human is alien to me," he is really saying, Nothing merely human is alien to me (—only a slave could have propounded such a piece of utter vulgarity!—); this is to say, every kind of "tyranny" is impermissible, protracted constraint is immoral, etc. Every monster that emerges out of freedom's pit *would have* to be designated "good"—; for it is a slave who does the designating. But *we* believe that slaves and "freedmen"—even the descendants of freedmen—see all things with jaundiced eyes: their judgments and evaluations result, really, from a kind of delirium, a sort of optimistic unreason and refusal (—who knows?

an inability?—) to see things as they really are.—Regard the framers of the U.S. Constitution from this perspective: a bit too wine-buzzed by prevalent French notions of liberty, *perhaps* without even knowing it, they imported not a few of these notions into that infallible document (—and *not*, mind you, by way of "emanations and penumbras," but directly into the Constitutional text—), enshrining, again, *possibly* without an explicit awareness of Gallicizing the fundamental law, the fantasist superstition, Rousseau's superstition, which believes in the primeval, *buried goodness of human nature* and ascribes all the blame for this burying to the institutions of culture in the form of society, state, and education.—Thus, the remedy for bad speech, at least according to those who stormed the Bastille, as well as our dear wine-buzzed founders, is not any restraint on speech, i.e., expression, but precisely *more speech*. Now, why is this? I have already divulged the answer to this question. Must I say it *again*? Because mankind is *by nature good*, all finite badness will be cancelled and swallowed up in the end. Good will prevail come what may. Moral: impugn traditional religion with its "fall of man," which stands in the way to man's perfectibility (—yet *another* French brainchild, that of Marquis Condorcet—).—In sum: the American founders had their reasons for making the First Amendment absolute, and thus granting unfettered liberty to the journalists. You say, "The press clause is not absolute." Indeed; but the journalist greedy-guts want absolute dominion, and according to the maxim, "*expressio unius exclusio alterius*," the text says this much.—But should it be absolute? Certainly not if defamation and privacy actions are justified, i.e., if a person retains an interest in protecting his good name and his standing in the community from unlawful incursion.—Therefore, our issue—and, by way of our rule, to return to our original question.—Do the abuses of the journalists *outweigh* those harms the press clause was intended to prevent? Very well; let us state our rule, then let every reader parlay his or her application and draw a conclusion.—*You must know constraint and obey someone: otherwise you will lose all respect and come apart at the seams.*

335

To resolutely refuse something one knows to be true, to act as if it did not even exist; then whenever it "demonstrates its existence" by accosting us and slapping us squarely in the face, we hurriedly slam the door and bolt it—or, better, run out the back door as fast as we can—: this, surely, is nothing other than the herd's right of self-defense. Just as in law, this right presupposes statutes and bodies of case law that created the right, so culturally speaking, there must be previously sanctioned grounds for the herd's right to exercise this awesome and awesomely familiar right of collective self-deception. These grounds are the idols any free culture chooses to worship.—Here, I assume a "choice" where there is none, for idol worship raises the question of ancestors and what is *passed down* to us as venerable, holy, immune from critical questioning.—I give an example: Americans *know* they have swallowed a rotten apple, know the tenuity of their morals (—specifically how easily they allow themselves to be *led by the nose*—): but this knowledge must be refused at every turn.—"A democracy cannot work without an informed populace," they will swear on their infallible Constitution under glass, "and so a democracy cannot work without laissez faire journalism."—Thus, as every American knows what journalism is after, *what* manipulatory capers are baptized lawful and "healthy for a free society," this knowledge is denied in the name of "freedom," and the vice-addicts of broadcast swine are *again* given a pass. It so happens that even if these freedom lovers gained a vision that the media were authoring military defeats, nothing would be changed as far as the swine themselves;—their hypocrisy and greed—: nothing *could* be changed, for a people's religious rituals are at stake. The pathos that is developed out of this is called "debate." The journalist class, and *only* the journalist class, must inform, direct, and instigate this "debate," which, we are told, is the essence and earmark of free government. What *is* debate?—Closing one's eyes, going along with everyone else, so as not to suffer from the sight of corruption.—What a journalist *contends* is true must be false. This is our *political* theory of truth.—The *peccatum originale* of those American founders who could do no wrong?—Not the press, but the *free press*: as aforesaid, the laissez faire attitude to the media filth machine.—What? The founders *wanted* an infantilized mob?—These press-pharisees, these blusterers with "righteousness" gushing from their lips; these pushers of every neurosis into the consciousness of those few *whole human beings* who still breathe: in the vicinity of these gnats and fleas everything healthy *must become ill*.

336

Picture for a moment Count Tolstoy and Gorky at Yasnaya Polyana; Jane Addams and Dewey at the Hull House. Their quest: to demyth Christianity and *exploit* this secularized new dogma, this dogma of dogmas. Another quest: to teach exhaustion: to unseat vitality and stand the human animal on its head.—Secularization is the necessary link between "Resist not evil" with its spiritual meaning and "non-violence" in its brutal, mechanical, even comical dress; "love they neighbor," a dictum that must have hovering before it and around it a God-relation, as Kierkegaard would say, *reduced* to "love," winnowed down and emasculated to the *aequales sunt* of all cows loving the same things and hating nothing.—Love becomes a campaign to extirpate "hate"! Non-violence the insectization of mankind! to *renounce* in the name of "passive resistance," to submit to exhaustion, to lie down on the nail-beds of scrofulous mahatmas!—Supposing, however, one leaves these reefs and goes so far as to regard the emotion of hatred as life conditioning; then one has sailed into dangerous waters;—and danger is a sin wherever enforced safety and timid uniformity are preached! wherever Tolstoyanism and Deweyism have become sacred dogma for sacred cattle.—Again: in authentic Christianity, humility and meekness necessarily flow off from the primary God-relation (—just as in Quranic Islam violence is always present, always a possibility—); in communism and pragmatism, weakness, as the secularized avatar of humility—for there is *no God* in the Hull House, no Orthodox icons at Yasnaya Polyana—becomes a *task*: socializing the desires, the feelings; banishing all possibility of distance between human beings; purging every incorrect thought; uprooting all sense of pride; renouncing resistance, enmity, and wrath as atavisms; demonizing every symbolization of father authority; rank confusion of the natural with the unnatural; primalizing the earth, the mother, the Earth-Mother: all these pathologies and neurasthenic states are but symptoms and preludes for the eventual triumph of *new supreme values.*

337

The ancient Greeks, accustomed to dangers, upheaval, and the ever-present possibility of dangers and upheaval, found in philosophy a kind of escape and refuge—a "rock of salvation."—The Americans, in an incomparably more secure position, turn this around and see philosophy, reflection, and a genuine, and genuinely critical, life of the mind as danger, and they escape this danger with their busy lives.—Not the first time minds strong enough and original enough to initiate opposite estimates of cultural rank will have to transpose up into down, fire into ice, degeneration into hope. Make no mistake: the time will come when "ancient" faiths will be emasculated and inverted, and religions led astray, leaving behind only persecuted remnants and colonies to remain pure.—Can't you hear the thunder?—The whole sky is darkened, the sun is a memory!—Nightfall; unending rain!—Not just ark-builders for the sake of the undefiled will be needed, but a new kind of thinker will bring forth new leaders, new forgers of constraints; mission-men and fasteners of brutalities will arise; bringers of wars will come, and the earth will tremble; not because of "man," but on account of the *earth* ... Now my brooding, hovering, uncanny, melancholy visions—depart! depart!

338

Only fools would consider something "true" merely because it makes fools happy or better, and in this substantive sense the pragmatists are foolish philosophers; thus they are *worse* than fools!—Are not the peddlers of foolishness worse than their intended victims?—Charles Peirce scratched his head and asked himself this question, "Seeing as how everything firmly believed will soon—*very* soon—be gone with the wind, a new foundation must be laid, a new fundamental must be found. How can I deny the fundamental character of existence? For a nature of existence *is* the fundamental we will overpower. How to deny this bugbear? How to bury it?—I shall posit my consequence analysis! Truth is *made* as money is made."—Well, we anti-pragmatists stand at the opposite pole and say, "Something might be true even if it is harmful, so harmful, in fact, that the most complete knowledge of it would destroy the initiate who professes his profound love for it."—In other words: so far from denying any fundamental character of existence, we perceive this nature to be the exact *opposite* of its commonly accepted interpretation. More simply: it has been attenuated ... *falsified*. Why has it been falsified? Human need. Specifically: the need to make fools happier and better ...

339

Consider the great stories of Kafka and Rilke. Next, contrast them with modern American horror stories.—It segregates humanity into two inimical wholes.—Let any representative of what I shall designate as the lower ring delve as he or she will into the worlds of the great Germans. He will say after reading a few of the stories, "Not as good as X. Mr. X keeps me on the edge of my seat, keeps my adrenalin flowing, keeps me turning those pages. Plot, suspense, simple and neat description.—I like these things. The ones you call great are too diffuse, too heavy. To be very honest, they make me think—and I don't want to think. I want to escape reality, to fly away into another world. Isn't this the purpose of *fiction*?"—On the contrary: even as Marilyn Monroe read Dostoyevsky on the set, she realized that she could escape and think at the same time. She escaped ordinary reality by way of the Dostoyevskian stagecraft; she was *drawn back into existence itself* by way of the marvelous idea-laden nature of Dostoyevsky's work. This simultaneous going in and going out is the formula for serious literary work: it is a two-way street: the one-way thoroughfare denotes the vacuity of cabaret narrative. Why does the *lower type* read merely to escape? Isn't it because the common natures, quite aside from not possessing ears with which they may *hear* literature, simply seek a rest from their labor, a respite from all their activities? To these natures, reading for a serious purpose would be onerous, would constitute *more work*. What? Once the long, dreary work day is finished, the worker naturally seeks more work? But he is already worked down and can barely raise his little finger.—Very well then, our conclusion: only a special type of human may enter the world of great writing. Common natures—if the embarrassing truth were known—are *repulsed* by the classics, by art. In such an environment, they are unable to find their world—alas! a world from which they would fain escape!—What world is this?—Why, it is the world of ceaseless activity, mindless activity, industrious pragmatism. The religious pragmatism of those twin demythologizing pastors William Ellery Channing and Ralph Waldo Emerson furnished the Americans with the bizarre idea that the solemn refusal of foreign literature is a patriotic act; that the American industry implicit in the conquering of the frontier was sufficient for the human type *least* suited for industry. As if a spark, thrown off by the awesome energy ignited by the will's fearful activity, would—somehow; no one knows how the light of genius is born—fly up to live in *another realm*. Or better: as if someone lost in a forest would strive in the wildest way to find a new pathway out. Entirely fitting that *such* a secular faith would inhabit the guilty breast of a godless preacher! But, oh! even a dab of genius with no ideas, no living link to the conversation of mankind;—a pretty picture signifying nothing.

340

One surely must get rid of the bad taste of seeing philosophy, especially Greek philosophy, as abstracted from the practical activity pragmatists fondly nominate again and again as the principal thing: one should not lay this imputation at philosophy's door, then saunter away, as Dewey does, wearing that complacent smirk, which of late, serves as a cue for the raising of ever more strident objections against his "wisdom." That philosophy is related to the world only as a pragmatist, who by his own admission, is out to revenge himself on its history and highest examples, asserts, specifically that it is not related, not connected to the "dirt of private fact," etc., is, as Comrade Kierkegaard would say, simply fantastic. Even the Seducer of Copenhagen politely *assumed* that what goes around also comes around. As one would expect, Plato assumed it.—Modern philosophers are fond of marking themselves off from all former dogmatic excursions and dogmatic flights, and indeed, modern philosophy is that which sees itself as essentially different from ancient philosophy, which took dogmatism to be its undisputed first principle, and medieval philosophy, which unfortunately, abrogated its right to be philosophy as it was, from beginning to end, subservient to religion. Yet, here, precisely where it matters most, a beer is a beer is a beer, and it is high time someone comprehends this! That there exists or does not exist a good-in-itself, that truths should or should not be true for everyone, that philosophy is remote or proximate, etc.;—these things are only stumbling blocks and deferments—only, as it were, fodder for professors' glosses and beer hall arguments—; for the time has arrived when philosophy will be seen even as it sees, when Sophia reveals her strong arm, and reaches out, once again, for her due!—But let us return to the wording of the indictment. Philosophy is accused of remoteness and aristocratism. Philosophy is accorded the victory of sublimity but also the defeat of ridiculousness, according to Herr Professor James, because philosophy is *drawn up and away* from the practical realm, divorced from the "concrete," abstracted from "experience." We will allow this much. For if philosophy transcends experience and then stops there, up in the clouds, "separated from particulars," as the anti-Platonists say, then, presto! the defendants are duly charged and bound over for trial.—Well, then! *Does* philosophy stop there? *Can* philosophy stop there?—Let us evoke a brief contrast with the law. Pragmatism's critique of law is essentially correct (—although, for reasons I don't care to discuss, it goes too far—). It is a fact—whether Catholic law schools admit it or not—that when law separates itself from society, jurists turn themselves into monks in ivory towers, working out legal axioms and corollaries which, even if true, don't meet the needs of the society law purports to serve. Legal rules are in a state of flux; this means that since law *follows* society, the job of judges is to overhaul the rules so that the rules keep pace with society. All the pithiest Holmesian obiter dicta—"The life of the law has not been logic it has been experience," etc.—are subsumed beneath this basic idea: when legal rules are abstracted from society they are ineffective, just as when Catholics are separated from their "Lady," *they* are ineffective.—But not so with philosophy. God pity our pragmatists and their Sancho Panza, John Dewey, when they say philosophy is no higher than law; but to *deny* philosophy its potency is precisely *what it means to be a pragmatist*.—What then *is* philosophy's potency? And to whom is her strong arm revealed?—American philosophy, so-called, Cambridge

Pragmatism emerged out of the agonal element in law; specifically: the exploiting of this instinct for adjustment of competing interests as a means for achieving two basic goals: a) to *geld* philosophy, to put it into a subordinate relation to science and legal method; b) to clear the way for associated living, for the rule of Deweyism. Pragmatism is thus touted as introducing a variation into philosophy: "love of wisdom" becomes a method to change the world, i.e., philosophy and social change are one and the same thing (—thus the natural overlap with Marxism—). Sophia's right to occupy a height and *look down* has been taken away from her and destroyed. There is no more philosophy. And what remains?—Science. Technosophy. Legalism. Popular culture.—Pragmatism must see social change as coming from below, from the sublunary realm, *never* from above: from the techno-planners and journalists with their fad-gizmos, "Constitutional mandates," and fake-images; from the legal profession with its "Brandeis briefs," monkeyshines, and showman's lies; from the pop icons, the scribblers, actors, moguls, and playboys, who "test consequences" as they scribble, dance, hoard, and playact. Let Langston Hughes peck out another be-boppin' boogie-ditty; let Richard Wright right another head-hung Tom Dooley wrong, and we've got a "movement." Let Hugh Hefner forfeit his favorite muff, a gold-digging spitfire on a round bed, and to compensate he launches a "revolution." Let Jerome Salinger bandy the word "phony" around for two teenybopperish minutes; let pop Professor Marcuse smoke a bowl of Columbian with those bereted Che Guevara look-alikes who call themselves "students," huddled in a circle, praying to Chairman Mao's buck teeth, and we inherit a "youthquake," dopey, clueless, and "committed" as all youthquakes are.—In one word: the pragmatists cannot recognize their pop icons as "abstracted from practical activity." The pragmatists know or should know the direct linkage between intellectual ferment and social evolution. Why, then, do the pragmatists deny this same kind of potency to philosophy? Because to affirm *here*, precisely here where the pragmatistic fears are acutest, would introduce an invidious bias into the happy herd of associated pragma-cows; precisely here philosophy must be halted at the gate.—The specific fear? The specific enemy?—*Greek philosophy.*—Aristotle must have been mentally ill to come up with that piece of subversion which says, "Leisure is the basis of culture." Philosophy unchained is the veritable womb of culture! The thinkers, the *higher men*, live beyond the rulers, and, as Nietzsche said so well, use the rulers as tools.—Yea, let us long for that *place* where free men and free women are found! Let us envision another kind of honor, another kind of courage! You, for whom this condition suffices, you fearless souls hovering above your brothers and sisters of action, the sullen, snarling, teeming mass of ordinary, and sometimes, extraordinary souls who ceaselessly translate your words into doughty deeds, your happiness alone consists in your "communication" of this heroic condition. Let this one thing be your free, exalted communication: that you have nothing else to communicate: thus, your privation and hope become one and the same! The long story you tell is the tale no one has yet told: that of two radically different kinds of freedom, the starkest contrast of actions and practices. You who think more and feel more, you who live in dark caves and perch on wild crags; you whose poetry is rehearsed for thousands of years—beware, beware! As the practical doers hate and contemn your dreamlike unreality, and do not understand how you create, so the age itself will hate you. The citizens of this age reject any higher type of man. They are the little people who no longer believe in the higher nature of the ruling caste; the bourgeois cattle who no longer believe in serene men and great saintly women; the technics and scientific planners who no longer believe in the philosopher.

341

I consider it a minor but at any rate significant event in the history of American attempts at philosophy and responsible thought, indeed an occasion worth celebrating, whenever one of those Quinean logical analysts, who since the day he was accepted as a budding graduate student has debased the philosophic spirit in word, example, and deed; who corrupts the youths by *sucking dry* the living potential for the philosophical life; who by his logical stultification of the field of vision prevents anything that passes for genuine insight into the human predicament;—I consider it worth noticing when this pompous, tasteless crew cut finds—via logic, of course!—his *locus paenitentiae* at last and carts off all his logic books in the direction of the university bookstore. Then my mood changes somewhat when I see this man, after his belated refutation of the entire "epistemological enterprise" as so much jejunity and futility, throw himself into narrative fiction as a drowning man hoists his better leg upon a piece of flotsam—the idea being that, since "knowledge" in the form of propositions and judgments is impossible, all humankind can do is recognize literature as a means of "furthering the human conversation"—and concomitantly recognize American Pragmatism as a unique "problem-solving philosophy" adumbrative of "human progress" and "evolution" in the service of the Deweyan mandate to breed and teach industrious herds how to be "happy" in a correct-thinking, pluralistic anthill—; it is then I think I am sitting in a jam-packed audience at Comedy Central.—And yet surely anyone who sees in Professor Rorty's celebrated conversion anything other than the same old analytic raddle-daddle and sly logical imposture of the Quines, Putnams, Goodmans, Kuhns, and Sellarses of the world and adrenalizes himself with dearly held fantasies over that crisis in disintegrity we now refer to as the "new pragmatisms" certainly either doesn't enjoy the best of natural eyesight or had better remove his blinkers. Assuming the chicken does indeed pre-exist the egg, it must be confessed that pragmatism is a specifically American *outcome* of skepticism; in this case, the new skepticism in epistemology. And the cocoon out of which classical pragmatism emerged? Precisely the skepticism in legal method. Everything happens as if this Rorty fellow has succeeded in *spoofing* himself into the presumptively dubious status of *primum inter pares* American celebrity intellectual. What is the difference between saying on the one hand, with Holmes, that the Constitution embodies only *relative rules of fundamental right*—that there are no legal absolutes; that the once crucial natural law has outlived its usefulness; that, *consequently*, natural rights have no metaphysical grounding and may survive, *mutatis mutandis*, absent such grounding, etc.—and claiming on the other hand, with the new pragmatists, that there is no privileged relationship between the mind and nature, and consequently, there is justification of rationality only *within* particular social practices, language games, vocabularies, contexts, paradigms, i.e., not outside them and between them? That an omelet is made from stolen eggs is one thing; that a logician's leg gets caught in his own web is another. Let us examine the nature of this notional mesh. Given epistemic skepticism, relativism (—a hopelessly muddled lay term Professor Rorty uses because he can get away with it—) *should* appear in some itchy form, but our pragmatist is not dismayed. Kuhn's paradigms and Wittgenstein's language games transport themselves into a multiplicity, indeed an infinity, of self-contained social worlds of reason-giving: eternal verities—and, quite unbeknownst to Rorty, with them the cherished rights of man—morph felicitously and pragmatistically into contexts, i.e., vocabularies. Now there can be no reasons outside these vocabularies for adopting any specific vocabulary for where is the grid of concepts that would mandate such adoptions? Like the truculent, frowning African philosopher who feeds on his revenge sandwiches—revenge against the White man's hegemonic concept of reason; that horrible blueprint for the master and his slaves—the new pragmatists seek a kind of moral politesse or queue of equal discourses, a castrated isopolity of participation and contribution (—I emphasize the word "castrated" for every contemporary "reconstruction" of Deweyan philosophy, believe me, is nothing other than a war against *male values* whether our literati, cosmopolitan big-heads, and

African frowners *comprehend* this or not—). And this, of course, is nothing other than a continuation of Dewey's war against the contemplative ideal, for what *is* the ideal of the primordial contemplator, i.e., the genuine philosopher who arrives late so he can *look down*; what can this lordly ideal be but the hated master-vocabulary of the despised philosopher-legislator who commensurates and hierarchicalizes the discourses and *imposes discipline* upon the rising, headily proliferating voices in the conversation of mankind?—No master vocabulary?—Away with all masters!—Whatever practices are endorsed by the ethnos: the lowlands of the herd conscience!—Whatever it is these blackleg philosophers do, whatever language games they tricksily play, I see but one foundational remissness in all their vaunted attempts to fabricate a political morality supportive of their precious discourse democracy; to wit: the glaring absence of any quest to *dig down* into the very artifacts they prize so dearly. Instead, I witness the same old story: business-as-usual for the briefcase carrying, never-to-be-ruffled-out-of-his-essential-coziness, professorial supposititian: the "philosopher" either demonstrates that an appeal to transcendent standards ought to be abandoned, propounds an unvarnished appeal to the practices and values of particular societies as the only answer, or gingerly threads a path between these alternatives; . . . when what nominally endowed, distracted, half-conscious observer will not confess that all this tedious business is as old as the rhumba! The incapacity for a truly critical consciousness consequent upon the abdication of the genuine philosopher's mission: *this* is the inherited stupor and stupidity of the new pragmatisms! this is the explanation for their obsession with fleeing an unhealthy relativism that would prevent them from putting *their* political morality on display; that would prevent them from touting *their* "vocabulary" as superior to other vocabularies (—when, forsooth, *within* this vocabulary the bare mention of something as superior to something else is greeted with fear, trembling, and "prior restraints on expression"—). Oh, you pragmatists! You childlike, erring, malicious pragmatists!

342

Everything happens as if this Habermas fellow—Dewey's "legitimate heir," this is to say the only legitimacy we will allow him—wants us to *forget* everything we have learned about democracy. For the goods on this maundering Teuton one need only consider the source. By nature, *another* liberal German theologian tutored to tell a good lie, this *theologus liberalis vulgaris* strayed into pragmatism by dreaming two not entirely unrelated dreams at once: the Marxian and the Deweyan; and not to forget, a *pious* German philosopher's need to rework the old categorical imperative.—Habermas observes from his bird's eye view, and hence from the perspective of his bird's comprehension, that political questions have a moral core susceptible to argument; that, pursuant to his *lofty* ideal of discursive democracy, the existing political culture can no longer be immunized against rational demands for legitimation. I suppose birds are apt to think such lofty birdlike things whenever they *fly over* socio-politico-legal landscapes: for birds are designed to fly over landscapes; as far as I know, they have never had occasion to dig down into the landscapes and sift through the practices they sing so prettily about. Once again: behind all the pragmatistic hand-wringing over practicalities we find nothing but im-practicality; the problem here being the amount of information cognizable within the discursive apparatus itself. In the age of Bodin and Locke, political philosophers could afford to talk about concepts: the general, confronting the particular as a superior force, commanded practice, and received the homage of social fact. To say the same thing: bird's eye view political philosophy worked in those days when arguments and "discourse" were sufficient, when debate was recognized as the self-corrective vehicle of a self-correcting system. What then? You pragmatists will sermonize about social flux and change and—in practice!—disallow the fact of change? Specifically the fact that democracy is alive and grows even as the common law is alive and grows (—that this kind of legal system is experimental and inductive as opposed to a Romanist system—)? Then you will admit that democracy changes; that the American democracy today is different, even (—assuming we dig down into the facts the concepts represent and exchange our wings for shovels—) *radically different?* Very well. Instead of talking in a vacuum, baptizing "debate" and receiving it into democratic procedures as the holiest of sacraments, Herr Habermas should clip his wings for the precise purpose of practicing a little political *downdigging*: if he wants to find the truth of debate as it is actually done in an advanced democracy today, let him consult the American Constitution, the acknowledged cornerstone of world democracy. (—Let him, if at all possible, consult the fundamental law not as a high school student or bleary-eyed journalist in j-school consults it; and certainly not as our amply-larded, smooth-jowled, golf club-swinging right wing radio windbag.)—Now, assuming our *profound* German philosopher, instead of merely thinking in broad outlines about norms, values, law, and policy, possesses a modicum of talent for sifting through relevant legal issues, let us look on as he studies the cases beneath the broad heading, Freedom of Expression. Then, not content to see principles applied to facts, we will go out into American society with a dogged determination to adhere to the main requirements of authentic philosophizing: first, courage; the courage not to keep any question back; second, to see everything others do not comprehend problematically as a problem to be investigated, and if possible, solved; finally, to forego every foregone conclusion, aim, and goal so that the problem under consideration is tackled by pellucid truthfulness itself (—note, please, that this latter element of authentic philosophizing is impossible for an orthodox or revisionist Marxist—). We will then notice exactly how the cases are applied, ever ready to measure the moral phenomena that spring up out of this soil.—And the verdict?—Precisely that debate in a democratic milieu has nothing whatsoever to do with truth (—*Invectives Against the Idols*, 2006—). Sad but true, the government by consent these pragmatists and political philosophers get so worked-up about is nothing other than *manipulated* consent.—Argument? Reasons? Oh, don't try my patience! Our tempo dictates, today our *nature* dictates, that we no longer possess any capacity to listen, let alone weigh arguments and reasons. And these last observations—unfashionable as they are—lead us straight into the belly of that nonstop, never-to-be-placated Filth Machine we know as American journalism. But why should I say more about this incurably depressing case of narcotica, exhaustion, and decline, especially when I have better, more cheerful things to do?

343

One certainly does not have to possess the best or biggest ears to continually notice that the word "context' has a way of lingering on the tongues of those loquacious Peter Pans recent American philosophy has dubbed the new pragmatists. After flying over the work of John Dewey for so many years these fairies concluded that it is time to revitalize and reconstruct the residue of his basic homiletic;—for even devitalizations need revitalizing from time to time; a periodic updating as a legal rule is updated by overhauling its core in the face of changes in the society; especially so once it is recalled that the genesis of classical pragmatism consists of intuitions about legal phenomena, viz: that the *interest* constitutive of public policy in tort theory of causation of attaching liability somewhere gets transmogrified, finally, into the "interest of the knower." Then, aha! We arrive at the real genetic meaning of the notion of context.—There even exist supracontexts out of which, and on account of which, a whole repertory of philosophies, I should say *possible* philosophies, make their appearance, rising as it were, out of human matrices like dead men emerging from the bottom of a lake. Not unlike literature, philosophies are reflections of a people, arise out of a people, and thus trace again and again invisible trajectories as proper expressions of their respective peoples. What then? Anglo-American analytic philosophy as it veers or might not veer off in the direction of pragmatism is there as a philosophy to shore up and legitimate science? Yet it is no accident that logical analysis is an Anglo-American invention, an English efflorescence (—and with regard to Wittgenstein it ought to be understood how easily the English temper is imprinted upon a mind; just look at the way, say, Niebuhr the German absorbed pragmatism as if by osmosis and incorporated it into his theology; e.g., his notion of the hidden Christ and his whirligig of the pragmatic "proof" of God—): obsession with language, the usages and meanings of words: this orientation, along with the aforementioned fixation on interest, suggests that this philosophy didn't emanate from science; that its trajectory isn't preponderantly and primarily scientific (—for the Continent was no less saddled by scientific method as England and America—). Therefore, I conclude that Anglo-American philosophy grew out of its Anglo-American "context," that is, the expression of its people, and that its trajectory, quite unbeknownst to the philosophers who cannot see *beyond* any trajectory—for how could *they* occupy such a God's eye view?—is the precise logical method that has informed such a hard-headed people obsessed with legal issues since Runnymede: the method of the common law.—Since philosophies do *not* come into the world arbitrarily and autonomously—the Hegelian conviction that they are connected organically is itself but an adumbration of a larger truth—but emerge out of the peculiar ethos of a race;—that the philosophical genius, not unlike the great artist and religious reformer, through cumbrances linked not to an outer but an excessively refined and delicate inner kind of torment, has drawn off from millions of ordinary souls the quantity of spirit nature failed to allocate evenly and democratically—; this fact is in the end demonstrated by the essentially *spellbound nature* of philosophers: however independent their critiques and coherences may seem, it is their spiritual surplus that drives them to dance around the same center and flesh out identical iconographies. Just as the surplus of spirit is innate, in like manner the relations of possible philosophies to an invisible center is also innate. So that when the philosopher thinks, I suppose, nay, whenever *any* thought is thought, it is in reality not an independent flowering or gushing up out of nowhere, but a kind of reminiscence and return to a fantastic parental hearth. In this sense, the philosopher is always turning to look at the past, even when he thinks he is courageously pursuing the future. (—By correlation, he perceives the energy he expends upon his work and wonders how this energy can be expended upon his life? Thus, there is a boundary at the very heart of being, and the whole problem of geist and leben is a reflection of this—). Again and again, artists and philosophers present their wonderful bouquets to humanity; humanity has provided for the flowers *beforehand* by supplying the soil, the sunshine, the rain; the artist-thinker furnishes merely the string to bind them. Perhaps this overstates this strange case a bit, but I trust you get the idea. How then to escape this dominating and directing hand? Well; . . . to this rather hasty and presumptuous question, I can only reply, "Strait is the gate and narrow the way, and *few* there be who find it." Suffice it to say that ideas most certainly do *not* come from any blank slate. Ah, but who lifts up his eyes to see this handwriting on the wall?—Given that philosophies are sign languages of and orbital motions about an invisible but felt center, one would do well to find the first falling domino. Without question this Anglo-American analytic pragmatism—and yes; Wittgenstein too—emerged out of that *fundamental attitude*, that all-important center of the English common law as opposed to the older, Roman conception. Logical analysis and American Pragmatism are products of the Anglo-American race revolving about legal method just as the new African philosophy is a by-product of invisible racial mechanisms. The African philosophers must trace again and again the same trajectory; and one ought to ask this question: at which point will the tediousness of all this begin to bore the finer minds? For surely all great philosophy is untimely. But with regard to Africa and African philosophy, the trajectory is destined for expansion, not abandonment. This philosophy is *race philosophy*, pure and simple: the "hegemonic concept of Western reason" is just another name for the colonizer: the rush to define the African intellect is the direct result of the presence of Western reason, i.e., the presence of the White man in Africa. Either the African mind is subjugated or segregated; and this on account of which one specific fact? The fact of European colonization and the African's sense of being violated (—which means, psychologically, the African congenital *inability to forget*—). Everything, philosophically speaking, is thus set up and prepared *in advance* for a succession of philosophic events; whether these events are or can be pridefully characterized as systems, bold architectonic, or some yet-to-be invented pyrotechnic to punish and repel the collective ghost makes no difference: everything comes under the spell of racial conditions.—When we turn to the phenomenon of race pragmatism in America, and take a leisurely, self-flagellating look at the *syncopations* of those ragtag "philosophers" in the Harvard Can't-Touch-This-Afro-American Studies department, this spell becomes a kind of seasickness. The power of this sickness has penetrated deep into the heart of America; and since Ellison's "visibility" as a racial salve is one of its many symptoms, we find this sickness nestling everywhere, and thus distorting everything. But isn't it the mission of "philosophy" in America, including, of course, that golden calf of political nervousness we call democracy, to distort everything? Well then, why raise an eyebrow at the race pragmatist's Marxianization of this calf as the great black hope? These race-baiters want to burn the image of their tightened sensitivities and constantly abraded feelings, the image of their self-fabricated "moral" lacerations into the hide of every soul that does not *look like them*; someone or something must be made to suffer for their malformation; they necessarily become the intellectual apology for the morally retarded, the morally insane. But they never call themselves the retarded, the insane, the decadent; they call themselves the good, the worthy, the "beautiful." Here in the black intellectual's *ghetto-world of imagined oppressions* a sense of cruelty parades about as justice; tolerance becomes intolerance of those who think differently; the will to persecute, specifically the privilege to *bless and curse*, to backbite, delate, dirtify, and calumniate as "racist" become desiderata of self-defense. With froggish cynicism, our intellectual for the bloodless, the weak, the self-subjugated scours world history to assess epochs, nations, individuals according to whether they were conducive of spiritual revenge or resisted it. Blessing and cursing are not enough: they must *perform miracles*: they must perform the miracle of falsification by translating the whole national past *into racial terms* so that today the entire culture seconds this falsification: the *lie* of this self-perpetuating, nauseous race swindle permeates every higher law with hieratic pomp and pedantic precision. For understand this: the racial advancement organizations have *dissanctified* every higher law. What are higher laws? A higher law is every law not called into being by the raceosopher's enmity. Yes, according to his own admission, our black intellectual is at war with society; what never gets noticed—and this is precisely because we are too busy formulating more ideological taboos—is that this war is waged not because the intellectual, like the Romantic hero, has truthfully adjudged the society to be "bad," but because *he* is bad. Generally, the trajectory this "philosophy" must continuously travel is the festering furor over slavery; specifically, it is the Hegelian master and slave as it actuated the racial imagination of W.E.B. Du Bois; thus actuating him to *numinize ancestors*. Finally: just as these trajectories—invisible to the philosophic laborers themselves whose lot in life *can* only consist in showing up, punching a time card, going through the motions, and trudging home for a mule's share of entertainment designed *for* mules—are appropriate to and adumbrative of the dawn of a *new age*, so the youthful Cervantic dreamers, at work even now, must wait patiently on *their* dawn; these new philosophers on an *untrodden path* shall complete the construction of a *counter-ideal*, a counter-reckoning to the triumphalist matriarchalism threatening our hemisphere with the reversal of all values! What I am saying is that the gradual matriarchalization of Europe and North America is at the same time an involuntary arrangement for the eventual appearance *somewhere* of a machismo philosophy; a *great* philosophy that will ground a political reaction such as the world has never seen: the awe-infusing facing off of diametrically opposed *states of soul*.—

344

It is never the philosophers, but only the *non-philosophers* who are congenitally bent on dethroning philosophy from its privileged position, i.e., the "professional philosophers," celebrity intellectuals, and certain temp-scholars with a flair for psittacism. Any real philosopher would never think of such a thing. Yet these polished academicians claim that such a reduction of philosophy is consequent upon the "end of metaphysics," the passing out of vogue of the correspondence-adequation notion of truth, the disintegration of the "old" language, etc. What? The end of metaphysical thinking must necessarily entail the reduction of philosophy to a literary genre alongside other literary genres for the most part there to please and amuse? The demise—or alleged demise—of metaphysical thinking has nothing to do with American Pragmatism's obsession to *do away with philosophy* by gelding the philosophers. Again: when philosophers advocate such abdication of mission, we have a new wrinkle in philosophy; otherwise, it's asinine business as usual. One could say, with some truth, that Dewey's leftist phobias were the necessary conditions for his dream of keeping the Americans un-philosophical, non-philosophical, the *anti-philosophical race* par excellence; oh, this dumbed-down race of gluttons grunting about equal rights!—One must, for example, cease seeing a contradiction in two contradictory things; *lest* some metaphysicalized aura attach itself to the things; *lest* we perforce spawn another hierarchy, another privileged class of thinkers (—for these thinkers, I can promise you, will work to undermine every value pragmatists hold dear—). Phobias aside, it could be the *profound* child-emancipator Dewey, that most *refined* child molester of human history, is only aligning philosophy with the tenderized and pampered taste of a mellowed democracy (—a tender democracy made tender by the morbidity of pragmatism, and not to forget, developments in the law inspired by pragmatism's progeny, legal realism—). Well, whatever the case may be, I can only reply that the pragmatist's campaign to reduce philosophy, to geld the discipline into the mellowness of an audience-pleasing literary genre, to thus corrupt the wild and sumptuous philosophic youth—and to tie all this in to a pragmatistic restatement of modern philosophy's lack of taste for foundationalism—; this commotion has nothing at all to do with *severity in the things of the spirit*; nay, it stands to reason that a genre of subversive philosophizing will come upon the scene; a deeper (—I say deeper, for depth in America today means first and foremost the capacity of an individual to penetrate behind and below "debate" in a society stretched to the limits of its "rationality"—), tenser, *wickeder* kind of philosophizing in view of the fact that the American scene has become tenser and wickeder. If your sheltered existence never once imagined how wicked philosophers can be, you had better take another gander at the pug-nosed old erotic of the Agora. Our mad and fascinating mask-wearing and adaptability, chaos of other-directedness, mingling in all directions, nomadism, racial restlessness, thought control, marriage of mediocritism and hermaphroditism;—in all this the spirit sees its advantage, and in the end, gives rise to that which the bland and somnolent encomiasts of mellow modernity would be least inclined to anticipate.—Meanwhile, we witness, we *must* witness, a devolution: the obsession with foundations turns into the search to relieve the obsessive agony; here the learned doctors in the seminar room prescribe two medications for relief: the twin notions of language games and vocabularies; medications that, if taken according to directions, produce a malady of a different kind, but because it *gives pleasure* to the agonizing and sick, isn't recognized as a malady. Indeed, the whole meaning and purpose of the thought of neo-pragmatist Richard Rorty is such pleasure taking (—while the consequence of such pain-killing is another matter; a matter for those philosophers who eagerly squint around the corner, seeking as all philosophers do, to concoct a name for the bogeyman, I should say bogeywoman, materializing before their innocent eyes—); whatever tickles the fancy of this Paracelsus in the seminar room is adopted as the latest therapy for philosophy; whatever he finds "liberating" is forthwith celebrated as redemption and transfiguration, as if *his* pleasure, *his* tinkering constituted an end of the affair! In all seriousness: even scholars should ask themselves this one question: is this Paracelsus capable of performing any new magic trick? Well, you savants who frown so easily will have to excuse me, but when Rorty mounts his high horse, he can only ride around and around the same logical-analytic epicenter. What is he saying that hasn't already been said? Even Heidegger has pronounced upon it. His famed "relativism"—in fact the whole neo-pragmatism ball of wax—is the unabashed christening of an ethnosophy, which, as I have said elsewhere, is the abdication of philosophy in the manner of the Greeks; this is to say a fallowing of the ground for the return of the ancient, pre-patriarchal religion: *here* contemporary American and French thought—with the new vengeful African philosophy—are three peas in the same pod. In fact, everything moves toward this one destination; and yes, you conservatives move with everything else. When the philosophers chant "farewell to reason," you can bet they have something up their sleeves (—whether *they* know what this something is couldn't be more of a non-question from the all-important standpoint of the future of mankind—). Just as, say, the freeing of sexuality from the hold of Christianity was probably intended by Nietzsche, he couldn't have intuited that his piping would lead *downward, away* from spirit and light, to the ultimate leveling decreed by the Great Mother herself. Yea, when the first blades of grass sprouted above Marx's coffin, Engels could hail her possible rule as the ultimate Marxist solution for the ultimate Marxist problem.—To return to pragmatist Rorty. What pleases *any* pragmatist is the practice of substituting vernacular for facts in such a way as to yield a profit. In other words, it is profitable to ignore facts. Why fool around with facts when you don't have to? Facts don't exist independently of the manner in which we reconstruct them using words. Again: our capacity for inventing new vocabularies to express human need outweighs the question whether our propositions comport with anything real. Consider this: disputes are based upon facts (—whether the actor makes a mistake and thus believes a non-fact to be a fact is another matter—). To solve the dispute, an untainted forum for the weighing of adduced evidence is created. Within the forum, this adduced evidence is not itself a fact or facts, but represents facts. The facts giving rise to the dispute are re-created inside the evidential arena and these dramatized occurrences *purport* to be representations of the "things themselves." But what happens in practice? The evidence adduced within the forum doesn't correspond to the facts, those unalterable events in the past, but with a tendentious reconstruction of the facts, i.e., a "theory" of the facts, a theory of the case, as it is known in the law. True evidence consists in the correspondence of fact A with representation B. False evidence is a lack of correspondence. Thus, with regard to direct testimony, if a purported witness didn't witness fact A but was told by another that A did indeed occur, the hearsay rule disqualifies the first declarant but not the one who actually witnessed the event, even though the disqualified testimony might have been perfectly true. Why would true testimony, absent the satisfaction of a relevant exception to the rule, be disqualified? Because the fact-representation correspondence has been ruptured; it does not, in fact, exist. Now it goes without saying that a theory of the case that can be *sold* to the trier of fact yields a profit, even though the case theory is at odds with the true facts. What then has been pulled off? Precisely the substitution of the reconstruction for the facts: the standard, yet at the same time, the ultimate pragmatist caper. The pragmatist wants plausible salability, "warranted assertibility." He must not merely make truth; he must *sell* it—and sell it for the highest profit. After all, a pragmatist does not philosophize—does not fabricate, buy, and sell—for *nothing*.—When Rorty gets worked-up over "language games and vocabularies" (—how long will it be before these philosophers realize that their magnificent obsession with language is a determined adversary of thought and is in truth a kind of convenient stand-in for an authentic relation to the possibilities of *practicing philosophy* in this getting-nuttier-by-the-hour nuthouse of modern ideas?—) he is functioning as an instrument or mirror, not an end in himself: he is, in short, a commentator whose *significance* consists in tickling his own fancy. This is done by effectively turning philosophy *into politics* so that the philosophical demonstration of the correctness of any intellectual choice has been "redefined" away. Philosophy becomes, as aforesaid, a kind of literary genre of quasi-private language that—via Rorty's tickled fancy—can do nothing but tickle readers.—"But," you say with a look of desperation, glancing at that stack of Kuhnian philosophy of science books by the window; "the linguistic turn is essential to the understanding of the *problems* of philosophy, the problems of knowledge over which I lose sleep and on account of which I pace the floor!"—Oh, you academic and "public" intellectuals! You who strain at a gnat and swallow a camel! You who send a contingent of rabble to perform kingly tasks! You'll wring your hands over the problems of philosophy, thus in some incalculable sense making yourselves tolerable to yourselves, all the contented while never once suspecting that it is philosophy as it is done in the United States of America—where the herd bestows the honors; where the religion of tenderness, mellowing, and sisterhood fanaticism hurls down its edict-taboos to achieve redemption from the guilt of the past, from the "columns of hell" as Hannah Arendt said so well, to erect the image of a savior, i.e., itself—; *this* is the beginning of the problem! No; not that there *is* no correctness; for philosophy, philosophy on its knees, philosophy that suffers from sluggish digestion, merely *seconds* all the edict-taboos that make genuine thought, genuine *anything*, well nigh impossible in this advanced democracy (—and by the time you read this we can dispense with the "well nigh"—).—Those who *allow* the smallest, the most vengeance-addicted, to lay down laws for them; those who *permit* the wracked, bungled, coke-corroded claque in our dearest Hollywood; those nervous, perpetually cocked and ready-to-accuse-and-destroy freemartins in the brotherhoods for racial advancement; those who allow such pitiful abortions to *dictate*; well: when you see for yourselves against the far horizon the rising of a cloud the size of a man's hand . . . *beware!*

345

What are the pragmatic logical analysts really doing? Formulating imagined positions then reconciling these positions with other positions. Yet is it any mystery that preference is the operative factor in all their reconciliations? The staking out of their theatrical formulations occurs within the context of a continual metastasizing of one central question: claims, i.e., formulations of the mind's potency or impotency to know the data independent of it. Then all this metastatistical rigmarole gets transported into a philosophical playpen for logicians: philosophy becomes the academic sport of academic egos (—remember the Saul Kripke, W.V.O. Quine, Ruth Barcan Marcus donnybrook in Boston; moral: avoid logicians with gloomy names—). The game consists of the identification of some top dog intellectual celebrity to broadside with neat formulations. Assuming there is no top dog for the logicians to dethrone, the materialists trudge to their drawing boards in hope of formulating ever more tedious positions regarding the mental:—eliminativism, reductivism, functionalism, and other physicalist hopscotch—; when every position constructed and theatrically bedizened with the form of logical unimpeacheableness is nothing but a product of the imagination (—no wonder Richard Rorty says philosophy is a literary genre—): specifically that tenebrous, never lifelike, notional imagination of the seminar room (—or, as the case may be, the stupefacient of yet another onslaught of "logically coherent," academically-worded papers—). Think of every *possible* logical-epistemological position as a demolition and rebuilding of an original Kantian sandcastle: same sand, different architectonic; and on until the imaginative appetite of the logical analyst is satisfied (—along with his voluminous argumentative appetite—). Then the circumlocutory gab determines the celebrity status; or is it the other way around? For, believe me, there are plenty of new American doctors, enthralled since their undergraduate days by the liberating notion of philosophy as a sport and not, certainly not, a serious undertaking reserved for gifted persons, ready to listen to the yips of a new dominant dog!—The entire enterprise of logical episteme is a hole the philosopher of science has dug for himself: a hole into which others might fall. Quite unlike the famous Thalesian tumble, this fall is the corruption of the philosophic youth, the turning around of every *potentia*. If philosophy gets mired down to science the way it was once mired down to religion, the relevant question is a question of philosophy's *destiny*.—Another thing: if Richard Rorty is sincerely interested in philosophy enough to be worried about philosophy losing its audience, a number of stern replies are in order. First, I consider it highly unlikely that anyone in the American seminar room can be sincere about anything once the *basic insincerity* is repressed and kept hidden: the corrupting discontinuity between lived experience and experience in the seminar room. Second, once philosophy's audience grows even the slightest bit larger than the elite of the intellectual class—C.S. Peirce's "one in a million"—then, well; what can I say? This ought to serve as our cue that there is some bad philosophy out there! Yea, we are rapidly reaching the point when even the intellectual class will cease thinking; yet this will surely happen unnoticed and amidst a veritable boom of thinking when everyone will be "thinking" precisely what they are told to think: more specifically, told what *not* to think. When sophistics try to be sophisticates, when pigs try to be philosophers, society becomes a preposterous pig pen; as was recently evidenced by a public exchange in the marketplace between the suave Indian "philosopher" Deepak Chopra and a first-year philosophy major from a small college in the Midwest.—"What does the earth rest upon?" the tyro asked the Mister-fix-it sage of the hour. Our millionaire gymnosophist flashed his slickest Wall Street glance at the expectant audience and replied in that Indianishly sonorous baritone, "Why an elephant, of course!"—"Yes, but what does the elephant rest upon, you son of a bitch?"—Since to imagine a position regarding the potency or impotency of the mind (—as aforesaid, a rebuilding of the sandcastle—) to know the data independent of it is a kind of sport or intellectual day job, and therefore stands at the opposite pole from the production of an idea, the distilling of the flux of immediate experience into a coherent train of thought, our gymnosophistical sage of the hour and the logical analyst in his ivory tower possess more similarities than differences. The revelings of the star in the seminar room is not at all unlike the joys of the pop sage: the one revels in a certain harmony between his way of "thinking" and his academic peers, i.e., those commonplace heads who have convinced themselves that the prolific professor is doing something in philosophy; the other in that harmony between "best-selling author" and public. But since the world we live in is chockfull of commonplace heads, these groupings point to other similar contrasts and chasms in the broad and capacious intellectual world. The pop writers—the novelists, our mired-to-cultural-correctitude playwrights, chained-to-correct-thought Hollywood screenhacks, financier-manques of political essayists, and certainly not to forget our frenetic, tied-in-knots horde of yapping journalists—come to mind, whose sole joy consists in selling themselves *to their contemporaries*. These groupings and types find meaning and justification only in this harmony with their "public." It is precisely this fact that occasions the fate that overtakes the genuine human beings who appear as kinds of accidents on this teeming scene: a great mind will only experience a *disharmony* with the public, and is able to find its joy, meaning, and harmonious life, only with another great mind. In this context, the vaunted "knowledge" of the logical analyst is restricted to what *serves his motivation*; he, quite like the others who revel in their own kind of harmony and so officiously pass it off as harmony as such, possesses no truly free knowledge, no purposeless knowledge, no knowledge ungoverned by motivation, i.e., those immediate motivations we fondly call practical. Truly *free* thinking is no less burdensome to him as it is to the denizens of the world of finance, the business people: their resolve is to get by with the *least possible* expenditure of thought: they think only as much and as far as their trade and business makes absolutely necessary.—What then? Is the thinker's urge to produce not motivation? The asking of this question is precisely an inquiry into the interestingly instinctual situation of the thinker whose drive to produce is so bound up with genius as to be taken for it: the production of ideas in the genius is of the same kind as the bringing forth of fruit or grain for harvest. Balzac said, "I am in love with a beautiful woman. Her name is fame." I can only reply that the great man coveted fame as a means to the favors of beautiful women; for fame is never certain—well, almost never—and is not, as we say in America, worth what it's cracked up to be. It's rather *instinct of a unique sort* that sets the genius' hands to his or her plough. Take Charles Peirce, our only genius: *what* was he doing in that cold room in Arisbe? *Who* was he speaking to? *Where* did his motivation lie? Let us take a look at this situation. As said elsewhere, Mr. Peirce was a man of wide experience who knew very little about the affectations, strutting, and effeminate face slappings in the American seminar room. He knew instead obloquies, woes, shipwrecks; . . . the game-playing shallowpates had cast him out, put it that way. To return to our question: what prompted Charles Peirce's productivity?—I have already answered this question. The genius produces as the tree bears fruit, *and precisely for the same reason*. The genius is simply NOT CONSCIOUS of any further motivation. It is as if a window has been opened on the top floor of a great house—a kind of tower, if you will—and the genius is standing at the window throwing things down to those on the ground as fast as he can because he knows the window will someday close. The people on the ground say, "Look! Up there! What is happening?" Well, indeed; what *is* happening? The genius produces for the species; always a kind of prophet, his vision is nothing other than a pair of eyes donated to mankind. (—In practice, however, this can only take place through the *catena* of other intellects—). What then impels the truly great man or woman to work in total solitude? How is this type able to work without praise, without reward, even in a worst-case scenario, *without any recognition at all* with not one whimper of a complaint? What allows this type to push on through the darkness with pack held high? Whence cometh his terrible glance, his burning gaze (—for he is gazing into Night, my brothers—), his awful realization that he might not live to see the dawn, *his dawn*? But all these questions have been answered.—To continue: for will he not someday exchange all his scornings and all his stripes for a crown?—In conclusion: the current aridities and tortuously circumlocutory imaginings of the American epistemological quest have turned their backs on what philosophy is and ought to be. Like the thinker who earns the gratitude of the age by keeping in step with it, the analysts earn, and can *only* earn, the gratitude of *each other*. Having learned philosophy, they never learn how to philosophize: for common heads know only what can be taught.

346

For a pragmatist to become a philosopher would require a forced occupation with things of no concern to him, for practice aims directly at individual things. The philosopher, on the other hand, wants to hover above the things like a hawk. Now this consists of a displacement of the normal relation of intellect to life: where the pragmatist sees intellect in the service of life, the anti-pragmatist employs the intellect abnormally; thinking becomes the main thing, hovering becomes the main thing, while life becomes the subsidiary thing (—and surely artistic creation is thinking here just as life is mere survival—). When intellect occupies itself purely objectively, it can do this only in view of the fact of abnormality: intellect exceeds the measure needed for living, and it is precisely the employment of this excess that produces art, poetry, and philosophy. If our pragmatism eschews this excess, and feels threatened by this glaring abnormality—and rightly so—how can it be proper to call pragmatism a philosophy? The pragmatist thinks just as a worker on an assembly line thinks: both are driven by interest, need: a thought has no other value, no value over and above its "cash value," as Professor James piously points out. Practical knowledge is linked to motivation, just as the worker shows up for work everyday because he needs cash; but an excessive intellect is impracticality itself. Now certainly this *excess of intellect* strives for knowledge and the kind of knowledge it strives after is free knowledge. (—Since Charles Peirce was an "outsider," those who offered financial help to offset the burden of such an excess, saw him in this way; and the simplest rationale for this aid was given by Anaxagoras when he chided Pericles.—) To state this another way is to say that even ordinary people possess some degree of leisure, which they squander on mindless things. This impractical free reflection, the contemplation Aristotle pronounced divine, is *subversion itself* to the pragmatist and the Marxist alike; for in the Marxian-Deweyan cosmos, everyone must go with the program, and pragmatists hate thinking outside the program. Just as Catholics burned heretics and Marxist-Stalinists "rehabilitated" revisionists, pragmatists dream of purifying thought, and they begin this doctrinal purification in the public schools. In other words, the pragmatist wants to conform all exceptions to the rule; his goal is to *exhaust thinking* so that there is no remainder, nothing left over once the homogenization sets in. *This* employment of the intellect always is concerned with material things, with everything pertaining to livelihood, personal drives, material welfare, and utilitarian concerns of every sort. Hollywood seeks to impose its jaded political agenda; race pragmatists can only be happy when everyone is smothered by the indecency of their anti-racism racism we know as the American version of Negritude; journalists want to keep us perpetually shocked, riven, and aflutter with their quotidian lunacy; television naïfwits want to reduce ruminative hours to split seconds; radio windbags want to keep as many minds as possible tethered to their rotten right-wing leashes; politicians fixate on the material externals of a problem, on the *outside* of a perceived harm, blissfully oblivious to the growing canker on the *inside*.—*Nec vitia nostra nec remedia tolerare possumus.*—To ask the questions how these indecencies are possible in a free society is to demonstrate the lethargy of the collective intellect: the intellect slides into inactivity once it's no longer in the service of the meager, this is to say practical measure required for living in an acquisitive, exclusively action-oriented society of non-critical drudges. Once the truths our pragmatists have "made" come off the assembly line, it's the business of philosophy to examine these truths, tying them with their consequences; and this in open violation of a multicultural society's ban on free thought. For how do you tell people what to think except by creating a situation that makes them hate everything that demands thought? That truth is made by man, the prettiest jewel in pragmatism's crown, cannot be legitimately conceived as an advance over any other conception of truth: if anything, this conception has only *democratized* the amount of dishonesty there is in the world, and has therefore only spread out the number of masks humans either already wear or are capable of wearing.—If, on the other hand, man could fly, we may legitimately imagine that the best flight would consist in the purposeless expenditure of excess energy (—just as philosophical thinking in its simplest, non-agonistic typification consists in thinking as Aristotle's thinker thinks, which thinking in its highest form, is thought thinking; or, if you prefer, man as "God," assuming God could be a mere thinking activity—), and to the extent practical considerations obtrude upon such an expenditure the activity would suffer attenuation, for it is not natural for man to fly. In other words, the *subjective* application is the natural one; whereas it's most unnatural to eschew and drive out everything related to interest. Indeed: the pragmatist and the normal man, the one being a copy of the other, exclaim, "Everything is interest." *Thus*, the classical pragmatic criterion of truth: truth is made. And, pragmatically speaking, such truthmaking is in perfect accord with all material matters and personal affairs in general. Therefore, we have the famous pragmatist dictum, "Truth is made as wealth and health are made." But it has always struck me as painful—and for that matter quite duplicitous since duplicity certainly consists in not telling the whole truth—the way the pragmatists consider *their* whirligig an absolute end of the matter. To be blunt: even assuming that truth can be made as wealth is made, this at its best only makes out the prima facie case that truth is being made, or as the case may be, that truth has been made in the same manner that money is made; for once the truth has been made, it would certainly upset this particular truth's applecart if some truth-seeker should come upon the scene to weigh and appraise the truth that has been created. In other words, if the subjective truthmaker were forced to do the impossible: take an objective interest in something;—as if aha! one could give a pair of wings to a pragmatist! as if one could hurl the subjective interest out the window!—then the truthmaker would become the seeker of truth, and would at least for the time being, extricate himself from the role assigned him, not by philosophy, but by the principles of pragmatism laid down in Cambridge so long ago by a tragic man of great mystery and personal charisma who was possibly insane, Charles Sanders Peirce. Those commissioned by pragmatism to "make truth" and those commissioned by philosophy—not traditional philosophy, mind you, but the spirit of philosophy—to seek truth: these types are *antithetical*; and it is high time philosophy learns to recognize and properly distinguish between the two. Whereas the one is nothing but activity—with the very word philosophy tacked on for emphasis and prestige—; the other gets translated into activity on account of the select few. Again: this is precisely the offense of philosophy from the standpoint of the logicians: these few may choose the avenue of rigorous method or they may legitimately choose to relinquish rigorous method. Two examples come to mind: Kierkegaard's prediction of television as a tool of dehumanization and Nietzsche's predictions (—to give only one: the rise and eventual fall of socialism—). Where is the logic in all this? Where is the vaunted method? And Heidegger. Isn't it a fact that the offense underlying the brief flirtation with Nazism is his grandiose conception of the philosopher? that he guards the ancient right of oracular pronouncement? that he *defends philosophy against its enemies*? that he by example extends the ancient, noble *gens* into modern journacentric, democratic culture dominated by a form of thinking that tears philosophy up at its roots and has promoted unto itself its own holy mountain of permissible thinking that must always lead to correct results? It should hurt and disappoint us that Heidegger was a Nazi; isn't it queer how it doesn't hurt us to see Ernst Bloch the unmolested unregenerate Stalinist? Does this mean that with Bloch we separate philosophy from politics? The best fascist is the one who gives to humanity because he *has* to; e.g., Hamsun, Pound, et al. The essence of politics is narrowness, seizure of the moment, and dirt. Therefore, the giving and the dirt are unrelated; but not so with Heidegger's pharisaical accusers: their real objection to him is *his* objection to their conception of philosophy. That Peirce hit his precious Juliette; that Schopenhauer threw the old woman down the stairs; that Leibniz was a toadying dandy; that the last act of Heraclitus was ignoble: all these things are forgiven with a tear or two, and in the case of the Greek, even a laugh; but he who forgives the motley quaestor his self-serving spleens is worse than a fool. Nay, if anything, it is Heidegger who sees the world objectively and not the pragmatist, whose total stock of knowledge is always and must always be circumscribed by naked interest; ... which brings us back to the truth question. Assuming truth is made as wealth is made, you pragmatists omit the next question: *what is it pragmatism has made?*—An American question.—A question for truth-seekers everywhere ...

347

Only the really *attuned* individuals, the rarest of exceptions, are led to philosophize. As for the great bulk of humanity, it is usually religion that takes care of their metaphysical needs. These attuned individuals, aside from the experience of merely knowing philosophy as the philosophy professor knows philosophy, and thus by virtue of the first potency of their attunement have passed from the idea of knowing *what philosophy is* to the practice of philosophy, it should go without saying, practice pure philosophy, or if you prefer, free philosophy. These true philosophers are free from the chains of interest: thus, they are forever free, liberated, and therefore liberating spirits. For these spirits, the whole experience of philosophy is a joyful experience (—for where is the man or woman who could entertain the slightest, chimerical doubt that such spirits as Socrates and Nietzsche were *full of joy*?—) as even the animal experiences joy when de-chained and truly liberated. Who among you can imagine a beautiful angel tied down and encumbered by chains? A demon, yes; but not an angel. It must have brought Socrates happiness beyond compare when, in the presence of his students, he humbled the proud by demonstrating they were good for less than they thought, or as the case may be, that they were good for nothing: that the wise are in reality not wise, and those who so pompously claim to know something really know nothing; yea, for he, the true philosopher, claimed to know nothing, save the fact of the knowledge of the herd's total ignorance, and ignorance of the most important matters. For the philosopher, it is true, is concerned with the most important, weightiest things. By contrast the philosophy professor, as well as his brother-in-chains, he who writes "philosophy" for mass consumption, inasmuch as his mind is put to practical use and is manifestly in service of interest (—if necessary to spell this out, the specific interest in getting tenure and accumulating a modicum of respect among peers—) cannot experience the joy of those who practice pure philosophy any more than the ant can repose faith in God. This true practice of philosophy is *opposed* to the practical stuff of life: it is its privilege to oppose it just as freedom, the free being of the true philosopher, casts off every denial of its freedom. When Nietzsche recognized Richard Wagner's Bayreuth as an encumbrance and a liability—a denial of his free being—he forthwith put everything Wagnerian behind him, lifted his eyes up to the horizon—*his* horizon—the horizon of the true hero who no longer has to pretend, and dared the Muse to love him as much as he loved her.

—*When the spirit is plunged into the bitter consequences of the flight from the practical life, it is precisely then that spirit magnifies itself and gives birth to culture, philosophy, and art.* Stated differently: spirit and life are *at variance*, and because of this opposition, we possess culture. Reconciliation of antinomies and incommensurables is the formula for cultural decline, impotence, artistic and philosophic exhaustion; for it is privation, not plenitude, that makes creation possible, and the stings of the Muse's whip are confirmations of unconditional love. Sometimes the consequences of impracticality do not supervene by the actor's own volition, but are cruelly thrust upon him or her by chance, or as in the case of Charles Peirce, a kind of demonic fate. Whereas with the German spiritual pain was *pursued* as a means of increasing the capacity for knowledge—the idea being that excessive self-cruelty brings excessive self-knowledge, and Nietzsche's self-knowledge, to which Freud attested, was greater and more refined than any human being who ever lived—the American, who saw himself as everything from inventor and fortune-seeker to scientist and mathematician, had to wait until the consequences of genius found him; which they did when he was forced to live with the people of the abyss on the horrible streets of New York. In one thought: Peirce's genius turned him into a philosopher; Nietzsche's philosophic activism turned him into a great genius. Thus, Nietzsche, that bird intent upon distant shores, became the greater philosopher precisely by the self-conscious *negation of all interest*, fashioning for himself an unimaginable intensity; while Peirce, primarily a scientist, could only find brief periods of respite from the demands of interest, and so could not enjoy, let us say, extended periods of the divine madness of philosophic ecstasy.—Sometimes, however, the one who dons the robe of philosophy and pretends to be what he is not, in fact, what he could never become, serves interest as a slave serves his master. Such a *slave revolt in philosophy* begins with Deweyism, the religion of political liberalism of this Deweyism, and finds its fullest, this is to say its gaudiest, most shameless efflorescence in race pragmatism: such revolt begins when pragmatist Du Bois, in the most gruesome exemplification of self-interest, dresses himself up as a slave, steps inside the *Phenomenology* as a slave, and with the calculating cleverness and rancune of a slave, waits on the dreaming dialectic to *transform him into the master*, the holy, the untouchable, the fanatical "blessed of God," the symptom-syndrome of the negation of all moral thought hitherto; this self-professed inheritor of the earth, this righteously serene Creole-epileptic; this resentment-convulsed, *priestly* writing-helot, who instructs even his nostrils to perform as the curse of correct thought emanating from the dialectic commands them to perform; this creepy art of revenge;—*become master*! One cannot read the words of this pragmatist without sensing a partiality for that which is never mentioned, never touched upon, never whispered about. Du Bois keenly understood the need to *distort*, hence every race pragmatist since has understood *him*.—But race pragmatists have their "equal rights" as enemies and antipodes of equality *before the law*; of equality of souls before integrity, liberality, and truth: away! away with all of it! One needs only a vampire to suck truth out of everything! A witch doctor to climb the Story Tree and hurl down curses! *One needs a Du Bois*.—Such witch doctors need a hostile external world, for the *act of self-creation has been inverted*. Moral: do not look to oneself, look to the outside world: react to external stimuli: as aforesaid, hurl down curses! Confront the "enemy" not because of who *you* are, but because of social justice, progress, goodness, and the perfectibility of man: in one word the lie of equality! Finally, the image of this external world is *falsified* by the hallucinations of the vengeful "public intellectuals"—they call themselves philosophers and theologians for they have seized upon the meanings of words and eviscerated these meanings, these substance-sucking ghouls of vampires, drunkards of God—; and these "public intellectuals" are everywhere, transforming everything into caricatures and monsters; i.e., mirror reflections of themselves! "Social justice"—only a *flatus vocis* for the establishment of happiness (—within the race!!—); and how is this happiness established? Is it established as happiness should be established? No! One thousand times, No! (—For *this* would mean the destruction of the public intellectuals, pseudo-philosophers and revisionist theologians laboring for the coming world order!—) *Happiness can only be established by an examination of one's enemies*!!—Moral: seek the chief, most natural part of a man in reacting to something perceived as hostile;—when the exact opposite is the truth: action, the *creation* of a situation, *self*-examination are primary (—precisely; the relation to primary and parasitic must be inverted, turned inside out and with the ceremony and moral stupidity of street demonstrations and placard-waving turned on its head—). The struggle against racism; the visualization of world peace; social justice; equal rights; fantasies of inevitable progress; human perfectibility; the forced evolution of law *away* from the venerated foundations, *away* from truth, from truth-telling as well as the forced evolution of the human psyche away from all discipline of spirit and moral loftiness; religious awe as linked to the sky, to light, to an above in sharpest contradistinction to a below, i.e., a deified, *necessarily* deified sublunary realm, to Mother Earth, the *Magna Mater* herself; the recrudescence of tribalism, animism, fertilityism; exultation in primitivism, sexual primitivism; the religious deification of the body; tribal tarantism; corybanticism; biologism—: these comprehensive states must be comprehended as quasi-religious after-images of an original race-gender symbolism: the simultaneous opening up and devolution of this symbolism, this war between right and wrong, good and evil, become cosmic, become necessary stages in this cosmicization: cocoon perspectives from which and out of which the great value-takeover, the reversal of "world history," of "man" through the progressive dirtification of everything that stands erect, everything that *wants* to stand erect.—Goal: to pollute the earth in the name of sanitizing "the planet."—Goal: the cyclopean disfigurement of the world's religions; the redoctrinalization of the earth, its mongrelization: the submergence of Christianity; the beleaguerment of Islam . . . We are now entering the time for which holy war was *designed* . . . Children of the patriarchy, tattered remnants of a heroic age! Lay aside your differences;—Unite!—Unite!—

On the Lumber of the Schools

348

Someone compared the San Francisco fog to a great, gray pearl that rolls in from the icy Pacific, engulfing Land's End, the Presidio, blanketing the avenues, moving greedily east in huge, cresting billows, finally to engulf the roofs and spires of that magnificent skyline in a pall of thick smoke. I have come to believe that the same kind of engulfing takes place, and is even now taking place, with regard to philosophy as it's done in America, obscuring the very concept philosopher in a stubborn, entrenched fog. Let us, therefore, blow away this stupid prejudice and misunderstanding. Let us erase the blackboard that has been marked and scribbled on for so long that it wears the sadly obsequious color of smoke.—To utterly misuse the name philosophy; to use Sophia's name in vain! How faint the heart grows, how benumbed the mind whenever one draws near the somnolent halls of philosophy in the great American universities! Closed windows, painted over. Heavy bolted doors. A sign above the main entrance: "Abandon all hope, you who enter here."—In such an enclosed environment, what kind of spirit or non-spirit practices philosophy?—American Continental philosophers so-called, the life blood of the field, the *reaction* to the sclerosis of analytic philosophy, that experimental, wilder breed of philosophy professor responsible for the belated reception of European thinking on these shores; doesn't the pathologist's cold scalpel reveal these reverse-gadflies, these "social philosophers," as a very narrow, hopelessly technical, and circumlocutory type of chained-up *cadaver* of a philosopher? Let us restate the old maxim of medical jurisprudence here: dead men do tell tales, sometimes whole volumes; and no, we by no means exclude our satyr-girls, those "female philosophers" whose hoary, dykey, mannish mugs resemble an aging Susan Sontag on a bad hair day.—The patient pathologist records in his journal the following: "Victims of cadaveric spasm. Curriculum vitae held high in the air at the moment of death."—But some truths lie beyond the reconstructions of forensic pathology. Here, for example, the good doctor didn't tell us that these narrow souls philosophizing on campus are really nothing but perpetual graduate students who dive down into texts of the "master thinkers" and smother themselves with glosses. And to what end? To which hope?—In the hope of producing more glosses! glosses upon glosses! Doomed to be day laborers in philosophy, they busily cram their graduate student heads with more knowledge, more doxa, more "profound" ways to elucidate texts (—as if elucidation *can* be profound!—). Thus, these antipodes of philosophers can only think with a text in their hands—or under their pillow—; and if they think while on the toilet—as one told me he had—holding a wad of toilet paper the same way he holds his Deleuze, his Lyotard, his Levinas, his Lacan, Derrida, Foucault, and all the other Fabricius Frenchmen they adore, what are they thinking *about*? What end and aim occupies their hairsplitting brains? Why, more glosses of more texts, of course! More notional palaver about truth claims, and praxis, and posits! More—and I cannot say this with sufficient horror—; more politicizing the genre (—which at bottom can only mean that that modicum of independence philosophy for thousands of years has managed to garner for herself through the renunciations, adventures, silences, intrepidities, and lofty seven solitudes of spirits such as Empedocles, Heraclitus, Plato, and Nietzsche, gets clumsily sacrificed to the tutelary divinities of the popular, legalistic culture—you know their names by now.—). *On the contrary*: a philosopher never dives down into a text, never feels a need to elucidate ideas not his own:—it is quite, *quite* enough that he elucidates his own; or, as Descartes said so well: *Bene vixit qui bene latuit*—; nor does a philosopher strain, squint, and otherwise harrow himself when he picks up a new text—if he does so decide—and chances are he doesn't—: his rare uncanny promptings and self-benefactions are more likely to come while he contemplates a Sonoma moon on a warm San Francisco night, a forest of sun-drenched Joshua trees, the sorrowful freighters drifting languorously for a paradisiacal Golden Gate. He feels no need to worm his way down, like a dung-beetle, into another thinker's words, phrases, imports, and implications; perhaps he is unable to take these bouquets seriously; for he, at last, knows too much: like a hawk, he hovers and *flies away*.

* * *

I hear the heavy bolt slide back. The door opens. Here one comes with a bag full of arguments, inductions, *a priori* truths, neo-pragmaticisms, and a cache of quite amorphous, "polymorphous doing." Condescension. Paternal smiles. "But we American Continental philosophers are original," says he, "whether you know it or not. Who are you to castigate with such a flurry of right jabs? After all, we professors know so many beautiful things, you so few."

—Show me one piece of originality in that pompous harum-scarum of imported tidbits you asininely refer to as your "work" the size of a hair from a philosopher's beard. Show me; I'm starting to get impatient with you.—

"Ah, friend! Impatience is no misnomer. You have the impatience of an undergraduate. I shall, therefore, treat you as one. To be eclectic is to be original. To be original is to be eclectic. Do you understand? I know your head is spinning. You are in the presence of brilliance. What we brilliant eclectics do is combine our marvelous knowledge of many things to create a living, breathing, embodied eclecticism, a phenomeno-eclecticism. If you will allow my profundity full sway: an eclectic eclecticism!—*provided*, of course, we publish enough commentaries in stuffy, uppity journals and write enough books for our many students to read; and, not to forget the principal thing: to sleep with our sex partners in a professorial, learned fashion."

—When did combining many ideas clearly not your own become original? You will reply that philosophers have always done this, but with the important minds, I sense something more than the sum of elements: the Eleatics plus the non-Eleatics do *not* equal Plato. With you, I sense the bare disparateness of the elements themselves.—

Laughter. Derisive frowns. "We scholar/philosophers know what's what, put it that way. What we do is fetishize a group of European thinkers, put them in a box—and if that's not feasible, a straitjacket—and apply their work to new facts. We apply their insights. This takes selectivity, hard work, and brains. Originality? Originality is in the application: we apply their thoughts to our thoughts, redolent of new states of facts. Or . . . is it the other way around? Well; minor point. The fact is that a philosophy that doesn't apply ideas is surely a dead scholasticism. Scholasticism is the opposite of originality. Therefore, we are very original people."

—Not quite. Your web of commentaries and readings mark time within the bounds of the traditional systems. You mistake adaptation and on-going synthesis for breaking out of the matrix.—

"Who have you been talking to? You're on the wrong track. Your wires are crossed. Besides, even if what you assert is true, our overall function in a free society is crucial, unmistakable. You see, our role is crucial in turning new ideas into old ones. Why, we'll take a new idea and contort it until it's finally a mere caricature of what it was before we started fooling around with it. We'll talk the thing to pieces; there won't be any flesh left, just bones so when we finally get through with this new idea, it's not new anymore. It finally dies, leaving room for newer ideas. Another thing: some people—especially those of the broader intellectual world—laugh at our incomparable brilliance because we are not known as intellectuals. True; we're not intellectuals; we're academics and leftists, good, true, mealy-mouthed leftists—and that may be enough for one clan."

349

Upon entering that wing of philosophy in America supposed to compensate for the aridities and general academic non-relevance found in the so-called logical positivist school, whose angels shimmying on pinheads are well nigh notorious today, one is stunned by the *smell* of the workman's tools, the workman's environment. It is as if these learned doctors could just as facilely have become salespeople, technological crew cuts, politicians, landlords, lawyers. What? Did they read their beloved Nietzsche with their dainty fingers crossed?—Can they actually believe they are "keeping the philosophical discussion alive" with that pompous crowing on dunghills they so innocently equate with philosophic thought?—Do they possess any conceptions of their own? Have they experienced one-ten-thousandth of the suffering, obloquy, and woe necessary for any aspiring initiate to *become a philosopher?* Then, be quiet, you roosters! Stand down from your gothic lecterns, your peripatetic pulpits, and take your seat in the pew.—How you hold yourselves aloof from the dogmatic aesthete who seems to practice philosophy but who doesn't know, who can't grasp, the historical trajectory of philosophy! Yet how are you any better than this practicing aesthete?—You *are* learned, I'll grant you that much. Your myopic labors have succeeded in drawing you as near the portals of philosophy's Muses as professorially possible; and there you congregate like spiders in a glass jar, quite incapable of pouncing upon any opponent, but ever ready to scare him with your hopeless circumlocutions, and if possible, *stare him down*;—then, if your lordly eyes are weakened by the writing of dissertations, colloquies, exegeses, papers, and, sometimes quite un-dramatic, non-scenic "novels," then by all means intimidate him with classroom histrionics and piquant disquisitions on how you came to philosophy (—from below, I conclude, never from above—); win him over with your ethnicity: are you from Athens? Rhodes? Were your ancestors there when the Mede appeared? Do you know Messina's narrow strait, with her Scylla and Charybdis? Have you, from a placid, moonlit Aegean, espied the jade, Lesbian Isle? Very well then; you'll suffice to have your learned redundancy showcased in the *Metaphysical Review*, the *Journal of Philosophy*, and those puerilely useless reflections of the popular idols you call philosophy books, those stuffy, non-relevant essays that make any genuine servant of Sophia cry out with Nietzsche, *Bad air! Bad air!*—For, believe me, the very men and women who beat on their chests and burnish their gleaming escutcheons as they go off to Paris for yet *another* seminar on "semiology and contemporary episteme," basking in the collective glow of their hermeneutical confabulations, post-structuralist structuralisms, those impossibly stilted conferences and colloquia on the destructured, decentered, detranscendentalized, deconstructed "self" of a philosophy professor's *Analecta Asinina*; these men and women are the culprits constantly on the lookout for any student impudent enough to *deviate* from their norm and veer skyward for Hyperborean Land.—And what are you pharisaic claptrappers doing when you spend hours on end in that little room breathing in Jacques Derrida's wine breath and measuring the shape of Foucault's head other than migrating to another end of the glass jar?—Let us be honest for once: these men and women—the insiders of philosophy's sorry state—exist for service and general utility, who *may* exist only for that purpose, and consequently, their pieces, papers, and glosses, all their "work," constitute a forlornly impossible *wish for the outside*, a vicarious longing to break out of the academic bubble! But comfort and frivolity prevent this! Yea, all their erudition is nothing but cowardice and vanity!—And not just any cowardice, not just ordinary vanity! All their running around, brandishing escutcheons (—and, yes; I do mean to say here shields, not swords: their erudition constitutes a shielding *from* philosophy—), and bonding has the effect of transfiguring their everydayness, as if poverty could mask poverty, and hence preserving the existing popular culture from *ruthless philosophic scrutiny*; certainly not the first time philosophy has ducked its mission by a shameful, toadying to the existing order! Therefore, in America and in Europe, "Continental philosophy" has *no moral prerogative*, no real exhilarating promise, over the old ossified and dead-ended analytic philosophy. First principle: when an educational endeavor becomes an educational system, is it any wonder, any cause for alarm, that thinking must at that moment die out and must begin again *from the outside*?—Oh, who has the slightest, most fancifully chimerical doubt that even Charles Peirce, a sunlit man of bravery, hardness, and magnificent self-severity—whose violent nature I do not apologize for—was a hundred miles closer to the *practice* of philosophy than these pitifully barren craftspeople whose main offense—I'll *repeat* it—is their pretension to wisdom? their horrible, little, bigoted claim to be philosophers!—Philosophers!—Reasonable minds may well wonder exactly when they became philosophers. Was it on the day their undergraduate noses turned brown? The auspicious day they entered graduate school and learned to play the game? Or was it when they put themselves on the auction block and some university said, "Come on down and do nothing except look important while we pay you. Come teach students how *not* to think by doing nothing!" Then maybe it was on the day they flew to Europe to bond and hob-nob with other important-looking sprites and do-nothings? later to accept speaking invitations and calls to man posts on "Comparative Literature," which, since they know nothing at all about literature absent Kafka, Camus, and a sprinkle of Dostoyevsky, would be an obvious shoe-in. Perhaps we will return to this interesting question.—The philosophy professor (—in this case, the professor of Continental philosophy, that new American philosophy, which doesn't see itself as academic or in any way abstracted from "life"—) stands in much the same relation to the authentic, "rare plant" we know as the real philosopher (—and may I please point out that the rarest of these rare plants recognize the need to live philosophy, and do so, frequently at the greatest hazard to comforts, satisfactions, and "best interests," for as we now know or should know, philosophy today isn't easy Boethian "consolation," not Platonic-Plotinian flights to "another world"—) as the popular writer of blockbusters stands to an accomplished artist of literary fiction. In the one case, the resonating worlds of *characters* are dunned and bullied by the monotonous vapidity of action plots: plot-driven novels are heinous and fascistic because the characters in them have no function, no choice, but to conform to plot. In the other case, philosophy is dunned and bullied by the drive to project glosses, by pettiness, and "debate," for the professors who thrive in an academic setting soon learn to see themselves as very important cogs and turning wheels in an evolving debate about philosophy (—which is itself a telling piece of evidence to suggest that if the professors are in a debate about philosophy, this fact would place them squarely at the opposite pole from the true *production* of philosophic conceptions; perhaps they mistakenly believe that these very different "points of departure" are the same when they are as different as night and day—). If, say, philosophy is bullied by religious dogma—doctrines cemented in place prior to any putatively authentic act of philosophizing—then the conceptions, certainly the conclusions, of this sycophantic philosophy are parasitic, artificial, and so many instances of special pleading; again: turning wheels and cogs at the opposite pole from the true, i.e., unfettered production of philosophic conceptions. Here an overarching analogy may be found, and *is* found, in the dictum of Saint Paul to the effect that the *traditions of men* have made null and void the living word of God. Not, certainly not, to offend any of you fine American postmodernists who have converted to "religion without religion," this pertinent, quite ignored Pauline passage points to the simple fact that the dead cannot be alive. Now what does this mean? At once, Hegel's university philosophizing comes to mind, but the real question is what would have happened to his philosophy (—specifically his uncritical acceptance of the "truths of the Revolution," and other unhealthy, cream-filled French pastries that informed and supported the whole system—) if he had, with Arthur Schopenhauer and his colorful disciple, Nietzsche, turned his back on the tradition, exited the glass jar, and gone over to the realm of the living? Suffice it to say that Hegel's timidity was bemoaned even by his wife. Scholars speak glibly about Goethe's period of truancy in Italy, and scholars are apt to say such things. The truth is this: the genuine artist's life is but one long period of truancy (—not to speak of that pupation period Goethe made famous—); and if this is true for the artist, it applies, *a fortiori*, to the philosopher who feels quite at home in the shadows, burrowing down into the bowels of the earth, so that, someday, his truths, and hence his name, shall be lifted high into the light of heaven. If authentic creation also involves destruction then what is it the philosopher *must destroy?* But I have answered this question.—What then? Is the act of creation, the authentic synthesis of philosophic ideas, denied the good professor? Is his sole art the art of nugacity? Must he eternally doodle inside the dim, gray walls of his philosophy hall? Must he forever filch other people's ideas, put them through the tenure-ringer, and bombastically nominate them his own? Yea, his cramping words never cease to flow, for he has lost control of them and instead of directing them is directed by them. It is precisely in this lack of control, in that which the Romans called *impotentia*, that the philosophy professor in America reveals his true nature.

350

The philosopher as we know him—as he or she *is*—has nothing whatsoever to do with the leftist sycophants and eclectic ants of our philosophically effete academia: the dirt of politics shall not receive any lip service and doctrinaire obeisance from such a spirit. This whole fracas over Martin Heidegger and the Nazis—let me refrain from offending *innocent* ears here—is symptomatic of that which will prove itself to be a greater "evil" than any pattern of evils perpetrated by any political party. The present scouring of philosophic texts for traces of what these sick sycophants call "racism" is only a kind of semaphore for the war being waged in the soul of every new philosopher, every *coming* philosopher!—which conflict is a mirror image of the war between authentic philosophy (—this is to say, to be very simple and brief, the spirit of the great philosophers, poets, and satirists of ancient Greece; the religious hermits, bird-spirits, and truth seekers: in one word, the entire courageous elite from Rome to Babylon—) and that pygmyish piece of fakery we know as the popular culture with its pantheon of idols and the culture-destructive *ideologies of these idols!* All the "evils" of the 20th century—children of the socialist experiment in forced progress—are *not to be compared* to the education and breeding of a correct-thinking *new race* of matrifocal helots! In point of fact: you Nazi hunters, instead of seeking out alleged links connecting Heidegger's political associations with his written philosophy, ought instead to see what manner of ways the Heideggerian corpus takes sides against the former religions and helps clear the way for the inevitable worship of the pre-patriarchal Mother with her nurturing values, fertility rhythms, and "non-violence." For the pre-Christian cults with their religious sexuality and the pre-patriarchal chthonic religion that triumphalizes natural, biological values and hates spiritual and intellectual values—in one word, individualism—will surely return as the beginning returns to the end.—Oh, I prophesy it!—And the Hegelian conceit of "cancelling and preserving" means very little here, for the Mother Principle will play the dominant role, will embody the blood-based, non-rational matriarchal law!—You are incompetent. You are simply incapable of *grasping* the situation. For all your "justice," you possess no sense of proportion. Very well; let us educate *you*: all the forces working for unity, peace, reconciliation, material happiness, material comfort, empowerment—what do the names matter?—; those forces put in place to *flood out* the old values connotative and constitutive of the Father Right—with its penumbra of names and designations that do not matter; can anyone deny that these counterforces will generate necessary reaction?—As the kingly Brahmins gave themselves the necessary task of nominating kings for the people, so you higher natures who choose the road to higher spirituality shall beget kings; yea, and more than kings for there shall be wars and rumors of wars! You, then; you who choose silence and solitude; you who know how to endure *just a little more*; you who put up with the bestial poverty of poorly fashioned souls; you who have grown accustomed to using suffering the way a mechanic uses tools; you whose conditions of life are so subtle as to be invisible to those who exist only for the general utility;—arise! as old Plato said you would;—prepare yourselves for future *rule*!

351

Having kept a close watch on American Continental philosophy for so long, I now stand ready to draw some conclusions. Any right-thinking observer would have to conclude that the grotesque self-absorption of these mirror gazers has an injurious effect upon the students. That philosophy (—for all the drum beating and ballyhoo about the wonderful prospect of making philosophy relevant to society—) is conceived as a "professional" flourish of eristic certainly affects the student's ability to think; as aforesaid, the student's ability to recognize the disvalue of tradition. But there is more: the reckless self-absorption of this cocky guild must have a necessary influence upon the student's ability to write. In philosophy, one *knows* how to write: one writes like everyone else, one writes as one is *supposed* to write: one writes as the teaching assistant writes, who writes as the professor writes, who writes as the other professors write, who write as professors have always written.—If the young Nietzsche had enjoyed perfect health at Basel, he would have come to the same conclusion about teaching: he had to get out of the classics business. Why? Because the business was getting in the way of his writing. Either he would duck his head and write like the professors—like Wilamowitz—or he would get out! Miss Gertrude Stein came to the same conclusion. She told Hemingway, "Get out of journalism or give up trying to write." When Plato argued with Socrates about continuing with drama because writing tragedy was his heart's desire, Socrates, we may legitimately imagine, propounded to the young writer the prospect of a synthesis of genres; and very much to philosophy's benefit, Plato chose to break free of formulaic plot-spinning and follow the call of the wild. This is precisely why the great Goethe *had* to reject philosophy as it was then done in Germany, and Goethe was not about to sell his writing potential to the Devil!—Question: are there any *good* American philosophy books? *Are* there any American philosophy books?—Yes . . . Confounded African-American protest! Philosophy of law! Pragma-notono-tism! And, not to forget, the very excellent philosophy one finds in *The New Yorker*: philosophy written under the influence of the two great American narcotics: politics and journalism.—How easy, how naturally the American Heideggerian falls for the heavy grotesqueness of Heidegger's writing. *He* thinks this is limpidity! After all, Herr Heidegger's pen doesn't splutter, and in America, spluttering pens come from self-absorption. But to say it again: the philosophy professor suffers from *stiff muscles*.

352

Yet the American Continental philosophy professors, the pragmatists, and our dear logicians, every single ill-informed one of them, wholeheartedly agree on one thing: that every *other* feeling for philosophy, every other "point of departure," is impossible, naïve, dogmatic, false, and fanciful to maintain. Thus, they preserve at least *one* practice of the ancient, noble *gens*. The question of questions regarding these "philosophers" is precisely this: what did they have to do to arrive, not at their own various positions, but at this very resoluteness, this severity in the face of every other possible philosophy, this certainty that *their* truths are the brightest and eclipse all others, all truths hitherto? (—I, of course, use the word "truth" in its most facetious, indecent acceptation—). What did they *have to do* to arrive at this kind of certainty so redolent of religious faith?—Turn the most basic philosophic evaluation upside down! *that* is what they had to do!—To deny, with the most nauseous sense of self-righteousness, that the philosopher is a rare plant; and as a consequence, to affirm that any Tom, Dick, and Harry can write a silly dissertation, gad up and down some university's hall of mirrors cum tenure papers, and presto!—you, wretch! mechanic; cook; janitor; caribou-faced teaching assistant; slack-jawed farmer;—you have become a philosopher!—Well; let me put it this way, you bores . . . There comes a time when the "American dream" is nothing other than a delusion and a snare.—My wish is that authentic philosophy, the spirit of philosophy, may someday be the only uncorrupted thing standing: for there must *be something* the impetuous, scurrilous masses must not touch, must not lick, fumble with, and "democratize." Are you listening, you *libres penseurs*? you who tremble and grieve at night over purple temple ruins! Listen to the call to be yourselves, to have enough joy in yourselves to run from thinking and acting like a herd acts and thinks, to have enough courage to take conventionality and throw it back in their faces; in one word, to be unafraid of the slings and arrows unconditional honesty would afflict you with; but this is your reward: to be youths for the rest of your lives! Has the prospect of *this* liberation not drawn your souls aloft until now? Break out of your chrysalises. Do not be afraid of the things that emerge on your mental horizon and make war on the coming age!—If I held in my left hand the universities with their grand tradition of learning, and in my right, the existence of philosophy on earth, and had to choose between the twain, I would unhesitatingly snuggle into Sophia's tress-bestrewn bosoms and ingest her heady perfume. Oh, that one philosopher, one genuine man of spirit to confound the wise and purify us of this accumulated filth, appear on earth and ten thousand universities perish! Oh, for the days when men of power saw philosophy as noble and divine, when the young Julius Caesar and Cicero veered their sails for Athens and Rhodes! When beautiful things were for the beautiful, noble things for the rare! But today! This petty, mean, miserable today! If the coarse clowns of this brutal gameplaying we politely call Constitutional freedom see nothing admirable in philosophy today, if the powerful see philosophy as a crock of armchairism and Ben Franklin nonsense, it's surely because they see a phantom sitting where a goddess should be! Sprites fill the lecture halls, elfish scholars crowd the conference rooms; every plastic-laureled peacock wants his Ph.D., and for what? To bless and perpetuate the scholarly and wan weariness of the lecture hall! To corrupt the pristine youth with this shrill warning, "American philosophy is practiced here. Relinquish all non-practical ideals. Love of wisdom is base, for there is no wisdom. Philosophy has outlived its purpose. Pick up your brooms, your dustpans, your mops, and polish these scientific halls. By all means, see to it that philosophy is not remote, not abstract, not divorced from concrete reality. Learn whatever the popular culture has to teach. Her ideals are there for philosophy to burnish, so bow down to her idols. But, above all, you philosophical thinkers-to-be . . . *Think as we do!*"—Thus, American philosophers of every ilk have passed the identical judgment upon philosophy: it is impotent, phantasmical, ludicrous.—And *how could they do otherwise*, infatuated with Bacon's prejudices, Bacon's limitations . . . The whole trajectory of Anglo-Saxon thought set into motion by an attorney? an unethical solicitor who by modern standards would be disbarred?—On the contrary: those called to power should bow down before the philosopher as before a well of tremendous forces. Yea, there's only *one kind* of force Alexander, Darius, and Napoleon to which would tamely bow before: Diogenes, Heraclitus, Goethe. But the passing of the age of kings and conquerors should not mean the slow death of the philosopher. Though the powerful today are the slaves to opinion, fashion, and the moment, the philosopher, as I have said, must not humble himself before the poorly fashioned golden calves of popular culture. It is not in his blood to compromise. Even Emerson could affirm the essential *dangerousness* of the thinker, how such a bird-spirit holds in his hands the lot of mankind, naming this spirit, before Nietzsche, a superman. Well then, if the thinker is the *most dangerous type*, it should become clear why our academic day laborers are not dangerous, are not thinkers, are not philosophers; for these most perfectly assiduous academicians raise no alarm, disturb no one: they have, by their example and by their writings, turned a beautiful goddess into an old hag: and this, my pampered Anglos, is the unforgivable sin!—So let the highbrow philosophic journals hum like deranged bumblebees.—I will be waiting backstage for the sounding of the belated alarm; waiting for *you*!

353

When from a lofty height the prophet looked down to descry the idol encircled by nude dancers carrying torches, and heard paeans of womanish wailing, his kindled anger caused the breaking of the tables of stone. One could say that, theologically, Moses was experiencing all at a rush the very contamination the later prophets would fulminate against. But I believe the Mosaic anger stemmed from the stark *lack of resemblance* between the idol and the God of Abraham whom Moses had just seen on the mountain top. Well, if Moses would come back to the earth, not as a prophet, but this time as a graduate student in philosophy (—transferring from Chicago to Columbia, finally to settle in Cambridge, having exposed himself to the rococo and rodomontade of our professional philosophers, proofreading their papers and pieces for publication in the highflown journals, editing their books, blurbs, and kickshaw professional reviews, and sometimes, accompanying them on the cocktail circuit—), we could rest assured that he would experience the same kind of stark lack of resemblance between the professional esthetes and the real philosopher.—The professional is lost and awash in knowledge and exegesis: his end and aim is to know many things and write glosses; whereas the real philosopher is devoid of scholarly exegesis and *employs* knowledge as a kind of coloring, shading, and means of expression for the communication of a vision. (—Suffice it to say that our professional tenure-chasers have no vision, let alone visions, unless we exclude the eye candy seen by the brothers who do "African philosophy" at Harvard when they get ahold of some bad marijuana—).—Our professors of philosophy are false and boring for one overarching reason: they *profess* philosophy. Conscious of having a boring content, they at least want to give this ugliness form: so they race around (—sometimes saddling off to stuffy board rooms of celluloid collared chief executive officers to give nifty little lectures on "ethics." This they do for extra pocket money; when they crave a little extra glory, they'll knead out exciting new glosses—) displaying their erudition with a special kind of decoration and ceremoniousness on and off campus. But this feverishly restless display of erudition does not give form; it merely conceals. One should see through the whole campaign as deriving from other sources; specifically from the indecent haste and breathless grasping of the popular culture: fashion, public opinion, instant gratification, non-stop mindless "news"—aha! our narcissist journalist pigs have struck again! Certainly, he who has to live among Americans, and not just philosophy professors, will either be blissfully unaware of this ossification of humanity or suffer from it; and since the artist must suffer, this constitutes a ready criterion for the recognition of bad art, of non-art. "Life is a journey," he will say with a wry grin and impish glimmer, "and not a destination," but since he has furnished this dictum of an overheated Lessing no critical thought (—then, too, was the good liberal theologian a little tipsy from a few German black lagers when he chanced upon this modern misconception?—) our good professor who shuns real journeys is armed with *a justification* for his racing around! Not truth, but the seeking of truth! Then, with the very same glimmer and grin, he'll ask, "What is truth?" And this is my reply: whatever truth turns out to be, either for overheated theologians or philosophy professors, the element of "journey," of seeking asserting its complacent precedence over possessing, is the surest excuse for keeping contemporary culture far away from philosophy's balances! It's precisely at this point that our grinning, glimmering professors think I am speaking Cantonese, and for this conveniently self-serving, sufficient reason: they are one and all good, dialectical leftists, and consequently, they believe that social "ills" are to be abolished and social lies defended, expounded, justified, and glorified; that a utopian vision of the Rousseauan kind is the *only* critique, the only *possible* critique; as if philosophy's *sole* purpose consists in Professor Dewey producing some socialist weasel like Sidney Hook, Professor Bloch indoctrinating a gaggle of gaga-eyed, 1960-ish Frankfurt Schoolish radicals at Tübingen, or dear Professor Marcuse going off to California to gather the students in a conspicuously neo-matriarchal huddle as a hen gathers her chicks, etc. (—and, finally, not to forget, certainly not to *offend*, those scholarly spoonies who comb through philosophic texts hunting for "racist" simulacra, banalizing philosophy with that slavish instinct for resentment that seeks always to pull down, never to build up—).—But let us return to the professional glossators who make up "Continental American philosophy," their many "readings" which muddy the philosophic stream, their "thinking," etc; and, of course, let us take up our question of the stark lack of resemblance between these passionate professional students-become-professors and the true philosopher. The scholar will brag that it is the better part of wisdom that affords him or her the luxury of open-ended experiment in ideas. Quite right, for it is not the scholar's ideas he is experimenting with; but it is surely scholar's bosh to say that the scholar, the philosophy professor, trapped in his herbarium of glosses upon glosses, possesses the luxury of not knowing where his thought is going. Such is to downplay the fact of routine and habit in a scholar's life. It's simply *shameless* for the scholar to grab with coarse, perfunctory hands a virtue he doesn't possess, is incapable of ever possessing! For the scholar is forced along many paths and channels, whether *he* knows it or not, certainly not the narrowest of which is the domain within which he has immured himself. Self-imprisonment is made possible by the scholar's denial that other domains exist! The scholar will say that he is so fortunate to be afforded the leisure for his "work." Absolutely not! Most perverse perversity! Happy marriage of self-delusion and pomposity! The scholar will have *nothing* to do with leisure for the simple reason that he does not know what to do with it! *Otium* is his bane, and thus his non-option, his flight-from! A good existentialist can lecture on dread and authenticity until his deceptively adventurous voice cracks, but like the mule who is immune from all the possibilities of vertigo, he is afraid of venturing out, and unlike this mule, he trembles at the thought of "the next day." He can only think of *this* day: his scholarly proclivity to explain, collect, sift, annotate, compile, examine, interpret, and patiently listen to *someone else's* thoughts. And for what? Precisely to evoke some kind of narcotic, some emotion! for *something* must inform the scholar that he is alive! some personal satisfaction regarding political sympathies, aesthetic preferences, etc.; and last but certainly not least, the consolidation of his position in the guild, quite oblivious of the fact that, although it's painfully true that scholars crave honors, recognitions, and offices, and every guild member must watch every other member like a hawk, man, even glossating man, must not live by bread alone.—In all that concerns the evolving philosopher, those who seem so sure that *they* are philosophers— the scholars and austere logicians who unravel alleged tangles in the sciences, the professors who pat-a-cake diverse elements of previous thought into unrecognizable wraiths of "higher syntheses" according to ethical, aesthetic, and political preferences, which by no rhyme or reason have nestled into the professional craniums, and which ultimately derive, as aforesaid, from the popular idols and icons of contemporary culture, i.e., non-culture—have an irrefragably harmful effect: their sharp, loud voices, congenital insensitivity, lack of comprehension of the philosopher's distress, etc., *grate on the nerves* of the genius: they either pass each other like ships at night or they fight!—And why? Precisely because of the antipathy to *original* thinkers, *that is why!* If a Socrates, a Nietzsche, or a Kierkegaard would turn up on the American scene today—either inside the herbarium or on the streets—; suffice it to say that a "free people" would brand such an unwanted misfit with every "ism" in the book. Socrates would *not* have lived to see 70, etc. And what does this mean? (—Aside from the painful fact that the *idea of correct speech and thought* has been accepted into the American marketplace and dominates without exception; and this in the face of all the shams of pitiful heartthrobs over Constitutional liberty, freedom to express and think, etc.—) Precisely that the conditions necessary for the production of the thinker have *not improved*, and have actually declined (—eventually they will cease altogether—). Like the Holy Fathers who prayed that Christ remain where he is and not return to earth—for a Parousia would mean the end of the temporal church at Rome—the sophisticates of the philosophy establishment wish never to see a *real* philosopher. Such a thing as a Socratic presence, a Kierkegaardian thrust and parry, a distressing crate of Nietzsche's dynamite, would imperil such an established guild's *existence*. For in that glorious day, philosophy would be *done* and not merely talked about and dickered with as if it, philosophy itself, has no real existence! No; one thousand times, No! If a philosopher showed up in the conference room—full of stern glances, uppity frowns, elevator shoes, and jacklegged, xiphoid-headed dolts writing inestimable doctoral dissertations on epistemological, cosmological, ontological, teleological nonsense—this philosopher *would not be recognized*. And why? A total lack of resemblance to the American conception of *who the philosopher is*. If recognition did someday come, he would be condemned for the simple reason that philosophy distrusts, and has always rightfully distrusted, the so-called values of the ordinary man; if, therefore, philosophy cannot accept these values, declaring them to be counterfeit and anti-values, philosophy must search above the heavens and below the earth for ways to expose the hypostatizations of these values: the popular idols before whom every free soul daily bends his epigonistic knee.—And please refrain from looking to the classicists for a better bill of health! Believe me, they zealously pursue culture and all its trappings, but *deny* culture three robust times before the cock crows. Classical culture belongs *to them* and must stand in the service of *their* requirements: they too are blithely involved in a basic misunderstanding. One of the problems here is satire, ancient satire (—a genre historically proximate to philosophy because of the bilious sharpness and offensiveness of its social critique; that wit and playfulness are only literary fronts for seriousness: that laughter is but a tool the satirist uses to *overcome* an obstinate unwillingness to criticize prevailing attitudes—). Again: popular culture has come to dominate the world of knowledge. Mr. Jefferson's question, "Whose foot is to be the measure by which ours are all cut or stretched?" may now be answered: the feet of the idols of popular culture! Ask any editor at a small press *why* anything but *correct* satirical work is unpublishable, i.e., why the press cannot touch it. The honest editor will say, "Satire as a genre is under a cloud in this country. There's a constantly expanding list of things the writer cannot say, etc." Here, *once again*, follow the evidence trail and you will find yourself right back in the laps of those who hunt for racial innuendo implied in literary texts. Yes, comrades, when you see some downfrowning bumblewit toting a placard that proudly proclaims, "Social justice," what he's really saying is, "Someday you will *pay* for my justice!" The relevant idol here, of course, was given life in the Harvard Law School and the courts: special protection for special groups. Well; let me say here that *he who pays* will someday—Oh, I prophesy it!—*require payment*. After all, what is the real difference, once your quiddities and aridities are laid aside, between the Voltairean ecrasez and a fascist club?—But let us return to the issue whether classicists, when they proclaim to the wide world they are affirming culture, are really affirming themselves. Classics study in the university today is a philosophic case in point. Same facts, therefore, same result: if Juvenal, the extraordinary writer who developed the genre by his peculiar *existence* and not just his keen power of perception, mastery of caustic wit, vituperation, etc., and brought it to stunning perfection, were to appear, *cum furor scribendi*, in the classics department of a major American university the great satirist would be condemned and forced to recant (—and if, by some excellent fortune, a few of the more hardcore Juvenalian barbs escaped academic condemnation, these verses would have to go up against the prior restraint censorship of the publishing world—). Why? Because he attacked the sacred cows of the protected groups! that is why! But that classicists have no sense for classics is a brute fact perfectly consistent with the *nature* of the classical scholar. Just look at the way they, the classical scholars, revile Theognis, Archilochus, Hipponax, and others . . . "Xenophobes, reactionaries, haters, impossible men," they will say (—now if some pudendum of a book worm would be so kind as to tell me what's wrong with xenophobia, reaction, hate, and being impossible, given the fact that literature is, and ought to be, amoral—). To keep it simple: Juvenal's anti-homosexual satire should be loved the same way, and for the same reason, that Theognis, the boy-loving homosexual, should be loved. Ah, but I am speaking Cantonese. Forgive me, my unconditional, unprejudiced acceptance of genius.—It is because of the arid self-satisfaction of the scholars that they fail to recognize the genius when they see him (—and once recognized, he is condemned—); or, the same: it is because he, the genius, does not resemble them that he is maligned, and his work, at least when it first appears, is treated with bovine indifference. Very well; but this is the question: what do these things *matter*? I mean, as long as the great exception is not derailed from his task! The solitaries, those who choose the tortuous, he-goat's path, and who, because of this destiny are unwelcome in their own age, are excommunicated, but once literary necessity has struck, they learn to adore it.—You have refused to fall in line and have gone your own way. Like Xenophanes, you toss yourself up and down the coasts of Greece, shying away from everything that would prevent the making of a philosopher! For the age only conceals who you really are; conquer it in yourself and the ghost you behold in the mirror will be a philosopher.

354

What have any of them to do with me, these lazily inactive, supine philosophy professors? They have turned philosophy into minutiae, concealing this outrage with pedantic precision. Conversely, if they possessed any knowledge, how could anything be *done* with this knowledge?—And don't forget their rakes, will you please? For their "work" consists of this: the raking together of something for themselves from the results of European philosophizing, science, contemporary feminist labors, and sometimes, as if to intentionally elicit curiously quizzical smiles from their more dialectical conferees, literature and art. Any observer can see—that all this raking together and synthesizing of ready-made, disparate elements is carried on beneath a luminous canopy, a great golden ceiling and many-colored dome beyond which their brilliant conclusions may not extend. So, what is this ceiling, this scarlet taboo not to be violated or ever questioned? As if the answer to this question really mattered, for if there exists a pre-established orthodoxy philosophy is not free to penetrate (—or, if you prefer, if philosophy will not and does not ever raise a finger to acknowledge or question the taboo—), then this philosophy is surely only special pleading, not philosophy. Nevertheless, I shall answer this pertinent question at once: the ideals—oh! did I say ideals, I meant to say *idols*—of the popular culture existing within the wider expanse of juridical culture, this is to say within the unquestioned matrix of the democratic ideals; *these legal totems turned moral* make up the canopy beneath which our dear philosophy professors perfect their studied glosses. Very well; the cramping depression and gloom any *free* votary of philosophy experiences the moment he or she sees with comprehending eyes that the professorial class is woefully remiss in its duty to *declare in practice what philosophy is*;

this natural vexation is explained by simply taking a peek at where the true allegiance of this professional class really lies.—Granted that this claque of bad thinkers who can only think popular culture and bow down before the idols of this culture has called down upon itself the curse of the ludicrous (—for who can deny that they *are* ludicrous, what with their fang-bearing social activism to the tune of "universal happiness" via "dialectical oneness" and other professions of lunacy on the outside and such obsequious quietude on the inside?—) must we also admit that they have called down the same upon philosophy itself? To the extent that this professional guild entrenches itself, any effectiveness of a true philosophy will be brought to naught (—or at least obstructed; for if any real philosophy wants to prosper today it must wage a war against the pseudo-thinkers in the American academy—). The cultural task of distinguishing between the real and the bogus in the realm of philosophy must first begin when the American pop culture *sees the approaching enemy*, and recognizes once and for all that there can be no peace between the true and the false.—What then is the *task* of true philosophy?—*A ruthless critique of the popular idols.*

355

My conception of philosophy is too antique, too pure for a thought-and-calculator machine mentality. Too antique, for you derive nothing but antiquarian knowledge from the ancient thinkers, no substance, no spirit, and certainly no direction: you cannot even *see* the ancients. Too pure, for popular culture has taught you to raise the most negative presumption against purity in any form. Moral: demonize purity. Purity breeds class bias, racial prejudice, religious fanaticism. The idea of pollution preached by the Hebrew prophets breeds intolerance. Conclusion: my philosophy stands squarely in the way of an emerging order that bullies the genuine human beings and causes them to lose faith in themselves. A philosophy of light and wind; of horrent resistance and reaction; of the *anti-matrist*: such a philosophy has, until now, been *lacking*...

356

What makes one regard university philosophy professors the way a hard-core satirist regards his target victim is not their curious ability to blend innocence with self-conscious weightiness, not even their seemingly natural capacity to look, sound, and seem profoundly deep when they are not; what impresses anyone who knows even a little about the world in which they live is their viscerally cavalier dismissal of the most important, most pressing matters (—I take special care not to say "problems," for their identifying trait is the identification of problems in a "text" where no vital problem exists—). If a real philosopher were to accost one of these good professors and slap him in the face; this is to say if a real practitioner would identify these pressing matters, and begin a careful discussion, even a politely Socratic discussion, both the real philosopher and his honest concerns would be dismissed, summarily dismissed.—And *why*?—Why would such Socratic honesty and forthright clarity be dismissed so cavalierly? Well, it seems that these good, devoted, brilliant philosophy professors—if I may seize upon a descriptive term popular in the East Texas oil field of the 1980s—are such *pussies* that if any spirit in their presence launches into a truly critical critique of our contemporary idols and taboos, such a critical critique would be branded mean-spirited and tyrannical; such branding has surely been inculcated by our legalistic, political culture, replete with its demonizing, "got-ya" mentality, which approximates, and must approximate, the worst aspects of the Athenian democracy. Philosophy professors, apparently, learn by osmosis. Political correctness, more correctly cultural correctness, has gone philosophical, and attempts at *cultural critique aiming at roots* is now not only not done, but expressly disallowed. Socratic gadflies; Kierkegaardian hornets; Nietzsche's heavy artillery—; such is taboo. This is the meaning of the indictment filed by those pop icons against the greatest exemplar of philosophy in Greece: Socrates was not really doing philosophy: he was operating a one-man show outside the ambit of popular philosophy, i.e., the kind of popular philosophy that taught aretē. Translation: the polar opposite of cultural critique aiming at roots.—The American Continental philosophy professors will say, rightly, that the logicians hung up on epistemic analysis are dodging the vital concerns of philosophy; then they will exclaim in that tone of half-thoughtless aplomb every student has learned to recognize as easily as he recognizes the sound of wind chimes, "Oh, do tell! Heidegger has ventured so far out, and has opened up such a vast terrain! It will be years and years before we will be able to appraise his work and issue a verdict!" (—Notice the "we"—). Then the same guild of professors will go back to the Husserlian paradigm and begin imagining things that never existed, that could never exist, inside the "act of mentation." The subject-object cramp gives way to the being-in-the-world question. This is to say: the same philosophy professors who reproached the sterile realists-positivists for their sterility and non-relevance; this same guild is now experiencing cramps of its own; to wit: they rush out to stake their claims in this vast terrain Heidegger has opened up. Who are the only worthy ones to survey this terrain, and thus, by the staking of claims on this territory, render a verdict on the *opaque* Heidegger? Why, our philosophy professors, of course! Then let every brilliant philosophy professor squabble with every other brilliant philosophy professor! These acts of scintillating exegesis can never be synoptic, can never reach out and grasp society. No; these acts are analytic, confined to a "terrain." As Burke said about the law—"the law strengthens the mind by narrowing it"—so now the logicians can turn and say, "Your skillets will reproach our pots for being black?" Quite right! The Heideggerian claim-stakers delve down; they use picks and shovels (—to be more precise: archaeological tools—) and shy away from artillery pieces. As aforesaid, they will cordon off a piece of this terrain and squabble among themselves over "place." One will say, "This is my place, here by the river." Another will retort, "No. Your place is across the river in the bushes. This here by the river is mine. I like to fish." All of this is based on imagination, you understand. Concede that Heidegger did open a terrain; what must be *done* with this terrain? There can only be one answer to this question: students must be taught to be synoptic for once and learn to think critically about this purported terrain. How is this feat pulled off? Precisely by *leaving the terrain!* If, say, one wanted to map a shoreline would the mapmaker count the grains of sand on the beach? Would he measure the height of the palm trees that dot the littoral, crack open the coconuts, and measure the precise amount of milk therein? Would he count the "mentative acts" of jellyfish? No; he would leave the shoreline to appreciate its configuration. But one other possibility exists with regard to Heidegger's "terrain." It was declared subsistent only as a means of satisfying the feverish needs of philosophy professors.—

357

You ask me about the *loves* of philosophy professors?—"Love of wisdom"—; what could this mean? Surely, it means to follow through, to go the entire distance, to hear the echo of the spirit groaning for truth, to fly up and out, unhindered by the comforts of common humanity . . . As Prince Myshkin says, "I have been happy in other ways." To say this in other words: the philosopher will never stop along the way. Specializing or compromising he cannot comprehend. Question: have you ever seen a philosopher do anything he cannot comprehend? These professors will say again and again—and in these very words—"Nietzsche is my first love." Or they will say in their inimitably childlike fashion, "I experienced this and that, but returned to Nietzsche, my lost love."—*I cannot convey the horror of such assertions!* Such delusional thinking is to *be pitied*. Count the times the philosopher Nietzsche was disturbed and shattered like glass; *therefore*, his philosophy consists of disturbances and shatterings: if Satan had tempted Nietzsche instead of Christ, the stones would have *remained* stones; and if Nietzsche returned to practice philosophy, as Christ returned, in Dostoyevsky, to the Church, he would have been rejected. "But," the philosophy professors would say, aghast, "your very presence in our groves will set back and thwart the work of philosophy. Return, O shattered one, to your double-mouthed, high cave on Lemnos, and leave us in peace."—*Nay, I have come to torment you before the time!*—I take it that any *professed* "love" of Nietzsche must be appropriated existentially, not merely comprehended, and hence felt in an abstract way. How do you appropriate Nietzsche existentially? Such an appropriation means to break from solid ground, and the "danger" Nietzsche continually warns of is the danger of vaporization. Wheresoever the self, in Nietzsche's cruel cosmos, has not been vaporized, there shall be no remission of sin. What difference can it make for the professor who will assert that such breaking from all solid ground is scarcely possible—as, say, in Heidegger's analytic, Dasein tears away from Das Man only, in the end, to be authentically reunited with a community, etc.—when, in fact, the good professor, again comprehending everything necessarily abstractly, has in no form or fashion broken from solidity *himself?* For a breaking here can only mean a spirit *continuing on its way*. What? Did you who *profess* "love" for Nietzsche really believe his metaphors were inexact, fanciful, inapposite, and out of place in the context of his whole philosophy? Come now; if you cannot appropriate Nietzsche existentially, how can you say you "love" him?—Do you love him? Well, batten down the hatches; you'll *sail away* with the next wind.—But you will *not* sail away; you will stay on the land, for there's safety and security on the land. If you choose to risk everything and, as he said, build your city on the slope of Vesuvius, you must one day leave the land: then there will be no more "land."—What? You love Nietzsche's solitude, his solitariness, the basis of heroism, the very heroism Napoleon saw in Goethe? Well, now, you'd make a fine hero, wouldn't you? You'd die of frostbite if you threw away those security blankets, those satin comforters! For the hero's essential solitude consists in this: he, the hero, has not a single companion truly of *his own kind* to console him. And between someone and no one there yawns a dark and foreboding infinity! Ah, that man who goes down into the caverns of the earth, that spirit who lives in labyrinths! Mark that spirit, for his intent is the overturning of the powers of the earth! So, I conclude you do *not* know what solitude is; you have no way to know. Nevertheless, you *do* know, I believe, what this solitude looks like, even what it sounds like: Goethe in the Campagna; Beethoven's masterpieces.—You say you love Nietzsche's example? *When have you ever once followed his example?* And yet you profess love for his example? How so? Once, in the flare of a fresh campfire, Jesus, alone with Simon Peter—for the disciples had journeyed to the nearest town to purchase meat—asked Peter, a rough man unaccustomed to searching questions expressed with such poignant tenderness, "Simon Barjona, lovest thou me?" Peter barked, "Yes, Lord." Jesus asked a second time. It was quiet for the fire had settled. "Peter," Jesus whispered, "lovest thou me?" And Peter said, "Yes, Lord." Peter fetched more wood. The fire had settled again. Jesus needled Peter, "Peter, lovest thou me?" Peter said, "Lord, you know I love you. If you go away, where shall I go? What shall I do? Thou hast the words of eternal life." Jesus said, "Then feed my sheep." Well, this sermon on love and its attendant discipleship should make you professors question yourselves; *when have you fed anyone's sheep?* Nine and a half times out of ten, you are too high and mighty to feed even your own students. And you . . . you are capable of *love?*—No; not that I expect a modicum of contrition. A philosophy hall is no *locus paenitentiae*. You, after a while, change your tune, and assert, "We can surely love what Nietzsche loved." You said this well; now let me ask you a question. What did Nietzsche love? "*Amor fati*" you answer, suddenly emboldened, "was his last love, and if this stoical love, this authentically life-affirming fusion of acceptance and conation, was his last love, this love of *fatum* was surely his greatest love." I grow so sad when I hear you professors spout off in this confident manner that reveals your learned innocence. Fate, here, has nothing to do with freedom, still less with unfreedom. Here Nietzsche has done no more than adopt Goethe's uncanny sense of *literary destiny*: the uncommon individual is possessed by a sense of his true destiny, an exalted, refined conception akin to religion. Stoical allusions miss the mark: Goethe and Nietzsche were professing a kind of Horatian faith, a beautiful conception adumbrative of the love of the Muses for a man. Yet, as with every expression of a pagan faith, doubt shadows belief (—This is not the time or place to delve into the precise manner in which Kierkegaard's celebrated Leap is at odds with Abraham's calculating faith; e.g., *if* the promise must come through Isaac, *then* even if Isaac dies, he will be resurrected; as is attested by the Abrahamic command to his servants at the foot of the mountain, "I and the boy shall return."—), and so to the degree that the evidence of the things seen preponderate over the evidence of the unseen;—suffice it to say that circumstances, sometimes, plunge the pagan faithful into despair. As just alluded to, Nietzsche chooses Goethe for his fideistic model. This brings, and ought to bring, any serious writer of serious work at first sadness, then in the very next moment, surges of infinite joy, when this writer beholds the great ones, inundated by the presentiment of a terrible and terribly lucid dread, scrambling about trying to save their feverish scribbling from the inquisitorial censors of silence and indifference. The same censors had put Schopenhauer in the stocks, had bound and gagged him, so that, through the little window of his dim prison cell, he was granted the exquisite torment of seeing the self-renewing nimbi glow iridescently about Hegel's frightful, bony head. Nietzsche knew how Goethe worried over the possibility of being unknown . . . *Goethe*! What a telling moment of truth when we see the *ardent* Nietzsche, torn from the university and from Richard Wagner (—who had secured for the young professor his first contact with the publishing world—), shotgunning queries, enduring the hauteur of the German commercial publishing houses, and finally, seeing his publisher almost exclusively occupied with proto-Nazi activities to the utter neglect of the contractual promotion of Nietzsche's earliest polemics against a rank Germanism he would finally come to hate. Ah, would his literary remains bear the impress of this all too agitated turmoil of literary doubt? Since faith—to the eternal chagrin of our puffy Tillichians—is the antipode of doubt, Nietzsche, out of the artistic religion of Goethe, would fashion his own private expression of Goethean destiny: *amor fati*. Thus, Nietzsche, the *great* Nietzsche, carries with him into the inaccessible boundary regions of alps and ice, the necessary anodyne and effective medication against the serious writer's greatest nightmare: not to be born while he is alive! But the philosopher grows in this faith and experiences death's foretaste as glorious posthumous birth! Like King Jehoshaphat, who gathers together his motley praise and worship team, a team that will go *ahead* of the army, Nietzsche sings of the coming dawn! *Amor fati*; this means: every roadblock, every closed entrance, is taken away in the twinkling of an eye, and a great stairway stands revealed. A "No" is transformed into a great "Yes." What? Didn't Nietzsche explicitly say that it is a *lack* that produces the artist, *and therefore, the philosopher?* And if a commoner such as a philosophy professor experiences a lack?—First of all, the lack of a common man is but a common defect; add to this the fact that every commoner experiences common things in a common way; then we will have at best a common thinker! To return to our question: what did Nietzsche love? Surely not just philosophizing, but creating great philosophy. Tell me, when has a philosophy professor created *any* philosophy? If the philosophy professor is incapable of loving what Nietzsche loved, how can the professor profess any love for Nietzsche? There are American Continental philosophy professors alive today who chewed on sauerkraut at Herr Heidegger's table; does this turn them into philosophers? philosophers, moreover, who philosophize out of a love for wisdom? How silly to say you love Nietzsche when you cannot experience what he loved and *how* he loved it. Nietzsche saw how creating great philosophy and *fatum* constitute the same thing, a *fatum*, for sure, no philosophy professor has ever experienced or is capable of experiencing. There are even examples of ambitious philosophy professors, who instead of professing a silly, chimerical love for Nietzsche, manifest a dishonest hatred of Nietzsche. Surely Heidegger saw Nietzsche, especially Nietzsche's honesty, as unendurable. Moral imperative for Heidegger: explain Nietzsche away! Gloss him to death! Heidegger the glossator will get rid of Nietzsche's honesty and replace it with *his* dishonesty. Question: what *is* the Heideggerian vision? Nietzsche spent his short life penning the original hashish visions experienced with his friend Wagner; thus, Nietzsche carries his readers through with this original shamanic vision, but Heidegger carries us so far and then drops us. Is *this* the reason to drop Heidegger? Don't be silly: if Heidegger's Being cannot be thought, Heidegger's Being, and hence Heidegger, should be dropped. The "end of philosophy" is Heidegger's futility; *therefore*, Heidegger's futility is the end of Heidegger. The whole corpus, absent his Unthought, is simply so many footnotes to Kierkegaard and Unamuno. The question is not, "Did Heidegger disavow Nazism?" The question is, "Did *Dasein* disavow Nazism?" Heidegger touches something and then spins a riddle about it, all this in face of the plain fact that philosophers have devoted their lives to unriddling things, and more often than not, the ominous riddles are *there* because of the monkeyshines of some professor who practiced before the mirror all the choreography of profound facial expressions, etymological poses that result in nothing, and, not to forget, flaunting his gamy little skullcap, which in reality is a dunce cap.—Then, too, the whirl of recent French thought emboldens the guild by bringing in more raw material: the glass jar is filled to the brim. This new material is guaranteed to smolder in the lillypates of our good, profound professors for quite some time (—indeed, maybe for all time, since there will always be new French thought, i.e., French thought about French thought; as Camus says, it's all about erotics and ideas; . . . in that order—), which guarantees in turn the professorial proliferation of ever new, exciting, colorful quiltworks pieced together from a variety of French snippets, which, on principle, fill out lacunas in Heidegger, and for sure, undiscovered lacunas in lacunas. Variety, local color, and second-hand gymno-notions constitute the spice of philosophic life, correct? Ever novel and intricate possibilities for philosophic dishonesty crowd in to fill the fermenting void, and thus scratch the powerful, and powerfully ineradicable, professorial itch. With one hand, the professors give grateful homage to Nietzsche's free spirit as the first principle of wild philosophy (—I take it that wild and French are perfect synonyms—); with the other, they concoct smorgasbords. At length, the professors convince themselves that they have escaped the glass jar when in truth even their next book on Lacan, Lyotard, and Levinas offers no such freedom. They need each other more than ever now (—even though knock-down-drag-outs *still* occur, and each professor regards the other as a) his intellectual inferior, and b) hopelessly tethered to Untruth—). Their "work" and "thought" become a kind of quietly desperate semaphore for American political liberalism, American political Deweyism, and all the other "isms" Nietzsche decried in every sentence he ever wrote;—still they *love* Nietzsche! No usable elements are refused. They'll mine the unbridled speculations of the American *theologus liberalis*, that rare bird of our exciting new thought, for special "insights" (—like that *rara avis*, Mark Taylor—the name is bland, but the beak is exotic—) culling every little usable piece of tasty pickled meat for the *expanding* philosophic smorgasbord. Question: are they unaware that Nietzsche had no patience with the *theologus liberalis*? that the profound, and profoundly clownish, David Strauss possessed *no intellectual honesty*? And, by extension, David Strauss' children—via Adolf Harnack—possess no intellectual honesty? Yet these professors *love* Nietzsche? Yea, the love felt by an undergraduate too inexperienced to understand Nietzsche, who feels an uncanny exhilaration at the bare mention of existential freedom, the freedom philosophy *promises*, is a thousand times more acceptable than the love professed by professors! For it's a fact: that very undergraduate will one day express *his* love for both Nietzsche and freedom when he throws up his hands at all the pompous pedantry, entertaining while he is still uncorrupted, all the bright and unique ways to be free of philosophy as it is done and, do not doubt it for one moment, as it will *always* be done in our fine universities!

358

How can we perpetuate the *lifestyle* of professorial philosophy? What can it mean for the continuation of an authentic Western philosophical canon when one gives a Continental hermaneuticist an inch and sees him take a mile? (—A mile that must be settled and homesteaded by droves of American Continental philosophy professors, whose profound glosses on tortuosity convince them of the critical nature of their "work."—) Well, for sure, the fact that the Continental takes a mile explains how the American Continental has a mile; but the inch, the inch! A half inch of linguistic obsession combined with an equal amount of seeing texts in a mechanical way (—connecting texts to an unconscious "text"—) renders one whole mile of hermeneutic possibility. A monstrous notion! Philosophical texts *belong* to the hermeneuticist! A pompous way of saying that written philosophy belongs to the philosophy professor;—a roundabout way of saying that the bare, bleak, philosophically lifeless Anglo-American world has the last word with regard to the meaning of a text! Or the same thing: a literary work's *reception* constitutes, *can* constitute, its meaning, vitality, substance, etc. And this in face of the fact that *philosophical texts belong to the one who intuits them.* Yet the philosophy professor comes to believe the opposite: texts have doors, and only the professorial clerisy may pass through these doors;—specifically: texts have wishes and desires, and thus hermeneutical acts become an exposure of the truth of the text's desire. Even assuming the possibility of such a self-serving fairy tale, the objection that the hermeneuticist is insufficiently honest to carry through with such an endeavor immediately flies up to fan the air like banners. To *expose the truth* of a text's desire? . . . What *is* this? As if such a trumped-up exposure accorded with a *pure* investigation into truth! As if the whole hocus-pocus procedural form of professorial hermeneutics is coldly and blithely unconnected to the mood of contemporary popular culture that causes us to notice some "problems" and not notice others! The very professors who wring their dainty hands over the non-relevance of philosophy—pointing a mean, self-righteous finger at the logicians, which, I will say it again, is the pot calling the skillet black—are the same professors who consciously or unconsciously import whole slabs of "modern ideas" into their pseudo-self-unwinding investigations and bow down unabashedly in unphilosophical obeisance to the golden calves and sacred cows of the popular culture.—In any case, the students, wherever there exist circles of serious students, i.e., students whose love for philosophy (—the desperate desire that philosophy be as genuine as it was in ancient Greece—) is of the kind that takes jubilant precedence over everything else; these students insist upon calling these self-satisfied professors who worry about philosophy's non-relevance even as their example tears the ground away from any possible relevance (—and who in this way turn the student's love into something ridiculous, unsung, and invisible—) by their name: the culture clones; and by culture the students mean precisely the circumambient world of popular values, the very ordinary values genuine philosophy deems meager and wretched. Through a superstition in the collective psyche of the culture clone, he identifies the sycophancy and phlegmatic lack of all feeling for courage and incautious honesty in the genre—the fact that on the day he became a graduate student, he began to see himself as an ineffectual, time-serving crew cut who plays a game and who must, on pain and penalty of immediate delation, play a game—with the spirit of philosophy as it has been revealed to us in the great thinkers. It is quite *possible* that these culture clones who call themselves philosophers really did learn something from the example of the young Nietzsche: when he turned his back upon the dreary scholastic spectacle, and thus enshrined and cultivated the values of courage and incautious honesty, he forfeited his professorial standing: he was attacked for being courageous *and* brilliant, honest *and* gifted. He was driven out by mean spirits; but, ah! I am being facetious. Nietzsche chose the stigma of obloquy the same way Socrates chose death. *And when Nietzsche chose to be different, he chose philosophy.* So, Nietzsche began to philosophize out of this formative experience: to leave the crowd, to forsake the things held dear by the crowd, to choose the high, unbeaten path of the prophetic type: *this is the beginning of philosophy!* Therefore, the problem encountered by genuine philosophy is precisely that of the un-genuine calling itself genuine: the culture clone fancies himself as the exemplar of genuine philosophy! But this apparently sincere fancy is also a sincere delusion: when the popular gruel of fêtes champêtres is mistaken for wreaths of laurel and clover;—on this day the Muses are mocked: when pigs consider themselves philosophers, philosophy becomes a pig pen.—The question that obtrudes itself more and more is the question of the *why*, and by correlation, the even more dramatic question of the *how*: why does the philosophy done in the universities submit time and again to the popular culture? What is this dynamic? These questions can only be answered if we glance at *the scholar's relation to the intellectual* in American life. First, the scholar feels himself to be a kind of all-knowing pygmy at the feet of the American intellectual. Perhaps this is the reason William James would not encourage W.E.B. Du Bois to enter the academic *profession* of philosophy. Perhaps the good pragmatist had the *consequences* of such a move in mind; put it that way. And yes; Du Bois did things as an American intellectual he couldn't have done as a Harvard scholar, who lives, and must live, in the glass jar. But to return: the professorial scholar feels shortchanged, and he *is* shortchanged. Continually hearing what the big truck drivers sarcastically refer to as "chump change" jingling in his rather large pockets, the scholar gazes up at the intellectual in an unfeigned—even if not always visible—spirit of adoration. The intellectual lives at the center; the scholar, the periphery.

The scholar thinks about thinking; the intellectual thinks, then does. Compared to the philosopher, who hovers, sometimes menacingly, above both these types, the scholar and the intellectual patently belong together in the same guild; and yet it's not the similarities but the differences that show the relation of the knowing, *analyzing* scholar to the more ambitious, *creative* intellectual. What is striking is that since the intellectual is a kind of artist, he may operate without intellectual credentials, even as an autodidact. Try to imagine the scholar naked, bereft of his degrees! Here we must visualize the intellectual class in America, the active clerisy, as artists in the *broadest possible sense*, for the guild includes historians, manufacturers of narratives of all types, the writers and actors of filmland, radio and television icons, judges, journalists (—the creators of history, story, images, juridical novelties, news—); the *creators of popular culture*, the active coiners of popular values. Is it any wonder that the more sedentary type casts an envious eye at the creative people? That the scholar, the professor who fills the scholarly journals with his all too tortuous, technical verbosity is, and by right ought to be, in a kind of puerile awe of those who occupy the limelight, move and shake the real world by their ceaseless social machinations, and who, like the dog, though cursed with a brain that is small, are blessed by virtue of a keen capacity to use what they do possess, with an adept and ambitious perspicacity (—which, to be perfectly frank, the others in the guild often, but quite erroneously, refer to as "genius"—)? Perhaps, also, the scholars envy the avowed ambition of the pop artists: to take absolute charge of the leisure hours, and hence the ruminative hours, of modern man (—I am impertinent enough to assume that *homo faber homogenens* still possesses leisurely, ruminative hours) and thus to stun and stunt this man of modernity. Since, say, the invention of celebrity culture by a virtually omnipotent Hollywood, the spectacle of the Washington press corp bringing down a president, and certainly not to forget the putrid arrogance of our novelists, the televised gladiatorial shows, and the doctrine of a correct and an incorrect speech sedulously planted by a multicultural-preaching federal judiciary intent upon the creation of a new kind of ruling case law that makes no bones about the law's right, and indeed the law's dictatorial duty, to jump ahead of the social ethic, etc.; since these stunning successes we refer to as "gains" and" progress" the new popular culture is all happiness, dignity, and poignantly exalted self-awareness. One might perhaps have expected that the more thoughtful of the cultivated Americans, say, our fine literary novelists, for instance, would have recognized the dangers inherent in such a *misuse of dignity*, or at least have felt this spectacle as painful: for what could be more painful than seeing perversity and deformity parade about as a superior state of human happiness and awareness? But our literary people are perfectly content to let happen what is happening, and have, in any case, quite enough to do with maintaining their august reputations writing spicy quidnuncs for the *Times Literary Supplement*, lamenting the disintegration of the literary novel in the *New York Review*, and other wise pieces for assorted journals (—could be *possible*, dear highbrows, that writing literary novels and concocting ever spicier quidnuncs do not mix; and thus what we really witness is not the "death of the literary novel," but the disintegration of *your* instincts, the vanishing of *your* literary integrity—) and are just too busy to look after the welfare of their country. In fact, the literary class is convinced that American popular culture is such a palpable advance over all previous cultures (—though their bitching over "Puritanical culture" and "Christian fundamentalism" is still quite the pastime—); that although "there's still a long way to go," it's the journey, not the destination, that is the fun of it; that, alas! the command of freedom to adapt to anything and everything is the most palpable proof of personal morality; that justice means tolerance, and tolerance means accepting all and rejecting nothing; that the greatest bulwark of our liberties is the "eternally vigilant" campaign to politicize every aspect of our lives so that the "real America" consists of one long, dreary, Dantesque cavalcade of journalistic side shows and Constitutionally-mandated feeding frenzies;— now with all this social justice happening, why should anyone, let alone our pampered highbrows, get up the gumption to care or do anything at all about the welfare of the American spirit?—Then, it is *possible* that the scholars admire the intellectuals, those self-satisfied, preeminently unphilosophical people who spend their lives creating and burnishing a popular culture, out of a kind of fear. I should think that those people who merely want to survive and live only for the moment are capable of inspiring a kind of fear. And why shouldn't our scholars, those who do philosophy within the university sanctums but have no philosophic spirit in them; why shouldn't these kittens be at least a little bit leery of the lions of the bold savannah, who, if they knew anything, would know one basic thing: it's best to live without any wonder, any true wonder at the world; and the most successful, "happy," popular artist is the one who wonders at nothing. Therefore, any attempt made to attack the self-complacent coziness of this elite would be punished swiftly and severely. This is to say: any scholar who dares to stand up and do philosophy as it ought to be done, as it has always been done by true philosophers, would be exposed to the very thing the scholar most fears: obloquy; i.e., he who attacks coziness and contentment shall have *his* coziness and contentment attacked, and this is dreadful. Well, then; witness the unabashed antinomy: while professing to hate fanaticism and intolerance, what the scholars really hate is the tyranny of the demands of genuine philosophy. Forsooth! the demands of genuine philosophy! This is to say unequivocally the demands of ancient philosophy as practiced by the leading spirits of the ancient world have themselves become fanatical and intolerant! No one is more aware of this than our dear scholars who must think as the popular culture tells them to think. Not to say, however, that they do only what they are told, for as aforesaid, the scholarly envy of the pop intelligentsia endears them to that culture created by those popular intellectuals.—Finally, whether it's jealousy, envy, fear, or some unknown prompting that governs the American scholar's strange relation to the American intellectual, you may place all your bets on one invariable certainty: when the time rolls around for the philosophy professor to concoct another one of his language twisting vanity-pieces, i.e., another volume of *profound* philosophy, its backdrop will always be the popular culture itself. Just as in law, a restatement is a kind of temporary codification of rules in an effort to delete the confusion in the case law, so the work product of the scholarly caste in philosophy becomes, and most certainly *is*, a nebulous, sometimes imperfect, even *unconscious* restatement of the popular values. What has been accomplished here? What has been *done?* Precisely this: a kind of philosophizing claiming to be philosophy is made to mirror the ordinary values, the philosophic cloning of the very phenomena philosophy is intended to expose . . . and *condemn.*

359

Ever since the suspicious schemas Kant went about peddling were finally accepted as the basis of a new kind of philosophy, the philosopher has dared to believe that *names* are sufficient, nay, more than sufficient, to confer real existence as regards phenomenology of perception. All the philosopher must do to solve problems and invent new ones is: invent terminologies; construct more schemas; and then fill in the gaps in these newly constructed schemas by inventing ever newer terminologies! Episteme says with a leering frown, "All my children have been named, dismembered, renamed, reconfigured, and named thrice more." Then, and *only* then, the philosopher bestows upon every existing thing the *wearisomeness* of his weariest smile, and says, "Ontology! The queen of the sciences, ontology! See how the argument has finally led to ontology!"

—Whence comest thy weariness, my wearisome friend?—"Herr Heidegger's imperative of death awaits!"

Yes, *how much* dreariness, how much weariness, the epistemological, ontological phantomry of philosophers has injected into philosophy; how much *depression*! This thing philosophers call ontology, this capricious itch we call ontology, what is it but an apprehension of fugitive shadows, a shadow play in a shadow world incident to the *old age* of philosophy? These flitting shadows in this philosophic Hades; are they nothing other than the darkest shadows of mourning for the sudden death of the old mental god of philosophy?—The ontologist does what he wants to do, and then retraces his steps—*as if* he is walking with Socrates—to provide ontological wherewithal for all his doing, all his desiring? Question: what are the *needs* of a budding ontologist? What are his needs today?—The day shall arrive, I promise it, when Heidegger, lifting up his weary eyes in a resurrection, shall see coming in the clouds and at the sound of a trump, *his* gadfly; as Herr Professor Hegel had his Kierkegaard so Herr Professor Heidegger shall one day find his suffering Dane.—Another question: what is the future reception of existential systems?—Heidegger chose death. Why? To rip poor Dasein out of Das Man; as if death were the *only* way to accomplish that! And the result? Weariness! Dreariness! Depression!—Listen! Can you hear the ferruginous pealing of the bells at the Church of St. Martin announcing the *revelatio continua*?

360

The genuine philosopher is ingenuous to the nth degree: he is always looking at the world for the first time precisely because he is overtaken by wonder. To say the same in other words: the philosopher is a poet whose poetry is his life. How is this done? By cutting oneself off from the past: by confronting the world for the first time *everytime*. Like our fabled Underground Man who refuses his "best interests" for higher, more dangerous values, the philosopher has put his best interests behind him. With regard to this severance from the past, the philosophy professor of late has been somewhat vexed. He has finally recognized that Herr Heidegger forgot the past by overemphasizing the future, so some say, "We must reconnoiter this forgotten dimension," and others speak of "nomadism," something, it must be confessed—despite his little trips to those places most exemplary of the nobility and savagery of the noble savage—again and again, the professor knows nothing of, for if he did know it, he would certainly be *less* of a professor for it. This is to say:

time-severance is the precondition of nomadism as wonder is the precondition for this continual cutting oneself off from what once was. True, Sartre *speaks* of some such severance, but he has never experienced it (—it is only, to be sure, one of his arguments for an absolute freedom that exists in his head; but not, incidentally, in Miss de Beauvoir's head—); and Heidegger's ontologic freedom;—what use is it to speak of being mired in a freedom one does not *use?* Precisely the problem with existential systems.—Since the tendency of the philosophy professor is to remain in his current state and not venture out, isn't it expectable that he never enters his own proper sphere, the sphere of true philosophy, i.e., the *ruthless Socratic mission?* Another question: exactly in which state or sphere of existence does the one who professes philosophy remain? I have likened this state of raw potential to a young, starry-eyed tyro who yearns to become a fiction writer. This tyro is in love; he is in love with the idea of writing, the romance of it, without considering there might be more to it than that; as the tyro, the romantic yearner, encloses himself within his self-made cozy world, his heart tumbles into vertigo at the bare thought of *another world* existing outside his self-made one. In other words, to enter the market means the certain recognition of his illusions *as* illusions, and hence the vanishing of the illusions. Likewise the whole tribe of philosophy professors, by fabricating a kind of interstitial dalliance and *interpretation* of philosophy, a kind of intersubjective romance with philosophy, intuitively recognize (—I say "intuitively" out of kindness; this possibility of philosophy slaps our professors in the face every day the sun rises over their hallowed halls of "philosophy"—) a genuine, albeit dangerous, risky, uncozy world, a world into which our tribe doesn't dare step. For to view philosophy as a Socratic mission, a Nietzschean critique of the dominant values (—in our case, *coming values*—), a Platonic assault of the popular values;—this means sacrifice, and the open-faced acceptance of a kind of life our professor recoils from in abject horror.—Here comes one now. He says, "We philosophy professors are hardworking hangers-on, delving deep into the meaning of philosophy in our noble effort, our noble undertaking to tell us who we are."—There you go again! You might just as well go up to a man being devoured by a serpent in the tropics and tell him who he is; I beg your pardon; since you'll see him not as a man, but as a splinter or walking shadow of Heidegger's Dasein, I should have said *what* he is; and I'm sure you'll get his attention with your asinine post-thises, post-thats, and all the hopelessly sclerotic scrimshaw of your hermeneutic cobwebs . . . How vain our philosophy professors are! How malicious! You ask me how they are malicious?—*They chase the best minds out of philosophy.*

361

I don't know what meaning philosophy could have for our time unless it is purposely directed against our time and is tended and nourished as a force against our time. You may say my view is quaint and dogmatic. I will reply that this "view" has the whole history of philosophy on its side. Here, I explicitly exempt the so-called Frankfurt School: the Marxist-socialist critiques should be seen as so many radicalized potentiations of the democratic ideals. These ideals speak—and most certainly are heard and obeyed—across millennia: they are calling the matrifocal, the *womanish* values back again. Thus, the final verdict—what philosophy must *do*—of philosophy's brief, almost inconsequential, history stands at the next great turning point of human history.—But I, the first and prophetic anti-matrist, seek disciples in the queerest sort of way: you must follow yourselves before you may share my vision and climb up to follow me . . .

362

Let us divulge a secret: the professor's fossorious capacity constitutes the apex of professorial achievement: connecting the galleries of Herr Professor Heidegger's catacombs by way of burrowing new hallways—openings large enough, that is, for a normal-size graduate student to clamber through; and, not to forget, the acquisitions editors at our university presses—replete with the standard and standard-baroque, Heideggerian convolutions, involutions, and necessarily obscure ornamentation;—this is the high tide of American Continental philosophizing! Adding new, vogued-in-France, hermeneutical, hermeneutical-semiological, structural, and post-structural dimensions to our basic, time-tested Heideggerian blueprint has lately been, and is likely to continue to be, the chiefest, and by the lights of a true philosopher, the stiffest, timidest, most *unseemly* form of self-pleasuring possible; . . . but fossorious! by all means! I provide an example: whenever a good professor stumbles upon a fissure, at least what appears to be a fissure to a philosophy professor, in the Heideggerian text (—and, please remember, this tribe *fetishizes* texts—); where a philosopher would see an inconsequential gap in the Troglodyte's lugubrious thought-train, our professor sees yawning abysses; where we notice mere predicatory hiatuses, our hardy hermeneuticist sees infinite possibilities. As the true thinker runs nimbly through the catacombs with a jealous eye to decide what has passed away and what is being raised in its stead, our professor, our bright-eyed dodderer beclad in his mantle of musky goatskin, and sometimes, a dainty skullcap, measures his steps in mute self-testimony of his cramps and pains. Not to intimate, however, that professorial wisdom can be spotted only by way of skullcaps, mantles, or timidity dressed up as learned method or brilliant capacities for an all-too-workmanlike thoroughness;—no, no! Our Heideggerian, like our conjurer of Being himself, is known for his idiomatic dexterity, his polished neologisms, his incomparable way with words! In fact, *he* thinks, all the daring elbow-rubbing with Herr Professor in the 1960s and 70s made him who he is today (—ditto the longhairs, angelic exponents of Marxist bildung sprawled about in opium-scented peace huddles at the feet of Marcuse and Ernst Bloch—). Well, he is who he is; let's leave it at that. When he sits down to write, he becomes that dashing, fabled playwright who enveloped two Manhattan models in his scarlet-lined cloak, sweeping them off to attend rehearsals of his new Broadway play. Yet the cloak, the leggy models, are but evanescent fantasies; what endures is the look on his face: it's as if he's presiding at a literary luncheon at the Algonquin or, better still, composing his features for a portrait: sometimes, if his office door is open, he puts on a wily, feral look to intimidate the students; other times, he makes his face resemble Heidegger's or Gadamer's. But there is nothing to commend such poses to the true virtues of philosophic writing, e.g., abundant power, boldness, nimbleness; no, not a trace of the spirit that once took up its abode at Nørregade, Ferney, Sils Maria, or the Agora, but plenty of cautious scrooching and straining; any semblance of the daring stride of one who plays with his material has become starchy constraint; love of truth—truthfulness itself—parades as the glairy bombast of prolific disingenuousness, and, not to forget, our newest avatar of sophistical "technique."—"But, but," our Heidegger-Gadamer look-alike retorts, "our investigations, though necessarily mannered to the hilt, and sometimes stilted, never descend to the gutter of shabby American jargon. Although we witness the sorry dilapidation of the American language day by day, we are not taken in." My retort: *tu quoque*. Mannered? Stilted? You are too kind; or are you *under the influence*? Another question: does anyone care to arrive at some kind of perspective on philosophical writing? Philosophical writing claims a just independence from what the great Arthur Schopenhauer referred to as the slime of newspaper language; but is this independence an immunity from another kind of slime? Where is the serious student of philosophy who does not sense the literary rescue effort of Nietzsche and Kierkegaard? This rescue consisted in the campaign not merely to dismiss lameness—impotence pretending to possess power; obscurity masquerading as lucidity, at least a lucidity for philosophic cave-dwellers, etc.—but *deformity* in philosophic speech! The mission? To replace bad air with fresh air: *to drain the Hegelian swamp*. Firm land at last; clear skies; a fresh horizon; the *sounds of the swamp* have been replaced by the whirr of crickets on a clear night, the plash of waterfalls, the cry of eagles. Then what? Out of the Black Forest, a hunchback comes swearing founderous locutions even as he reads Sophocles and Hölderlin! Yea, a hunchback who says by every word he writes, "I thank God for my magnificent hump!" What *then*? Precisely every philosophy professor not of the analytic school is converted to this guff. These enraptured professors, whose most conspicuous exemplar is that shofar-tooting Emmanuel Levinas, see this newest swamp not in any sense objectionable, but as stimulating refreshment! As prime and, without question, *preferred* locutions for philosophical discourse! Question: how does one *write* for the highbrow philosophy journals? One *reads* the philosophy journals: one accustoms oneself to the same manner of philosophizing, i.e., the same words, phrases, locutions (—Need I add here that the books a professor of philosophy publishes grow out of this same rut?—). This manner of expression defines the guild; the philosophy professor learns finally to listen for its endless repetition, and experiences pain in the absence of such tintinnabulation. *Therefore*, woe to the stylist who avoids these professorial locutions, and for the simple reason that he, the real stylist of philosophical writing, finds the whole extravagant and extravagantly pompous mosaic sickening. Precisely the experience of a genuine philosopher prevents him from ever recording this experience the same way a professor (—who, I will repeat as many times as necessary, *has no real experience*, no matter what kind of globetrotter he may be, and for this reason: he is and remains self-tethered—) tries to record his dancing angels on postmodern pinheads. Then, in the classroom, the conference room, or on the lecture circuit, these same soulless elves will ominously say, "A writer of philosophy imitates his various models." Bosh! Professorial bosh! Any writer of philosophy who writes outside the glass jar writes as his personality *compels him to write*. When we read Montaigne and Nietzsche, we are looking at their insides; this idea of self-confession is what makes a classic writer classic. Montaigne's experimentalism—his invention of the essay—is a result of his natural gaiety, charm, and stubbornness, i.e., it's an expression of his moods. The marvelously ferocious later Nietzsche springs directly from the burial of his name during his lifetime in absurd silence. This is what I meant when I said a moment ago that you professors of philosophy are one and all under the influence: all your written work could have been composed by the same professor; and this is professionalism! This is *philosophy!* Is it any wonder then that the philosophy professor derives comfort from the fact that all the philosophic world writes as he does? Is it any wonder that this world consists perforce in the working out of his logical tangles and the assuaging of his imaginary cramps? Finally, isn't it *necessary* that the truly forceful and uncommon thinking expresses itself outside this corrupted world? For, isn't it far more likely, as Montaigne taught long ago, that the pupil is naturally apt to gain more profit from the uncouth language of taverns than from the artificially constructed syllogisms whose sophistical quibbles lead him astray through their fallacies? These factitious syllogisms had *their* day, so the cobwebbery that grows in unventilated basements will have *its* day. Then again, as long as these catacombs exist—and do not, finally, fall into a twilit desuetude—there will be monks eulogizing bones.

363

With a vacant, forlornly sensitive look on his face, the professor of philosophy will speak in affectedly sonorous tones we should reasonably expect to issue forth from one so self-exalted and sagelike, saying, "From the very beginning of my philosophical life—"—Stop right there!—The good professor meant to say, "my life," or better still, "my time spent in university philosophy." For a professor of philosophy, a man or woman who *teaches at a minimum* and thinks more of tenure and the next cozy, wheyfaced driblet for the journals;—well, when one of these strutters and crowers, struts and crows about a "philosophical life," any serious student destined for a philosophical life must call down the strutter and demand an accounting. Perhaps the professor is intentionally confusing a philosophical life with an academic life: that the Academy *is* philosophy, that miring oneself to the Academy *is* an answer to philosophy's call. Is there an *honest* confusion? Self-deception?—Go on, professor.—"From the very beginning of my philosophical life, I have found myself drawn to phenomenology because—"—Stop!—The professor is saying he is drawn to a school. How can a schoolman possibly answer philosophy's call? By working in the school, for the school, on behalf of the school, in light of the school, examining the life of the school? Very well, by applying the insights of the school! But to what end?—Continue.—"This method respects the reality of experience and empowers subjectivity in its struggle to twist free of the cultural interpretations oppressively heaped upon it." Yes, yes; but what does this mean? That one must climb Husserl's ladder and think as Husserl thought to twist free of the restrictions non-philosophers wallow in? One must enter in at the strait gate of Husserlism as the only way of freeing oneself? Let us assume you *are* free; free to do *what*?—"Well," he says, "free to critique the culture, the society."

What you say and what you do, Herr Professor, are clear polar opposites, for your "critique" will do nothing more conspicuous than grovel at the feet of the popular idols. Therefore, I say that it's a demand of culture *that philosophy be free of our Academy as it now exists.* Lest the curse of the perfunctory that the representatives of this Academy have called down upon themselves strike at philosophy itself and bring to naught both American *and* European philosophy. But who will hear this voice crying in the wilderness? Can the ant turn and rend the hill it has erected? Nay, things in philosophy are glacial, and we may have to *wait for a long time.* But this Professorial Tower of Babel will come down;—its uselessness unmercifully exposed; its fancy gossamer, its disgusting non-relevance seen as gossamer and frivolity.—Oh, yes, philosophy will wrench itself free, some fine day; the glass jar will be seen even as it now purports to "see," and will become a mere artifact in the history of philosophy, as say, those disputatious, arabesque-spinning monks of dialecticians, strung out on the ivory tower aridities of a rank canon law, were buried by the eventual crowing of the Cartesian rooster!—But, ah! I am being facetious. Although the gossamer arabesques, the angels on pinheads, the marshaling of finespun arguments for the sake of subtlety, etc., constitute the similarities betwixt the monks and fastuous professors, *this time* the monks of Heideggerians are working toward an unarticulated even unconscious goal!—Before we reveal what this *unconscious* goal is, we will allow the good professor to continue with respect to Heidegger's question, the question of Being.—Herr Professor? Go on!—"The question of Being demands an open hermeneutic receptivity to whatever might come, whatever might emerge, from the self-concealing origin of openness into which the question throws us. The question whether Being is speaking gets resolved into the question of whether we are listening. This hearing, then, belongs to alterity." Then, the good professor, with the goal of combating the evil and violence "some of us see in the world," launches triumphantly-timidly into a Levinasian ethics. It should be plain to anyone, well almost anyone, that the professor has but a nebulous notion where he is going, and an even foggier idea where his Heidegger is going (—the question whether Heidegger himself knew should probably be answered in the negative—). Heidegger's thinking is a road, and the piper himself seemed quite certain that the future world would inevitably come tramping down this road. But to which possible destination? The essence of Heidegger's thought is "listening" and "waiting," and this *inedita* is adumbrative of an unwitting evocation of long dormant matriarchal values. These *new values* will then serve as authentic guardians of Earth. Consequently, only one lost in the details, only a foggy-eyed professor, would nominate Heidegger as a major thinker. Heidegger's thinking—how shall I say?—services one side of the conflict: the all-out war between the old male values and the promised matrifocal holy order. The final conflict is the war of religions. Does anyone understand this? Even Nietzsche had his grand formulations, his grand *plans* for man, but Nietzsche never expected the return of the *Magna Mater*: the insidious resurrection of the pre-sky god chthonic myth. Therefore, the question—*our* question—is: what can philosophy do? Within the helices of the *strong* species whose fertility and power keep the faith in the male values, in the male idea of light, spiritus as opposed to the swamp of impotence with its new nurturing morality, etc., and the emerging Mother-worship, philosophy must choose sides in the greatest, most momentous conflict the world has ever witnessed, a gigantomachy of light versus dark. Everything moves toward the decisive Yes or the decisive No. Unity *against* division; division *against* unity: that is the law of this conflict and all intellectual values are at stake! As aforesaid, this university philosophy has taken sides whether it is aware of it or not; as I have pointed out, it is the side of the popular idols of decadent *demos culture*. Indeed, the whole juridical machinery of democracy appears as another tool to be picked up and used in the struggle for the new passive order. Nothing is wasted; every event *means* something; every soul, someday, will be counted. The fight against the active energy of everything dominant and everything with the spirit and strength to stand erect, the seduction of valuing the exceptions as a *means* to suffocate the exceptions finally in the mass—: the apotheosizing of the "deviant," the "pervert," the half-god, half-satyr-hermaphrodite, the trannie-eunuch as a "higher form" of human, hatred of the normal, the square, the "straight" as forms of oppression, intolerance, violence, etc.—; yea, this today is full of gods and demons, powers warring for *mastery of the earth!* Presently, the worlds of politics, law, journalism, new ethical theory, and contemporary theology struggle to winnow the old values, for before the new temple can be constructed, the old one must be destroyed. How to destroy? Discredit. Slander. Demonize. Hands and feet are moving, tongues are wagging, minds are machinating, but why? *Why?* If philosophy, the sworn enemy of the popular culture of every epoch, casts its lot with the ever expanding matriarchal ideals, and therefore *works* for the eventual extermination of the individual and his spiritual, suffering nature—whether beneath the umbrella of an enticingly decadent new French thought or the *essential passivity* and earth-numbness of a Heidegger listening for new divinities—well, philosophy has been forewarned!—With the notable exceptions of Nietzsche and Kierkegaard, the Parmenidean confidence has entailed the so-called reconciliation of opposites as a kind of corollary. Nothing syncretic is alien to me, Plato said, and this dictum begins its march through the millennia culminating in Aquinas and, of course, Hegel. What am I saying? Simply that philosophy, as if at the behest of its nature, its overweening need to prove to itself that erecting cathedrals is *the* way to demonstrate its power over "reality," will seek out ways and means to synthesize the waning values with the miraculous return of the emasculate values in the unmistakeable avatar of a new world order. What can philosophy do? What *will* philosophy do? Synthesize. Synthesize *what?*—*Opposites!*—While the suffocation of spirit exalts similarities, not differences, the resistance—the *necessary* reaction to all this accumulating miasma—will and must exalt differences! The will to difference, the demand of intolerance, purity as the highest principle of life, as the divine itself hiding from the contrary principle of reconciliation: this is incorruptible religion, the *prophetic* hatred of pollution. More: whole cultures must resist the coming flood, and this resistance is nothing other than their last ditch efforts to *remain* cultures! First: equal rights, the consolidation of mediocrity in desires and aims (—all the while glorifying "dreams"—), maintaining and increasing the flow of Mother's milk, i.e., the steam of new things, new ways of putting to sleep, i.e., the narcotica of technological teetotums, the extirpation of suffering, green pasture happiness for all, absence of insecurity, the extirpation of "hate," insensate glorification of hermaphroditism in every possible form, the condemnation of every war as unjust (—consequently the inability to fight—), the psychological demand that everyone be seen as a victim, that everyone be regarded as dysfunctional (—the consequent demand for everyone to serve as nurses—); the demonizing of all patriarchal religions as so many atavisms to a brutal past, as glorifications of violence, oppression of women, domination of children and animals, as man's own self-alienation in the *male gods*. Then: a reversal of the reversal: the formation of iron brotherhoods for the purpose of combating the womanish values, nation-cults for the maintenance of *grand souls*.

364

When we have our grand expert on the Middle Ages, that quasi-Catholic magus, perfectly content to dwell in some gloomy Thomistic hole in the morning and devour the newspapers in the evening, maintaining all the while his acute interest in hoisting himself up to a little system of metaphysics, when every thinking person has abandoned both systems and metaphysics (—so prettily decorated and crowned with those mental deities who, as Kierkegaard preached, should be offended to have their existence demonstrated every single time a philosopher feels like it—) in light of the known fact that such idle constructions, such airy castles, besides making the tourists dizzy, will soon be of no interest to anybody. This decorated doctor, whose work is well known to the likeminded professorial elite in Europe, will rear back in his high chair and say, "The Middle Ages said such and such on this point and the Middle Ages said such and such on that refined quibble," when if this four-eyed time-server had really wanted to know what the Middle Ages *said*, he would have learned to read feudal law.—My hopes are dashed; he crawls back into his hole—yes, the *same* hole—to gloat over Aquinas in the original (—no wonder I hear such experimental vivacity crackling in his innumerable maxim-bestrewn disquisitions!—), swearing up and down *he* enjoys the beatific interpretation of the beatific vision! Yes, he'll kick around the forced abstruseness of medieval theology all day and night—sniffing every quiddity and haecceitas the way a stray dog sniffs a bitch's rear—never once happening upon the real issue—I should say the *vital* issue—in the totality of medieval thought (—and he never discovers this issue precisely because Professors Maritain and Gilson, being good Catholics first, special pleaders next, and "philosophers" last, either never discovered it themselves or were too learnedly pigheaded to explicate it—): *whether philosophy pollutes faith*; whether your papally glorified *ratio* denatures revelation; whether Luther and Calvin were *made inevitable* by the syntheses inaugurated by the very first theologians, who, as sowers, sowed the seeds of the doctrine of works; whether the Reformers were made possible and necessary by the greed and drunkenness of the canonists determined to introduce Roman methods of administration into the Roman Church; whether the central issue of religious syncretism produced eventual corruption the same way syncretism in ancient Israel *made the prophets necessary*; whether Athens, as Tertullian said so well, has anything at all to do with Jerusalem; whether Kierkegaard's either/or is the religious equivalent of Elijah's either/or.—Later, the good professor converts to Heidegger, our modern analogue to Meister Eckhart. He worships the masterfully concocted myth of Being for what seemed to the students a short while, is finally disillusioned of Being's nimbi, then apostates—presumably on account of Nazi hunters whose principal thesis seems to be that only a fool is foolish enough to view any thinker apolitically;—when it's precisely only a fool who is slavish enough to perform shameful sacrifices to the popular idols by politicizing everything;—yet Nazism is Nazism; so what is a disillusioned professor to do? Well, he satisfies his many philosophic needs, I meant to say his many professorial needs, and runs for shelter beneath the rainbow of a

Levinasian ethics, primarily because the novel idea, *he* thinks, of an obligation grounded not in spirit, but in flesh, in a completely finite transaction of flesh to flesh, turns the good professor on; to which I reply that Thomas Hobbes is the hare and Levinas is the tortoise.—Now, alas! hasn't our professor come full circle? Having left the Thomistic hole for Heidegger; having left Heidegger for an ethics of flesh; well, our good professor is left with the newspapers!

365

Not that university professors, whose life in the glass jar tricks them into every pose and every mask that justifies and, in the end, sanctifies every scandalous bit of dishonesty about themselves—most notably the piece of presumption that they are *philosophers*—; not that these fine, self-puffed pseudo-seekers don't at certain times entertain a desire for an independent existence. There are even cases in which university professors have acted upon such daring, unconventional ambitions. Take the case of the English chappie, who be-bopped across the Atlantic just to get a peek at the world-renowned wealth and poverty of our North American wilderness. Always under the influence of journalists and journalism, he'd "learnt" about the "racism and xenophobia" of the people—especially the horrible racism and xenophobia in the American South—; consequently, he had in the meantime, following the airing in Britain of a journalist's perspective on the "civil rights movement," come to believe that he, precisely in the capacity of a self-puffed pseudo-seeker doing philosophy in a wild, unkempt wilderness that needed him, could with some diligence, a great deal of persistence, and even more gambler's luck, produce a bit of reverse racism and xenophilia that would have two, at least two, immediate consequences: 1) it would prove to him that he'd made it not only across the Atlantic, but out of the glass jar; and 2) he'd actually done something to improve our wild, unkempt North American wilderness.—Well, you had better believe that this ambitious, starry-eyed Englishter, who had no desire to get rid of his punchy, carpetbaggerish accent, couldn't wait to write a fresh little piece in the journals telling, I should say *listing*, all the things he had "learnt," and in so short a time. First, he found out where the philosophy department in Memphis, Tennessee was (—but this special knowledge and understanding of the geography of our wilderness didn't, unfortunately, tell our good philosophy professor where *he* was—); and he soon took professorial notice that the blues, and jazz, the music so evocative, at least according to Hesse the novelist, of the doom and twilight of ancient Rome, were sung on the wrong side of the tracks, the poor side, the Black side, the swinging side according to our good professor. He'd delegate more and more work—if a rational being can call it work—to the t.a. just so he could have the leisure time to stroll through the real Memphis, the earthy Memphis, the Black township he called heaven. Not to say that our good professor didn't carry his security blanket around town. He was fearful of ever assimilating to the extent that he would lose his punchy Englishness. No, our professor was too afraid, too ashamed, to walk into a club as a mere White man. Once, as he exited Antone's on K Street, a short, thick Black man surlily accosted our timid professor. Jazzed-up and a might whiskied, his fear of the natives came to a head. He cowered when he heard the belligerent demand for "change," when he saw the pugnacity of the man's features, when he noticed that no one was around and nothing moved, save the gaudy flash of blue neon above their heads. *Shall I die in this strange North American wilderness?* He stuttered, stammered, tried to decamp.

"Hey, man," said the panhandler, rubber-faced in a laugh, "let me tell ya next time a man want some money, ya know what ya tell him next time that happen?"

Our professor shuddered.

"You tell him I'm broker than a piece a-glass!"—Though our good professor had disabused himself of religion while still a boy in merry ole England, he took a hankering to the Black churches. Fearful that the young preacher of the Ebenezer Baptist Church, who had a peculiar way with words and quite a style of delivery, might subliminally sway him, might perchance hoodwink him into believing that Jesus Christ was more than a man, might through sheer histrionics engender a *lapse*, he took to the habit of reading the slimmer works of Paul Tillich during the sermons, and sometimes, the ravings of Jimmy Baldwin, the manifestoes of Frantz Fanon, the dark race-treatises of Du Bois, the striking words of Langston Hughes. He joined the Frederick Douglass Society, dated a Black woman who taught him that the secret of serving delectable pigs' feet is simply to season the feet with bell pepper and onion, befriended a young rapper name "Forty" (—Forty always carried a forty-ounce bottle of Schlitz Bull—), read the slave narratives (—although the one-sided nature of these stories never dawned in his brilliant mind—), and mulled over the civil rights documentary in the most serious fashion, the most *philosophic* fashion (—never once realizing that journalists are in the image and propaganda business intent on one thing and one thing only: shaping policy—). His incessant mulling resulted in this: whenever he sees a poor Hispanic, a poor White, he feels nothing but indifference; the poverty of *this* man, the situation of *that* man, says not a thing to his exquisitely refined sensibility, his social awareness, but when he sees a Black man stumble out of the Thunderbird honky-tonk on East Main, he starts an interior monologue about "hatred, bigotry, lynchings, oppression, White demons burning crosses," etc. When he *imagines* the same man accosted by the Memphis police, he thinks how the environment—"institutional racism"—determines a man; specifically, how institutional racism made a man drink himself to oblivion and resist arrest (—Or was it the downers, the cocaine? Well, as they say around Memphis, "Same difference."—); how the perfection of justice, and most especially in the North American woods, is the ability to *shift off* responsibility for an act to society, to the *other* man, to the *other* side of the tracks; and social justice means so much to our good philosophy professor, especially in his adopted country, precisely because, as he preached in the classroom, it had so very little of it.—Our acute Englishman's high-falutin ideas of criminal law aside, he finds that his reading of Tillich during the sermon is no longer *necessary* (—which means the sermon itself has come to satisfy his innermost desires even more than an integral existential theology satisfies, and has always satisfied, his innermost desires—); the preacher is setting forth the gravamen that the Western canon of philosophy *excludes* "Egyptian philosophy," i.e., excludes *him*, specifically as he thinks of himself and sees his black face in the mirror every morning in Memphis, Tennessee, and especially Sunday morning, when as God, or is it Osiris, gives him specific utterance to preach to Black Egyptized Christians. So the question for our White philosophy professor sitting in the Ebenezer Baptist Church on K Street is: is the refusal of nothing the ultimate justice? (—Hence the definition of a "bigot" is one who doesn't adapt to anything and everything.—) Stated differently: what is the connection between the Black African's—this is to say the sub-Saharan African's—reaction to Western man's imperial colonization of Africa and the paradigmatic imperial role of reason in philosophy? But this is not the *only* question for our gifted philosophy professor, who insists that the overriding issue is how the Western philosophical tradition relegates African philosophy to the back of the bus;—a specific location on the bus that a philosopher not caught up in the fisticuffs of Africa, and by simple and inevitable extension, African-America versus the West, is not at all prone to admit its innate inferiority to the front of the bus.—Or: what specific historical fact in Western experience accounts for the Western exclusion of African oral traditions, which manifestly contain much moral philosophy, from the philosophical canon? The answer (—at least the answer for guilt-ridden philosophy professors obsessed with race—) is: *racism* . . . the great, unintelligible, indefinable naught . . . *racism*! His proof? Precisely that the imperial paradigm of Western reason denigrates pre-philosophic African myth; that the Western tradition excludes myth, story, maxims, moral beliefs, et-African-cetera. As if our canon does not have an inherent right to do this; as if it is unjust (—bigoted, oppressive, prejudicial, racist, etc.—) for this tradition to make a beeline for Greece when there *is* a beeline for Greece: i.e., the purposeful exclusion of oral traditions; unless one says that everything is, in some sense, philosophic and is therefore philosophy: that the rabbit that escapes from the fox has an escape philosophy or a rabbit philosophy, and this is what accounts for his success or failure to escape from the fox, who we can be sure has a fox philosophy and a rabbit-eating philosophy.—With *The Souls of Black Folk* in his left hand and a sleuth's magnifying glass in his right hand, our professor determines that in former centuries, the bigoted West determined to "restrict philosophy to a linear tradition beginning in Greece." What? A *linear* tradition? Precisely so! For the professor's unspoken yearning is not for a straight line, but a circle. To say the same: African philosophy is matriarchal. To *want* to undermine the "unity of Western philosophy" is tantamount to the professor's contemptuous attitude for the idea of *distance*; not that the unity of philosophy is the real problem, but the *integrity of units*; stated religiously: the purity of doctrine; philosophically, the principle of individuation, the life-affirming tension of strife; distance in a word. The forces that stand in the way of the production of the authentic philosopher are the *same* forces that blunt the effect of great philosophy. The existence of the philosophical genius is one thing; but a cluster, an efflorescence of philosophical geniuses confined to one specific period and one specific geographic location, which taken together with the simultaneous efflorescence of literature, art, political innovation, freedom of conscience, the bold letting loose of the individual for the first time in human history;—well, this sort of thing is more than enough to engender a tourbillion of modern resentment! Nay, that one magnificent peak should stand out surrounded by valleys; that one magnificent giant should arise amidst a common, all too common, concatenation of lunar seas and desert intervals! This suggests, this *demands* the construction of the world-process not as a straight line going forward, a "human spirit" marching forward—God marching through History, as Hegel would have it; and as our dear American Deweyites would have it, exalting biological values over intellectual values, the matriarchal principle of nurturing and the mere corporeal as *opposed* to the male principle of spirit, light, and distance, etc.—but a fantastic nightscape of waves and undulations, peaks and valleys, over which the great historical spirit-dialogue transpires. To draw a line back to *Greece* is the confirmation of those insufferably prejudicial callipygian strokes and squiggles, we turn and nominate "history." That a *people* constitutes such a peak is an offense against modern decency; excuse please, I meant to say modern indecency. On what platform can the modern sensibility shun the exemplariness of the Greek genius and avoid the very propounding of the idea that one thing might be superior to another?—Progress; but of course! An essential "equality" of all "contributions," leading via an assured meliorism to some phantom of a climactic end of history; not a wavy line in any sense, but a straight line to—a goal! The world as a series of monads devoid of process—and hence devoid of any faith in progress—is a world that is finished at every peak and eternally completed in every dell: there is no envisaged salvation in the process, there can be no salvation in the process. Thus, to contemplate the men and women living at the crest of an apogee reveals more than contemplating future years conceived either as a unit or units (—which could possibly contain one high, one low, or many of the same kind—); and this series of singular universals finalized in each and every moment is the enemy of the idea that whatever follows must be more valuable, as if a valley could be higher than a peak, as if a peak is a stepping stone to something higher, i.e., another valley. When our philosophy professor says the linear tradition beginning with Greece must be discarded, he is surely under the influence of the popular idols: to restrict philosophy to a peak, indeed our highest peak, is xenophobic; more: it is *racist!* Everything our professor sees and hears lately is racist. Does he have race on the brain? Yes, whenever images are seared into the mind of an individual or a people, then surely the mind contains the content of those images; with this result for our professor who can't stay out of the blues clubs downtown, who can't eat enough collards, cornbread, gizzards, black-eyed peas, purple hulls, pig feet, etc.: whenever he refuses a panhandler, he feels guilty; whenever he gives a small amount of money or a generous amount, he feels guilty. The hidden assumption of journalists is that they make the news available to the people, when it is only entertainment they are offering, a kind of dancing, copulating unicorn whose one exalted horn is the desperate attempt to make policy. Deception, out and out deception, is the end here; is this understood? The press is the false alarm that leads the people off in the wrong direction. The truth value in a bit of news is always, by the miracle of the many techniques employed by the journalist class, an entire panoply of legerdemain lifted from the American trial bar, techniques, and time-tested tools of art to *move the triers of facts*, in other words to persuade, to push the minds of "the people" into that *passivity of acceptance*, which is the essential trait of our dear advanced democracies;—this modicum of truth is far outweighed by the stock tonnage of deceit and lies. The people must learn, someday, to suffocate of the journalist's impure breath. The deception endemic to the modern democracies, the root of all democratic evil, is precisely *where the genuine philosopher's disgust commences*; and who in the democratic cosmos knows how to flaunt this evil the way the journalist class flaunts it?—But since our philosophy professor who calls himself a philosopher is not a genuine philosopher, can under the circumstances never become a genuine philosopher, these things never occur to him. That he refers to himself as a philosopher is, quite tragicomically, some kind of midpoint between his conceit (—this is to say his certain knowledge that he is a scholar but certainly no philosopher—) and his actual credence (—this is to say he listens to others in the glass jar and finally comes to believe what they say; to wit: that scholars are philosophers in some sense; when philosophers would never grub around among other people's thoughts for the express purpose of spreading narcotica over these very thoughts, and thus putting people to sleep—). Consequently, for all his pomposity in the form of "cultural critique," he never makes it around to an examination of journalism; and rightfully so, for if it ever dawned on him that journalism is a form of theft, that journalism of every political persuasion *dehumanizes*, he wouldn't be the agent to carry forward an examination. Why? Because he is the pawn of the popular values: journalism to him is a good thing, blameless in the eyes of truth. Which brings us back to our philosophy professor who eats pigs' feet and thinks that the African philosopher's search for an "African cognition" (—a search, incidentally, which either will be successful or unsuccessful; if unsuccessful, this is to say if the African philosopher doesn't find a specific cognition endemic to the African psyche, the African remains subjugated by the paradigm of Western reason; if successful, if the African philosopher does find such an animal, then the African philosopher has segregated the African psyche—) is the greatest, most momentous gambit in philosophy since Descartes threw everything out the window but God and the *cogito*. Quite so; yet all the pigs' feet in Tennessee and all the *nzagwalu* in Africa—at least as the idea of pigs' feet and the ground for African philosophy exist in the mind of our Memphis philosophy professor—are emotionally parasitic upon our professor's conclusions, I meant to say our professor's journalist-foisted *fixation* on the American civil rights movement. One must say, indeed, that this movement stripped our Memphis professor of any potential for critical thought about his adopted country (—I assume here that sunlit shafts of insight *can* penetrate, from time to time, the horribly suffocating black cloud of American political liberalism; that our titularly religious, hard-headed political conservatives, those manicured mavourneens of intellectual torpidity, *can* be taught how to think someday—); that this movement wears such artificial and unnatural finery—the archetype of which is Afrocentrism's attempt to *inflate* Egyptian philosophy out of all proportion to its real influence and *what it really is*; and, not to forget, the African and African-American conceit of relocating Egypt to correspond with the Afroist's feelings duly recorded as glossolalia and psittacism; for believe me, African-American-Harvard-Princeton philosophy is based upon how Kwame Appiah feels on a given day—; that a less guilt-ridden and agitated posterity will reproach our age with being to an unheard-of degree distorted and degenerate. The time is past for the raising of objections to this pseudo-philosophy among many American pseudo-philosophies. Now is the time to examine consequences. Although, I will admit, it is a bit early to examine the consequences of these consequences. At any rate, let us begin in the most general way; let us *fly over* this idea of American pseudo-philosophy before alighting on the sturdiest branch of the holy Gandhi tree we affectionately know as the American civil rights movement (—I say fly over not to be poetic or bombastic, for as Socrates was the patient examiner of things above the heavens and below the earth—things his Athenians held in the dearest embrace and thus never dreamed of scrutinizing—the first thing an independent observer indifferent to the tide of public opinion notices is the fact that the Americans have *exalted this movement to the skies*—). A good place to begin is to propound a few simple, but not immediately comprehensive, statements: how odd and oddly frenetic, how capricious, intemperate, barbaric, and vain these Americans are!—thus speaks any observer from a foreign shore—How the essence of the American dream consists in the flirtation with counterfeit philosophies! Oh, where is the modern Lucian who will write the satire of *this!*—Now these foreign observers come to this conclusion by way of a vantage point: they are able to see the Americans as, say, the people in the American heartland see the Californians, especially the denizens of our chilled and foggy abode of eternal youth, San Francisco, where everyone, even Dorian Gray, goes to escape the past. I will be the first to admit that every satirist and every philosopher works from a vantage point, I meant to say *atop* a vantage point. It seems to me of the first importance that there should be created outside those Americanisms calling themselves philosophy today a higher tribunal whose function would be to supervise and judge this pseudo-thinking, e.g., the philosophy of the political liberal, the political philosophy of American Pragmatism (—which *is* the philosophy of the political liberal all over again—) the philosophy of the political conservative, the skewbald J. S. Mill phlegm of Hugh Marston Hefner, and say, the mule skinner notions of Ayn

Rand (—our dizziest Russian émigré, cow-eyed chain-smoker, who in her trashy novels first baptized the dollar "Almighty"—) with a view to *exposing the kinds of education these philosophies are promoting*. For when the foreigner hears about all these Americanisms;—well, that is quite enough to raise some foreign eyebrows. That there is something called honesty, and that it's even a good thing belongs, I know, in our age of journalist-run Constitutionalism and streamlined mass opinion to the private opinions that are strictly taboo. In view of the glaring absence of honesty, the philosopher expects at least a kind of reasonable honesty with regard to the dishonesty, but he will not find *such* reasonableness in America; not today. If the cornerstone of civil liberty the Americans call "freedom of expression" has broken down, the truth requires silence and listening, not, most assuredly not, idle prating and sillily enameled encomiums on our evolving democracy, namely, that this democracy is evolving in the right direction when, in point of brutal fact, it has been snowballing in the *wrong direction* ever since the young, brash Thurgood Marshall entered the Supreme Court building and serenely unsnapped his shiny brown briefcase. If our self-flagellating liberals in their imbecilic "think tanks"—who ever heard of thinking in a tank?—and our self-decorating functionaries in the stingy-machine who call themselves conservatives do not know this it is surely because they have never been told. Are you so naïve, are you so hopelessly brainwashed, as to believe Thurgood Marshall's proferance of his arguments before the High Court based upon how the children *feel* did not contain implicit reference as to how *he* feels? And how *did* he feel? Let me answer this question by asking another question: how does the Africana scholar, the African-American "intellectual," the man or woman on the streets of our First Amendment thumping society;—how do these people feel when they encounter offensive language in a literary text? We must learn to see the well nigh sacred Brown case as *containing* a host of things not originally contemplated by the judges; but Thurgood Marshall; *he* contemplated them, and to this extent precisely: plaintiffs were keenly aware of fashioning a rule for future cases and hence for future conduct. Plaintiffs were keenly aware of steering the democracy in a new direction: specifically: plaintiffs were keenly aware of incorporating premises the hundred-year conclusion of which no jurist dared draw. But Thurgood Marshall; *he* drew the conclusions. Very well; we have again arrived at the portals of our question. In the same way as, say, the right to publish and distribute pornographic material—material not adjudged obscene and therefore protected material—*contained more than the granting of that right* (—the idea being that pornography bid adieu to the shadowy corner and came out into the daylight of everyday mainstream

America—), so it is with regard to the now enormous body of case law and statutory law we refer to as civil rights law. Law, especially law in a common law democracy, is fraught with continuing consequences. The American collective psyche as it is, we see a collective ignorance as to the existence and meaning of these "social consequences." Conceive the matter this way: the people make their mistakes; this, as Holmes reminded us, is the people's right under the theory of the Constitution. But what Holmes didn't notice was this: the mistakes, after being duly and assiduously recorded in the official mistakes of the people book, never get a chance to teach anybody anything; in a word: the mistakes of the people book is a book that is never read, and with this consequence: the people retain not merely the right to make mistakes, but the ostensibly even greater right to commit the same mistakes again and again.—Then, when Marshall came to the Court, he would sit up like a wise ominous owl and warn of the "chilling effect" some piece of legislation would have on speech, when just between you and me, what could be more chilling than some alabaster-browed, self-appointed mandarin who, in his capacity as head of some racial "advancement" association or some African studies department, arrogates to his "dignity" the summary right to pass on the propriety *vel non* of a word, a phrase, a setting, plot, character trait, implication, "innuendo," connotation, etc., while the person who seeks imprimatur sits stricken with morbid suspense, cowering in the dock? Oh, there very well may come a day when a writer must first go kowtowing off to the W.E.B. Du Bois Institute for Afro-American Research at Harvard University to get permission to use what he or she selects as *le mot juste*. "May I please use this word? I see . . . Well; what about *this* one? This plot here . . . Opinions may differ as to what constitutes a slur . . . No? Well, should I rewrite the story? What should I do? What did you say, sir? You think I should sell used cars?" Later, as the managers at the local car dealership read the sad resume, they glance at each other knowingly and gaily intone, "Of what possible value is that infinitesimal atom, the individual writer, when compared to the *race!*"—How simple it is to identify thought and expression; and, by correlation, to identify all the shocking surprises lurking inside one shiny brown briefcase! What the Florentines did when, under the influence of Savanarola's preaching, they made that celebrated holocaust of books and paintings; what the emperors of Rome did when, under the influence of their paranoia, they exiled Juvenal, Epictetus, Ovid, Saint John; what Nero did when he ordered the suicides of Seneca and Lucan;—were all these glorious acts not done to control the *contents of minds?* Yes, surely, but for political purposes. When Abelard was forced to recant in the face of the delations of

Bernard; when Wyclif was exhumed and defaced; when Huss was burned; when Martin Luther was chased into a dark castle;—these things were all done in the name of doctrine. But oh! Our race-baiter;—*he* is driven by race! All his twisted thoughts are on past wrongs; all his tightened, sick sensibilities are centered on slavery. In the end, slavery becomes his most precious possession, for its purpose, its excuse, is spiritual revenge in the grandest style. Our race-baiter must use the *law* for the realization of his purpose. Here we touch the base upon which the civil rights movement rests: *change must come by law*; change must only come through legal process. Thus, the civil righter has wrested social change from its rightful natural environment and placed it in the arms of compulsion. He has divested *human* evolution of its naturalness and substituted cold, factitious force in its stead.—What the Brown decision did:—the legislation of pluralism: the *wickedization* of a dominant culture (—and on its heels the dominant sexuality *as* dominant, the dominant race *as* the dominant race—). Thus, the Court, not merely in effect, but by judicial intent, legislated in the very pragmatism that had been so patiently waiting in the wings, the Deweyism that had been coiled like a black and tan copperhead at the judges' feet. Did this poisonous snake coiled at the feet of the already pragmatistically-minded judges, who had no qualms over issuing in another kind of American reality, another kind of fate for America;—did this snake, full of the venom of a false philosophy and full of its *own* hatred, its *own* love of "justice and equal rights," have its eye on *bigger game* than the justices' ungainly toes? Oh, yes! One thousand times Yes! This was the same weapon forged long ago when Pierre Bayle saw the comet's blue tail fly over his native France! This was the door through which Voltaire lowered his irreverent head to pass; and Rousseau with his Babeufists; the materialists; the angry, torch-carrying mob! Yes, Professor Dewey's first love and last hope: to exploit the religion of the Evangel as a means of issuing in a *new religion as preparation for a new consciousness*. Oh, these philosophers! these malicious philosophers! I read their palms the way a blind man reads Braille.—What a strain it is on intelligent men and women in America today to listen to our bumptious conservatives incessantly rail about judges legislating from the bench. How insufferable it is when some power-suited, fast-talking nitwit insists on wearing ignorance on one sleeve and obtuseness on the other;—how pitiful!! What underlies this conservatism? Would you throw everything, every issue you deem socially portentous, to the states? What would this accomplish? Let's learn to frame the issue the proper way: the question can *never* be, "Does the judge legislate?" This is the way backwoods, churlish Americans think (—who pronounce subpoena as *subpeenie*, warranty as *warran-tee*, etc.—). The question for Holmes was precisely this: can the Court enact Herbert Spencer? This is to frame the issue properly: did the Court *look outside the Constitutional text*? The question of judicial legislation, once it is allowed that the rule of the case applies to other facts besides the instant facts, cannot be a question. And if not a question, then it is meaningless conservative babble. The next issue is: if the Court confined itself to the text, did the justices jump ahead of the social ethic? And with specific regard to Brown, these twin questions—the question of confinement to the text of the written document and the question of social ethic—have been asked and answered. Yet Thurgood Marshall and the racial advancement organization he fronted for *wanted* something in Brown. What did they want? A remedy. What kind of remedy? Specifically: racial commingling. Has any empirical investigation ever been launched at the mystery of why the African wanted commingling as a remedy and the Chinese did not? The Brown decision should be distinguished from the case of Yick Wo of San Francisco. Well; for those of you who are new to this, let me distinguish these cases this way: if I were to commingle with Mssrs. Rockefeller, Dupont, and Perot, would I after, say, 50 whole years of commingling, be able *because* of this commingling to open one bank account? Yick Wo is a case of empowerment; Brown is—if I may use a phrase Holmes used on his death bed—a bunch of damned foolery. But sufficient unto the case, in this case, is *not* the evil thereof. The flood of litigation dissenting judges direly predicted in the old English cases and on this side of the Atlantic, say, since Holmes sat on the Massachusetts bench, is now a reality. You will object, "Anglo-Saxons are a litigious people, and this flood would have come sooner or later, etc." The answer to this objection is yes and no, Mr. Attorney. *What the Brown case did was to lay the foundation for an exclusively legalistic society, a society that transmutes all questions into quasi-justiciable legal issues;*—precisely the situation in ancient Athens prior to the reactionary philosophy of Socrates and Plato. America needs new intellectuals, new philosophers, iron natures who will ask themselves what the consequences of such an involvement could be for culture; whether such a preoccupation chases out the possibility of anything higher.—The great leaders of the civil rights movement, the thinkers and, finally, the doers, pointed the way; their "dream" of universal progress constituted the goal—and no one can doubt for a moment that the erection of signposts and, if sufficient "gains" are made, even milestones are more than sufficient to guide mankind along definite channels. More "gains" are desired; more doers arise; even those who claim to be thinkers are called once again to the forefront of the movement, for the goal still shimmers far out beyond the yellow horizon. They say in fervent, quavering voices, "Keep the dream alive. Keep hope alive." And, alas, there is so much dreaming and so many hopes aiming for the yellow horizon that the movement becomes a kind of surrogate religion. The struggle must go on, they say, for the gains are in constant jeopardy; the well-meaning men of zeal threaten retrenchment; the battle cry is renewed, "We will never go back!" and thus thought and action press ever onward, ever *forward* toward the goal. The noise of the tinkling word-bells, the gestures, the haste, the giving of new hearts to the cause, the very moving of the movement itself;—these integral components of the dream suck them down into a dreamlike stupor so that, after a while, the stupor of the dream and the dream itself become one and the same. The gestures and tinkling are going on and on, the vertiginous haste pressing for the flicker beyond the horizon: finally, aloneness and quietness too are seen as the enemy; only shouting can be heard, as if listening and quiet threaten to awaken the dreamers to a new kind of life! So that the striving for what is *ahead* of them blinds them to what is *above* them. True, experiments made in multiculturalism have the effect of tightening the sensitivities, but life in the herd dulls sensitivity, makes animalic, mimetic, one-dimensional. Only the well-being of the racially circumscribed mass matters; the ultimate goal—and this in face of a shroud of unconvincing disclaimers—is the development of great racial communities. Thus, once the advancement of the race reaches a certain point, specifically the point at which it is seen that commingling in and of itself cannot satisfy racial pride, education comes into view and is finally trusted as the great deliverer. This education is both general and multicultural. The general education consists in this: that the individual, at least that one whom we may designate an individual, must be able to assess himself, in light of his general education, with regard to whatever position or status he has a right to demand of life. Formerly the "dream" was to walk hand in hand with another human being of another race; now the dream is all about status. Education? Why, education means intelligence. Status? Why certainly status means property. There therefore exists a quite natural connection between intelligence and property; if you prefer: a necessary connection exists between education and "the dream." But what does this education include? What does it reject? Education gets bound up with production, demand, profit. This is the scandal of the advanced democracies, you understand; this attests to the fact that the dream has crossed the Red Sea and stands proudly at the gentle banks of the River Jordan. Can you spy the white-robed priests wading out? On the other side of the river, American political liberalism, that Ark of the Covenant wherein the dream had its holy abode for so long, meets American political conservatism. For it has always been the fundamental belief of our dandies of the right that the greed—excuse, please; I meant to say enterprisingness—of the money-makers possesses the right, indeed the duty, to dictate to culture its proper standards and objectives, as if a pig has the right to tramp into the parlor and go about rearranging the décor. It is from this quarter that there comes our formula: education = production = profit. Education is the insight by means of which one best acquires all the ways and means of making money; making as much money as possible in the shortest time as possible. The most immediate influence of the profit side of the equation on the education side of the equation is precisely this: the education should be *as speedy as possible*. (—Not to give the rightists full credit, however, for the idea that the wealthiest strata, as if in *exchange* for its assistance of culture—all those gaudy balls at the Kennedy Center for the Performing Arts—should dictate to culture, for our nearsighted Kennedy clan has attracted and purchased many a fine scribbler.—) The goal is to manufacture as many people who resemble minted coins as possible; and, according to this conception, the more of these minted coins it possesses the happier a nation will be. Thus, the sole intention behind this education should be to assist everyone in becoming minted coins, to educate everyone in such a way that they can employ the degree of knowledge and learning of which they are capable for the accumulation of the greatest possible amount of happiness and profit. Thus again: intelligence = property; wealth = culture. American education: a kind of liturgy for the worship of the great god speed. Very well; as the morality of speed and the specifically American *moral necessity* of instant gratification gain the ascendancy over the older, uncorrupted, more leisured kind of non-entrepreneurial, non-scrambling morality that took the sharp cleavage of spirit and matter for granted, the hatred for this latter type (—for I speak of a different, *radically* different, type of human—) is based upon the fear the herd feels whenever the solitary being comes upon the scene: a being whose morality proposes long-term goals, who spooks the herd by his uncanny if not otherworldly capacity for waiting. Sometimes, this fear leads the multicultural herd to classify this type as sick (—thinking differently in a multicultural society, the ability and *longing to think differently* is a pathology the multiculturalists must attempt to cure: one must think the party line when it comes to race, sex, gender, etc.—) when the real sickness is the indecent haste and breathless grasping of the correct-thinking slaves of the moment, opinion, fashion. Here one easily passes from the general education to the multicultural education: the concerted effort on the part of the multiculturalist black shirts to enact Social Deweyism; to say the same in other, more easily understood, words: *to diminish willpower and strike at the roots of the capacity to resist!*—Multiculturalism, specifically the kind of multiculturalism inaugurated by the civil rights movement (—as I have said, Dewey and his cohorts laid the wood, the kindling; the Supreme Court decisions mandating racial integration and the prayer decisions functioned as the match; this is to say, Constitutional text quite aside, the real *ratio decidendi* was the pluralism of American Pragmatism. That philosophy—or religion, moral principles as distinguished from moral sentiments etc.—should *not* function as grounds for the decisions of cases is explicit Holmesian, i.e., pragmatistic doctrine; but when American Pragmatism, the philosophy of O.W. Holmes, is the philosophy in question, the specific philosophy providing the ground of decision for a particular case;—well, that is another matter—), wants to dissolve a dominant culture, a dominant race, and most certainly a people's dominant *religion*. To be quite succinct: *the framework of a multicultural society had to be put in place if America was going to participate in a grand synthesis of all religions*; specifically, the return of the long nascent pre-Christian cults, Gnosticism, etc., as a kind of presageful aromatization of the final construction of a new matriarchate. But *how* the civil rights movement spawned a kind of secular theology is not merely a tale yet to be told; it's a tale that cannot be told in the present day. To return to education: the multiculturalists in education want behavior modification. What kind of behavior modification do they want? Atonement. Purgation. Exorcism. The "education" that passes muster for the multiculturalist exists as an *act of exorcism*. Again, this is an extension of the popular culture: humans are there to be conditioned, programmed, reconditioned, reprogrammed. But this presupposes victims and predators. Who is the predator? What class of persons steps into the formidable role of predator? Well, the predators are the ones who go on purity crusades, upholding the "good" and excising the "bad" (—precisely in relation to the victims the good is bad and the bad good—). To give an example: the Volstead Act was enacted at the behest of those who saw drinking liquor as evil, but finally the purists were portrayed as predators and themselves evil, preachers intent upon "legislating morals," etc. Then it was proclaimed that after this noble experiment of enforced purity, America never again would embark on such purity crusades. Yet who is doing the preaching now? The political left *against* the purists. This idea of declaring something wrong when the political right is to blame but morally right when the political left performs a perfect analogue of the same action finds its parallel in American Constitutional Law. During the era of the famous Holmes and Brandeis dissents, from what exactly were the dissenters dissenting? The intrusion of the *preferences* of the majority in their legal reasoning. The majority preferred the side of capital to the side of labor. When pro-labor legislation from the states came to the Court, the justices would strike it down (—this is to say the law was invalidated in light of its collision with a higher principle of the Constitution, i.e., freedom of contract—). But Holmes declared against the majority, claiming it had slyly substituted pro-business proclivities for an actual Constitutional provision; therefore the collision with a fundamental right was illusory; and, of course Holmes was correct. Later, because of the dissents, it was taken for granted by serious Constitutional scholars that the judge may not intrude his preferences as a means to invalidate otherwise Constitutional legislation. Yet, in practice, what the scholars took for granted was not a rule proscribing intrusion for all judges, but only judges deemed non-progressive (—when Holmes' "judicial restraint" did not say this—). The upshot? The liberal majority on the Court may read preferences deemed progressive, i.e., expansive of rights, into the "emanations and penumbras" of the Constitutional text.—To return to our exorcists. *What* is considered progressive here? Social Deweyism and every word in the mouths of Thurgood Marshall and Martin King. Therefore: to educate is to *exorcise unwanted thoughts*—not merely groups granted special protection under the law, but groups launching out on purity crusades! Not liquor, this time around, but speech, communication, and thought! (—*Invectives Against the Idols*, 2006—)—But why? As is so often the case with human beings, the answers to their questions lie already concealed in their thoughts, sometimes on their tongues. We so desperately seek an answer only later to find we have already noticed it, and on some level, already spoken it. When the Christian prohibitionists sallied out against the evils of liquor, i.e., against liquor itself, when say, Justinian and Theodora closed the doors of pagan learning in 529; these repressions were done to win converts, to create a favorable environment for decision (—of course, Justinian came out against the "pagans" for the same reason the pagan Cato advocated the expulsion of the Greek philosophers: Christians and Roman youths alike should be protected from the enfeebling of morals brought on by the eristic skepticism of a decadent Academy—). In some sense, our civil righters, embattled behind the breastplates of their racial advancement organizations, wearing large imposing frowns on their faces and tiny chips on their august epaulettes, seek converts, but it is not the prospect of converts that animates them, no; let us even pass over the motive of revenge and proceed toward some deeper, perhaps unconscious, possibility. The inheritance of a diversified descent devolved upon our Black brothers the moment our ignorant, Sabbath-keeping White forefathers moored their ships at the foot of the great green forests of Virginia. Contrary drives and values began their pull, their veritable war on the inside, marking off, I should say reserving the black soul for, and indeed *as*, a scene of conflict. The struggle goes on: these drives and values rarely leave one another in peace. For it is a rather brutal fact—is it not?—that the black souls didn't arrive in this wilderness by virtue of choice. Meanwhile, the Blacks embrace the dominant religion, and develop as a protest against suffering, the so-called Negro spiritual (—and ignorant theologians even today seek the spiritual in the Negro when if they were interested in the truth, which they most assuredly are not, would seek instead the Negro in his spiritual—); but this protest against suffering; is it not also a plea for *peace*? A plea that the war on the inside may someday, someday, when the "sweet chariot swings low," when the preachers descend from the mountaintop to preach deliverance to the captives, come to an end? Yea, the preachers have *been* to the mountaintop and have preached deliverance to many; the sweet chariot of fire has swung so low it has singed the eyebrows of a nation; and still, *still* the war goes on!—Question: what to *do* with this war once the guilt that keeps our sacred, blemishless lamb we call the civil rights movement *in* movement, has finally expended itself? This, psychologically considered, brings our forbidden inquiry back to the rather bashfully broached question of theological influence. For it is possible to map the grounding of the question. Given the perpetual struggle of contrary drives and values inside the man of diversity; given the need for happiness, the need for peace, the desire that the war *come to an end*;—precisely now a venerated species of thought-medicine aiming at repose, at tranquility in the soul, begins its subtle work. Plato and the early Christian theologians—most notably Origen and Augustine, those personifications of inward strife—prescribed for themselves this holy sedative. What is this sedative as a mode of thought? Unity at last attained. Theological synthesis. Cultural syncretism. Precisely the kind of peace the great Hebrew prophets fought against. But where is the man with one-tenth of the hatred of contamination that once welled from the souls of prophets from Elijah with his intolerant either/or to Mohammed who wasted no time enshrining his precept of doctrinal purity? What kind of man is able to stand against the contrary doctrine of coercive tolerance spreading across the West like a plague, threatening to suffocate the once vital, once *masculine instincts* in the sickly-sanctimonious ague of guilt-and-atonement over the Holocaust and that reciprocal lust for guns, profit, and rum we mawkishly refer to as the slave trade?—It is a curious fact: there's *a difference* between Christian morals and secularized Christian morals. The civil rights movement took Christian morality and succeeded in secularizing these values. The movement released a new force upon the people; this force now combines with others for the purpose, the *destiny* of new evaluations, the creation of new values out of the old (—as I have said, these *coming values* are nothing but the pre-Christian values *rematerialized*—). Thus, Christian morality, as this morality proceeds directly out of religion (—out of Scripture, if you prefer—), is branded as *productive* of Holocausts, of segregation, prejudice, bigotry, hate, and intolerance. Indeed, patriarchal religion is so branded; its doctrines given over to calumny precisely in direct proportion to the gathering strength of the coming values; e.g., warlike values versus nurturing values, the restriction of sexuality versus the declaration that the old taboos are meaningless, etc. All this creates the necessity for new theologies—African-American theology, liberation theology, feminist theology, indigenous theology, the reappearance of long buried myths, etc.—finally, to coalesce inside the pregnant belly of the Great Mother. Meanwhile, behind the furor of political pie-slicing, as well as the legal scramble over the expansion of key Constitutional phrases and provisions with the proviso that such expansions serve the one moral purpose of marginalizing the old dominant religion and expunging the old patriarchal culture—and certainly not to forget, those swift, merciless strikes at the public schools made by our lords and saviors, the race, gender, and lifestyle pragmatists, the grenadiers of Dewey, who *first* gave them the right to uproot, plant, and build; these grieving pragmatists feel wronged by the very possibility of independent thought, thought that is *free*—; behind all this the look-the-other-way morality that first began in dear old decadence-lusting San Francisco; the obedient, modest, self-effacing disposition; the "mellow" over-tenderness—*again* San Francisco!—that is truly ashamed of severity in any form and learns how to take the side even of the one who *harms* such a society, the criminal;—in one word, the morality of sheep comes gradually to the fore, flourishes, and reaches its pinnacle. This pinnacle is that point at which the thinking and baaing of every lamb is "equal" to and indistinguishable from the thinking and baaing of every other lamb: so that the climax and end-point of the "diversity" worshiped by an advanced democracy, I meant to say a secular theocracy, is precisely and ineluctably a *lack* of diversity.—This morality of sheep, the morality that refuses to question because it refuses to stop, look around, look at itself, and listen; the morality of the *sacred* civil rights movement; the morality that animalizes man to the pygmy animal of equal rights and equal thinking; the morality of redemption from all the guilt of the past (—for what greater proof of *devitalization*, of exhaustion and true *lack of morals*, could exist than that a people chooses to suffer one ounce of guilt, one batting of an eyelash, over past wrongs?—); *this morality has vaporized the former morality of hardness and command!*—Today, the Americans must constantly watch their step and go around on tiptoe. The experiments in thought control in old Europe and in America—the whole green-sick, quicksand spectacle of crucifixion and redemption over the Holocaust and slavery—: this first-falling domino, this gruesome *last gasp* of independent thinking: how all this suits perfectly our old maidish university professor, our professor of *philosophy* . . .

366

Show me the prophet who kept a map for his journey, the man of God who knew every detail in advance. There will come a time in the life of spirit, of which the life of the mind is but one special calling, in the life of *freedom*, when it seems that everything is lost, for the spirit who bears the demands of the spirit is himself lost. Quite different from Kierkegaard's loss of self consequent upon the vaporization of extremist freedom, this lostness is reflective of the very nature of prophecy as a journey. The Kierkegaardian deification of journey is misleading, especially if we see in it more than it is: a kind of intelligence agency in the service of God, viz: a daring escape from the engine of titanic ideas, and hence, an experience of freedom (—as in the Pauline journey, the singing of praises unhinged the prison's doors and the captives were set free—). But Kierkegaard is existentially correct: God would not allow Abraham the "objective certainty" of a road map. Here the medieval conceit of *intelligo ut credam* shows itself for what it truly is: a conceit of medieval theology; i.e., a "proof" of the extent to which the theologian needed reason to theologize: for if, quite contrary to the history of theology, the *intelligo*, so far from enriching the *credo* and possessing value as a scrutinizing tool for the positive examination of any revelation, detracts from and denatures the *credo*, then Kierkegaard is again correct; . . . as is Martin Luther—who perhaps, first got an inkling of this subversive theology, this anti-theology, from Tertullian: for what *does* Athens—or Rome for that matter—have to do with Jerusalem? The Holy Father condescends with this answer: *everything*. Quite incorrect, Your Holiness, for the "traditions of men" and a road atlas have much in common.—When, as in an experiment, this road map idea is applied to the practice of philosophy, we come face to face with the most basic thinking of Nietzsche, as this thinking is a thinking about the existential category of possibility: *to become who one is, one must not have the foggiest notion who one is!* Precisely the kind of critical questioning Socrates instilled into the young Plato (—and as this was essentially *at first* a literary question it involved the switching of genres; simply put: the writing of dramatic narratives was an intellectual trammel; Plato would break the chain and follow the call of the wild—): *the great affirmation could come only in consequence of the great negation.* Thus, Nietzsche's dictum, lifted from Pindar, "Become who you are!" is precisely the Socratic call to the young writer of drama. It is the call of philosophy: *the call to throw away all maps and become lost for a time; for once to experience the agonies and the ecstasies of being alive!* Now you must descend to the depths of "existence." Now is the appointed time to sail the sunless seas! Fit the sapphire ring and kill the fatted calf! For he who was found has become lost again!—But notice the sigh of relief when we enter the halls of university philosophy, where freedom is traded for bread everyday, where the professor says to himself, "Thank goodness I am no philosopher, but a professor in a university. Thank goodness that with a snap of my soft, uncalloused fingers, I can turn these stones into bread!"—Nietzsche's demand that you *become* who you are can only mean this: you don't know who you are inasmuch as nothing, absolutely nothing, stands between you and things, between you and the world. But since the professor, who before he became a professor was a crew cut functionary on his way to becoming a professor, lets an education in philosophy—and hence not philosophy as it is lived which means *open horizons*—stand in his way between himself and the world, he cannot become who he is if, precisely, he already *is* it, i.e., a university professor whose horizons never were open, and to be frank, could open only on one condition: that he *leave the university!* Leave the meretricious pack of cowardly hyenas unfed for one second—; deny them all prospect of place and position within the academic-bourgeois superstructure; cease to dangle before their squinty little flint eyes the enticements of salaries, book deals, honorariums, speaking engagements, press releases, distinguished chairs, and all the rest of the *curriculum mori;*—you will see the mice run for their holes! Yes, the poor pseudo-philosophers will seek a roof and a computer to play with wherever they can: one will become an import car mechanic, another will try to write screenplays, still another will saddle off to the nearest menagerie of chattering journalists to write editorials and op-eds: every learned shallowpate will have flown the coop! Every whited sepulcher will become a stinking open grave! For it's easy to get rid of bad philosophers and Pharisees who call themselves philosophers: stop rewarding them. Now that the fair green shoots of Derridaism and the whole once tempting postmodern harvest have come to nothing, it is understandable that a few of our professors of late have been writing feverish queries to Hollywood script agencies and reading the want ads. More: they'll cozy up to Nietzsche the way a mangy cur dog mounts a bitch in heat, traveling to Sils Maria to sleep in the bed in which Nietzsche once slept, hike along the Alpine trails, where he first met tightrope-dancing Zarathustra, and for what! For what! To burnish their escutcheons with another philosophic pictorial? To elicit even more envy and contempt from the faculty? Conceit! Professors' conceit! They'll say, "Nietzsche taught me perspectivism." Surely; but *which* perspective? The gaining of one perspective means the relinquishing of another. How have you relinquished the perspective gained when you do nothing but gaze out your university window? Unless you are seeking a way of gaining a thought without a thinker, in which case I suppose you will strut around bragging about having a window and no eyes with which you may see out of this window. This is why some professors roundly say that Nietzsche is "still a metaphysician." I will eagerly admit that nothing is more metaphysical than a thought without a thinker, a perspectivism without a concomitant stance that has relinquished every vestige of the abstract. No; Nietzsche has not taught any self-consciously sanctimonious egocentric how to *gain* perspectives, and for one reason: our self-consciously sanctimonious egocentric has, again and again, refused to learn. After all, when has the heart of such an egoist been aflame? When did he leave his father's bailiwick to sleep on a distant shore? There will be found in the university philosophy professor's desk drawer panoplies of critiques and critiques of critical critiques, such that a microcosm of the history of philosophy speaks from the desk drawer. And yet *where* is the thinker of all these fine, soporific thoughts? Is he also tucked away in the drawer? Well, wherever he is, the only critique of a philosophy that proves something is the *experimental attitude* of trying to see whether one can live in accordance with it. And you are going to tell the world how Nietzsche, who lived his philosophy more than even a Plato (—and I say this simply in view of the fact that the Nietzschean philosophy is ten thousand times more dangerous than the Platonic—), has taught you something?—*you?* The one thing Nietzsche has for you to learn and relearn has not been learned: the shame of thinking that one is doing philosophy when one is only pasting words together and swimming in miasma. Unless, of course, philosophy really is and ought to be words about words, and swimming through tediousness.— "What then?" you ask, smiling insinuatingly, "Is there *no good at all* in the philosophy departments of America?"—If you are impertinent enough to ask such a question, I am impertinent enough to answer it. For whatever good that remains after all the word pasting and bombast (—after the sower has sown among thistles and choking thorns—) is washed away by the tremendous dispersing power of the crowd and drowned by the seductive voices of the culture (—for the fowls and ravens have devoured the seeds, and now nothing is left but barren soil—). The self-seeking impules, vanities, and above all, the temptation to think correct thoughts, and hence, the interdiction of all tabooed thought; these seductions of the popular culture gradually estrange the solitary one, the wanderer who has been left behind, who has *left the others behind*, from that concealed, nameless something he most certainly *is*; but this rare, courageous one is returning for his due, returning for his *antipode*. Everything else is pandering, reaching out to an audience, "literature," lack of breeding. Everything else falls into the news-gutter and is talked to pieces.

367

The notion that the philosophical jobber and pieceworker in America should be confused with actual philosophers, while blasphemous, is not entirely out of place in a culture that has for so long made a practice of confusing surface for core, shallowness for substance and depth, even collective sickness for general health. The question ought to be asked whether the confusion in America over *who* the philosopher is, is good for the scholar and bad for the potential production of new philosophers. Whether a scholar can become a philosopher is only a foreground for the asking of the question, "Do philosophic scholars obstruct potential philosophers from becoming who they are, philosophers?" The heraldry, fanfare, and panache of the scholar's credentials, I believe, could serve as a deterrent for any young spirit, who after receiving his or her "education" in philosophy breaks out of the abhorrent bubble and sails away for *new worlds*, gazing with Julien Sorel's dark, manifold eyes on great, manifold expanses, after having traversed those expanses, and conquered those great expanses!—Then what?—What, pray tell, is next in the education of a philosopher? That he or she has received the freshman year equivalent of a philosopher's rightful education—for, believe me, other blue Aegeans and pink-beached Cycladic spires await you stormy and stressful Goethean youths! you flower-garlanded, voluptuous daughters of Hipparchia!—; is this piece of petty presumption *worth anything* on your untimely application for graduate school? Nay, I think not, my far-seeing, far-reaching adventurous one! You are like the fabled Renaissance scholar who, after many quixoteish travels to the world's end, returned to the University of Paris and was appalled to discover the philosophy professors still discussing the very same problems; aha! had this scholar-turned-entry-level-philosopher caught our educated knaves *flagrante delicto* at last!—Think of the unbending manliness of the young Charles Peirce with his prim unpretentious B.A., leaving the security of the university to explore the Pacific Northwest's majestic, thick forests and navigate her wide, pearly rivers. That the university, in the end, had nothing to do with Charles Peirce, and the only genius America has ever produced had nothing to do with the university, ought to tell you professorial moles something! While you moles are feeling around this truth, consider old stoney-eyed Wendell Holmes with his bloodstained epaulettes; compare this man to the opaline bloodlessness of John Dewey and the puerilely fastidious snobbishness of the James boys. Peirce's *lack* of credentials in philosophy—his divorce from the university—served him the same way the jawbone served Sampson. (—Remember Nietzsche's lack of credentials in philosophy, his rejection by the philosophy department at Basel, and *his* divorce from the university—).—This is the personal quandary, something the students are not expected to *see*. Very well; what can they see, appreciate, and finally seal with a dolorous spirit? Here is the situation. The spirit of the cloister, Heidegger's frustrated Catholicism, which is *dungeon air*—bad air!—; this spirit has fathered the new popular French—Derridaism, Saint Foucaultism, and all the rubicund déclassé Gallicisms of our day—. Thus, the hue and cry went up in the American universities, "This is the future of philosophy! *This is critique itself.*" Critiques of interpretation, critical exegetical constructions placed upon other interpretations, are not critical enough, and certainly cannot be mistaken for critique itself—as satisfying the end and purpose of philosophy—except by impish elves bred in the dungeon (—and, thus, quite incapable of distinguishing fresh air from dungeon air, specifically, here, the cyanotic exhalations of a gradually disillusioned, resentful candidate for the priesthood—). Catholicism is, after all, the propylon for medieval dungeons; do I hear any objections? How then will Heidegger fight back? How will he humble Mother Church? At the risk of smiles and grimaces, let us first see that he didn't have to invent any new thing, for the modus had been consecrated from eternity: like the existential theologian, the Magus of the Black Forest, I meant to say dungeon, will counterfeit religious dogmas; thus, his Being of beings takes the place of God; thus, the hermeneutic of this heuristic chimera becomes big business for the elves. What does this mean? What does this elfish activity, this clubbing and networking of American Continental philosophy, this feeding upon the cold, dead bodies of Heidegger's once rosy-faced children, *amount to*? Again, the general situation from the bird's view of a higher crag: it took an unprecedented aggregate of honesty and logical bulldogging to *oust* the absurdities of medieval theology and philosophy. Building upon the demolition work of the logicians, Descartes, with his stringent method, deleted the aerodynes and one could breathe again. But this temporary paradise contained the seeds of trouble: drunkenness; sobriety;—the debauch of Hegel. Then, when nothing good came of this rampant Hegelianism, with Schopenhauer's literary bent as the accusing witness, Nietzsche and Kierkegaard, whose first task was the razing of the dark, dank Teutonic castles, cleared the air this second time. New pathways, formerly mist-enveloped, revealed themselves. Philosophy could *breathe* again. Next, enter Heidegger the *resentful* Catholic, Heidegger the *medievalist*: and clarity is lost, freshness polluted, the nasal passages restricted, the veins full of German beer again, Catholic-Medieval stodge again . . . *again!* Now, Heidegger's children, the French, make a great noise and commotion about philosophy *coming to a head in their investigations* when in truth philosophy has been obfuscated with words, positions, pseudo-thought-experiments, muddy clarifications, acrobatics, bedizenments, high chairs, high claims; i.e., philosophy hasn't been augmented, but *postponed*. Seeing all these contortions of episteme, the American professors come around for their piece of pie: they get in on the act by coming into contact with as many new French positions as they can, which they then interpret, they say, in a sense useful for their "perspectives." Interpretations abound; they are collated in papers, picked over, danced over, desultorily pullulated, placed in newspapers, etc. But there are gaps in their many interpretations of the Continental practitioners, holes. Then it is the filling in of the gaps that constitutes, and must ever constitute, the primary business of philosophy! Think of it! Philosophy, that which purports to be, and is, an *original intuition of the world*, reduced to gap-filling! Philosophy castrated to an interstitial nitpicking of text-worms! Problem: how is it possible for a philosophy professor to gain an original intuition of the world? He is simply not cut out for such a thing. Finding holes and filling them is enough to win him renown among his colleagues. Why bother with anything *more*?—This, then, furnishes an answer to our original question: once the true ultimacies of university philosophy are seen through; I beg your pardon, I meant to say: once the shams of such hermeneutical brilliance, such professorial quacksalvering, are duly registered in the curious, curiously fresh and penetrating minds of the alert students;—well, this is the end of the huff and puff. Even the most promising of spirits, who like the young Plato drank deeply from the springs of wisdom even as rash and restless youth burned within; the beautiful charmer whose heart thrilled to the prospect of *another* hour in Montaigne's tower, one *more* walk with Nietzsche in the

Alpine ice and over the leaden hills of old Genoa, yet another breathless encounter in his professor's book-lined office, which he was wont to liken to the pleasures of a beautiful woman's form and face; such a spirit will perforce shake his fist at philosophy's door and leave the scene altogether! And, oh! How such an one's heart will ache! The philosophy he once loved has turned out to be nothing but the hermeneutical delineation of officiating djinn on pinheads, "truth" a general show of words by generalists divorced from any idea of flesh and bone, "concrete reality" the cautious cultural correctness of the scholar's dim lecture hall, the quintessentially philosophic values of independence and courage pronounced impracticable, puerile, of antiquarian interest only, and thrown out with the other outdated, impossible dogmatisms. Finally, the stalwart minions with moss on their humped backs (—for carrying around so many hermeneutical coils and webs have made them stooped—) will roundly reply, "Our many and varied investigations, taken intelligently as a whole, help to tell us who we are!" I take this show of breadth to mean who mankind is, for it is a preliminary question who exactly *you* are; next question: who you are *not*.—Both questions have been asked and answered.—But some may say my intuition of philosophy is too classical (—I have spelled out elsewhere how classical civilization has ceased to affect scholars, let alone *set an example* for scholars—); that I fail to appreciate how professors have so masterfully integrated linguistics and comparative literature into philosophy's realm, and this to the incalculable enrichment of the latter. Well, I can tell you with a sure confidence that this obsession with language and with "signs" is a curious analogue for the obsession the logicians have with their endless delimitations of episteme, and does not in any manner benefit philosophy. Here you will bark, growl, and say, "This is my favorite bone and I refuse to let it go!" And here is my reply. If you professors are really concerned with words, why must you employ such circumlocutory insipidity and tail chasing in your effort to say one thing instead of using a few words to say more? Ah, but the philosophy journals must be filled! There must be meat in thine house! What? Is it impolite to ask about the *relation* of a professor to his exsanguinating circumlocutions? Very well, you may have your bone and chew it too, but all your mastications, believe me for once, are at the *expense* of philosophy. And comparative literature? The bare presence of the word literature in the mouth of an American philosophy professor is enough to make the hackles on the necks of every true lover of literature the world over rear up like the quills of an affrighted porcupine. Here you may retort, "But Professor Walter Kaufmann knew as much literature as philosophy, and he tenderly introduced many students to novels and plays of ideas." Yes, and this is my reply. You are no Kaufmann. If philosophy in America, i.e., university philosophy, has *purported* to find its way to life only by politicizing both philosophy and life, this is to say by the perversion of philosophy and life, what right does this philosophy possess to *annex* literature, the epitome of life? You curtly deny, saying, "We in no way shortchange life. We *begin* with Heidegger's analytic. Our concern is with the self in the world." Etc. Still, the question ought to be asked whether Heidegger's attempt to *codify* Kierkegaard's life-explorations is an unwitting regression to abstract philosophy. Any analytic-conception of freedom is at best an abstraction, and in no way drops the "all men everywhere" tag; Sartre's conception of it is ludicrously abstract, proving once again that even phenomenology and philosophy of existence can be used to prove what the philosopher, for the overriding purpose of his polemics, must prove. For there certainly is no "freedom," only shades, gradations, and degrees of freedom. To say that I possess freedom absent an ability to *use* freedom is the very kind of abstraction "existence" eschews; and if existence, then philosophy of existence. What? Freedom is this very ability? Then I do not possess "freedom," only a foolscap prognosis of abstract feasibility.—Assume this analytic *captures* life. It does so tangentially, temporarily, and then only for philosophy professors.—Finally, and to keep this very simple, why should it matter that philosophy professors, philosophy journals, and even major universities with vigorous philosophy departments exist as long as real philosophers exist? Can the professors, the journals, the departments, and the monkeyshines make even one philosopher? You accuse me of being simplistic and naïve. You retort, "Teachers such as Aspasia must have influenced Socrates in his great task of distracting philosophy from cosmology to ethics, from heaven to the streets; and wise Anaxagoras must have incited in the younger man an anti-sophistic animus; then, too, if what they say is true, the great Parmenides taught Socrates the value of trances, otherworldly ambitions, dialectical logic, and midwifed the possibility of attracting like minds to carry on the vital work of philosophy once he flew to heaven on Orphic wings to test the great Greek heroes and wise men to see whether they really possessed wisdom and courage." Indeed, what you say is true, but the teachers who happened to touch Socrates surely did not *make* a philosopher. If you insist on your point of teachers as influencing students, we come back around to our original question. Do the philosophic scholars today, simply by their illiberal, mousey, impossibly perfunctory antics so out of line with what philosophy is and has always been; *do these scholars obstruct the production of new philosophers?*—

368

It has rightly been observed that when the cat's away the mice will play, and it is no secret that on the very day of American Continental philosophy's birth, Heidegger had just been pronounced a dead cat. Yes, it is a fact that Heidegger's departure, in effect and certainly in the harum-scarum conceits of the university professors, passed the baton—I take scrupulous care not to say laurel wreath—to the academic day laborers, who instantaneously and with the pomp and hermeneutical circumstance such a momentous occasion in the history of philosophy required became "philosophers." On that auspicious day, the birthday of American Continental philosophy, *parasitic intuitions* transmuted themselves—again, instantaneously—into original intuitions; the traditional dues every real philosopher since Thales walked with Solon *had* to pay were cancelled, and general philosophic merriment supervened, not over the fact that anything had been "let be," as the old Marburger would have it, but that much had been *let loose*. Every professor worth his tenure rejoiced over the post-modernist, post-Heidegger, soon to be post-structuralist, post-everything, but no one shed a tear over philosophy's sudden loss of clarity; specifically clarity as a goal of philosophic discourse. The new post-Heidegger goal? To use verbosity to look profound (—in, perhaps, unconscious contradiction to a professor's sincerely held belief that he *is* profound—). "Language running riot," Professor Russell observed, and for once Bertie is correct! The basic problem with the "thinking" of the post-everything university professor? Intoxication. His thinking is the thinking of an *inebriate*. His philosophic word games are more than games: the professors believe their glosses are *advances* beyond the original intuitions of the primary thinkers (—as, say, the way case law fleshes out the bare bones of a statute and in this way cancels and surpasses the statutory law—) when in reality these inebriates are only *rewriting texts*; for what is a gloss but a *writing over an original*? Not original intuitions about the world, but parasitic intuitions about texts, interstitial intuitions by parasites! This constitutes the *profound* wing of American philosophy today! (—And let the Devil take the other wing.—) Smoke and vapor of the brain: this is American philosophy today! No one has the slightest inkling how the seriousness of philosophy differs from the seriousness of a vulgar, ballyhooing journalist; in fact, the spirit of journalism is penetrating the universities more and more: witness the way these Heideggerian crew cuts chatter about justice, international peace, the United Nations, human rights, philosophy's duty to make the loudest anti-war noise, and that naïve wambling puffery bestowed upon a Constitutional law these "educators" have never really seen. How *could* a political event ever touch upon philosophy? (—Whether genuine philosophy touches upon political events is another question.—) But for the graduate student content to write astute "egalitarian" harangues to the effect that the political is the essence of philosophy and is philosophy's "mission," let this astute graduate student write his smoke and vapor doctoral dissertation and become a philosophy professor in an American university!—(—I am thinking of that crypto-Bolshevik, John Rawls, whose pitifully obscene ethnic guilt is tantamount to the torments of our Tolstoys, John Browns, and Harriet Beecher-Stowes; ... whose "theory of justice" *he* never treated as a theory. Believe me, such abortions of fully realized human beings, such deformity and exhaustion of the human species masquerading as "progress" atone for their sorry inner state by adorning these venomous distresses in pretty gowns and verbal fineries. Yes, all their "justice" has a goal and must be recognized as the time-bomb it most certainly *is* . . . If the theory of justice amounts to the *training out* of the barbaric male values—and I can easily see how the opposition recognizes holy intolerance, the tendency to preserve the vital instincts by honoring the fearful substratum of *distance* that separates man from man, the noble man's reverence for reverence and the higher man's wonder at wonder, the audacity to stand erect and not bow down before every new thing because it is new, i.e., the *capacity to resist invasion*;—I can easily see how all this may be nominated barbaric—then the real essence of the theory is surely the degrading and overpowering of these values. Yea, these progressive decadents represent the bottle-necking and suffocation of humanity. Their humane sermons aiming to uplift and refine humanity constitute the opposite of that which is proclaimed, its deterioration. Collective mediocrity and effeteness *has* to consider itself a goal and a pinnacle. Then, as this shame turns its inward eye to *religion*, the pollution of purity—but first the *demonization* of purity—is its proud "humane" desideratum, its "justice." Here the coming grand synthesis of all doctrines past, present, and future awaits enactment; here the gradual nebulafication of the patriarchal religions of the world constitutes the goal, the highest hope. What is the meaning of present-day "nihilism" but this? The unhurried, step-by-step intensification of the horrific conflict between the long-buried sacred vulva and the beleaguered sacred phallus!—)—Let us say, arguendo, that the philosophy professors someday succeed in their apparitional task of rewriting the text of the whole history of philosophy itself, expurgating, of course, all those incorrect elements not in strict accord with their political liberalism. What kind of philosophic accomplishment would this be in light of the fact that no one listens to a philosophy professor except other philosophy professors, graduate students who will one day become philosophy professors, and confused undergraduates, who once their confusion abates, will perforce listen with a sieve? Could this lack of an audience for their "work" have anything to do with the fact, the tradition, that a philosopher worthy of an audience and who, sometimes, draws diverse peoples after his example, *teaches by example* and not merely by books, papers, pieces, etc? How invisible the philosophy professor is in America today that we should know him only through his books, papers, and pieces, and not by courageous example? You say with a complacent grin, "How can we philosophy professors not be visible when we flit across oceans for our endless seminars, conferences, and colloquia on the most vital philosophic subjects, networking with other brilliant minds in the most brilliant fashion? Why, some of us, on some lucky occasions, have snuggled in so close to Professor Derrida's elbows that we could sniff his toilette!" Yes, and this kind of visible example can only produce more university professors and more professorial philosophy. Teaching by example means, among other things such as dress and demeanor, the natural ability to express the profound with simplicity, but this natural virtue is something that professorial philosophy *abhors*; it wants instead to call as much modal involution and ontological complexification into the picture as possible; I meant to say, into the text, to produce the inevitable multiplication of texts about texts, networking about networking, colloquia about colloquia, et-sickening-cetera. The true thinker always cheers and refreshes, but the professor has no cheer no matter how many times he will confirm his satisfaction with being a professor. In every professorial piece, in every book written by professors to get tenure (—so there may someday soon be more pieces and more books, so there may be more professors, more tenure, and more scholarly writing—), there in the white spaces between the learned black lines, one will always find the white effluvia of the professor's lack of honesty about his own inadequacy. Is this the crack through which dishonesty first crept in ? Yes, you know all the names and will toss these names around like beach balls, but if you take any honest writer on philosophy—from Plato and Diogenes to Montaigne, Descartes, Kierkegaard, Schopenhauer, and Nietzsche—you will divine that these solitaries wrote first and foremost for themselves, and only later for an audience: *and this fact is precisely how they gained audiences*! In fact, writing philosophy consists in this: a thinker is speaking to himself. Even Charles Peirce wrote this way, and we must conclude that a philosophy professor *has never written one line of philosophy*. The philosophy professor never speaks to himself when he writes, but only to other professors and to students who will someday become professors who will speak to other professors, who will speak to the next generation of students who will become philosophy professors! The pretender who does not write for himself, and thus speak to himself, wants to cut a figure, and such figure-cutting is always punished. The real philosopher, forgive me for saying, writes with Horace's bronze and the Pyramids in mind; he writes the way the Romans erected structures: for, and on account of, eternity. But that man or woman who wants to cut a figure is no more mindful of eternity, of the writer's ambition for perpetuity, than an armadillo is desirous of eternal life. Correlatively, if a philosopher enjoys too much attention in his lifetime, he, nine times out of ten, will have to pay for preferring the limelight to the true light, which if it be true philosophy, is nothing other than his own light. In this sense, philosophy professors are magi of darkness, who when bathed in light, look more like cogitating ragamuffins. They are always in their every movement and whim jockeying for approval from their universities and their peers: seen from a real philosopher's eagle perch, they *burn themselves out*; and precisely with this proviso: Professor So-and-So lived a long life, was granted tenure whenever he needed it, wrote many books on philosophy, shepherded many grateful graduate students through the mill, rounded up the posthumous papers of some famous pragmatist for publication, was good to his dog, and collapsed while riding his bike on the way to an important seminar held in his honor. While the true philosopher, as Aristotle and Nietzsche said so well, holds himself aloof from honors, especially petty honors (—again, excuse me for saying, all honors are petty to a philosopher—). Whereas the philosopher harbors no desire to deceive anyone—quite unlike, say, the orator, the sophistical writer, the advocate and the judge, the statesperson, the journalist, etc.—including himself, the philosophy professor constantly deceives others as to his real abilities, resorting, as aforesaid, to crooked, unseemly locutions to appear profound; and he even seizes upon a special security when he deceives himself as to his true abilities, and must always practice this self-fooling as regards *who he is*. The philosophy professor may very well be simple and honest in his life, but has thrown out every trace of simplicity and honesty in his thought; what is as unsettling as the vacuous spume of his impossible opacity? Simplicity is prohibited, déclassé. Honesty has no place in the popular pantheon of hasty neon gods, and since the philosophy professor never once veers from the popular culture; well, you draw the necessary conclusion.—The philosophic establishment in America has unquestioningly absorbed Alain Locke's perverse obsessions with multiculturalism the same way a sponge absorbs dirty dishwater (—and incidentally, everything else in this Harlem-Harvard degeneration of instincts has been embraced and declared the most American of American idols—). Whenever any dogma *crowns itself as critical reason itself,* this act means the invalidation and driving out of every *other* perspective and possibility of critique;—meanwhile, "the people," adrift on a current they cannot escape, learn the quintessential American art of adapting to everything that calls itself new, as the philosophy professors, deaf to every other matter but blurred bits of minutiae they have aptly nominated the "ready-to-hand," drone on over "textualities" and "othering" as final bastions of philosophical forgetting. Consequently, diversity is expunged on account of diversity; freedom is blotted out in the name of freedom. Make no mistake: *Daseinism* is, in practice, a diverting of minds, a postponing of philosophy, the same way the Kantian epistemic cramps diverted and postponed for a century the great ruthless social investigations of the latter half of the 19th century, possibly the boldest victory ever handed over to philosophy since philosophy took bodily form to roam the streets of Athens and the bright Aegean world. This vaunted Daseinism produces inebriates who lose their way in the cul-de-sac of the abstract textualism of philosophy's newest contentious monks, the professors of American Continental philosophy. Yet this contentious "experimentalism," this post-Heidegger pseudo-transcendence of the old existential phenomenology, is surface only: university philosophy lies lankly, passive and mute at the golden feet of the popular idols.—As the ever increasing velocity and shameless bongoization of American life dictates the eventual flowering of nervousness as the future of literature, so contemporary philosophy and literature together, even unconsciously, work for the cursing of the old and the blessing of the new: the renunciation of resistance, enmity, and wrath: weakening of the instincts—exhaustion—demonization of distances—the glorification of equality—; all of this and more as necessary preconditions for the consolidation of integral neo-matriarchalism. Our Heidegger gazers look for intentions, never consequences . . . Deification of the earth!! Passivity before gyneolatrous numina!! The unseating of the old mythology and hence the male values!! *Where are the barbarians of the third millennium?*

Epilogue

A philosopher?—A philosopher is one who recognizes predecessors and pretenders; one who discerns such dissimilarity in a glance (—Germ of the Socratic cockcrow—). While the hand of the one never rests from its cunning in taking, the other never rests from giving, from deigning to bestow the life-milk he has sucked from Sophia's breasts. The one does not know the happiness of those who receive; the other is a glutton who dishonors and bites the hands that feed him. Oh, how *great* the gulf betwixt this giving and this receiving! Such is the icy loneliness of stars! Such is the self-combustive heat of suns! Thus, fire and ice, storm and purpose, move our weary world! Thus, the philosopher is the artist who stitches together accidents, and fragments, and lofty dreams. What? Are you offended when I proclaim to you that all the planets revolving in the void reflect the light of higher men? Why so smitten? Why that crestfallen look? Is it not enough for you that your task consists in creating warmth out of that which shines? Where is your happiness over the prospect that something is better than nothing?—My conception of the world as an overworld of inspired higher men and an under-realm of *passive* utility-men and near-men has not been conceived. I am flattered that Plato—and Pythagoras before him—perfected a plan to *grant power* to a ruling spiritual caste in some distant, perhaps never realizable, future time. I merely point out that it is quite impossible to bestow upon grantees that which they already possess. Political philosophy at *this* juncture misses the mark; pragmatism and the helter-skelter *mis*-conceptions of the Americans cannot see or hear beyond the profits of a self-induced fog.—The synoptic/analytic opposition is helpful here: *the philosopher points the way*. A philosopher first sees the way: a philosopher is a surveyor, a reader of epochs, a diviner of historical entrails. Therefore—Pay heed to these tripod-headed ones with plumb bobs in their hands, these modern Chaldeans and rigorous, silent, severe, self-exalted transcribers of Sibylline scribblings, these Supermen!—Where is the sensitive soul who can doubt that the harvest of Nietzsche has not yet come? that Kierkegaard's day of overturning has not yet dawned?—I tell you: the hour will come, and now is, when I will be remembered as the developer and continuator of these "representative men."—*I teach you the Supermen.*—The day of critique-in-permanence must come . . . *will come*!! The prophecy of nihilism, this first and foremost idea, was the first attempt to make out the ominous silhouette of a black cow in the dark. Nihilism? Nihilism of *what*?—What is the what and the who—even the where—of this earth-moving "ism"??—You say, "The Superman is only a metaphor."—You scholars are apt to prattle such trash.—For Supermen *exist*. Their floruit is yesterday, today, and tomorrow. I cannot very well provide such spirits with eyes and ears, yet I can provide the mirror, the means by which they may take a long, leisurely look at themselves. Truly, before me, these tender ones who inhabit the sunrise, these emeralds of our race, did not possess a mirror. And yes;—as you may have guessed—when they think and create they are listening and speaking to themselves. Thus, the ears, the eyes; the tongues that proclaim distant futures as well as the necessary reaction to these futures. I have even recently discovered the precise manner in which these sunlit-natures are *open to suggestion*. This discovery provides a clue as to *what must be done*. Condemned to suffer an overabundance of vision and power, their cravings for love have, if I may be blunt, turned perverse; consequently *they* have turned perverse; in constant giving they forwent their sense of shame and turned perverse. Will these bestowers of soft words, these bestowers of purpose, suffer annihilation in this our madhouse of "modern ideas," drowned by the coming flood of Matrism, as you all will be drowned?—My readers must patiently wait on the apocalyptic details of this gigantomachy . . . I am leaving now for the deserted Isle of Patmos.